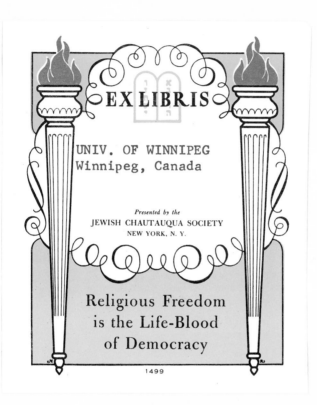

THE
SAMARITANS

The Earliest Jewish Sect

Their History, Theology
and Literature

The Vale of Shechem from the West.

THE
SAMARITANS

The Earliest Jewish Sect

Their History, Theology
and Literature

BY

JAMES ALAN MONTGOMERY, Ph.D.

Professor in Old Testament Literature and Language,
Philadelphia Divinity School

INTRODUCTION BY
ABRAHAM S. HALKIN

KTAV PUBLISHING HOUSE, INC.
NEW YORK

First published in 1907

New Matter
Copyright 1968
Ktav Publishing House, Inc.

Library of Congress Catalogue Card No. 67-30121
Manufactured in United States of America

THE JOHN BOHLEN LECTURESHIP.

JOHN BOHLEN, who died in Philadelphia on the 26th day of April, 1874, bequeathed to trustees a fund of One Hundred Thousand Dollars, to be distributed to religious and charitable objects in accordance with the well-known wishes of the testator.

By a deed of trust, executed June 2, 1875, the trustees, under the will of MR. BOHLEN, transferred and paid over to " The Rector, Church Wardens, and Vestrymen of the Church of the Holy Trinity, Philadelphia," in trust, a sum of money for certain designated purposes, out of which fund the sum of Ten Thousand Dollars was set apart for the endowment of THE JOHN BOHLEN LECTURESHIP, upon the following terms and conditions:

" The money shall be invested in good substantial and safe securities, and held in trust for a fund to be called The John Bohlen Lectureship, and the income shall be applied annually to the payment of a qualified person, whether clergyman or layman, for the delivery and publication of at least one hundred copies of two or more lecture sermons. These lectures shall be delivered at such time and place, in the city of Philadelphia, as the persons nominated to appoint the lecturer shall from time to time determine, giving at least six months' notice to the person appointed to deliver the same when the same may conveniently be done, and in no case selecting the same person as lecturer a second time within a period of five years. The payment shall be made to said lecturer, after the lectures have been printed and received by the trustees, of all the income for the year derived from said fund, after defraying the expense of printing the lectures and the other incidental expenses attending the same.

" The subject of such lectures shall be such as is within the terms set forth in the will of the Rev. John Bampton, for the delivery of what are known as the ' Bampton Lectures,' at Oxford, or any other subject distinctively connected with or relating to the Christian Religion.

" The lecturer shall be appointed annually in the month of May, or as soon thereafter as can conveniently be done, by the persons who for the time being shall hold the offices of Bishop of the Protestant Episcopal Church of the Diocese in which is the Church of the Holy Trinity; the Rector of said Church; the Professor of Biblical Learning, the Professor of Systematic Divinity, and the Professor of Ecclesiastical History, in the Divinity School of the Protestant Episcopal Church in Philadelphia.

" In case either of said offices are vacant, the others may nominate the lecturer."

Under this trust, the Rev. James A. Montgomery, Ph. D., was appointed to deliver the lectures for the year 1906.

INTRODUCTION

At present, the Samaritans are a small group numbering several hundred souls. At about the time this book
was published (more exactly, in 1907) , they counted only
152 individuals, 97 men and 55 women.* In the more
recent years they have been growing more numerous;
they were 212 in 1935. Since the establishment of the
State of Israel, the Samaritans who lived in the Jewish
state have in some cases married Jewish girls, and the
birth rate has increased. Reports from Israel indicate that
the contemporary Samaritans are being encouraged by
the authorities to assure their preservation and that they
feel quite comfortable as a negligible minority.

The concern of Jewish leaders for the survival and
welfare of the Samaritans is a new attitude. Relations between them and the Jews were not always friendly.
Whether the rise of the sect about 350 B.C.E. came as a
decided event or whether it was a gradual development,
it was the construction of a temple on Mt. Gerizim which
formalized the split. But the hostility between the two
groups dates even earlier than that. The account of the
Samaritan origin as recorded in the Bible, in the book of
II Kings, is the oldest document providing the grounds of
the estrangement. From chapter 17, which reports the
exile of the northern tribes by the Assyrian king and their

---

*In the middle of the past century, the well-known scholar
Abraham Geiger expected the group to disappear in two or three
generations.

replacement by peoples from distant lands, we are forced
to conclude that a new, alien group now constituted the
population of the country. This conclusion is strength-
ened by a statement which the leaders of these aliens
allegedly made centuries later when they came to plead
for permission to participate in the rebuilding of the
Temple under Persian authority. They declared: Let us
build with you; for we worship your God, as you do, and
we have been sacrificing to Him since the days of Esarhaddon king of Assyria, who brought us here.

It is doubtful that this account represents an adequate
explanation of the ethnic composition of the Samaritans.
It can hardly be contended that the native Israelites were
either all banished by the conquering Assyrians or that
they all perished in battle. It is most unlikely that the
countryside was entirely emptied of its former settlers.
Similarly, the story related in that chapter in the book of
Kings of how these Samaritans became worshippers of
God—including the judgment that "God they were fear-
ing, and their own gods they were serving, according to
the custom of the nations whence they had exiled them"—
is the product of strong hostility. It is more reasonable
and more likely that these aliens, brought in place of the
banished leaders, in order to stave off rebellion, came into
an environment of God-worshipping Israelites and were
gradually won over to the faith of the land, even if, at
first, not to the utter elimination of heathenism. Moreover, intermarriage probably kept pace with the religious
assimilation.

The opposition and the harsh judgment manifest in
these early records were implicit in the treatment of the
Samaritans by the superior Jewish group and in the relations between them. Soon after the latter won their independence from the Seleucid overlords they undertook the
conquest of central and northern Palestine, including
the Samaritan area, and demolished their temple on Mt.
Gerizim (c. 125 B.C.E.). Under the Romans several
clashes occurred between the two, undoubtedly not initi-

ated by only one side. The reluctance of the Samaritans to join the Jews in their uprisings against Rome only exacerbated the hatred between the two. Thus all feeling of kinship between the two peoples was wiped out, and the persistent Jewish charge that their neighbors to the north were worshipping a pigeon only added to the dislike.

Over the centuries then, the steady estrangement and suspicion resulted in ignorance by each of the world of the other; ignorance and indifference. Although it may be unwarranted to argue that the separation was air-tight, or that no influence and effects penetrated from the Jews to the Samaritans, it is nevertheless true that formally the former regarded the latter as an outside religious community. Jewish leaders certainly knew that their neighbors cherished a Torah very similar to theirs. One Rabbi even praised them with the statement that whatever precept they practiced they fulfilled more punctiliously. But no feeling of common origin survived, nor were they regarded as coreligionists since they were believed to be "proselytes caused by lions" (II Kings 17, 25-28), and as such were not acceptable. There was no concern, no desire to argue with them. A Karaite heresiographer, Kirkisani (10th cent.) lists them among the sects which developed within Jewry, but he does not polemize with them, as he does with the Rabbinites.

The legal position of the Samaritans as the Jews defined it is detailed in a small tract supplementary to the Talmud, called *Massekhet Kutim,* a monograph about the Samaritans. It is a compilation of Rabbinic rulings culled from the Talmud and from no longer extant sources, and it is given in an annotated translation in this book from page 197. Of its many regulations, the last paragraph is significant (p. 203) : "When shall we accept them? When they renounce Mt. Gerizim and recognize Jerusalem and accept the belief in the resurrection of the dead." The demand of belief in the resurrection of the dead as a condition to acceptance by the Jews is surprising. Without doubt this article of faith was included in their creed by the time this tract was compiled, the sixth or seventh century at the earliest. The possible explanation of the inclusion of this prerequisite is either that this paragraph of *Massekhet Kutim* was copied from a quite ancient source, or that the Jews, who associated the resurrection with the Messianic age, were not impressed with the Samaritan belief. It was not original with them, as our author points out, but it began to develop among them about the beginning of the common era probably under the influence of the Jewish doctrine. In his exposition of Deuteronomy 32:35 ff., the fourth century author Marka describes the "day of vengeance and recompense" (in the Samaritan version) as "the day of resurrection for all men, the day of regret for all the wicked, the day of reckoning for all things done, the day of recompense for the good, etc." (ed. Macdonald 4.12). This is also the view of the event expounded by the eleventh century Samaritan scholar Abu-l-Hasan of Tyre. In his commentary on the last three chapters of Deuteronomy, when he explains the thirty-ninth verse of chapter 32, which he treats as part of Moses' prediction of the future, he identifies it as a statement of the last judgment. God will then raise all the dead, and will decide every individual's fate unto eternity, whether reward or punishment. And the judgment will involve body and soul. He rejects the opinion of a group he calls the Dahriyya (in Islamic theology they represent different positions) who believe that only the spirits will be judged. In view of this development of a dogma, one prerequisite of the two needed for Samaritans joining the Jewish community could probably be eliminated.

But the issue of Mt. Gerizim is an insuperable block which nullifies any likelihood of an eventual reconciliation. The controversy over the identity of the "chosen place,"—i.e. the location of the sanctuary,—dates from the time when the Temple on Mt. Gerizim was constructed by the sect. It is reflected in the Samaritan Pentateuch. The last of the Ten Commandments is a compilation of

verses from the Torah,—almost all from Deuteronomy,—
instructing the Israelites to erect an altar on Mt. Gerizim
(Deut. 27.4; the accepted text reads: Ebal), and identifying it by means of Deut. 11.30. The several occurrences of
the phrase "the place which He will choose" are altered
to read "the place which He has chosen," since they con-
tend that Mt. Gerizim was designated by the Lord as His
favored site at the beginning of time. In the writings of
all Samaritan authors, whether in Christian or in Islamic
times, the devotion to Mt. Gerizim, the certainty that it
is the Chosen Place, the blessed spot, occupies a prominent position. Marka, in his rhapsodic composition on
Moses, gives an entire chapter,—out of six—to praises of
that mountain. As time passes, the honorific epithets and
the events alleged to have occurred on that site multiply.
It is the House of God, the gate of Heaven. It was from
the dust of the mountain that Adam was fashioned. Enoch
was buried at the foot of Mt. Ebal—opposite Gerizim—
which was given the name on account of the mourning for
him (note the confusion of the two words). Malchizedek,
who met Abraham with bread and wine after his return
from the pursuit of the Sodomites, was king of Shalem,
near Shechem. This is the same town that Jacob came to
after his departure from Esau. (They treat the word
Shalem, Genesis 33.35 as a proper noun; Jewish tradition
takes it to be an adverb meaning *safely*). Isaac was offered
as a sacrifice on Gerizim; Abraham and Jacob prayed
there. In a word, they heap praise and glory on it very
generously.

Step in step with the growing reverence of Mt. Gerizim,
the ill will toward Jerusalem became more and more
intense. In the Samaritan chronicle published by Neubauer in 1873, called the Tolida, Hadrian is said "to have
captured *cursed Shalem* (Arur Shalem, a parody on
Yerushalem). In Shechem he set up a bronze tablet on
which he inscribed 'No Jew shall dwell in Shechem,' on
account of his wife, because it is settled by Samaritans
(Hebrew: Shamerim = guardians). Abu-l-Hasan of Tyre

explains the verse 22 of Deuteronomy 32 to speak of the burning of Jerusalem as a manifestation of God's rage. A full-length account of how the "outrage" of Jerusalem and the Temple was committed is contained in a Samaritan legend, which has been preserved in the *Asatir*, a Midrashic elaboration of early Biblical history (ed. ben-Hayyim, 13-14 and 30-31) and in the commentary on Genesis by Meshalma al-Danfi and Ibrahim ibn Ya'akob. The version here follows the latter. In its exposition of Jacob's blessing (chapter 49), it cannot very well distort the meaning of the first two verses of the prediction to Judah (49.8-9). But beginning with verse 10: "the scepter shall not depart from Judah, nor the ruler's staff from between his feet," it expounds the remainder to match the sectarian rancor. It interprets 'until Shilo comes' as referring to Solomon, whom it condemns for the practice of magic and the unlawful knowledge of the language of birds and animals and the consequent control and domination of them. Solomon acquired this unholy skill from Ahidan ben Bered ben Tubal Cain.[1] Solomon went to Bet Miktash (a parody on Mikdash—sanctuary—it means "pest") and it is well known in Arabic by name. He attached himself to it, following in this the confession of Ahidan ben Bered. It is he who built Zion, whose name is Bet Gafna, and it is Bet Miktash which we are discussing. This Ahidan, may God curse him, used to work with the art of magic and astrology. Remember that the numerical value of Miktash is 760, which is also the numerical value of Esh Tmida (perpetual fire), and the equation of something with the fate which awaits it is fully legitimate. With the art of magic, Ahidan set up a large rock, suspended, neither on a structure nor on pillars. Most of the people who looked at what this was followed him voluntarily and unashamedly. This place bears another

---

[1]My friend Prof. H. L. Ginsberg suggests that Ahidan may be a corrupted form of Hiram, king of Tyre, who aided Solomon with the building of the Temple.

name, Bet Gafna.[2] This is the reason Scripture says: He
ties his "city" to the Gefen (vine) , intimating that when
he desired what he should not have desired, it led him to
set up this town of Gafna and to choose it as his object of
belief, and to reject the belief in the chosen place and the
mountain of God, the place which God was to choose.
The entire body of Jews were enrolled in it. And an act of
this kind will alienate you from the start.

For it is well-known that most of those who followed
him from this people are descended from Perez and
Zerah, the children of Tamar, with whom Judah had
illicit relations. This is known to us from the Torah and
from Tradition. If you examine the meaning of the word
Shelah you will find it to mean "remover"—the same
meaning as "remove (shal) thy shoes"—i.e., remover of
the truth and inventor of the false. This is indeed appropriate for those of whom it is said: "For their vine
(gafnam) is of the vine of Sodom, and of the fields of
Gomorrah," to the end of the verse about the branches
and their bitterness. They miss both worlds. For in this
world they are far from the Chosen Place and the holy
religion, and in their afterlife they will be far from Paradise. The fire of hell will burn them and their people.

Undoubtedly this condemnation is not the expression
of one man's sentiments but the crystallization of tens of
generations and hundreds of years. It can be readily
understood that the rejection and the abuse of Jerusalem
led to the denigration of the people in whose life it is
central. We find a genealogy of the Jews similar to the
preceding one in a liturgical composition by Abraham
ibn Ayya (18th century) , in which the following appears:
The seventh of the trials of Jacob is the action of Judah
when Tamar stopped him on the way, and he, believing
her to be a harlot, cohabited with her and she conceived.
Woe to him! Offspring came, bad seed, thorn and thistle

---

[2]According to Asatir, Gafna is the name of a woman from Babylonia whom he took for his son Asur.

grew. From it the Jews sprang, and the land was filled with defilement. It is clear that the possibility of reconciliation and reunion between Jews and Samaritans can become a reality only if this cardinal issue dividing them ceases to play a part. This can happen only if the Samaritan faith should lose its appeal.

Demographically and economically, the most striking feature of the Samaritan community is its amazing shrinkage. It may be true that during the period of the Christian domination of Palestine before the spread of Islam a considerable portion of its population was lost by slaughter and by conversion. Yet in the early years of Islam they represented a sizable portion of the country's inhabitants, and there were also groups of them residing in Egypt and Syria. In a work on the Samaritans, the late President Isaac ben-Zvi, of Israel, listed over seventy locations in which they resided, and many of them also existed in the Middle Ages. Of their position in Damascus and Cairo we have quite a bit of information. Professor Montgomery utilized the contents of the Samaritan chronicles in his sketch of their history (pp. 148-153). Some Jewish travelers in Palestine and neighboring lands likewise observed them and left us some reports regarding them which shed light on them. The first is in the travelogue of Benjamin of Tudela (ab. 1167) who noted some of their religious and cultural characteristics: He found about 1000 of them in Nablus, who "have priests descended from Aaron; these do not marry Kutheans, but only among themselves. . . . They offer sacrifices and burnt offerings in their place of worship on Mt. Gerizim . . . and they bring sacrifices on Passover and other holidays on the altar which they erected on it. . . . They do not pronounce the three gutturals *he, het, 'ayin,* . . . by this they are distinguished from the Israelites, because they know the Torah of Moses save those three sounds. They guard against defilement from contact with the dead, skeletons, or graves, when they go to their places of worship, they remove the clothes which they wear ordinarily, they bathe and put on others, and they do this at all times."

Isaac Helo, of Aragon, who traveled in Palestine in 1333, still found numerous Samaritans in Shechem. As for Mt. Gerizim, he relates that "facing this mountain, which they call 'the blessed mountain,' is Mt. Ebal, which they name 'the curse mountain.' . . . Although they observe the Torah of Moses punctiliously, they still have an idol in the shape of a dove. They lack the guttural letters in their alphabet. Their script is also different from ours. I was unable to read even one word in their Torah."

An expression of the resentment felt by the Jews towards the Samaritans is voiced in the sketch given of their situation in Cairo by Obadia of Bertinoro, author of the most widely used commentary on the Mishna, who visited that city in 1487 on his way to the Holy Land. "In Cairo there are about 700 Jewish households, 50 of them Samaritan, called Kutheans, and 150 Karaites. . . . The Samaritans possess only the Five Books of Moses. They do not use our script . . . but they have the same sacred language we have, except that they draw it out in their reading. . . . Everywhere in the Torah where the Tetragrammaton appears they read *Asshema*. They are hated by the Jews because they offer sacrifices on Mt. Gerizim. Many of them traveled along with us from Egypt on their way to Mt. Gerizim, where they have their sanctuary, to offer the paschal lamb. They observe the Sabbath only from noon Friday to noon Saturday. They are just a remnant now, having, so one hears, only some four hundred households all over the world. . . . The Samaritans are richer than all the Jews of Cairo; they perform all the tasks of the ministers and are their treasurers and agents."

An account of Samaritan hostility towards the Jews in Cairo is preserved in a historic work by Elijah Capsali (16th cent.) : "Muallim Sedaka, the Samaritan,—may his filth and his rage always be remembered—went to the Egyptian leaders and informed them quietly: 'Do you know that the Jews are proud enough to kill the Muslims?

They have rebelled against you and joined Selim (the rival of Tuman bey). If you keep silent you will be found guilty.' This blood-thirsty scoundrel Sedaka, a man as rich as Korah and Haman, important in the entourage of the king and one of his counsellors, testified before his ruler when the officers informed him of the plot of the Jews, and he succeeded in his conspiracy." While the relations in the past between the two groups very likely fluctuated, it should be a source of gratification that the usually latent animosity which endured for hundred of years is now being replaced by a kindlier and more cooperative spirit.

The Samaritans offer a good illustration of gradual diminution rather than of wholesale destruction. It is true that they suffered calamities, whether they resulted in death or in conversion. But with full recognition of this, the decisive factor of their numerical reduction is what may be called assimilation, i.e. voluntary conversion. It is not easy for all the members of a despised minority, whose history has been almost one unrelieved tragedy, to remain staunch in their faith in the face of dazzling victories by a taunting challenger who jeers unceasingly at the oppressed minority and scorns their folly. Most probably there was a continuous stream of defectors who joined the majority.

Nevertheless it must be borne in mind that those who remained steadfast clung tenaciously to their practices and doctrine. Their previously cited praise by the second-century Rabbi could be repeated throughout their history. Their creed, similar in form to Muslim declarations, is a brief formula: "I believe in You, O Lord, and in Moses son of Amram, Your servant, in the holy Torah, in Mount Gerizim Bet-El and in the day of vengeance and recompense."

Their belief in God is absolute monotheism. Even if they combined their worship of God with idolatry in the early years of their history, as the Bible reports, it was probably sheer calumny when they were charged, in Christian times, with honoring a pigeon in their sanc-

tuary. In their writings which have survived, whether
from pre-Islamic or Islamic times, one will not come
across a trace of paganism. The contrary is true. These
extant texts are fanatically zealous, almost polemical, in
their insistence on the unity of God to the exclusion of
any modification of this doctrine. Under the impact of
Greek philosophy via Islam, they, like their Jewish and
Muslim contemporaries, defined their beliefs, more ra-
tionally, emphasizing God's singleness, and incorporeality. They became interested in the problem of God's
attributes, they discussed revelation and prophecy in
philosophic terms. But essentially they adhered to the
orthodox position.

Their adoration of Moses goes beyond the great esteem
in which the Jews hold him. He has become an almost
divine creature. Since they recognize no later prophet he
is the bearer of not only the title of prophet but also the
unique role of law-giver, the *nomikos*. He is the choicest
of men, whose life from birth is distinguished by the
miraculous and the supernatural. Beginning with the
paean of glorification sung to him by the fourth-century
Marka, the admiration and the legend grow to almost
modern times. One will hardly go wrong in theorizing
that, like some Jews under Islam, they consciously or unconsciously sought to emulate the claims made by the
dominant religion for its founder.

Their inclusion of the holy Torah as an article of their
creed is a reflection of the tremendously important and
lofty position which the Five Books of Moses hold within
that community, although competition with Islam's holy
book may also be seen in it. Since, unlike the Jews, they
possess no other holy book, save the Torah, they bestow
all their love and reverence on it. It is the source of all
their beliefs and all their views, the authority for all their
doctrines and practices, the depository of all their hopes
and expectations in the future. They know of nothing else
in the world as holy as the Torah. While it is essentially
the same text as the Torah of the Jewish Bible, it deviates

from it in numerous details and in a few more serious matters. Originally their scrolls were written on parchment. A fragment of one such is said by them to have been written by Abi Shua, the grandson of Aaron the high-priest. For some time now they have been using paper for their copies. A curious device which they have introduced into their copies is called *Tashkil*. In the middle of any of the Five Books of Moses—preferably Leviticus—they interweave in the text the name of the scribe, the date of writing, and the name of the person who ordered the scroll. The procedure they follow is this: the column, or columns in which they wish to include the information are written with the lines broken into two halves. In one of the lines they may find that a letter at the beginning or at the end of the two halves is the first letter of the word they want to build; in the next, or a few lines below, the second letter, and so on. In this way, sometimes over several columns, information is provided which is gleaned by reading the letters from the top of the page down, perpendicularly. Such built-in words have the advantage of preventing falsification or theft.

To this belief in Torah they join the doctrine of tradition. As in the case of the Jewish Oral Law, it was the desire to be guided in their behavior by God's will, and the difficulty of discovering in the text what instruction they sought, which compelled the growth of tradition. It is of interest, however, that in its development one recognizes the influence of the Muslim concept. They derive their knowledge from the statements and practices of Moses, as the Muslims claimed they were guided by Muhammad and his companions. The knowledge of what Moses said and did is, of course, incorporated in Torah, and the Samaritans utilize every possible indication in the text in order to learn what to do. It is clear that their means of expanding the divine law differs considerably from the logic of interpretation which the Rabbis applied to the reading of Scripture. The Samaritans even adopted the Muslim standards for establishing the authenticity of a tradition.

The teachings regarding the Day of Vengeance and Recompense were discussed above. But it should be pointed out that in their vision of the future they have also introduced the belief in a kind of Messiah. They hope that eventually a redeemer will arise, whom they call the *Taheb,* the returning one, and he will work a radical change in the fate of the community. His appearance will mark the end of the age of *Fanuta,* or God's anger, which is the character of the present relations between God and His people, and will inaugurate the age of *Rahuta,* goodwill or well-being. It will be an earthly change, and it will mark the triumph of the Samaritan community—Israel—over its enemies, and the life of peace and prosperity. The sanctuary on Mt. Gerizim will be restored and with it the full sacrificial service. The nations of the world will then realize, and accept the true religion. After a long duration the Messianic age will pass, to be followed by the judgment of the day of vengeance and recompense. Then a general resurrection will take place, but only for the purpose of being assigned by God to eternal sojourn either in hell or in the abode of the righteous.

The Samaritans by James Allen Montgomery appeared in 1907. It reviews the history of western interest in the remnant of a sect from the first attempts, in 1584, by the orientalist Joseph Scaliger to become acquainted with the group. Prof. Montgomery further summarizes the history of the Samaritans from their rise as a separate community to the present time. He also offers a digest of their theology, sub-sects, and their languages and literature. He includes the text as well as an annotated translation of the Rabbinic tract *Kuthim,* which regulates the relations between the Jews and the Samaritans. An appendix offers a full bibliography up to the date of publication of studies in modern times on various phases of their history and culture. In this undertaking, Prof. Montgomery gathered all the available material on the sect, both primary sources

and secondary works, and presented a reasoned appreciation of their past as well as their contemporary life and
situation.

Some sixty years have passed since the publication of
this book, and the decision to republish it is wise and com-
mendable. In the world of scholarship, it is useful to provide summaries in the various fields of research of the
achievements and conclusions reached over a given period
of time. Even in subjects where the progress is rapid, as in
the sciences, and the danger is real that handbooks may
become quickly antiquated, it is beneficial to have these
epitomes as records of the development in them. Certainly in studies where, without revolutionary changes in
the amount of information and attainment, there may
still be a modest increase of knowledge and perhaps also
modifications of points of view, such manuals are valuable. They save the reader or the student the time and the
energy needed to peruse all the accumulated bibliography.
An examination of the list of books and articles read by
Prof. Montgomery will demonstrate how grateful we
ought to feel to him for summarizing the results of the
research contained in the hundreds of items by scholars
who preceded him, which he utilized for his book.

With the development of the offset-process, reprinting
a book is a relatively simple matter. In the scholarly
world, particularly in the humanities and the social
sciences, there have been certain works of investigation
which are deemed "classic." Such is Gibbon's *Decline and
Fall of the Roman Empire,* or the researches of Zunz in
Medieval Hebrew poetry. In the past, the esteem which
books of this rank enjoyed induced scholars and pub-
lishers to prepare and issue revised editions which still
have the name of the original author. Gesenius' Grammar
of Hebrew, which appeared in twenty-nine editions, is a
good example of this policy. At the present time it is
faster, and much less costly to reproduce the book as
originally offered by the author. In the case of the present
work the disadvantages resulting from this recent change

are few. Continued study of the history and culture of the Samaritans has not produced any startling revisions since the first publication of this volume. A few corrections of detail may be necessary. Views may differ on the history of the beginning of the sect or its ethnic constituency. More of their texts in Samaritan or in Arabic have been published. More recent studies have advanced the knowledge of the grammar of Samaritan Aramaic, or the influence from Judaism and Islam to which they were subject. Above all, a bibliography brought up to date would be helpful.

Compared with these few and relatively unimportant changes which ought to have their place in a more recent edition of Montgomery's *The Samaritans,* the benefits to the scholarly world resulting from its re-issue are many. It is a judicious, interpretive condensation of their history, theology and literature, the fruit of the author's painstaking search and analysis of the contents of both primary sources and secondary studies. It represents the result of dedicated application and of integrity. It inspires the reader with the confidence that the book he is reading is authoritative; that it is the work of a scholar who is not pleading a cause, nor defending a stand, but presenting a documented account. It is not tendentious. Without doubt he expressed his own view where a conclusion had to be reached, he chose to support one possible interpretation over another which seemed less likely to him. But at all times the student trusts that the author's personal predilections did not consciously affect the reasoning. He knows that conclusions were not hastily arrived at, that for every statement evidence was utilized. He realizes that the author composed the work with no other motive than to tell the story as honestly as he could. It is the highest tribute to the book that sixty years after publication it is still cited in references and relied on for facts. Its reappearance will make it accessible to many who wish to own it.

A. S. Halkin

PREFACE.

The following work has grown out of the author's desire to gain an answer for the question: Who are the Samaritans? He publishes it in the expectation that the same question may be of interest to the intelligent public, while withal he hopes that the collection of material here presented may be of use to the scholarly world.

In large part this work is a digest of the labors of many scholars for over three centuries; in so far it is the result of painstaking investigation in a widely scattered and recondite literature. At the same time, while he has made no pretence at original hypotheses, the author believes that he presents ampler treatment of the subject as a whole than has yet been attempted. The difficult problem of the origin of the Samaritan sect has been here discussed in the light of modern criticism as a preliminary to the subsequent history. Their own Chronicles have been carefully explored for historical data, illustrating or adding to the foreign sources which up to within fifty years have been almost the sole means of information. The Jewish, Christian, and Muslim references have been collated, and a digested treatment of the Talmudic references is offered. The Samaritan theology has been treated formally and at some length, with a full apparatus of citations to the literature, especially the Liturgy, the theological importance of which has hardly yet been recognized. The Chapter on the Literature seemed a necessary supplement, although it can give only an outline of the results of the many specialists who have worked in this field. In fact, Samaritan study still lies in the primary stage of manuscript investigation, and the student who has not access to the original material must recognize that at best he can be only an encyclopædist in the subject.

It is hoped that the constant references to the literature, and especially the Bibliography at the end of the volume, will be of use to students. The history of Samaritana gives many instances where first-rate scholars have entirely ignored the labors of other specialists in the same lines.

My thanks are due to Professors Hilprecht, Jastrow, and Clay, of the University of Pennsylvania, for their great and unfailing kindness to me in my course for the Doctorate in Philosophy, the first Chapters of the present work containing the material presented as my thesis for the degree. I have also to express my deep sense of obligation to the Committee of the Bohlen Lectureship, for the dignity they have conferred upon me in appointing me as Lecturer on that honorable foundation. To my friends, Prof. W. Max Müller and the Rev. Dr. Julius H. Greenstone, my thanks are due for much kind assistance, and I am deeply indebted to Newcomb B. Thompson, Esq., for his critical reading of both MS and proof.

JAMES A. MONTGOMERY.

Philadelphia Divinity School.
July 28, 1906.

TABLE OF CONTENTS

XXVII

LIST OF ILLUSTRATIONS

BIBLIOGRAPHICAL' ABBREVIATIONS.

Abu'l Fath: Vilmar, *Abulfathi annales Samaritani.*
AJ: Josephus, *Antiquities of the Jews;* **BJ:** do. *Jewish War.*
Baedeker: K. Baedeker, *Palästina und Syrien;* ed. 5, 1900.
BR: E. Robinson, *Biblical Researches,* Boston, 1841, **LBR:** do. *Later Biblical Researches,* Boston, 1856.
BS: M. Heidenheim, *Bibliotheca Samaritana.*
Chron. Adler: E. N. Adler, *Une nouvelle chronique samaritaine* (cited according to the separate imprint of 1893).
Chron. Neub.: A. Neubauer, *Chronique samaritaine,* in *Journal asiatique,* 1869.
CS: W. Gesenius, *Carmina Samaritana.*
DB: Hastings, *Dictionary of the Bible.*
DVJ: (Heidenheim's) *Deutsche Vierteljahrsschrift für englisch-theologische Forschung und Kritik,* 1861–1871.
EB: *Encyclopædia Biblica.*
GJV: E. Schürer, *Geschichte des jüdischen Volkes,* etc.; ed. 3.
HG: G. A. Smith, *Historical Geography of the Holy Land;* ed. 7, 1901.
Hist. Sam.: T. Juynboll, *Commentarii in historiam gentis Samaritanæ.*
JAOS: *Journal of the American Oriental Society.*
JBL: *Journal of Biblical Literature.*
JE: *Jewish Encyclopædia.*
JQR: *Jewish Quarterly Review.*
JZW: *Jüdische Zeitschrift für Wissenschaft und Leben.*
KAT: E. Schrader, *Keilinschriften und das Alte Testament;* ed. 3, 1902.
Lib. Jos.: T. Juynboll, *Chronicon Samaritanum — Liber Josuæ.*
Marka: the text of Marka given by Heidenheim, *BS,* iii (cited according to the MS pagination given in margin).
MGWJ: (Frankel's) *Monatsschrift für Geschichte und Wissenschaft des Judenthums.*
N. et E: de Sacy, *Correspondance des Samaritains de Naplouse,* in *Notices et Extraits des Manuscrits de la Bibliothèque du Roi,* vol. xii, 1831.
PEFQS: *Palestine Exploration Fund Quarterly Statement.*
PSBA: *Proceedings of the Society of Biblical Archæology;* **TSBA:** *Transactions,* etc.
RE: Herzog and Plitt, *Real-Encyklopädie für protestantische Theologie;* ed. 2 (unless otherwise indicated).
REJ: *Revue des études juives.*
REJud: Hamburger, *Real-Encyclopädie des Judenthums.*
Repertorium: (Eichhorn's) *Repertorium für biblische und morgenländische Litteratur.*
Sam. Targ.: J. W. Nutt, *Fragments of a Samaritan Targum — With an Introduction.*
Sam. Theol.: W. Gesenius, *De Samaritanorum theologia — commentatio.*
SBOT: P. Haupt, *Sacred Books of the Old Testament.*
SWPM: Conder and Kitchener, *Survey of Western Palestine Memoirs,* vol. ii: *Samaria.*
ZATW: *Zeitschrift für die alttestamentliche Wissenschaft.*
ZDPV: *Zeitschrift des deutschen Palästina-Vereins.*

" And he was a Samaritan." (*St. Luke,* 17, 16.)

THE SAMARITANS

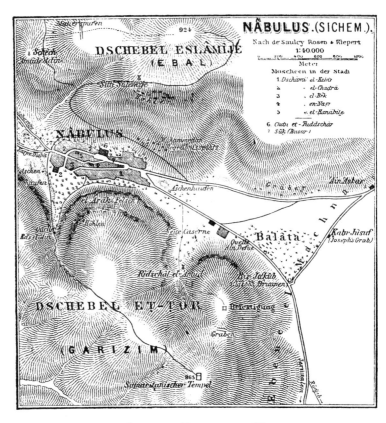

MAP OF SHECHEM-NABLUS AND VICINITY.

(From K. Baedeker, *Palästina und Syrien.* By permission.)

THE SAMARITANS.

CHAPTER I.

THE RE-DISCOVERY OF THE SAMARITANS.

The existence of a peculiar sect native to Samaria, the central region of Palestine, is first noticed in the Old Testament, 2 *Ki.* 17, where they are called the Samaritans.[1] This record narrates that the land of the northern Kingdom of Israel, having been denuded of its population by the Assyrian conqueror after the fall of the capital, the city of Samaria, in 722 B.C., was repopulated by heathen colonies transferred thither from distant parts of the empire. The deities of the respective colonies are then named, and the narrative proceeds to relate how upon the outbreak of a plague of lions the newcomers bethought themselves, in true primitive fashion, of the claims of the neglected god of the land; in consequence of their distress they sought, with the patronage of the Assyrian King, to learn the way of the God of Israel, and added his worship to their respective cults, the result being an eclectic form of religion, abhorrent indeed to Yahwe and to all who found in him the One True God.

After a lapse of two centuries the people of Samaria appear again as the opponents of the restored Jewish state, and especially as objecting to the re-building of the temple at Jerusalem.[2] The history of the Jews as continued by the Books of *Maccabees* and the works of Josephus, abounds in references to the Samaritan sect, whose members always

[1] For the names of the Samaritans, see Additional Note B.
[2] *Ezra-Nehemia, passim.*

I

appear as the arch-enemies of Israel. The historians of the Pagan empire ,of Rome give some data bearing upon the sect, while the Byzantine chronicles and edicts of the IVth, Vth, and VIth Centuries have much to report upon the obnoxious and rebellious nature of the people.

To the man of average information the sect is mostly, if not solely, known, through the contact which Jesus several times had with the Samaritans and from his parable of the Good Samaritan. It is characteristic of the Christ's gentleness that these evangelical accounts alone, to popular knowledge, redeem the ill-fame of that sect. He himself even was given the opprobrious epithet of " Samaritan." A chapter in the *Acts of the Apostles,* and then, particularly in their comments upon Biblical passages, the Church Fathers, throw some light upon the relations of the Samaritans with Judaism and Christianity.

Many references to the sect are found in the Talmuds, Midrashim, and other Jewish literature, and there is a small tractate bound up in the Babylonian Talmud which treats of the Samaritans. But the Talmud still remains a wilderness to general Christian knowledge, and the Jews have felt, until very recent times, but little interest in digesting the information at their hand concerning " the foolish people who dwell at Shechem " (*Ecclus.* 50, 25), — which city has been from the beginning the headquarters of the sect.

Thus it came about that when the dark veil of Islam separated the East from the West, the Samaritan sect, despised and abominated by Jew and Christian alike, fell into deep oblivion so far as the western world was concerned. Those intelligent observers, the Arabic geographers, historians and philosophers, recorded valuable notices of the Samaritans ;[3] the Jewish traveller, Benjamin of Tudela, brought home some exact information concerning them.[4] But mediæval

[3] See below, p. 134ff.
[4] See below, p. 136.

Europe was too sunk in barbarism to have its curiosity awakened; even the Crusaders utterly ignored the Samaritans, although the sacred city of the sect, which since the Roman period bore the name of Neapolis, was one of the gay centres of those marauders. Among the many travellers who in the spirit of adventure visited the Orient, after Islam had recovered its own again, only two before the XVIIth Century seem to have noticed the Samaritans, Wilhelm von Boldensele, of Lower Saxony, in 1333[5] and the author of the more or less romantic work ascribed to John Mandeville, composed between 1357 and 1371, and widely read in many editions and languages.[6] What the entertaining Sir John has to say about the Samaritans — how that they are a distinct sect and wear a red turban — is very accurate, but probably it was all taken as one of his "traveller's tales." The Samaritans became to Christendom as real, or as unreal, as the Lost Ten Tribes who dwell beyond the fabled river Sambation.

The dense darkness was at last penetrated by the genius and the will of "the greatest scholar of modern times," Joseph Scaliger. In 1583 was published his immortal work *De emendatione temporum,* in which he asserted the rights of the Orient to its place in universal history, and the value of all oriental chronicles for the scientific historian. It was evidently this *magnum opus* which determined the author to explore the Samaritans, for in conjunction with it he set agencies in motion which in the following year, 1584, brought him from the Samaritan colony in Cairo two cal-

[5] See his *Hodæporicon ad Terram Sanctam,* in Canisius, *Thesaurus monumentorum,* ed. Basnage, iv, 353. See *ZDMG* xvi, 710.

[6] On authorship and bibliography, see the articles on "Mandeville" in *Encyclopædia Britannica* and *Dictionary of National Biography.* The passage is found in Halliwell's edition, *The Voyage and Travaille of Sir John Maundeville,* London, 1839, p. 108. Kootwyk (Cotovicus), who travelled in Palestine in 1598, refers to the Samaritans as a sect of the Jews; see his *Itinerarium Hierosolymitanum et Syriacum,* Antwerp, 1619, p. 342.

endars, and a copy of the Samaritan *Book of Joshua*.[7] The great scholar's appetite was now whetted for the possession of a copy of the edition of the Pentateuch, which he heard the sect possessed. His ambition was not rewarded, because the Samaritans refused the boon of their holy Law to an alien. But his search had its fruit in two epistles of the date 1590, one from a Samaritan of Gaza, the other from Egypt, and these documents were the beginning of an extensive correspondence with European scholars, which for nearly 250 years was almost the sole source of information concerning the contemporary condition of the Samaritans.[8]

The next European to gain undying merit for himself in investigating the Samaritans was the great traveller Pietro della Valle, who is also immortal and of special interest to present-day scholarship as the first to acquaint the western world with the Persian cuneiform inscriptions, which have at last given the key to the decipherment of the literature of Babylonia and Assyria.[9] Upon the commission of Achille Harlay de Sancy, the French ambassador at Constantinople, that he procure a copy of the Samaritan Pentateuch, della Valle made the Samaritans a special quest of his travels, and in 1616 visited their communities at Cairo, Gaza, Shechem (the modern Nablus), and Damascus, in which latter city he at last succeeded in his search. It may be worth while to repeat part of his quaint description of the visit made one summer day to the Samaritan community housed in the suburbs of Damascus. "One morning," he

---

[7] For Scaliger's work, which in the later editions published the calendar material — the first appearance of a Samaritan document in print — see Chap. XIV, note 80, and Bibliography.

[8] These letters, which were called out by the efforts of Scaliger's friend de Peiresc, never reached him, as he died before they arrived at their destination. A Latin translation was published by Morin in Simon, *Antiquitates ecclesiæ orientalis*, 1682, p. 119. The text, with translation and notes, was finally published by de Sacy in Eichhorn's *Repertorium*, xiii (1783), 257. For the history of Scaliger's efforts, see Juynboll, *Lib. Jos.* i.

[9] See Rogers, *History of Babylonia and Assyria*, i, 16

writes, " I was consoled for all the discomforts brought me by that illness by being taken by Father Michael and by a Hebrew, my friend and interpreter, to see outside the city in the gardens certain small houses which were there, belonging to the Hebrew Samaritans, beside the pleasure which I had in seeing those gardens, and those houses, which within were most gay, in spite of making a very poor appearance without, all filled with pictures painted in miniature, with their Samaritan letters engraved in gold, and so also their synagogues." He then proceeds to describe his inspection of the Samaritan books, he being the first Christian scholar, so far as we know, to become acquainted with them since the Roman rule, even as he was the first modern Christian to come into intimate intercourse with the sect.[10]

Della Valle was able to purchase two copies of the Samaritan Hebrew Pentateuch, a copy of the Targum or Aramaic translation of the same, and some other books. The discovery of these literary treasures set all learned Europe agog, for they became an additional apple of discord in the wordy and voluminous strife between Catholic and Protestant theologians as to the text of the Scriptures and the Church's authority in defining her Canon and its text.[11] Once again the Samaritans played their historic part as disturbers of the peace, but now in the distant academies of Europe.

At the end of the same century three travellers visited the Samaritans, the first of whom, Huntington, gave renewed stimulus to the interest awakened in the sect. The two others wrote brief descriptions of the Samaritans at Nablus; one of them was Henry Maundrell, the predecessor of Hunt-

[10] For the editions of della Valle's *Viaggi*, see Bibliography. The above passage appears in the XIIIth Letter, " from Aleppo." I owe my translation to the kind assistance of E. H. M. For the recent discoveries of house inscriptions like those described by della Valle, see below, p. 277.

[11] For these MSS and the resulting discussion, see Chapter XIV, §§ 6, 7.

ington in the chaplaincy at Aleppo, in 1697, the other the Frenchman, A. Morison, in 1698. These seem to have been almost the last direct observations upon the Samaritans until the visits of European travellers in the XIXth Century.[12]

But the laurels in the quest after the strange sect fell to Robert Huntington, later Bishop of the diocese of Raphoe of the Church of Ireland (d. 1701). When chaplain at the English " factory " in Aleppo, he undertook a visit to Jerusalem in 1671, and on the way visited Nablus.[13] The Samaritans were astonished at his interest in them and at his acquaintance with their literature and script, and they assumed that the Israelites in England, of whom the clergyman spoke, were their brothers. By nursing their self-deception he obtained a copy of their Pentateuch, and soon afterwards, at Jerusalem, received from them an epistle addressed to their " Brethren in England." Before an answer arrived, the Samaritans addressed to him another letter written at Gaza in 1674. The first epistle came into the hands of Thomas Marshall of Oxford (rector of Lincoln College, 1672–1685), who in 1675 addressed a Hebrew epistle to the Samaritans, which informed them that the writers were of the race of Japheth; its substance was a pious attempt to proselytize the sect for the Christian Messiah. Huntington forwarded this letter, accompanied by one from himself inquiring concerning the alleged dove-cult of the Samaritans.

The latter immediately replied, in 1675, with a curt response to Huntington, expressing their surprise at his inquiries and their amazement at the lack of information concerning the Brethren in England. The earlier correspon-

---

[12] Maundrell, *Journey from Aleppo to Jerusalem at Easter* 1697. Oxford, 1703, etc.; the reference is under date of March 24. A. Morison, *Relation historique d'un voyage au Mont Sinai et à Jerusalem*, Toulouse, 1704, p. 234.
[13] See T. Smith, *R. Huntingtoni Epistolæ*, 1704.

dence had been couched in Hebrew, the mother-tongue of
the sect, and written in the peculiar Samaritan script; this
letter was in Arabic, the vernacular in Palestine. The reply
was accompanied by two epistles, addressed to the Brethren
in England, the one in Arabic, the other in Hebrew. Another Arabic epistle for the English Brethren was addressed
to Huntington in 1688.[14] Huntington's deceit was an unfortunate one, for it established in the Samaritan mind a
well-founded suspicion against the Europeans.

In the same decade with the epistles last mentioned falls
the correspondence between Job Ludolf, the Amsterdam
scholar, and the Samaritans. He availed himself of the
services of an itinerant Jew, who was acquainted with the
Samaritans, to forward them a Hebrew letter. In the following year, 1685, the Samaritans replied with two epistles,
containing largely duplicate matter. Ludolf again replied,
and in 1691 received a third letter, of date 1689.[15] A lull

[14] For the correspondence since Huntington's time, the fullest authority is de Sacy, who has also edited most of the Samaritan epistles.
See his invaluable *Correspondance des Samaritains de Naplouse,* in
Notices et Extraits des Manuscrits de la Bibliothèque du Roi, xii
(1831), p. 1. The preface gives an account of the Samaritans and the
correspondence; the body of the article, almost all the epistles, along
with translations, except those to Scaliger and Ludolf. All the Huntington correspondence, with the exception of Huntington's letter concerning the dove-cult, is found in Nos. xvii–xxiii. Of the Epistle of
1672 the English scholar, Edward Bernard, gave a translation in Ludolf, *Epistolæ Samaritanæ Sichemitarum ad J. Ludolf.,* Zeiz, 1688, p.
26; in *N. et E.* it is No. xvii. The Epistle of 1674 appeared in German
translation by Schnurrer in Eichhorn's *Repertorium,* ix, 8, and with
text and translation in *N. et E.* xviii; the Epistle from Marshall, in
like forms, in *Repert,* ix, 11, and *N. et E.,* No. xix; the Arabic Epistle
of 1675 in *Repert.* ix, 16, and *N. et E.* xx; the Arabic Epistle to the
Samaritans in England of the same date, and the fragment which has
alone been preserved of the fellow Hebrew Epistle, in *Repert.* ix, 22,
55, and *N. et E.* xxi, xxii; that of 1688, in *Repert.* ix, 36, and *N. et E.*
xxiii.

[15] The first two of these Epistles appeared in Ludolf, *Epistolæ Samaritanæ Sichemitarum ad J. Ludolf,* 1688 (bound up with Cellarius, *Collectanea historiæ Samaritanæ,* of same date). The third Epistle was
not published in full until the appearance of Bruns, *Epistola Sam.
Sichemit. tertia ad J. Ludolf,* 1781, which work was republished in
Repert. xiii, 277. Cellarius had published some extracts from it in his
Historia gentis et religionis Samaritanæ, 1699.

then fell upon this learned intercourse, until it was taken up by the French savants of the XIXth Century.[16] But the new information had the effect of stimulating some of the encyclopædic scholars of the XVIIth Century, the great lexicographer Castellus, that prince of archæologists Reland, Cellarius, and others, to the accumulation of all the material concerning the strange sect; but we must pass over the labors of many indefatigable scholars and travellers of this earlier period of research. One note recorded by Kennicott[17] is worthy of citation because of its reference to an attempt to acquire the sacred Nablus codex. Kennicott relates that word had been received from Mr. John Usgate in 1734; that " he had been at Naplose, the preceding February; that several families of the Samaritans then resided there; that they had still their old MS. of the Pentateuch, some passages of which were so effaced as to be scarce legible; and that he had made proposals and hoped soon to agree with them for the purchase of it; of which he would send Mr. Swinton notice. But no such notice has been since received; the purchase being probably prevented by the unfortunate death of Mr. Usgate, who was afterwards cut to pieces by a party of Persians."

The next stage in these epistolary relations, and the one yielding the most scientific results, was under the auspices of the First Empire; the initiative was taken by the distinguished Henri Grégoire, Bishop of Blois, revolutionary, senator of the Empire, and author of the *Histoire des sectes réligieuses,* with the aid of de Sacy, the illustrious Arabist,

[16] However, Samaritan Epistles seem to have found their way to Europe in the interim. Heidenheim has published in his *DVJ* 1, 78, the *Schreiben Meshalmah ben Ab Sechuah's an die Samaritaner*, apparently addressed to coreligionists in Europe. It is subsequent to the failure of the highpriesthood in 1623. In 1790 the Samaritans addressed a letter to the Brethren in France, which, found again in Holland, was published by Hamaker, in *Aanmerkingen over de Samaritanen*, 1834. This Epistle I have not seen.

[17] *State of the Printed Hebrew Text, Diss.* II, 541.

who was the writer of most of the French documents, and became the editor of all the correspondence. After some futile applications to French consuls in Syria, Consul-general Corancez at Aleppo addressed a letter containing categorical questions to the Samaritans, and this drew from them, in 1808, a full and direct reply. But the answer only provoked further questions, and these were drawn up by Grégoire and de Sacy in a memoir containing sixteen questions. Direct answers thereto were received in a long Hebrew letter, accompanied by a short one in Arabic, of date 1810. Ten years later, in 1820, there reached de Sacy an Arabic letter, accompanied with a table of contemporary astronomical observations, and also a Hebrew epistle addressed to the Brethren in Europe. Finally in 1826 there arrived a Hebrew epistle addressed to the Samaritans in Paris.[18]

These Samaritan epistles, dating from Scaliger to de Sacy, are most valuable in the information they give upon the theology and the contemporary condition of the Samaritans. The latter answered the questions addressed to them with great intelligence and frankness, while the sincerity of the information is the more evident because many of the letters were addressed to the assumed Brethren in Europe. Further, in the scholarly study of the sect it was these epistles which constituted, alongside of the Pentateuchal codices, almost the sole knowledge scholars pos-

[18] For all this correspondence of the French savants, see *N. et E.;* the letters are given under Nos. iv–xvi; xxiv–xxv. There is also to be noted an epistle obtained by Kautzsch, of date 1884, from the Samaritan highpriest, published in *ZDPV* viii, 149. It contains answers to questions concerning the numbers of the community, their inner legal relations, and the Taeb or Messiah, giving an interesting definition of the latter term; see below, p. 246. A Samaritan letter addressed to the author appears in Rosenberg, *Lehrbuch d. sam. Sprache,* 1901. There exists a petition addressed to the government of Louis Philippe, in 1842; see below, p. 141. A letter of the Samaritans to the English government of date 1875 is in the British Museum, catalogued as *Or.* 1381. Almkvist has published a congratulatory Epistle to King Oscar (see Bibliography).

sessed on the subject, until the opening up of more extensive and immediate information in later years of the XIXth Century.

But there was a more direct way of learning about the modern Samaritans than by their literature and epistles, namely through the close study of the sect in its home by trained orientalists.   The few earlier travellers had noted only things which lay upon the surface.   Edward Robinson, who visited Shechem in 1838 and 1852, left scholarly accounts of his brief sojourns there.[19]   But Heinrich Petermann, the distinguished orientalist, was the first to take the pains to devote considerable time to a visit to the Samaritans.   In 1853 he spent two months among the people, making there, despite many difficulties, a systematic study of all that he could learn.[20]   He had already in the spring attended the Samaritan Passover, his party, which included the English consul Finn, and the German scholar and consul Rosen, being the first modern Europeans to witness that ancient rite, which in the Jewish Church had ceased for 1800 years.[21]   In the same year with Petermann the French abbé Bargès visited the Samaritans,[22] and since that time the ancient sect has been an objective both of curious tourists and of well-trained scholars.   Among the latter may be named Rosen, John Mills, Hammond, Dean Stanley, Firkovitch, Warren, Conder, and the Americans Trumbull and Huxley.[23]   We may record here the visit of a fugitive Samaritan to the west; in 1855 Jacob esh-Shelaby went to London, having with difficulty escaped assassination by the Muslims at home, and interested many philanthropic Eng-

---

[19] *BR* iii, 96; *LBR*, 128.
[20] Petermann, *Reisen im Orient*, i, chap. vii.
[21] *Ibid.*, 233.
[22] See his *Samaritains de Naplouse*, 1855.
[23] See the Bibliography. I have not attempted there to record the visits of all travellers to Nablus, but only, as a rule, the accounts of those who have attended the Samaritan Passover.

lishmen — among them Lord Shaftesbury — in his people's cause, for which he made some extensive collections.[24]

Further, in consequence of the renewed interest of the western world in the sect at Nablus, and through the opening up of the treasures of the Orient in the last century, scholarship has become enriched with a great quantity and variety of Samaritan manuscripts, which have manifolded our means of studying the history and the genius of the sect. Partly by infiltration from unknown sources, partly by direct purchase, this literary material has been slowly flowing into European libraries, and it proves the Samaritans to have been by no means ignorant of letters. Beside many texts of the Hebrew Pentateuch and its Targum, we have extensive theological treatises and Midrashim, commentaries which show some exegetical skill, chronicles whose defect is their chronology, grammatical and scientific works, and, most important of all for studying the spirit of the Samaritan religion, tomes of their liturgy. The chief collection of this material is found in the British Museum,[25] which is now rivalled, in quantity at least, by the Royal Library at St. Petersburg, containing the treasures found by the great Karaite scholar Abraham Firkovitch.[26] Alongside of these should be named the Bodleian Library at Oxford,[27] and then the libraries in Cambridge,[28] at Leyden,[29] Paris,[30] Rome, Berlin, and Gotha. Pieces of the literature are to be found in many other collections, private

[24] See Consul Rogers, *Notices of the Modern Samaritans*, etc., 1855. Shelaby's coreligionists charged that he kept the money for himself, and when he returned, he had to retire to Jerusalem.

[25] Margoliouth, *Descriptive List*, 1893, and *Catalogue*, 1899. (For these catalogues, see Bibliography.)

[26] Harkavy, *Catalog*. Cf. the digest of the collection given by Harkavy in Nutt, *Samaritan Targum*, Appendix i.

[27] See the Catalogues of Nicoll and Pusey, 1835, and Neubauer, 1866.

[28] Wright and Schiller-Szinnessy's Appendix to the Trinity College Catalogue.

[29] De Jong, *Catalogus Codicum Orientalium bibliothecæ academiæ regiæ Lugdun.-Batav.*, 1862.

[30] Zotenberg, *Catalogues*, 1866; Steinschneider, *Supplément*, 1903.

as well as public. This extensive material has by no means as yet been worked out, although it has engaged the interest of many Semitists, some of them the peers of the scholars of the XVIIth Century, such as Gesenius, Juynboll, Kuenen, Nöldeke, Geiger, Kohn, Neubauer, Heidenheim, Clermont-Ganneau, Cowley, and many others, the long list of whom shows that Samaritana evoke the attention of specialists in many different lines. It may be said that we now possess enough material to recover the history and depict the character of the Samaritans so far as literature can give the means, until the archæologist's spade shall turn up in Palestinian soil ancient monuments which can make revelations concerning the darkest age of Samaritan history, that of its beginnings.

Fountain in the Vale of Shechem.

CHAPTER II.

THE LAND OF SAMARIA AND THE CITY OF SHECHEM.

ἡ δ' ἄρ' ἔην ἀγαθή τε καὶ αἰγινόμος καὶ ὑδρηλή·
οὐδὲ μὲν ἔσκεν ὁδὸς δολιχὴ πόλιν εἰσαφικέσθαι
ἀγρόθεν, οὐδέ ποτε δρία λαχνήεντα πονεῦσιν.
ἐξ αὐτῆς δὲ μάλ' ἄγχι δύ' οὔρεα φαίνετ' ἐρυμνὰ
ποίης τε πλήθοντα καὶ ὕλης· τῶν δὲ μεσηγὺ
ἀτραπιτὸς τέτμητ', ἀραιὴ γλυφίς, ἔνθ' ἐτέρωθι
γῆ διερὴ Σικίμων καταφαίνεται, ἱερὸν ἄστυ
νέρθεν ὑπὸ ῥίζῃ δεδμημένον· ἀμφὶ δὲ τεῖχος
λισσόν, ὑπώρειαν δ' ὑποδέδρομεν αἰπύθεν ἕρκος.

(Description of the Vale of Shechem by the Hellenistic poet Theodotus, in Eusebius, *Præp. Evang.* ix, 22, with Ludwich's emendations.)

The central district of Palestine is Samaria, one of the three divisions of the Holy Land well known to all students of the New Testament. But the name Samaria as applied to the district is comparatively recent; it is the Hellenized form of Shomeron, the capital which Omri founded in the IXth Century B.C.,[1] and the name of the city was extended to the district only towards the end of the following century, when the Assyrian advance cut off from Northern Israel Galilee and Across-Jordan, and reduced the once proud kingdom of Israel to a dependent province named after its one important city.[2] The older name of the land is Mount Ephraim, or more correctly the Highland of Ephraim.[3] It is the northern section of the rugged upland region, whose

---

[1] 1 *Ki.* 16, 24. See Additional Note A.

[2] Amos uses the word only of the city, but Hosea, writing after the land had become an Assyrian dependency (739 B. C.), always — six times — of the land.

[3] Highland (*har*) of Ephraim, *Jos.* 17, 15; also once the Highland of the Amorite, *Dt.* 1, 7, and later the Highland of Israel, *Jos.* 11, 16.

southern part bore the corresponding name of the Highland of Juda,[4] the two sections being connected by a narrow neck of land, from which deep wadies descend eastward and westward, forbidding communication across the border except by that rocky ridge.[5]   And alike and unlike, connected and separated, have been the two lands since the beginning, as well in politics and religion as by nature.   The reader of the Old Testament recalls that ancient monument of Hebrew literature, the Song of Debora, in whose count of the tribes Juda is missing, while he knows how the ancient separateness of North and South was perpetuated by the fateful schism under King Rehoboam, which caused the Judaite historians to look upon the North as schismatic and renegade.   In the history of Judaism, Southern Israel's precipitate of the people of Moses and David, Samaria appears almost as a blank upon the map, and the student of the New Testament likewise knows how, while the Gospel history is enacted on Judæan and Galilæan soil, and even in half-heathen Peræa, it refers to Samaria only in episodes. Jesus himself, like any Jewish rabbi, was an unwelcome guest in Samaria; it was an epoch in his Church's life when it established itself in that hostile region.   The absence of information concerning Samaria and its people in the historical sources that are generally accessible to both Jew and Christian, naturally prompts the question: Who were the Samaritans?

But if left stranded by subsequent historical developments, and ignored by orthodoxy, the people of Samaria may claim the privileges of both nature and early history. In marked contrast with rocky and barren Juda, Samaria is a verdant hill-country, in which the traveller marks a constant succession of smiling valleys.[6]   Even the eastern

---

[4] Highland of Juda, *Jos.* 11, 21, etc., cf. *Lu.* 1, 39.
[5] See G. A. Smith's brilliant chapters upon the comparison of Juda and Samaria, *HG* xii, xvi, xvii.
[6] Buhl, *Geographie des alten Palaestina*, 21; *HG* 324.

slopes, which in their southerly prolongation end in the waste and precipitous Wilderness of Juda, are gradual in their fall and contain many a fertile spot.[7] Unlike Juda too, Samaria is rendered accessible by the valleys east and north and west, which keep the land in easy communication with the world beyond. This comparative openness of the district may have contributed to the depravement of Israel's religion and morals, through the ready contact with the Mediterranean highway, heathenish Galilee, Tyre and its seductive Baal-worship, Damascus and its luxuries (*Am.* 3, 12). It was Juda's geographical isolation which contributed to its final spiritual development and the preservation of its sacred fruit. But withal this catholicity of the northern land has given a richness to its history and literature which we miss in the South. Except for the episode of David and Solomon, the North occupies the stage of history until the city Samaria's fall; there was the seat of the early prophetic guilds, with their seething life, pregnant of weal and woe for Israel's religion. The contrast may be most clearly marked in the comparison between the one writing prophet of the North, Hosea, and his southern contemporary Amos. Both insist equally on the exclusive claims of Yahwe and his righteousness, but it is the former who preaches the long-suffering love of God, with a depth of passion and a variety of imagination, which outbid the colder South. And the divine Heart never lost its sympathy for the North: " Go," speaks the Voice to Jeremia, " Go, and proclaim these words unto the North: Return, Backslider Israel, says Yahwe!" (*Jer.* 3, 12).

And along with the charms of nature and the corresponding endowment of a richer, more passionate character in the people of the land, is associated the privilege of history. Straight into the inviting uplands of Ephraim went the tribes of Israel, or such as were associated under the leader-

[7] Robinson, *LBR,* 296; Buhl, *op. cit.* 22.

ship of Joseph; their objective was Shechem, the natural capital of the district (*Jos.* 1–9). Upon its two holy mountains was performed, and this according to Judæan tradition, the first formal covenant of the people with Yahwe in their new home (*Jos.* 8, 30ff; *Dt.* 27). In Israel's memories or legends of the past, Mount Ephraim was the land frequented by Abraham and beloved of Jacob, and many a site might be pointed out where Yahwe had appeared to his favorites. And now again the land was consecrated by the graves of Joseph and Joshua and Eleazar (*Jos.* 24, 29ff), even according to an early tradition by the tombs of all the Twelve Patriarchs (*Acts,* 7, 16). This was the land of Gideon and Samuel and Saul, of Elija and Elisha, in a word the land of *Israel,* whereas the South possessed no better title than its tribal name Juda, a provincial designation, over against the noble succession of the North. If holy places were counted, Juda could boast only of Hebron and Beersheba, and of the very modern sanctity of Jebusite Jerusalem, but the North was full of sanctuaries where Yahwe had appeared and where his heroes lived and died. Strange outcome that the one-time separatist tribe became the Church of Israel, while the North has at last given home to the smallest and most insignificant sect in the world!

But only in one place is the modern remnant of that ancient sect to be found, in historic Shechem, once the capital of the tribes of Israel,[8] the sanctuary of their Covenant-God;[9] and thither they have drawn back to die in the first home of national Israel. In Shechem and its neighborhood is the quintessence of the natural charms and historic traditions of the land of Samaria. As the traveller from Jerusalem pushes his journey northwards along the barren ridge which connects Juda with Samaria, at last his eye, wearied

---

[8] Add to previous references, 1 *Ki.* 12, 1, 25.
[9] It contained the sanctuary of Baal-berith, or El-berith, *Ju.* 9, 4, 46, *i. e.,* the God of Covenant.

MOUNT GERIZIM AND MOUNT EBAL

with stony ledges is refreshed, hard by the village of Kuza, with the view of a long and broadening valley, rich in season with waving grain.   Eight miles or more the fair sight stretches before him to the north, and in direct alignment beyond appears the snowy peak of distant Hermon.   Into this plain, al-Machna, he descends, and on the left there begins to loom up a pair of promontory-like mountains, which, as he approaches them, reveal a narrow vale nestled between their steep slopes.   Under the eastern front of the first of the mountains, Gerizim, he makes his way, and, whether Jew or Gentile, doubtless pauses to rest at Jacob's Well, where once Jesus as he sat, held converse with a Samaritan woman in words which alone would immortalize her sect.   From this point he gains a full view of the vale of Shechem stretching to the west, and turns in thither between the heights of Gerizim and its northern mate Ebal, by the road which from immemorial times has connected northern and southern Palestine.   For a mile and a half he proceeds into the narrowing valley, through fields of grain and olive orchards, with the walls of his destination lying before him — ancient Shechem, the modern Nablus.[10]

Travellers rival one another in describing the charms of Shechem and its vale.[11]   Its climate is attractive, the mountains warding off the chill winds of the north and the hot blasts of the south.   The abundant waters of the valley, springing from Gerizim's side temper the dry air of Palestine, which here, for one spot at least, is enriched with the

[10] Nablus, properly Nabulus (as Abu'l Fida points it), is the Arabic corruption of Neapolis, the name — more fully Flavia Neapolis — which Vespasian gave to the new city with which he replaced the elder Shechem; see below, p. 89.   This is said to be the only case in Palestine where the Arabic nomenclature has preserved a Greek place-name, in lieu of its Semitic predecessor.

[11] It is impossible to enumerate the descriptions travellers have written; for a few, see the Bibliography.   For brief objective descriptions of the town and its sights and inhabitants, we may note *Baedeker*, 246; *JE, s. v. Samaritans.*   For the topography, consult Rosen, *ZDMG* xiv, 634; Guérin, *Samarie*, i, cc. xxii-xxviii, and *SWPM* ii.

2

atmospheric effects which only humidity can give. The
water and the warmth of the narrow valley, which in one
place is only 100 yards wide, nurse a luxuriant vegetation,
both in grain crops and in orchards; no place in Palestine
would be more fitting for Jotham's Parable of the Trees
(*Ju.* 9, 7ff). The more picturesque descriptions tell of the
myriads of birds singing amidst the trees, among them
the bulbul's voice being heard.[12] The streets of the city
are cooled with the water-channels that run through them,
from the fifteen springs that are found in the town and
from others outside.[13] Above the town lie green fields and
orchards, while higher up again the more genuine Palestinian scenery reappears in the steep and stony heights of the
two mountains, a contrast which must make the oriental
Neapolitan more than ever content with the beautiful valley
in which his lot is cast. "Little Damascus" the town has
been fondly called,[14] and such an epithet, the Prophet of
Islam being witness, is the highest compliment an oriental
can pay. At all events to the senses of the wearied traveller
it must appear as a veritable Garden of the Lord, while
the thriftiness of the town is a welcome relief to one who
is accustomed to the ruins and desolation of the ancient
cities of Palestine.

Shechem is not only at the heart of Samaria, but is also
the junction of the natural routes traversing this hill-country. Through it runs the ancient highway connecting Juda
and Galilee, on the line of which the Romans built one of
their noble roads. Its springs feed the Wady ash-Shair,
which runs northwest, giving the natural road to the ancient city of Samaria, and finally to Cæsarea and the cities of

---

[12] For impartiality's sake, I should refer to Mills, who gives a much
more prosaic account of Nablus' charms: *Three Months' Residence at
Nablus*, 29.

[13] Rosen gives a list of these springs, *l. c.*

[14] Mukaddasi, quoted by Le Strange, *Palestine Under the Moslems*,
511.

the northern Maritime Plain. Just east of Shechem is the watershed between the Mediterranean and the Jordan, and the Wady Fara here affords easy access to the latter valley, while the great plain of al-Machna is the natural confluence for many roads from all directions. Shechem's commercial importance in modern times is signified by the fact that it is the junction of two telegraph lines from the west, one coming up from Joppa, the other over the western heights from Galilee, meeting here, and thence running across the Jordan to as-Salt.

The early existence of Shechem is proved by the traditions concerning Abraham (*Gen.* 12, 6) and Jacob (*Gen.* 34), and also by two extra-Biblical references of the IId Millennium B.C. Knudtzon now reads the name in a Tell-Amarna tablet,[15] and a reference to it and its holy mountain is found in the Papyrus Anastasi I.: " the mount of Shechem " (Sakama).[16] The Old Testament is witness to its importance in Israel's history, at least before the rise of the new capital Samaria, which eclipsed it, until with Samaria's decay in the IIId and IVth Centuries A.C., Shechem again outstripped the rival and recovered its position as the chief city of the district.

In this connection reference may be made to the question whether Shechem always occupied its present site, for in the Orient the identity of name does not involve continuance in the same locality. Nothing in the Old Testament disproves the identity of old Shechem with Nablus, and the scene of Jotham's parable capitally suits the present site of the city. However it is to be observed that Josephus and

---

[15] Knudtzon, in *Beiträge zur Assyriologie*, 1899, p. 112, to Tablet B. 199 (Winckler, 185), lines 21–24. He reads: "Lapaya and Shechem (mat Shakmi) have given (pay ?) to the Chabiri." See Steuernagel, *Einwanderung der israelitischen Stämme*, 120, who connects the passage with the transactions in *Gen.* 34.

[16] W. Max Müller, *Asien u. Europa*, 394; Sayce, *Patriarchal Palestine*, 211. The date of these *Travels of a Mohar* is about 1300 B. C.

Pliny assign Vespasian's foundation of Neapolis to a place originally called Mabartha.[17]   Shechem may then have lain more to the east, and if it is to be placed on the watershed already described, its name, " shoulder," can be explained. This distinction between the elder Shechem and the " New-City " of Vespasian is borne out by Patristic authorities and also by archæology. The Pilgrim of Bordeaux (*circa* 333) writes as follows: " Civitas Neapoli. Ibi est Agazaren (Gerizim). . . . . Inde ad pedem montis ipsius, locus est cui nomen est Sichem. Ibi positum est monumentum ubi positus est Joseph, in villa quam dedit ei Jacob pater ejus. . . . . Inde passus mille, locus est cui nomen Sechar, unde descendit mulier Samaritana ad eundem locum." Eusebius writes (*Onom. s. v.* Συχεμ): " Sychem and Sikima, which is Salem, Jacob's city, now deserted."   The Mosaic Map of Madaba likewise distinguishes between Neapolis and Sychem. The archæological evidence obtained by the English Survey may also be quoted here:[18] " The ruins of Nablus extend for a distance east of the modern town.   Vaults were excavated in digging the foundations of the barracks [about half-way towards Jacob's Well], and persons in the city claim to have title-deeds of buildings and shops in the same direction.   A long mound with traces of a rude wall exists between Balata and 'Askar, and there is a tesselated pavement just east of Joseph's tomb, in which neighborhood ruins are mentioned in the fourteenth century, and were supposed to be those of ancient Thebez (Marino Sanuto)."

In this connection rises the question concerning the identity of the city Sychar of *Jn.* 4, 5, which it has now become the fashion to identify with the Ain Askar lying 1250

----

[17] *BJ* viii, 4, 1: Mabartha, so Niese, var. Mabortha; Pliny, *Hist, nat.* v, 14, Mamortha. This name is doubtless to be explained, with Schwarz, *Exercitationes historico-criticæ in utrumque Sam. Pent.,* 25, as representing the Aramaic Ma'abarta, i. e., Pass.

[18] *SWPM* 206; cf. Rosen, *ZDMG* xiv, 639.

meters NE of Jacob's Well. As we have seen, the Bordeaux Pilgrim distinguishes a Sychar apart from Shechem and Neapolis. Also Eusebius, treating of Sychar, says that it is " before Neapolis, near the place which Jacob gave to Joseph, his son." On the other hand Jerome knows nothing of a place Sychar, and insists that it is a mistake for Shechem, which he also identifies with Neapolis.[19] These IVth Century authorities therefore by no means agree. It is to be observed that the elder Shechem once lay as close to Jacob's Well as does Ain Askar, so that the Samaritan woman could easily have come to draw water at the former place. Further, the Fourth Gospel describes Sychar as a Polis, and there is absolutely no evidence for the existence of a *city* Sychar. As to the dispute between Jerome and the opposing authorities, inasmuch as Jerome takes pains to make denial of the existence of a Sychar, it may be argued that he is right, and his opponents were rather depending upon some tradition originated in support of the Gospel text. Finally, while it is quite possible that Askar is an Arabic corruption of Sychar, nevertheless in its simple meaning of 'askar as a camp, may it not be the later Arabic translation of *machna*, the name of the plain, which itself in Hebrew means a camp?[20] Ain Askar would then be the Well of Al-Machna. It appears to the present writer that a strong case can still be made out for the identification of Sychar with Shechem, on the supposition, with Jerome, of a text-corruption in the text of St. John,— Συχεμ, a variant of Σιχεμ, having accidentally become Συχαρ. The reception of Jesus in the home-city of the Samaritans would be no more strange than the hospitality accorded to Simon Magus or to the Jerusalem Apostles (*Acts,* 8).[21]

[19] *Epitaphium Paulæ; Quæstiones in Gen. ad* xlviii, 22; *Onom.* lxvi, 20 (in Migne, respectively: xx, 888; xxiii, 1055; 965).
[20] I find that Conder has already suggested this etymology; *PEFQS* 1876, p. 197.
[21] G. A. Smith sums up the case for the identification of Sychar with

Nablus itself is a long narrow town, about two-thirds of a mile in extent, surrounded by a dilapidated wall. In strategics the town has always been weak, as it lies in the hollow of an indefensible valley, and its walls could never have amounted to much more than police barricades. Indeed the history of the town shows that it never was strong enough to necessitate regular siege, its conquerors always easily pouring into its undefended bounds. This natural weakness was one of the calamities of Northern Israel, which was finally forced to leave its ancient capital for the new city of Samaria, whereas Shechem's southern rival Jerusalem again and again stood the siege of invaders when the rest of the land had fallen to the foe. Nevertheless Shechem has survived, in that way peculiar to oriental life, whereby a city is re-born like the phœnix out of the fire of destruction, and it contains within its walls the only fragment of the Hebrew race which has survived by unbroken succession on Palestinian soil.

In its structures the town does not differ from other oriental towns. It contains five mosques, four of which were originally Crusaders' churches, one of them going back to a foundation of Justinian's. The great arched bazaar which occupies a section of the principal street is said to be the finest in Palestine, and even to rival those of the largest cities of the Turkish empire. The shops are well-furnished with a great variety of commodities, while the productive power of the community finds vent in extensive manufactures of woolens and soap, the latter product being famous all over Syria.

The population of Nablus numbers about 24,000.[22] The

Askar, in *HG* c. xviii. Cheyne has a good review of the data in *EB* *s. v. Sychar*, and concludes with the view above preferred, insisting on the purely Arabic character of 'askar. The earlier students of the question, such as Robinson and Guérin, rejected the identification of Sychar and Askar.

[22] These and the following are Baedeker's figures, ed. 1900. The town

great majority are Muslims, the remainder consisting of about 700 Christians,[23] 152 Samaritans (in 1901), and a number of Jews.[24] The town and district are under a local Mutesellim, who is subordinate to the governor of Jerusalem; with his Diwan, or council, are associated representatives of the Greeks, the Samaritans (including the Jews), and the Protestants, as according to Ottoman rule each community must have its responsible spokesman.

As in many another earthly paradise, so in Nablus, "only man is vile." No town in Palestine has so bad a reputation for the ill-disposition and violence of its citizens, and the Ottoman government handles the local elements only with greatest delicacy. Since the day of Lapaya, the marauder of the Tell-Amarna period, Shechem has been the scene of violence and murder. Here occurred the one blot upon the peaceful scutcheon of the patriarchs (*Gen.* 34); here the headstrong Abimelek made himself king, and fell into feud with the rebellious citizens (*Ju.* 9); here the tie with the Davidic dynasty was snapped, and the secession baptized in blood (1 *Ki.* 12), while its priests became notorious for murderous violence (*Hos.* 6, 9). It would be impossible to enumerate the conflicts which have taken place at Shechem between Samaritan and Jew, Samaritan and Roman, Samaritan and Christian; and when Islam conquered the region, although the turbulence of the Samaritans was then cowed forever, the Arabs too fell subject to the atmosphere of the place, and the town and its district have been notorious for the lawlessness which the inhabitants have shown toward the Ottoman rule.

seems to have grown considerably since Petermann's visit, when the calculations given to him by the residents varied between 12,000 and 20,000.

[23] Mostly of the Greek Church, but some of the Latin Rite, along with 150 Protestants.

[24] Baedeker says merely "some Jews." According to Petermann they numbered some 200. The Jews did not return to Shechem until the third decade of the last century, under the Egyptian *régime*.

CHAPTER III.

THE MODERN SAMARITANS.

In the southwestern quarter of their ancient city, close to the path which leads to the holy place on Gerizim's top, is the Ghetto of the Samaritans.[1] They live crowded together, being quite segregated from the Muslim population, not only out of desire of separation but as well for fear of their violent neighbors. According to statistics of 1901[2] they number 152 souls, and the doom which confronts the community is presented in the ‘proportion of males and females, the former numbering 97, the latter only 55. They do not marry outside of their own body, the Jews, the only race with whom they might intermingle, of course refusing such alliances. The people call themselves by the ancient geographical appellative, Samerim, which they interpret however as meaning " the Observers," i.e. of the Law.[3]

Concerning the ethnology of the Samaritans, Robinson makes this observation: " The physiognomy of those we saw was not Jewish; nor indeed did we remark in it any peculiar character, as distinguished from that of other na-

[1] Called Charat as-Samira, the Quarter of the Samaritans, although incorrectly, not being a proper city-quarter. The name also appears as Charat as-Samâra, SWPM 204. Rosen vocalizes it as Sumereh.

[2] Reference is here made to the valuable statistics and anthropological tables presented by H. M. Huxley in JE x, 674, the materials for which were collected by the American Archæological Expedition to Syria in 1899–1900. (The publication of the full material by Huxley is promised for an early date as Part V.) The figures given by travellers in the XIXth Century are discrepant; Robinson estimated them in 1838 at 150, BR iii, 106; Petermann, in 1853, at 122 (Reisen, i, 265); Mills, in 1855, at 150 (Nablus, 179); Rogers, in the same year, at 197 (Notices, 16). SWPM gives 135 for the year 1875, 160 for 1881.

[3] See Additional Note B.

24

Pal. Ex. Fund.   A Group of Samaritans.

tives of the country." [4] But this judgment has been controverted by almost all other visitors to Shechem, who remark upon the distinctiveness of the Samaritan type, and bear witness with some surprise to its comparative nobility among the races of Palestine; the representatives of the priesthood, the only educated ones, have called forth much admiration for their intelligence of expression and dignity of bearing. The Rev. John Mills, who lived among them for three months, also paying them a second visit, and who seems to have been a very intelligent observer, writes as follows of the race:[5] " I had seen individuals, among Arabs and Jews, of as noble aspect as any one of them; but as a community, there is nothing in Palestine to compare with them. A straight and high forehead, full brow, large and rather almond-shaped eye, aquiline nose, somewhat large mouth, and well-formed chin, are their chief physiological characteristics; and, with few exceptions, they are tall and of lofty bearing. They seem to be all of one type, and bear an unmistakable family likeness. In this they differ from the Jews, who have assimilated in physical as well as in moral qualities to the nations among whom they have long dwelt."

These impressions of travellers are corroborated by the exact figures and scientific observations that are reported in the article in the *Jewish Encyclopædia,* above cited. I refer the reader to the tables contained there, and quote here only the summary, as follows:

" The general type of physiognomy of the Samaritans is distinctly Jewish, the nose markedly so. Von Luschan derives the Jews from ' the Hittites, the Aryan Amorites, and the Semitic nomads.' The Samaritans may be traced to the same origin. The ' Amorites were men of great stature ' and to them Von Luschan traces the blonds of

[4] *BR* iii, 106.
[5] *Op. cit.* 180; cf. 182, 184.

the modern Jews. With still greater certainty the tall stature and the presence of a blond type among the Samaritans may be referred to the same source.[6] The cephalic index, much lower than that of the modern Jews, may be accounted for by a former direct influence of the Semitic nomads, now represented by the Bedouins, whose cephalic index according to measurement of 114 males, is 76.3.[7] The Samaritans have thus preserved the ancient type in its purity; and they are to-day the sole, though degenerate, representatives of the ancient Hebrews."

The principal employment of the Samaritans is petty trading, a few of them being engaged in manufacture, especially of woolens; none of them are agriculturists. Their past history shows that their *forte* has lain, like that of their Jewish relatives, in finance, and they appear to have maintained an honorable reputation in the handling of moneys, for down into the past century individuals of their number have regularly acted as the fiscal agents of the local government. Travellers vary in their impressions concerning the virtues of the Samaritans; many are disgusted by their participation in the everlasting oriental demand for bakhsheesh, "the one Arabic word the traveller never forgets," as a French scholar has said. But while ready to drive hard bargains for fees and manuscripts, and equal to deceit in imposing upon the credulous tourist, no charges of commercial dishonesty or faithlessness have been laid against them. The retention of their sacred volume of the Law of Moses against the captivating attempts that have been made for its purchase by European scholars, is demonstration that they can put principle before Mammon. Some travellers speak very warmly concerning the social traits of the perishing community. The violence and extortion from

[6] Earlier in the same article it is shown that the Samaritans are the tallest people in Syria. Also the figures given for pigmentation reveal "a distinct blond type noticeable in the race."

[7] That of the Samaritans is 78.1, of the modern Jews, 82.

which the people of Nablus have suffered in the XIXth Century have reduced the Samaritans to a condition of poverty.

The Samaritans have adopted the Arabic vernacular to such an extent that only the few learned ones among them carry on the tradition of the Hebrew and Aramaic which were the earlier tongues of the people.[8] Every Samaritan man possesses two names, one of which is generally composed of names taken from the Pentateuch, especially from its heroes, while the other is drawn from the common Arabic nomenclature for persons. Despite the assimilations with the Muslim population into which the Samaritans have drifted, their political masters have taken pains to keep them conscious of their inferior position. Following the principles of the caliph Omar, who required distinguishing costumes for unbelievers, an Abbaside caliph ordered that the Samaritans should appear in public with a red turban on the head, a regulation which has been more or less stringently enforced, according to the temper of the government.[9] Their native costume, especially on gala occasions, is white.

We come now to the consideration of the inner life of the Samaritans as a religious community, and this phrase means, it must be remembered, for an oriental sect practically the whole of the community's life. Here a thesis must be advanced of which the whole of the following work gives proof, and to which all modern investigators bear testimony. Even as the Samaritans are shown by anthropology to be Hebrews of the Hebrews, so the study of their religion and manners demonstrates them to be nothing else than a Jewish sect. This is not the traditional view concerning their origin, nor is it as yet generally known to the lay mind.

[8] For the languages, see Chap. XIV.
[9] Not as Petermann, *op. cit.* 274, says, a "Mamluk Sultan," but the Abbaside Mutawakkil; see below, p. 129.

Samaritanism is still commonly looked upon as a mixed religion containing elements of Judaism and ancient heathenism, and although the compound is not supposed to have been analyzed, it is considered to be full of theological heresies and moral corruption.

Subsequent chapters will expand and substantiate the points at present only summarily given. This chapter will treat only of the customs of the Samaritans as they have lain under the observation of Europeans for over three centuries. But their religion may be summed up in these few words. It is a monotheism identical with that of Judaism, whose very terms they use throughout, while it bitterly opposes any attempt to associate with God other deities, as in polytheism, or to find in him any distinctions, as in Christianity. It is a spiritual religion, which not only rejects any representation of Deity, but even eschews, after the letter of the Second Commandment, all pictorial designs.[10] It is moreover an ethical religion which has flowered in just such virtues and which is circumscribed by just such limitations as mark what is known as orthodox Judaism. We will now consider those points of the life of the Samaritan community which come under the eye of the observer, and mark, as we proceed, wherein they agree with, and wherein they differ from, the forms of Judaism, leaving to subsequent Chapters the history of the sect and the formal presentation of its theology.[11]

The intelligent visitor to Nablus naturally soon takes his way to the Samaritan quarter, and discovers their synagogue, which is called after the same name used by the

[10] Petermann, *op. cit.* 282, relates that on the visit of the highpriest to his room, the latter requested him to turn the face of some hanging portraits to the wall.

[11] The facts in the following pages are drawn from the statements of the travellers already cited, from the Samaritan correspondence with Europeans, and in some cases from other Samaritan literature. In moot questions or points of particular interest, reference is made to the authorities, all of whom are listed in the Bibliography.

Jews for their places of worship, *Kenîsat as-Samira,* the Samaritan Synagogue. It is also commonly called among themselves *Bit Allah,* the house of God.[12] This is a plain building, of no great antiquity.[13] It contains a room whose greatest length is 37 ft., 5 in.; on its right hand and running for about two-thirds of the length of the main portion is an extension with a raised floor. On the left is a curtained recess, about 4¼ ft. sq. There is no adornment, and light is admitted only by a glazed circular aperture in the roof.

Entrance is had upon application to the highpriest,— Kohen hag-Gadol, he is called in Hebrew, or in good Arabic, the Imam. He is of the blood of Levi, the direct Aaronic line having failed, according to Samaritan testimony in the XVIIth Century, although this fact it has become the fiction to deny.[14] With him is associated a Levitical relative, the Shammash, or minister, who performs most of the service, but the priest is required for the blessing.

This great man, who always appears in robes of white, is not too dignified to demand of the visitor a large bakhsheesh for the privilege of inspecting the synagogue. The terms of the bargain having been arranged, the stranger desires to look upon the sacred roll of the Law of Moses, the greatest treasure of the Samaritans. This is contained in the recess already mentioned, which is called the *muçbach,* or altar, even as the Jews call the synagogal ark containing the scroll the *heikal,* or temple. The recess has an important function in the services, as it corresponds to the

---

[12] Mills, *op. cit.* 222.

[13] The Samaritans claim that the neighboring mosque, Chizn Ya'qub, was originally their synagogue, which was confiscated about 1300; see below, pp. 134, 273. The present synagogue contains an inscription recording the restoration of the building A. D. 1711, and asserting that it had been built 320 years before. The inscription is given by Rosen, *ZDMG* xiv, 624.

[14] See p. 139.

michrab of the Muslim mosque, that is, the niche which indicates the *qibla,* or direction of prayer — for the Muslim towards Mecca, for the Samaritan towards Gerizim; the whole congregation face this point in their devotions in the synagogue. The recess contains a plain chest, which holds rolls of the Law of Moses, unimportant copies of which are shown to the ignorant tourist, but amongst them the greatest treasure of all, a codex which, it is claimed, was written by Abishua, the great-grandson of Aaron.[15] How old this roll is cannot be ascertained, for it is never submitted to examination, only a section being exposed to view at a time. But its sacredness in the eyes of the Samaritans and its appearance of relative antiquity naturally arouse the ambition of scholars for its acquisition, or at least for its inspection, a wish that may never be gratified until the community has perished. The exhibition of one of the rolls, although not of that sacred codex, is an important part of the Sabbath service. At the proper point, the minister brings forth the roll, and presents it to the congregation, opened at the Aaronic blessing, *Num.* 6, 24–27, which passage is then kissed by the worshippers.[16]

It has been said that these rolls contain the Law of Moses. They are indeed codices of the Hebrew Pentateuch, containing a somewhat variant text, with a few intentional alterations made in support of the peculiar tenet of the Samaritans concerning the holiness of Gerizim,[17] along with many textual variants, and written in the Samaritan script, an alphabet derived from the Phœnician and more antique than the Hebrew square character.[18] The Law of Moses is the Samaritan Bible, and herein is the first great difference between this sect and the Jews, who

---

[15] See Chap. XIV, § 6.
[16] Hence in many copies of the Law this and other sacred passages are found blurred to illegibility by the contact of the faithful.
[17] See Chap. XII, § 6.
[18] See Chap. XIV, § 4.

include in their Scriptures, although on a lower plane than the Law, the Prophets and the Hagiographa.

The services in the synagogue are said to be decorous, although the rendering of the service and the music sound barbarous to European ears. The Samaritans once possessed an extensive liturgy,[19] much of which in its written form is now lost to them, and is probably to be found only in European libraries. The portions that are still used are always recited from memory, and concern the chief solemnities of life, the feasts and fasts, birth, marriage and death. But probably the Samaritan memory has retained but a small part of its one-time liturgical wealth. As the language of all their offices is in either Hebrew or Aramaic, tongues for centuries lost to vernacular usage, and as in the last half of the XIXth Century there has been a sad decline in the learning of the priesthood, the majority of the people know nothing of what is said in the services, and the ministers themselves have often only a superficial knowledge of the words they use. The Law, it may be said, is read through once in a year, thus differing from the Jewish arrangement which distributes its sections over three years. The lections are begun with the month Tishri.[20] There is also a rude kind of music, with a number of various airs, for which the Samaritans claim a high tradition.[21]

We have seen that the Samaritans possess three of the great institutes of Judaism, the synagogue, the Law of Moses, the priesthood, the last of which has only a traditional survival amongst the Jews. The highpriest is the theocratic head of the community, he is the authority both spiritual and secular; after the rule of the old Jewish state and of the early Christian Church, believers dare not go

[19] See Chap. XIV, § 10.
[20] For the order of lections, see Cowley, *JQR* vii, 134. The lectional divisions are called qaçin.
[21] Grove (*Nabloos*) and Mills, *op. cit.* 230, seem to be the only ones who have noticed the music.

to law against one another before infidels.[22]   The priests also combine both the sacerdotal and the teaching functions; the sect has never developed the difference between the priests and the doctors of the Law to the extent which marks Judaism, and in modern times the former possess all the learning of the community, although the literature shows that in earlier days laymen were also masters in theology.[23]   The old Nazirite rule is still observed by the priests, that no razor shall touch their head;[24] they are specially careful about defilement, and avoid contact with a dead body.   They always wash before handling the rolls of Scripture.

The laymen also possess their traditional claims.   They are all of the tribe of Joseph, except those of the tribe of Benjamin, but this traditional branch of the people, which, the Chronicles assert, was established in Gaza in earlier days, seems to have disappeared.[25]   There exists a strong aristocratic feeling amongst the different families in this petty community, and some are very proud over their own pedigree and the great men it has produced.   In the services the laymen also wear white robes, and have some antiphonal parts to recite, either from memory or with the use of books.   They do not use the Tephillin, the frontlets or phylacteries of the Jews, nor the fringes, nor the Mezuzot, or prayer-boxes for the door-posts.   The reason given by them for the non-use of the Tephillin is such a one as a Christian would give, that the law is to be spiritually observed.   The priest wears at the reading of the Law a talith, but without fringes.[26]   The women are not admitted

---

[22] See the Samaritan Epistle to Kautzsch, *ZDPV* viii, 149.
[23] *Abu'l Fath*, 129, speaks of the Wise Men, adding that "the priests as a body are not called Wise Men."
[24] There seems to be a reference to the Nazirite profession in *Chron. Neub.* 459.
[25] See p. 149.
[26] See *N. et E.*, 123, 218; Mills, *op. cit.* 192.   The former passage seems to indicate the use of some kind of fringes, but the custom was denied by the priest at Mills' visit.

to the synagogue, even as the rule is amongst the oriental Jews to this day. They, as well as the men, have a morning prayer to recite, in this differing from Jewish custom. They also follow the ancient custom of keeping their hair,[27] which they never shave off, as do the Muslim and Jewish women upon marriage. There is no *Minyan,* or minimum of ten persons, as in the Jewish law, for the observance of a service.

Mention has already been made of services on the Sabbath. This cardinal Jewish institution is observed by the Samaritans with like solemnity to the Jews, but with far greater rigor, for the former have never developed that casuistry, which Jesus so often attacked, whereby the explicit directions of the Law could be circumvented. They stay strictly within doors on the Sabbath, except to go to the synagogue, and have none of the Jewish fiction of the Erub, whereby several houses or a whole street could be artificially designated as a single tenement; nor is there any " Sabbath-day's journey." They follow strictly the injunctions of *Exodus* not to light a fire on the Sabbath, nor may they procure the service of Gentiles for this convenience, as in Judaism; nor may they use any contrivances to keep their food warm, which must all be cooked the day before. It is thus seen that they are purists and literalists, and closely resemble, in their lack of a tradition of the elders which mitigates the rigor of the Law, the Sadducees, with whom, as we shall later see, they are historically connected.

From the weekly Sabbath we naturally pass to the sacred year of the Samaritans. The Samaritan year is of the same nature and has the same months as that of the Jews, the secular or economic year beginning in the autumn, with Tishri, the ecclesiastical year in the spring, with Nisan. The months have 29 or 30 days, and a second Adar is intercalated when necessary to avoid the variation of the lunar

---

[27] Cf. 1 *Cor.* 11, 2ff.

3

year from the solar, which would result in the gradual recession of the sacred seasons through the year. The times of the new moons and of the beginning of the two kinds of year are calculated by the priests in advance for a short period, and the results used to be announced to the scattered communities. The Samaritans appear never to have adopted the Metonic Cycle, by which, in the IVth Century, the Jews finally regulated their year, but still depend upon empirical observation. As late as 1820 such a table was drawn up and sent to the supposed brethren in Europe.[28] The Samaritan Passover and other feasts therefore do not necessarily coincide in date with those of the Jews.

The Samaritans celebrate the seven sacred seasons appointed in the calendar of the Law, *Lev. 23*. Three of them, those which in ancient times were the chief feasts, namely, Passover, Pentecost and Booths, are always celebrated on Mount Gerizim, unless, as often has happened, even for terms of years, they are prevented by Muslim fanaticism; in such case the solemnities, including the Passover sacrifice, are celebrated in the town.[29] We must accordingly make a diversion to observe Mount Gerizim and the sanctity which it holds in Samaritan eyes.

The article of faith in Gerizim is the great differentiating tenet between the Samaritans and the Jews; if they yield this heresy, teaches a Talmudic tractate, they can be readmitted to the true Israel.[30] Doubtless since prehistoric times both the mountains of Shechem, Ebal and Gerizim, were counted amongst the most holy of " the highplaces " of Palestine; as we have seen the Egyptian traveller of the XIIIth Century B. C., makes an allusion to one of them.[31] Of the

[28] See quite fully on this subject, Mills, *op. cit.* 240. See further Chap. XIV, § 12.
[29] For the interruption of the visits to Gerizim, see p. 141; for the celebration of the Passover in Shechem, *N. et E.* 72.
[30] See Chap. XII, §§ 2, 6; Chap. XI.
[31] See above, p. 19.

MOUNT GERIZIM.

two Ebal is the higher (3076 ft. above the sea), and the more commanding in its noble prospect, while Gerizim has an altitude of only 2848 ft.[32] According to Hebrew tradition, upon the conquest of the land, these two mountains formed the amphitheatre for the great convocation of all Israel, when the curses were recited from Ebal, and the blessings from Gerizim (*Dt.* 27; *Jos.* 8, 30ff). The comminations alone are given in the story of the rite, a fact which gives greater prominence to Ebal; this was felt by the Samaritans doubtless because of Jewish taunts, and they deliberately altered the text in *Dt.* 27, 4, so that the stones of Jordan and the altar should be reared on Gerizim.[33] There can be no doubt, despite the assent of such a scholar as Kennicott, that the Samaritan reading is a falsification. But the reason why Ebal was chosen for the curses, which appear as the more important part of the ceremony, was simply due to the fact that it lay on the north, the side of ill-omen. Gerizim then would be the auspicious one of the pair for worship, and the Samaritans have in all probability preserved the ancient tradition concerning the relative religious worth of the two.[34] On Ebal's top only ruins of a very rude construction, a great enclosure 90 ft. sq., have been discovered,[35] while the ruins on Gerizim are much more extensive and of considerable architectural importance.

The easiest path from Nablus to Gerizim's top is one which leads from the Samaritan quarter up a defile; following this the traveller, after nearly an hour's climb, reaches the eastern summit of Gerizim, upon or near which are

[32] The Samaritans deny the greater height of Ebal, in fact hold that Gerizim is the highest of all mountains.

[33] See Chap. XII, § 6, for this falsification, and also for the Samaritan legends connected with Gerizim.

[34] This superstition as to points of the compass would be enhanced by the comparative bleakness of Ebal's southern slope, seared by the sun's heat; it is also more difficult of access.

[35] *SWPM* 186.

found all the sites and ruins of interest. At the northern and eastern end of the natural platform lie the remains of what once was a massive and noble structure. The history of the building is a story common to the holy places of the Orient. One compartment of the enclosure is now used as a Muslim mosque; the octagonal building situated in the midst is doubtless the Church of the Virgin Mary erected by the emperor Zeno, which succeeded a Roman temple, while this heathen structure was preceded by the Samaritan temple, destroyed by John Hyrcanus in the IId Century B. C., and built according to tradition by Sanballat the reputed founder of the sect in the time of Alexander the Great. And behind the history of these respective fanes stretches the succession of primitive cults, of Yahwe and of Baal and of many another deity, back into the beginnings of history. But it is only probability that leads the archæologist to find here the site of the Samaritan temple; no local tradition corroborates it, and the Samaritans ignore it.[36]

On the west side of these ruins are the Twelve Stones, which according to Samaritan tradition are the stones Joshua brought from the Jordan and set up in this place, *Jos.* 4. These seem to be the remains of an upper tier of stones forming the edge of some ancient platform. At a distance of 240 ft. to the south of the ancient temple lies the holiest spot in Samaritan eyes; this is a platform of natural rock, about 48x36 ft. In its southern end is a hollow, like the depressions which are found in many of the Syrian rock-altars, designed doubtless for the collection of the sacrificial blood. At the northwestern end is a cistern lined with primitive masonry, which may have been a natural cave. To the Samaritans this stone, the Sakhra,[37] is

---

[36] See, for the ruins and holy sites on Gerizim, C. W. Wilson, *Ebal and Gerizim,* in *PEFQS,* 1873, p. 66 (with plan), containing the results of explorations made by Wilson and Lieut. Anderson in 1866; Guérin, *Samarie,* i, c. xxv; *SWPM* 187.

[37] The priests are sometimes designated as Priests of the Stone; see *JBL* 1906, pp. 34, 36.

the Holy of Holies, which a member of the community approaches only with bared feet; the tradition is that the temple was built over the cave. This stony projection with its cave and pool for blood reminds us at once of the corresponding Sakhra, or holy stone, and cave which have been the immemorial sanctuary on Mount Zion. In the south-eastern quarter of the top of Gerizim, according to tradition, was the site of Abraham's sacrifice on Moria, while the seven steps leading down into a neighboring trench are those by which Adam descended when he was expelled from Paradise. For almost every sacred incident from the beginning of history to its consummation is connected by Samaritan credulity with the top of Gerizim.[38]

Strangely enough it is not at these sites consecrated by tradition that the Samaritan celebrates his holiest rite, the Passover. But the celebration takes place at a point which is reached by the path above described about ten minutes before arriving at the top of the mountain. There is nothing distinctive about the spot, which is surrounded by dilapidated stone walls and contains some sunken trenches. Probably it has been the malice of the Muslims that has driven the sect to this insignificant piece of land. We read in a Chronicle how a benefactor from amongst them in the middle of the XVIIIth Century bought from the Muslims a piece of ground on the mountain,[39] and we may suppose that this is the lot which the Samaritans still use in lieu of the holier sites from which they have been debarred.

It is within this enclosure that the Samaritans celebrate their only sacrifice, the Passover, and here alone in the world is that historic rite of Israel maintained.[40] No wonder

[38] For lists of the other holy places as claimed by the Samaritans in the neighborhood of Shechem, see *SWPM* 218f; Conder, *PEFQS* 1876, p. 192.

[39] See p. 139.

[40] The family Passover of the Jews is only a symbolic rite, not a sacrifice.

then that both lovers of the Bible history and students of
antiquity have eagerly availed themselve: of the opportunity
to witness the survival of this decaying ceremony, so laden
with historic memories. Petermann first, and many observers since have witnessed the Samaritan Passover, and
the reader is recommended to turn to their easily accessible
descriptions for graphic accounts of the ceremony.[41] Here
only an outline of the function can be given.

The solemnity is a veritable *Haj,* or pilgrim-feast. The
whole community proceeds to the place of sacrifice on Mount
Gerizim, allowing abundance of time for the preparations.
The tents are pitched, and all eagerly await the appointed
hour, which occurs at sunset,[42]— for so the Samaritans interpret the phrase " between the evenings," *Ex.* 12, 6.[43]   A
number of lambs have been carefully selected from those
born in the preceding Tishri, and of these so many as will
suffice for the worshippers are destined for the sacrifice,
generally from five to seven, although others are at hand in
case anyone of them is ritually unfit. Some hours before
the sacrifice two fires are started in the trenches above described; in one of them a caldron is heated for boiling the
water necessary to fleece the lambs, in the other a mass of
fuel is kindled to make the oven for roasting the lambs.
All these preparations are in the hands of young men (cf.

[41] For descriptions of the Passover by eye-witnesses, see the Bibliography under the titles: Curtiss, Grove, Macewen, Mills, Moulton,
Petermann, E. T. Rogers, Stafford, Stanley, Thomson, Trumbull, Warren, Wilson. The notice by the young American scholar, Moulton, is
based upon particularly critical observation.

[42] Variations in this appointment, however, are caused by the inci-
dence of the Sabbath. If the 14th Nisan is a Sabbath, the feast takes
place the day before, in which case the functions must be proceeded
with at earlier hours so that all may be over before the advent of the
Sabbath; if the feast falls on Sunday, the preparations may not begin
until Saturday is past, the days being measured of course from sunset
to sunset.

[43] The Samaritan use here agrees with the Sadducæan as against that
of the Pharisees, according to whom the sacrifice should be made between 3 and 6 p. m.

Ex. 24, 5), who sometimes are clad in blue robes.[44] Coincident with the starting of the fire the service begins, and this is kept up until the lambs are put into the oven; it consists in the reading of the Passover lections from *Exodus,* and ancient Passover hymns. A certain number of representative men render the antiphons. In the service all turn towards the Kibla, the top of Gerizim. At sunset the sacrifice takes place, not on an altar but in a ditch; the throats of the lambs are deftly cut by a young man, not by the priest.[45] The ritual inspection then takes place, the sinews of the legs are withdrawn (*Gen.* 32, 32), the offal removed, and the lambs fleeced by aid of the hot water. The lambs are then spitted with a long stick run through their length,[46] and are conveyed to the heated oven, over which they are laid, the spits protruding on either side, while above them is laid a thick covering of turf to seal the oven. The process of roasting takes three or four hours, during which time the worshippers may rest, the service being mostly intermitted. When it is deemed the proper time, the lambs are withdrawn, and present a blackened and repulsive aspect. A short service then ensues, the congregation now appearing with their loins girt up and their staves in their hands (*Ex.* 12, 11), and when the service is over, veritably " eat in haste," for they fall ravenously upon the coal-like pieces of flesh, devouring it and taking platters-full to the women and children, who remain in the tents. When all the flesh is consumed, the bones, scraps, wool, are carefully

---

[44] So Mills saw them, *op. cit.* 253, although others witness to white robes, in which the community appear. For the use of blue in sacred vestments, see the Samaritan Epistle, *N. et E.* 123.

[45] Petermann saw individuals applying the blood to their faces, and parents streaking it on their children; Moulton, the most recent observer, saw nothing of this, and learned that this rite had been omitted for some years for fear of the Muslims.

[46] The statement of Justin Martyr, a native of Neapolis, that the Passover lamb was trussed on a cross-shaped spit does not, as is usually noted in this connection, refer to the Samaritan sacrifice, but explicitly to the Passover at Jerusalem; *C. Tryphon.* c. 40.

gathered up, and thrown into the still smouldering fire, until all is consumed, " so that none of it remain till the morrow." After the meal ablutions take place, and the ceremony is concluded with further prayers and chants. According to the prescriptions of *Num.* 9, the " Second Passover " is allowed.

In close connection with the Passover is the feast of Unleaven, or Massot, which is reckoned as the second sacred feast, being distinguished from the Passover, although coincident with it, according to the language of the Law. On the 13th of the month a careful search is made for all leaven, which is scrupulously removed, and from the 14th day till the 21st no leaven may be eaten. The 21st is the great day of this feast, and on it they make pilgrimage to Gerizim, reading through the book of Deuteronomy on the way and at the village Makkada, where they finally halt.

The ensuing Pentecostal period, which is measured not after the Jewish method from the second day of Unleavened Bread, but literally according to *Lev.* 23,15f from the morrow of the Sabbath in that week,[47] is an especially holy portion of the year; on the third day before Pentecost is celebrated the third great feast, that of the Stay of Moses upon Sinai, that is of the beginning of the Lawgiver's sojourn in the holy mount. On this day the whole Law is read.[48]

The fourth feast is that of Weeks, or Pentecost, which is reckoned as above stated. It is celebrated by pilgrimage to Gerizim, where the whole Law is again read. Its primitive character as a harvest feast is particularly observed, with regard to *Dt.* 16,9ff. The fifth feast is that of Trum-

[47] This was also the method of the Boethusians and is still that of the Karaite sect.
[48] This feast does not appear in the lists given in the Epistles, *e. g.*, *N. et E.* 76, 157, 176; in these lists it is difficult to discover how the seven feasts that are claimed are actually counted; probably the 8th day of Weeks is reckoned the seventh feast.

pets, the New Year's day, falling on the first day of the seventh ecclesiastical month. But the Samaritans do not regard this so much as a New Year's festival as rather the beginning of the great penitential season of the year.[49] The sixth holy season is the solemn fast of the Day of Atonement, the Jewish Kippur.[50] The day is most strictly observed; none, man, woman nor child, is allowed to eat, drink, sleep, or converse for the whole day; all adult males must spend the whole day in the synagogue, except, according to Mills' narrative, for a solemn excursion to the tombs of certain of the prophets. The service consists in the reading of the whole Pentateuch, and in the singing of special hymns, which are by far the most spiritual of all in the liturgy, dwelling as they do most earnestly upon the need of repentance, and likening the fast to the great final " Day of Recompense and Vengeance." Towards the conclusion of the service occurs the most solemn event of the year, the exhibition of the ancient roll of Abishua, which occurs only on this occasion. More than usual ritual solemnity accompanies the rite; the priests are clothed in light-green satin dresses, and upon emerging from the recess with the roll are covered with a talith. Before the exposed roll the congregation repeatedly prostrate themselves, then press forward to touch, kiss, caress it, the cynosure of all eyes.[51] This solemn day makes the month the holiest of all to the mind of the Samaritans.

The feast of Booths completes the circuit of the seven seasons, and is observed in close accord with the Pentateuchal regulations, the booths being erected in the courts of the houses. Each day of the first seven they make pilgrim-

---

[49] Cf. *BS* ii, 96, line 14. Herein doubtless ancient Semitic usage is followed; cf. the first month of the Muslim year, Muharram.

[50] Called Kippurim, as amongst the Jews.

[51] The only eye-witness of this celebration I know of is Grove, in Galton's *Vacation Tourists*. Azazel, the " scapegoat," is known correctly enough — only, as a demon. See below, p. 219.

age to Gerizim, and abstain from all work throughout the week; the eighth day, " the last, great day of the feast " (*Jn.* 7,37), is sabbatically observed in the synagogue. Among the minor days are to be reckoned the New Moon feasts, which are observed in the afternoon of the day following the appearance of the young moon.[52]

We turn now to the observation of the functions of domestic life, every detail of which is also consecrated by religion. In connection with birth the laws of purification are scrupulously regarded. The male child is always circumcised on the eighth day, no postponement being allowed as in the Jewish rite. The priest generally performs the operation, and at home;[53] the cruel act of " tearing " performed by the Jews is not observed. The naming of the child takes place at the same time. The redemption of the firstborn, formerly practised, is now omitted because of the poverty of the community.[54] There is no initiation into the community like that in Judaism which makes a boy Bar Miswa, a child of the Law; the child's accountability begins with his " knowing good and evil." Marriage takes place early, with boys in the 15th or 16th year, with girls in the 12th; celibacy is abominated in this declining community. Divorce takes place at the pleasure of the husband, who gives a bill of divorce, according to *Dt.* 24;[55] but because of the paucity of females, if for no better reason, such separation rarely occurs to-day. Polygamy is allowed only

[52] See Mills, *op. cit.* 238. The same authority also refers to a celebration of Purim, which is held, not as by the Jews on the 13th Adar, but on the last three Sabbaths of the preceding month, the mission of Moses to deliver the Israelites being the object of commemoration. The Samaritans interpret the word Purim in the sense " rejoicings " (the root *pa'ar ?*). Petermann, *op. cit.* 290, describes the two tithing days, the Summot. Also for the order of the seasons and their services, see Cowley, *JQR* vii, 128.

[53] It was once performed before the community; see the anecdote of Bishop Germanus, p. 101.

[54] Mills, *op. cit.* 191.

[55] *N. et E.* 122.

in the case of the barrenness of the wife, when a second wife may be taken, but a third is not allowed. The Samaritans strikingly differ from the Jews in the interpretation of the law of the levirate marriage, according to *Dt.* 25,5ff. They regard as the " husband's brother " the coreligionist who lives in the husband's house, and whose duty it is to marry his widow, if childless; if he refuses, the contemptuous ceremony of Chalisa follows theoretically, but is never now practised.[56] The law of prohibited degrees is strictly followed, and the marriage with a niece is prohibited.[57]

The Levitical laws of defilement are scrupulously regarded, both in respect to all natural defilements, and in the purifications required before participation in the rites of the community. Large ablutions of water are used, and in earlier days fire was employed as a purifying agent.[58] The early Samaritan sects developed the notion of " baptisms " to a great extent, and have probably affected the orthodox community. According to the Epistle of 1672 the lustral water made with ashes of a red heifer was still used, but this had been given up by the age of the Epistle of 1810.[59]

Upon death the corpse is carefully and ceremoniously washed; it is not forbidden to the Samaritans, as has been frequently stated, to handle their dead, except in the case of the highpriest. Candles are burnt at the head and foot of the corpse before burial. Coffins are used — an exception in modern Palestinian custom. The mourning ceremonies last until the following Sabbath, the community going each day to the tomb, where they read and pray. On the Sabbath the community again visit the tomb, where they partake of a meal, while further appropriate services are

---

[56] *N. et E.* 123; Petermann, *op. cit.* 280. Earlier there was a different interpretation of " brother's wife "; see p. 184.

[57] *N. et E.* 179. Marriage with a niece was a bar to the priesthood in the early Catholic Church; see *Apostolical Canons,* No. xix (Fulton, *Index canonum,* 87).

[58] See Additional Note C.

[59] *N. et E.* 178, 127.

held in the synagogue. The Samaritans appear to-day to make a point of forgetting their dead, and have no subsequent commemorations, except their visits to the tombs of the Patriarchs. However the liturgy contains requiem hymns. They are said to share with the Jews the custom of burning combustible articles at Joseph's tomb.

Finally a word remains to be said concerning the ethical quality of the Samaritan religion, for the elaborate system of cult and custom which envelopes the sect might be considered to tend to the deadening of all true religion. But both their literature and the reports of travellers who have spent any time with them show that the Samaritans have developed a spiritual appreciation of the essentials of religion, which finds utterance in phrases frequently equal to the best in Judaism and Christianity. The practical cessation of sacrifice has led the Samaritans, as in the Jewish synagogue, to replace the primacy of the rite with the worship of the heart; so we read of " the altar of prayer," and " the altar of conversion," " tears of blood "— i. e. in place of bloody libations, —" drink-offerings of song."[60] Much is said about the circumcision of the heart, and prayer must be made from " the heart and soul." The sense of sin is strong, appearing especially in the liturgy for Kippur, when a call to real repentance is made; God alone can forgive sin (although the saints have certain merit), and no rites of religion replace true conversion and God's merciful forgiveness. Many expressions are akin to those in Christian usage, as the " being clothed with faith " (cf. *Eph.* 6, 11ff); " the bread of forgiveness "; " the clothing of atonement " (cf. the clothing with Christ's righteousness).[61] The Samaritans have not developed the hardness of Rabbinic exegesis, and they have given large play to allegorizing, which

[60] *BS* ii, 154, line 17; p. 202, line 1; p. xlii. Cf. Hosea's "calves of the lips," 14, 2.
[61] *BS* ii, p. xlii; 197, v. 24.

with all its absurdities often contributes a poetic touch to their hymns. At the same time their exegesis is frequently rational and spiritual, as in their interpretation of the frontlets between the eyes, or in finding, after the example of Jesus, a proof of immortality in the verse, " I am the God of thy father, the God of Abraham, the God of Isaac, and the God of Jacob."[62]

The facts given in this Chapter abundantly prove the thesis that, whatever its beginnings, Samaritanism has become and is a Jewish sect. The history of its origin must now be taken up.

[62] So Mills relates, *op. cit.* 219.

CHAPTER IV.

THE ORIGIN OF THE SAMARITAN SECT.

§ I.   TO THE FALL OF JERUSALEM, 586 B. C.

When the present writer took up the study of the origin of the Samaritans, he naturally began with a consideration of the differences which distinguished the histories of the two sections of the Hebrew people, Israel and Juda, the North and the South.   It seemed antecedently probable that the Samaritans must be the heirs of the peculiar religious characteristics of northern Israel; they would be the lineal successors of the church of Elija, Elisha and Hosea, and of those Yahwe-enthusiasts, the family of Jehu.[1]   But the results obtained in this field of investigation are entirely negative.   When at last we come upon definite information concerning the Samaritans, of the kind that gives some description of them, — and these authorities belong to the Christian era, the New Testament, Josephus, the Talmud — the Samaritans appear as nothing else than a Jewish sect. The one essential difference between them and Judaism is that their cult centres on Gerizim, not on Zion; minor differences there are, but almost all of these can be shown to represent elder stages of Judaism and often to correspond with the tenets which distinguished the conservative Sadducees from the progressive and finally triumphant Pharisees.

It is not necessary then to ascend into hoary antiquity to

[1] This theory has been attempted, but unsuccessfully, by Lincke, *Samaria und seine Propheten.*

ascertain what ancient cults upon Gerizim may have given a peculiar coloring to the worship still connected with it by the Samaritans; between the rise of that sect and antiquity has entered the cleft of Jewish monotheism and iconoclasm. Nor is it necessary — interesting as the task would be — to expatiate here upon the original differences between the North and the South in the matter of religion. These differences have been too much exaggerated; northern Israel has been condemned because orthodox Juda has written the history. But a comparison need only be made between the two great prophets who preached the fall of their respective states, Hosea and Jeremia, in order to make it clear that while in both kingdoms there was a spiritual remnant, incarnated in those respective prophets and their partisans, religious and moral degeneracy marked the South at the end of the VIIth Century B. C. as luridly as it stains the pages of the last days of the northern kingdom a century before.[2] In the providence of God Juda was given a respite of a century and a quarter beyond the fall of Samaria before her own ruin came; her spiritual fruit had greater time to ripen, and became crystallized in the Deuteronomic reform, so that when the stroke fell there was a spiritual germ with vitality enough to withstand uprooting and transportation. We have to add to these considerations the more benevolent conditions of the exile under Nebuchadrezzar, and the auspicious political circumstances of Cyrus's conquest, in order to understand the perpetuation of Juda's community and its final restoration to its native seat. These factors of history, simply fortuitous as they appear to some, providential as they prove themselves to other minds, help us to understand why of the two "Sisters," Israel and Juda, "one was taken and the other left," and why Juda's church finally dominated in the ancient Holy Land.

[2] See Jeremia, *passim,* and especially 3, 6ff, for Yahwe's change of heart towards Israel.

The period in which we must look for data concerning the origin of the Samaritan sect is a lengthy one. It extends from the time, about 722 B. C., to which the description given by 2 Ki. 17 of religious conditions in Samaria after the Assyrian conquest assumes to belong, down to the age of Alexander the Great, in whose reign the Jewish historian Josephus places the rise of the Samaritan sect and the building of its temple on Gerizim. Yet the data bearing upon our subject for these four centuries are most scanty and meagre, while most of them are involved in disputes of Old Testament criticism which are kaleidoscopic in their variety and show no sign of speedy settlement. We will observe first the classic passage 2 Ki. 17, which, more than any other document, has controlled the traditional theories concerning the Samaritans.

The pertinent data in this chapter are as follows. After a three years' siege the capital of the Northern Kingdom, the city of Samaria, fell to the Assyrian king, who deported Israel, and settled them in various specified places, both in Assyria proper and in Media (v. 1–6, cf. 18, 9–11).[3] But the land denuded of its inhabitants required new citizens, so we learn that " the king of Assyria brought men from Babylon, and from Kutha, and from Awwa, and from Hamath and Sepharwaim, and placed them in the cities of Samaria in place of the children of Israel; and they possessed Samaria and dwelt in the cities thereof " (v. 24). But the newcomers " feared not Yahwe," that is, did not worship him, because as strangers they knew not the cult of the native god; " therefore Yahwe sent lions among them, which killed some of them." The settlers thereupon prayed the king of Assyria's assistance, and he responded

[3] The problem of these " Lost Ten Tribes " does not concern us here. A tradition concerning their maintenance of relations with the Jews is preserved in the Book of Tobit; Tobit is of the tribe of Naphtali, descended from an Israelite taken captive by Shalmaneser, 1, 2, and having social relations with Israelites in Media.

to their implied desire by sending back to Samaria some of the deported priests,[4] who should teach the people "the custom of the god of the land." So the priestly deputation returned to their native home, and settled at Bethel, where they taught the foreigners the way of Yahwe (v. 25–28). The following section, v. 29–33, is evidently drawn from another tradition, for it contains a different story concerning the origin of the priests amongst the new colonists.[5] On the one hand, each of the imported races set up its own cult, and established its peculiar deities, which are respectively named; and on the other hand, they worshipped Yahwe, overcoming sacerdotal deficiency by making priests for the native cult out of their own number,[6] and these continued the rites of Yahwe along with the new cults of the foreign deities in "the houses of the highplaces" throughout the land. And so "they worshipped Yahwe and yet served their own gods." The picture here offered represents the land of Samaria as wholly inhabited by foreign colonists, who have adopted a syncretistic religion, compounded of their ancestral cults and of that native deity Yahwe, whose worship superstition caused them to accept.

Let us now turn to the Assyrian accounts of the fall of the city and its results. Sargon (722–705), the Assyrian king who captured the city, and not Shalmaneser as the con-

---

[4] The text fluctuates between the singular and the plural as to the number of the returned priests. With Josephus and several modern critics, e. g., Stade in *SBOT ad loc.*, I prefer the plural, supposing that "one" was inserted to minimize the amount of sacerdotal "succession." A legend of the Syriac Church has it that its version of the Old Testament is due, at least in part, to this priest from Assyria, whose name is variously given as Asya, Ezra, Uria, etc.: see Bar-Hebræus, pref. to *Horr. myst.; Hist. dyn.*, ed. Pococke, p. 100. For the Rabbinic traditions concerning the names of the priests, see below, p. 254.

[5] See Stade, *SBOT ad loc.* N. B. the parallelism of the participial constructions in vv. 29 and 33.

[6] This is a repetition of the tradition concerning Jeroboam's priests, 1 *Ki.* 12, 31.

4

text of the Biblical passages leads us to infer, has left a fairly detailed account:[7]

L. 11. " Samaria I besieged and conquered ...... 12 ...... 13 ...... 14 ...... (with the help of Shamash?) who gave me my strength ...... 15 ...... 27,290 people I took into captivity, 50 chariots for my military use I removed ...... 16 ...... I renewed, made it higher than before; people out of all lands, my captives of war, I settled there; my officer I made governor over them, tribute and taxes like the Assyrians I laid upon them."

A parallel but briefer account relates:[8]

L. 23. " Samaria I besieged, and conquered. 24. I took into captivity 27,290 of those who dwelt there, and removed 50 chariots. The rest I let keep their property (?). I set my officer over them and laid upon them the tribute of the former king."

According to Sargon then no complete deportation took place; he removed only some 27,000 natives, mostly without doubt from the capital, whereas we learn from a passage of contemporary content, 2 Ki. 15,19f, that the land contained some 60,000 well-to-do landed proprietors.[9] It may be believed that amongst the exiles were found all the priests that the conquerors could capture, for these were the mainstay of the fanatical opposition of the petty Syrian states against the Assyrian empire.[10] But the bulk of the Israelites still remained behind, in the condition prophetically described by the prophet Hosea, " without king, and without prince, and without altar, and without sacrifice, and without pillar, and without ephod or teraphim " (3,4). Moreover it is most improbable that the five peoples mentioned in 2 Ki. 17 as imported into the land at this time

[7] *Annals*, 11–17. (I refer for these passages to Schrader, *Keilinschriftliche Bibliothek*, ii.)
[8] The so-called *Prunkinschrift*, 23–24.
[9] See Buhl, *Die sozialen Verhältnisse Israels*, 52.
[10] Cf. *KAT* 95.

were actually introduced then. Apart from the general
phrase "people of all the lands" Sargon names only one
people as settled at this time in Hatti-land, i. e. Syria,
namely the Tumuna, possibly an eastern Aramæan tribe.[11]
In truth, the data of 2 *Ki.* 17 have focussed events which
were spread over a good part of a century, and actually
summarize the historic fact that several importations and
deportations of citizens occurred under Assyrian rule.
These events we must briefly review. In 721 broke out
the serious revolt of Ilubidi of Hamath, in which, strange
as it appears, Samaria took part.[12]   We learn at the same
time of an importation of people from Urartu into Hatti-
land, and may suppose that Samaria received some share
of punishment.

With the year 715 Sargon began his campaigns against
the Medes.   For the following year, 714,[13] the conqueror records the colonization in Samaria of the tribes Tamud,
Ibadidi, Marsimani, Haiapa, the distant Arbai (Arabians?),
whom he describes as people of the desert, hitherto independent and even unknown.   Now the settlement in Samaria of these wild tribes may have been in compensation
for the Median deportation of Israelites claimed by 2 *Ki.*
17, which deportation is to be included among the people of the lands transported into Media as a result of
Sargon's conquests in that region.[14]

After a lapse of several decades we read, in a much later
Biblical passage, *Ezra,* 4,2, of the colonization in Samaria
effected by Esarhaddon.   The gloss in *Is.* 7,8: "and within 65 years shall Ephraim be broken in pieces so that it shall

---

[11] *Annals,* 20–23; see Winckler's revised translation, *Alttestamentliche Untersuchungen,* 105.
[12] *Annals,* 23ff.
[13] *Annals,* 94ff.
[14] *Annals,* 67ff; *Prunkinschrift,* 59ff. This combination of data has
been suggested by Winckler.

not be a people," may have reference to some chastisement of the land undertaken by the monarch named.[15]

Finally *Ezra*, 4,9f, gives a list of peoples settled in Samaria by Asenappar, who is now unanimously identified with Asshurbanapal.[16] The list of peoples as given by the Massoretic text of this passage is a mass of barbarous names, but is now generally interpreted as follows:[17] " The Persian judges, the Persian secretaries (?), the people of Erech, the Babylonians, the Shushanites, that is, the Elamites." In accordance therefore with this passage, which purports to be a document of the age of Artaxerxes I., the colonists settled in Samaria included both Persian officials, and Mesopotamians from Babylon and Erech, along with Elamites from the old Elamitic capital Susa. With this reference to colonies settled in Samaria by Asshurbanapal from Babylon and Erech, we have doubtless to associate the reference to the colonies from Babylon and Kutha in 2 *Ki.* 17, for which deportation there would be no place in Sargon's history, although it could well have been part of Asshurbanapal's chastisement of Babylonia for its participation in the civil war raised by Shamash-shum-ukin.[18]

[15] I see no reason to change the name, with Josephus, *AJ* xi, 4, 3, to Shalmaneser, or with Winckler (*op. cit.* 98ff) to Asshurbanapal, to make it agree with *Ezra*, 4, 10. The two passages are critically distinct. If a change has to be made, Sargon is the easiest makeshift.

[16] The identification was first proposed by Bosanquet in G. Smith, *History of Asshurbanipal*, 364. For the proper vocalization of the first syllable, see the texts of Baer and Ginsburg; for the Persian origin of the last consonant, see Meyer, *Entstehung des Judenthums*, 29.

[17] I follow Meyer, *op. cit.* 35, and on the "Tarpelites," Marquart, *Fundamente israelitischer u. jüdischer Geschichte*, 64, who proposes a corruption of the Assyrian *dupsharru*, tablet-writer.

[18] I can only briefly refer to Winckler's notable essay, *op. cit.* 98, with its drastic criticism of the narrative of colonization in 2 *Ki.* 17, a piece of criticism which has been largely adopted. He holds that v. 24 originally read: Babylon, Kutha, Sippar, but that the latter word was confused with the Sepharwaim, *i. e.*, the Syrian Sibrain, of 2 *Ki.* 18, 34, which confusion dragged into our passage the two other cities mentioned in the latter passage, Hamath and Iwwa. Against this plausible critical theory is to be placed the fact that four out of the five

There was thus more than one deportation of the inhabitants of Samaria, along with several colonizations in the land to replace the citizens who had been lost by captivity and the calamities of war. Still, there is no reason to think that these movements absolutely changed the character of the citizens of Samaria.[19] The conditions there must have been parallel to those in Juda after the fall of Jerusalem. From what we read on the surface of the Biblical records, we are led to suppose that all the Jews were transported to Babylon, the remainder perishing, and that those of the Return were the sole progenitors of the subsequent Jewish church. But it is now recognized that the poorer classes of the country and villages largely remained behind, some of them amalgamating with and being lost in the peoples who entered the depopulated territory, others being finally saved to Judaism through the religious intensity of the Gola, the returned exiles.[20] In like manner it is to be presumed that a very considerable remnant of Israel remained in Samaria. Yet possessing neither spiritual nor secular heads, they must have been both politically and religiously a weak community.[21] Without doubt many of them — how large a proportion there is no means of judg-

deities named in 2 *Ki.* 17 for the Syrian cities can be connected with the Syrian pantheon. Adrammelek, a corruption for Adad-melek, and Anammelek, for Anu-melek, are syncretisms of the Assyrian deities Adad and Anu (who were son and father in the Assyrian pantheon) with the widespread Syrian deity Melek. Tartak is Atargatis. (For the origin of the latter word, see Baethgen, *Beiträge,* 68.) Ashima has now been proved to be a Syrian and Hamathite goddess; see Additional Note D. This verisimilitude in the names of the Syrian deities increases the probability of the historical worth of the statement concerning those Syrian cities as contributing colonies to Samaria.

[19] So Hengstenberg, *Authentie des Daniels,* 177.

[20] Indeed some scholars now go to the extreme of arguing that there was no Return under Cyrus, that the Jews left behind in Juda were the continuators of the Hebrew commonwealth.

[21] Jeremia ignores the existence of this remnant in Samaria, and regards all Ephraim as in captivity, c. 3. But in like fashion he looks upon the remnant in Juda as utterly worthless, "bad figs," not to be accounted for, c. 24. For other references in *Jer.* to the restoration of Northern Israel, see c. 31 ; 33, 7.

ing — amalgamated with the new settlers, and syncretized with them in religion, thus giving a basis to 2 Ki. 17 and to the later Jewish tradition that all the Samaritans were idolaters.   Yet we must believe that some few thousands of the succession of Elija and Hosea, " that had not bowed the knee to Baal," must have remained faithful.   However there is nothing definite to show for any spiritual power in this remnant.   Certainly we may not hold that there arose in the North a spiritual and monotheistic institution like the Jewish Church, which pursued its parallel but independent course, and which finally resulted in the spiritual religion of Samaritanism.   Nor can we argue that original Samaritanism was a syncretism of heathenism and Yahwism, out of which the latter element finally emerged triumphant, establishing a pure monotheism for the northern sect.   This would assume a greater spiritual marvel in Samaritanism than in the development of the Jewish religion, and none who knows much about the Samaritans would assign to them any extraordinary religious genius.   But the key to the problem of the continuance in the North of a remnant of Israel true to Yahwism and able to resist the temptations offered by aliens, must be found in the support offered to those weak brethren by the more persistent community of Juda.

This hypothesis, likely in itself, is borne out by some facts. Hosea, the last northern prophet, condemned the northern political constitution (8,4), even if his Messianic references lie under critical suspicion.[22]   The fall of the state must have turned the minds of sincere Yahwe-worshippers in the North to the Davidic commonwealth of the South.   On the other hand Juda would have prospected the possibility of the ultimate re-incorporation of Joseph in

[22] See Harper, *Amos and Hosea,* p. clix. But the prophet who condemned the house of Jehu (1, 4), could have been bold enough to cherish the hope of re-union with Juda.

its kingdom. A tradition to this effect is contained in 2 *Ch.* 30, in the narrative of Hezekia's great Passover.[23] King Hezekia invites all Israel to take part in the Passover which he intends to celebrate in connection with his religious reforms. He sends his invitation through Ephraim and Manasse and into Lower Galilee. The messengers are said to have met with ridicule in Mount Ephraim, yet one statement declares that " certain men of Asher and Manasse and Zebulun " responded (v. 11), another that " many of Ephraim and Manasse, Issachar and Zebulun," participated (v. 18). The Passover was also postponed to the second month (v. 2), probably for the convenience of the northerners.[24] This religious interest of Hezekia in the northern Israelites was also part of his political policy, for we know from Sennacherib [25] that he attempted the unsuccessful *rôle* of conqueror and dictator in South Syria. Further, if the Chronicler's report about Manasse's imprisonment in Babylon, 2 *Ch.* 33,11, be accepted as history, we may suppose that he took advantage of the revolt of Shamash-shum-ukin, 652–648, to regain the old northern Israelite land. Probably the importation of Babylonian colonists into Samaria at this time[26] was accompanied with the exile of rebellious citizens of the land.

The next information we possess concerning Samaria comes from the period of the *mêlée* of the nations, when the Assyrian empire was fast crumbling to pieces. Josia, the martyr-king of Juda, played the same part as did such greater men as Nabopolassar and Necho; he attempted, if not foreign conquest, at least the recovery of Israel's ancient territory to his crown. It is in the light of this claim

---

[23] The writer does not accept the position of the dominating body of critics who find in the Chronicler's statements only reflections of contemporary history; he is inclined to let this tradition speak for itself.
[24] The season in the North is a little later; cf. 1 *Ki.* 12, 33.
[25] *Prism,* ii, 69ff.
[26] See above, p. 52.

and probably even of possession of the Ephraimitish highlands in part, that we may explain Josia's foolhardy attempt to stem Necho's march through the historic land of
Israel as he pressed on his way toward Nineve, falling
himself in battle at Megiddo, in the Valley of Esdraelon.[27]
This royal reformer, according to 2 Ki. 23, extended his
reform into Samaria. Bethel is particularly named as the
scene of his most violent iconoclasm (v. 15ff), and all the
northern sanctuaries are said to have been destroyed;
Bethel, it may be recalled, was the seat of the syncretistic
cult established by the colonists (2 Ki. 17,28). The violence exercised against the highplaces of the North was a
counterpart of the destruction of the Judæan highplaces;
we may not argue from the terms of the narrative that there
was no genuine old-fashioned Yahwism left in Samaria.
Juda's dominance in Samaria lasted for less than two decades, but we are justified in assuming for this period some
rapprochement between the faithful of Joseph and of Juda,
which augured greater possibilities in the future.

The hypothesis that a considerable number of northern
Israelites adapted themselves to the religious hegemony of
Jerusalem is substantiated by an anecdote belonging to the
time of the fall of Jerusalem in 586. From *Jer.* 41,4ff we
learn that after Ishmael's assassination of the Babylonian
governor of the Jewish remnant, the Jew Gedalia, " there
came men from Shechem, from Shilo,[28] and from Samaria,
eighty in number, with their beards shaven, and their
clothes rent, and having cut themselves, with meal-offerings
and frankincense in their hands, to bring them to the
house of Yahwe." This must refer to the ruined temple

[27] Winckler, *Forschungen,* ii, 289, *KAT* 105, follows Herodotus, ii,
159, who makes Magdolos the scene of the battle; this place Winckler
identifies with the later Stratonis Purgos, which name he considers to
represent a Semitic Migdal Ashtoreth.
[28] Graf prefers the Salem of Gr. B; but see Giesebrecht, *ad loc.*

at Jerusalem,[29] while the mourning of the party seems to relate to the desolation of the Holy City. This reference to a considerable body of northern Israelites expressing a sympathetic interest in the fate of Jerusalem at such troublous times, is only incidentally recorded, but may have represented the sentiment of many in Samaria.[30]

§ 2. FROM THE FALL OF JERUSALEM TO THE BEGINNING OF THE GREEK AGE.

In the preceding pages evidence has been offered for the hypothesis that after the fall of the northern state those of its citizens who remained faithful to its ancestral traditions turned for help to Juda, whose holy city and dynasty Yahwe had wonderfully preserved in the Assyrian wars, thereby setting his seal of approval upon the southern institutions. On the other hand both political and religious ambition incited the Judaite state to reassert its claims over the northern territory which was once part of its dominion.

We now come to the most difficult field of the whole of our historical quest, the age in which we must look for the definite separation of the Samaritan community. This is the " Dark Age " of Jewish history, covering the Exile, the Return, with its several stages, and the remaining obscure period until the fall of the Persian empire. There have survived many prophetic books and fragments belonging to this age; its history is set forth in the Book of *Ezra-Nehemia*. But nowhere, in the eyes of Biblical criticism, does so much uncertainty lie concerning the worth and meaning of the historical data as with regard to this latter

[29] Sacrifices were offered after the Return in the ruined temple, *Hag.* I, 4; 2, 14. The Mishna allows the possibility, *Eduyot*, viii, 6.
[30] Some scholars, Giesebrecht, *ad loc.*, and Cheyne, *Jewish Religious Life*, 26, take this house of Yahwe to be the ancient sanctuary at Mizpa. But apart from the difficulty of allowing a Jewish writer so to speak of a "highplace," it is most unlikely that after Josia's iconoclasm such a highplace should still have existed upon Judæan soil.

book; and nowhere is there such confusion and conflict of critical theories attempting to reconstruct the actual history, as amongst the studies of this period. It would be impossible here even to describe all the different reconstructions that have been attempted, much less to criticize them. However, fortunately many of the Jewish problems can be left to one side, while only certain leading facts need be set forth, concerning which there exists the minimum of critical dispute.

In the first place, while it is popularly assumed that the adversaries of the Jews in their pious attempts to restore Jerusalem were the Samaritan sectaries, it is to be observed that this supposition rests upon a very few statements, all of a doubtful nature. In general the adversaries of the Jews appear to be the political chiefs of the Persian province of Abar-Nahara, i. e. Syria, as in *Ezra*, 5–6, or more particularly the Persian officials and Babylonian colonists in Samaria, as in 4,7ff, and as in the case of Sanballat, of Bethhoron on the Samaritan border,[31] who had behind him the support of what is generally translated "the army of Samaria," a phrase which may mean "the aristocrats of Samaria."[32] How far the same Sanballat made friends with those of the Jewish type of religion in Samaria who dissented from the Jerusalem Church, will be considered later. But he appears as an entirely secular and worldly-minded noble. Two other passages have been especially referred to the Samaritan heretics, *Ezra*, 3,3, and 4,1ff. The former passage reads: " They set the altar upon its base, for fear was upon them because of the peoples of the lands." The Hebrew actually makes still worse sense, and the critics have arrived at no approved emendation.[33] In

---

[31] I see absolutely no reason with Winckler to explain "the Horonite" from the Moabite Horonaim, or with Kamphausen, from Harran.

[32] I owe this suggestion to my friend Prof. W. Max Müller.

[33] See Guthe-Batten, *SBOT ad loc.*; Bertholet, *Esra u. Nehemiah, ad loc.*; Torrey, *Composition and Historical Value of Ezra-Nehemiah*,

any case the peoples of the lands could refer to many others than the Samaritan sect. The other passage, 4,1ff, relates how " the adversaries of Benjamin and Juda " proffered their help to Zerubbabel and his fellows in the re-building of the temple, saying, " Let us build with you; for we seek your God as you do, and sacrifice unto him since the days of Esarhaddon king of Assyria, who brought us hither." Their offer is proudly scorned by the Jews. But the passage has been subjected to unsparing criticism since Schrader's essay upon it,[34] and it is unreasonable to construct much history upon so doubtful a passage.

The explanation of the opposition to the Jewish restoration on the part of the Persian officials, from the satrap of the province down to the local bureaucracy of Samaria, is to be explained simply as on the score of political envy against the privileges received or assumed by the Jews. We know little about the constitution of the province of Abar-Nahara,[35] but we may suppose that with the fall of Jerusalem, the land of Juda came more or less under the control of the officials in Samaria, whose dominion fluctuated according to the greater or less independence that the restored Jewish community was able to gain from the Great King. The hostility to the new Juda was, in a word, of a political, not a religious character.

We have next to consider the changed social conditions of Palestine. The new complexion of the population of Samaria, due to the Assyrian captivities and colonizations, has already been noticed. A like process went on in Juda

Giessen, 1896, p. 13, who discusses the passage at some length. Grätz, quoted by Torrey, actually reads, " All the peoples of the lands were coming to them and helped them,"—the very reverse of the usual interpretation!

[34] *Dauer des zweiten Tempelbaues, Theol. Studien u. Kritiken*, 1867, p. 460. Kuenen took a somewhat milder view, *Hist.-Krit. Onderz.*[2] i, 505, and Bertholet defends the passage, *ad loc.*

[35] See Meyer, *Geschichte des Altertums*, III, i, 136; Hölscher, *Palästina*, 1.

from the day of Jehoiakim's revolt against Nebuchadrezzar. There was no importation of new settlers from distant parts, as in Samaria; this was unnecessary, for the districts left vacant by the Jews in the wars with Babylon and finally with the captivity of a great part of their number, were rapidly filled up by the Edomites and Arabians pressing in from the south, while it is probable that Trans-Jordanic tribes like the Ammonites crossed the fords of Jordan and settled on Israelitish soil. These newcomers were designated as " the peoples of the lands," as we find in *Ezra-Nehemia*. The intruders took the lion's share of ancient Juda, so that the district which the Jews occupied in Nehemia's time consisted of not much more than Juda and its suburbs, lying between Jericho and Mizpa on the north, and Beth-Sur on the south.[36]   In this district to which the Gola, or returning exiles, came back, remained those of the Jews who had not the good fortune of enjoying the Babylonian captivity. Thus before the return of the exiles, Juda was in like social condition to Samaria; it was dominated by alien peoples, but also contained a considerable element of the old Israelite blood.

It is to be observed that the irruption of the peoples of the lands pushed the centre of gravity of the Judæan element to the north, toward Samaria. So we find that the seat of Gedalia, the governor of the Jewish remnant after the fall of the capital, was at Mizpa to the north of Jerusalem, *Jer.* 41,1. Now it can hardly be denied that their common misfortunes must have brought together the unfortunate remnants of Joseph and Juda; distress made friends of those who had been so long sundered by sectional jealousies. It is to be held then that the gloomy period of the Exile, and also of the following century, until Jewish rigorism expelled all doubtful elements, tended toward the

---

[36] See Meyer, *Entstehung des Judenthums,* 105, and map at end of volume.

amalgamation of the Israelites both in Mount Juda and Mount Ephraim who in any way maintained their ancient religious traditions and political hopes. Both Judaism and Samaritanism go back to a common foundation in the circumstances of the age of the Exile in the VIth Century.[37]

There existed then upon Palestinian soil in the century of the Exile the two distinct factors of the imported or immigrant Gentile races and the remnants of the Hebrew race scattered throughout the highlands of Juda and Ephraim. A third factor has now to be considered, namely the reaction upon conditions at home exerted by the Jewish exiles in Babylonia. It is to the efforts of the exiled community that the resuscitation of Palestinian Israel is due. According to *Ezra-Nehemia* there were two distinct epochs when this influence was exerted.[38]

The first of these periods is that which followed Cyrus's edict of emancipation of the Jews, issued soon after his capture of Babylon in 539. According to *Ezra,* c. 1–3, a large number of Jews took immediate advantage of the king's edict and returned to Jerusalem, under the leadership of Sheshbazzar, probably a Davidic scion.[39] Little was accomplished by this advance-guard. But the climax of the patriotic agitation of this period did not come until the reign of Darius, in 520. The political leader of this move-

[37] Observe that Jeremia's bright hopes for the future equally included the land of Ephraim, c. 31. For the authenticity of this passage, see Duhm, *ad loc.*

[38] I follow the broad outlines of the Biblical narrative. Despite Kosters' argument (*Die Herstellung Israels,* tr. from the Dutch) against any return of the Gola in the VIth Century, I believe that this is vouched for by the presence of Davidic princes, Shesh-bazzar and Zerubbabel, in Jerusalem. If Kosters' theory is accepted, it only enhances our estimate of the vitality and spiritual capacity of the remnant in Juda. As for the Babylonian influence in the middle of the Vth Century, Nehemia is a sure historical figure, while the question of the actual relations of Ezra to the governor does not materially affect our present study.

[39] Following the identification by Howorth, Meyer, and others, with Shenazzar, I *Ch.* 3, 18.

ment was Zerubbabel, the Davidide, and the stimulus to the intense agitation which arose in Jerusalem was due to the prophets Haggai and Zecharia.[40]   So far as we can judge, the agitation was Messianic, nationalistic; it appears that Zerubbabel was the hope of the Jews, patriots or fanatics, whichever we call them.   He is the Messianic " Branch " (*Zech.* 3,8) ; he and the high-priest Joshua are " the two Anointed Ones," i.e. Messiahs (4, 14) ; if we follow Wellhausen's brilliant emendations in 6,9ff, the crown was intended for Zerubbabel's head.   The agitation produced the result desired by Haggai : the temple was built.   How much farther the frenzy went we do not know ; Sellin has argued for an assumption of Messianic claims on Zerubbabel's part which was violently suppressed by the power of the Persian empire.[41]   At all events the furore did not abide for long ; within five years, 516–5, the dark veil again settles down upon Juda, and it is not lifted until the age of Ezra and Nehemia.

This first attempt at a restoration may be definitely described as political; and it possessed the liberalism which inspires politicians but is ignored by ecclesiastics.   Consequently its aim would have been to include the diverse elements of Palestine, not to exclude any, least of all members of Israel.   It appears that some of the non-Israelite races to the south which had pressed into Juda after the fall of Jerusalem, such as the Calibbites and Jerahmeelites, were assimilated in this period to the Jewish community.[42]   We have to assume then that the anticipations awakened by Zerubbabel welded still more closely the separated ele-

[40] *Hag.; Zech.* 1–8; *Ezra,* 5–6.
[41] Sellin, *Serubbabel,* 1898; *Studien zur Entstehungsgeschichte der jüdischen Gemeinde,* 1901.
[42] Meyer, *op. cit.* 114.   Bertholet, in his valuable work, *Die Stellung der Israeliten und der Juden zu den Fremden,* 123, holds that those who returned in 538 held aloof from the local elements, as is shown by the care concerning the family registers, *Ezra,* 2, but that a far freer disposition toward the homeborn came in with the agitation of 520.

ments of Israel, and that the Judæan, Samaritan, and Babylonian Israelites forgot old differences in the new enthusiasm. This then was another of those periods of unification which bound together Juda and Samaria.

But our sources fail us, from 515, for the results of this movement. We must pass on to the next chapter in the history as described by *Ezra-Nehemia,* which now introduces to us the figures of the two men whose names are given to that book. The first agitation had failed; the Jews at home were in great distress, the walls of Jerusalem were in ruins (*Neh.* 1,3). The secular ideas of Messianism had proved a failure, the Jews of Palestine had shown themselves incapable of establishing the desired restoration. The ecclesiastics and theologians of Babylonia next took up the forlorn cause; they utterly eschewed politics, except to gain the Persian king's favor. Their aim was to institute a religious community at Jerusalem with sufficient circuit of territory to establish " a state of the Church," over which the ecclesiastical administration could exercise the civil control necessary for its jurisdiction, for religion could not be conceived of except as a civil institution. The guiding-strings of the new administration were to be in the hands of the Gola in Babylonia, for this body alone possessed, in its own conceit at least, and probably actually, the spiritual capacity for the fresh undertaking; moreover it controlled the financial means and the political influence which were prerequisite conditions of success.[43] As a corollary, the remnant in Juda would have to submit to all the conditions laid down by the spiritual lords in Mesopotamia; the most essential of these requirements and the one which would prove the most onerous was that which regulated the purity of the holy seed.

[43] Ezra's expedition, if its historicity and the Biblical date, 458, be accepted, followed the revolt in Egypt of Inarus in 460, and was commissioned by the royal policy to offset the disaffection in the southwest.

The restoration of the Judæan church as proposed by the Babylonian Diaspora and effectively undertaken by Ezra and Nehemia was ecclesiastical; it was a proposition not of the family of David, nor of the highpriests, for these were likely to be as secular-minded as royalty, but of the doctors of the Tora, whose schools flourished in the new home and produced as their *pièce de résistance* the Law, or at least its first draft in the Priest Code. We can imagine the opposition to this policy produced in the minds of the people in Judæa, the Am-ha-areç or Boors, as they were contemptuously called by the Babylonian exiles.[44] The majority in any church is worldly-minded, does not easily or for long acquiesce in Puritanism. But now the social liberties of the Palestinians were to be restricted, their franchise in the community reduced to little or nothing. Rebellion to the Babylonian policy, feud between the elements of the community, excommunication of the dissatisfied, — these were the results of the second restoration.

How far " the Law of the Lord which was in the hand of Ezra the scribe " met with success we cannot judge, but that ecclesiastic evidently failed in the matter nearest to his heart. He attacked with burning zeal the practice of intermarriage with the peoples of the lands, requiring that all such unions should be ruthlessly broken. The people seem to have sullenly allowed the appointment of a commission to settle the grievous matter. And then the history abruptly concludes (*Ezra*, 9–10). As Nehemia had to solve the problem afresh, we must conclude that Ezra failed. The ties of humanity outwitted the priest.

Ezra's successor, the governor Nehemia (445–433), was a far more strenuous yet withal more politic ruler. Backed

---

[44] The term, which was once simply a social one, "the country-people," may have largely obtained its sinister meaning through confusion with the other, "the peoples of the lands," designating the Gentile colonists; the various texts and versions of Ezra-Nehemia evince this confusion in the varying use of the singular and plural.

by the king's commission and the support of his brothers in Babylonia, and relying upon his own strength and conscience, he did not first consult with the dissenting people he came to govern; he acted and ordered, and things were done; those who disobeyed found it wise to leave his jurisdiction, otherwise they were punished or banished. Rigorous as he was, he seems to have proceeded with greater caution in the matter of the mixed marriages, only forbidding such unions in the future (*Neh.* 10). But the cleft made between the factions of the native Jews by Ezra's course was not healed by the governor. Further he had to encounter the united opposition of the peoples of the lands and their ambitious chieftains, who, along with the self-seeking Persian bureaucracy, had everything to lose if a considerable slice of territory and the fair city of Jerusalem were to be excluded from their control and become an aggressive and arrogant *imperium in imperio.*

We learn the names of three of these antagonistic politicians, and hear much of their ways and wiles. There is Sanballat the Horonite, doubtless of the Gentile colonists in Samaria; Tobia, who was closely allied to the Judæan aristocracy and priesthood (6,17ff; 13,4ff), although himself an Ammonite (2,10); and Gashmu the Arabian (2,19; 6,6). These gentry dared not oppose the Persian governor openly; they had resort to ridicule (4,1ff), or attempts at intrigue and assassination (6,1ff, 10ff). But their chief engine for undoing Nehemia's work was the encouragement of the laxer party of the community which opposed the new order of the day. They became the more or less open heads of the revolt which was simmering against the administration. It was not difficult to find allies; apart from the easily persuaded Am-ha-areç, the Hoi Polloi, they had their long-standing connections with the Jewish nobles and priests, in his disruption of which relations Nehemia appeared to the easy-going ones as a meddle-

5

some innovator. These worldly-minded Jewish aristocrats had doubtless no intention of breaking with the governor, although they hoped to make his position impossible. But those arch-intriguers, particularly the cunning Sanballat, led them farther than they expected. For politics is often the major factor in schism and heresy.

We now come to the climax of the story. Nehemia briefly relates the following anecdote (13,28f) : " And one of the sons of Joiada, the son of Eliashib [i. e. the high-priest], the son-in-law of Sanballat, — him I chased from me. Remember them, O God, because of the defilement of the priesthood and of the covenant of the priesthood and the Levites." That is, Sanballat, probably taking advantage of Nehemia's absence (13,6), had formed the bold plan of allying himself with the hierarchy through a union of his daughter with a possible heir to the highpriesthood itself. Sacrilegious as the attempt appeared in Nehemia's eyes, it is but one instance of the countless ambitions which since the days of David to its cessation sullied that high office; Nehemia, not the popular sentiment, expelled the unworthy priestling.

The Old Testament vouchsafes nothing more about this scandal, and in no way connects it with the Samaritan schism. Our authority for such an identification is found solely in Josephus, whose story may be summarized as follows.[45]

The highpriest Eliashib's great-grandson Jaddua finally succeeded to the highpriesthood, and his brother Manasse gained as wife Nikaso, the daughter of one Sanballat. This man had been sent into Samaria by the last Darius (i. e. Codomannus), and was a Kuthite of the same stock as the Samaritans themselves. Sanballat arranged this marriage, recognizing the political importance of Jerusalem, and hoping by the union to gain the goodwill of the Jews.

[45] *AJ* xi, 7, 2; c. 8.

But the marriage brought upon Manasse the odium of the Jews, who gave him the choice between abdicating his priestly rights and the divorce of his wife. Manasse laid the case before his father-in-law; the latter promised to procure for him the dignity of highpriest and the succession to himself in the governorship of Samaria, also undertaking to build for him a temple upon Gerizim, as soon as the permission of Darius could be secured. Meanwhile many of the priests and Levites in Jerusalem seceded to Manasse, and Sanballat gave them lands in Samaria. The intriguer waited for the outcome of Darius's expedition against the conquering Alexander, and when the former was defeated at Issus, he renounced his liege-lord, and upon Alexander's entrance into Palestine, hastened to the conqueror with the offer of his troops, and gained from him as recompense the boon of building a temple on Gerizim. This construction Sanballat hastily accomplished, but died within nine months, at a good old age. Further dealings of Alexander with the Samaritans are then related.

Josephus thus gives some very exact details concerning the origin of the schism. The recusant priest is named Manasse,[46] and his wife's name is also given; Sanballat secures the Jewish priest as his daughter's husband, and builds for him a temple on Gerizim. But the cardinal discrepancy lies in this that the date is of the age of Alexander the Great (332), a round century since our encounter with Sanballat in Nehemia's autobiography!

Despite this discrepancy, the identity of the two stories has been generally accepted.[47] There could hardly have

---

[46] It is the tradition of this name that suggested the Massoretic change of Moses into Manasse in *Ju.* 18, 30; see Moore, *ad loc.*

[47] *E. g.* by Wellhausen, *Israelitische und jüdische Geschichte*[4], 180. However, especially by reason of the exigency felt by some critics for a later dating of the codification of the Pentateuch than the age of Nehemia, several recent discussions accept Josephus's date and hold that Josephus has unwarrantably combined with this history the story of the highpriest's grandson in *Neh.* See Steuernagel, *Einleitung in*

been two Sanballats in succeeding centuries, each of whom married his daughter to a member of the highpriestly family, an offence in each case visited with excommunication. In our piecing of the two stories together, we find a very brief statement from Nehemia's pen of an event which belonged to his immediate cognizance, while Josephus adds to this some details, and contributes the important key to the story that the Samaritan schism grew out of the affair. Two pertinent questions may be asked. First: Why did not Nehemia narrate the fatal sequel? But then how many important things are omitted in the Scripture history! And further the consummation of the schism may not have ensued for years after. The other question is, Why did Josephus err so sadly in his dates? The answer to this is, in the first place, that Josephus, like all Jewish literature of antiquity, is absolutely irresponsible in Persian history and chronology, and as the Ezra books name no Persian king between Artaxerxes I. and the last Darius, he ignored the suppression of a century which he was perpetrating.[48] In the second place the story of the origin of the Samaritan schism has been drawn into the great vortex of the Alexander Legend. The age of the Conqueror is the one bright point in the reminiscences of the ancient world, and was a shining mark for the art of legend-manufacture. Just as the Jews had their legend concerning Alexander's favor to Jerusalem, so the Samaritans told their fables concerning his connection with their sect and temple; probably in this point Josephus was depending upon some Samaritan tradi-

das Pentateuch, 276, and Bertholet's review in Theologische Literaturzeitung, 1901, Sp. 188. Hölscher, op. cit. 37, takes the ground that the datum in Neh. has nothing to do with the Samaritan schism, while Josephus's story is an unhistorical Midrash on that passage, the schism taking place later in the Greek period.

[48] Josephus's arrangement of Persian history can be observed in the way in which he constructs the Persian dynasty from the Greek Esdras; thus as the latter names as the second Persian monarch Artaxerxes, Josephus identifies him with Cambyses.

tion, which he, or rather the legend-cycle which he followed, brought into connection with the history of Sanballat.[49] It may be argued that the rejection of part of Josephus's story condemns it all; but there is generally some fact in fiction, and it is safer for criticism to save whatever is possible out of the ruins.

If this combination of the passage in Nehemia and the story given by Josephus be allowed, there still remain many questions for the answers to which no data exist, so that only a speculative reconstruction is possible. The malcontents in the Jewish community in Palestine were now reinforced by a serious defection in the hierarchy; moreover they had the powerful assistance of political magnates who were ready to manipulate religious feud for private ends. From the dependence which the separated faction ever afterwards exhibited upon the spiritual primacy of Jerusalem, it appears that the crystallization of the dissenters into an independent sect was due rather to their excommunication by the Jewish church than to their own will. But driven out and held aloof by Nehemia's strong will and policy, as long as this continued the policy of subsequent administrations, the separatists were forced for religion's sake as well as for self-preservation to establish an organization with an independent cult. While the party had its followers in

[49] Another Jewish tradition has it that the famous Simon the Just (*circa* 200) was the contemporary of Alexander; *i. e.*, Josephus's line of legend took for its hero the last Biblical highpriest, while another line took the most famous priest in the Greek period. Josippon ben Gorion makes the highpriest Onias his contemporary. It is impossible to discuss here the Jewish chapter in the Alexander Romance. The argument for its historical worthlessness is well summed up by Niese, *Griechische Geschichte,* i, 83. On the other side see Heinichsen, *Das Verhältniss der Juden zu Alexander dem Grossen, Theol. Studien und Kritiken,* 1871, p. 458; Mahaffy, *Empire of the Ptolemies,* 85. The Samaritan chronicles draw all their material on the subject from Jewish legend, and have absolutely no independent historical information; only the history is more terribly mixed up than in the Jewish stories, for Sanballat and Zerubbabel appear as adversaries before Nebuchadrezzar, *Lib. Jos.* 45. According to *Chron. Neub.* 438, the Samaritan highpriest at this time was Hezekia.

Jerusalem and throughout Juda, the erection of a new sanctuary on Judæan soil was impracticable, even impossible, as long as the Jews stood well in the royal favor. The land of Samaria however was independent of all Jewish jurisdiction; here a home offered itself through the political favor of the political leaders and officials of that district, who were bent on doing mischief to Jerusalem and its church. Here too, if Jerusalem was out of the question, could be found a fitting sanctuary, for Samaria possessed most of the traditional sacred sites of Israel's history. Bethel lay too near Jerusalem. But Shechem, always an open town to foreigners in ancient times, offered itself, perhaps contained many of the dissident faction. Its ancient and sacred highplace again became an Israelitish sanctuary, the centre of the cult of the new sect. The people came generally to be known as Samaritans, or by a more appropriate geographical designation used by Josephus, as Shechemites. In their own conceit they called themselves Israel, leaving the name Jews to their opponents, thus perpetuating in word at least the ancient primacy of Joseph over Juda.[50]

With regard to the Samaritan temple, it is now very generally considered that there is a distinct Biblical reference to it in the *Deutero-* or rather *Trito-Isaia*. The passage in question is *Is.* 66, 1: " Thus says Yahwe: Heaven is my throne, and the earth is my footstool. What manner of house will you build me, and what place shall be my rest? " The would-be builders of this house of Yahwe are then associated with the participants in the abominable cults which are described in 65, 1ff, and would be the same as the bastard-brood of 57, 3ff. Accordingly the original Samaritan temple was one devoted to polytheism and various obscene rituals. Despite the assent that has been

[50] See Additional Note B.

gained for this view,[51] I must hold to the interpretation that is as old as St. Stephen, and which is still maintained by Wellhausen,[52] that the passage, 66, 1ff, is a prophetic flight concerning spiritual worship which has its parallels in the Prophets and the Psalms, the full fruitage coming in Christianity. Against the prevailing exegesis it is to be noted that the prophet belongs to those who are excommunicated (v. 5), not to the triumphant party which cast out the Shechemites.[53]

It has been suggested by Bertholet[54] that the formation of the new sect really cleared the air for Judaism, and created a safety-valve against the danger to which the latter lay exposed in the admission of aliens. As for the relations between the two communities after the separation, it is not necessary to hold that the schism from the beginning excluded social and religious intercourse. We possess no further data concerning the Palestinian Samaritans until the IId Century B. C., in the period of the Maccabees. But the intervening age was not one that was committed to the rigorism of Ezra and Nehemia, or of the Chasidim and Pharisees of the IId Century. The fortunes of the Jewish Church were chiefly in the control of the highpriesthood, which appears in general to have been utterly worldly-minded.[55]

After all, a branch of the Jewish highpriesthood reigned in the Samaritan sect, and, as what cannot be cured must

[51] First suggested by Duhm, and since more or less positively accepted by such scholars as Meyer, Cheyne, Kittel, Marti.

[52] *Acts,* 7, 48ff; Wellhausen, *op. cit.* 165. See also Kleinert, *Die Profeten Israels,* 160: " Das Wagnis Duhms, wider den klaren Wortlaut," etc.

[53] If Duhm's view is correct, an explanation is required for the transition of the idolatrous Samaritan community into a sect imitative of Judaism, a phenomenon, which, as already remarked, would be a spiritual marvel.

[54] *Stellung,* 176.

[55] N. B. the scandalous histories of the priesthood narrated by Josephus *AJ* xi, 7; xii, 4, and the utterly Pagan character of the hierarchy in the time of Antiochus Epiphanes.

be endured, family ties doubtless kept communication open and easy. We may compare the parallel phenomenon of the erection by a scion of the priesthood of another rival temple, that at Leontopolis in Egypt, which does not seem to have provoked any extreme exasperation.[56] The close relationship in theology and practice of the Samaritans with the later Sadducees, who were the party of the hierarchy, can best be explained by the supposition of the maintenance of intercourse between the priests of Jerusalem and of Shechem. In addition to this worldly-minded party there was also the spiritually noble " Broad Church " section in the Jewish community, which, following the cue of much prophetic teaching, insisted more on the catholicity of the ideal Israel than on its necessary rigorism. The spirit of this school of thought inspired *Deutero-Isaia;* it produced the prophetical romance of *Jona,* while the Book of *Ruth* is now attributed to it by many scholars.[57]   A more prosaic yet equally ethical offshoot of the same school was the Wisdom literature.   With the triumph of Pharisaism in the Jewish Church this party was suppressed, most of its writings condemned. But enough of its product remains to warrant us in speculating upon the possible affiliations between the liberal tendencies in Judaism and the schismatic yet monotheistic and ethically earnest sect of the Samaritans. In more than one party of Judaism for various reasons the Shechemites must have received comfort and so have found the door kept open with the mother-church.

For from all we know of Samaritanism there can be no doubt that it remained under the steady influence of Judaism, and that this spiritual patronage was so strong and so necessary that even after the complete excommunication

[56] Josephus, *AJ* xiii, 3.   Many scholars refer the favorable comment of *Is.* 19, 19, to this Egyptian temple.   The event belongs to the early part of the IId Century.

[57] In this period was established the proselytizing propaganda of Judaism; see Bertholet, *op. cit.* 178.

of the schismatics in the IIId and IVth Christian centuries Rabbinism still infiltrated into Samaria. The proofs and fruits of this spiritual connection are found in the Samaritan possession of the Jewish priesthood, of the First Canon of the Jewish Scriptures, of most of those tenets that marked earlier, Sadducæan Judaism in distinction from the Pharisaic development. Because of the persistence of its original type, largely contributed to by its continuance throughout the centuries in its original habitat, the Samaritan sect stands as a monument of early Judaism. Its value in this historical regard has not yet been appreciated by scholarship.

The light thrown upon the date of the codification of the Law is a moot point in Pentateuchal criticism. It is argued that the Law must have reached its final form by the time of the exclusion of the priest who became the leader of the Samaritans, *circa* 432.[58] Other scholars think that the data bearing upon the origin of the Samaritan sect are too frail to control our Pentateuchal chronology.[59] In any case we know too little of the relations between the Jews and the Samaritans for at least 200 years to say that the Pentateuch could not have been further revised after the schism, on the ground that the Samaritan copy would give a much older and different text. It is possible that further revisions at Jerusalem, as in the case of *Ex.* 35-40, were readily accepted by the spiritually dependent community at Shechem. But with the Jewish promulgation of the Second Canon, that of the Prophets, about 200, a definitive break must have separated the two sects on the question as to the extent of Scripture. The northern community could not accept the Second Canon with its pronounced proclivities for Juda, David, and Jerusalem.[60]

[58] So Wellhausen, *op. cit.* 180; Carpenter, *Pentateuch*[1], i, 179.
[59] Kautzsch, *RE*[2], xiii, 344; Steuernagel, *Einleitung*, 276.
[60] There are doubtless many Biblical passages which, if we had the key, would throw light upon the relations of Jews and Samaritans

between Nehemia's age and 200 B. C. But in their present state they give room only for speculation. Reference may here be made to Hölscher, *op. cit.* 30, " Die Juden nach Nehemia," who argues that the Book of *Judith* in its geographical data assumes the Jewish control of Samaria in the late Persian period, and that the symbolic act, in *Zech.* 11, 14, of breaking the staff to portend the breaking of the brotherhood between Juda and Israel, refers to the schism. Hölscher would date this event about 300, but the date of *Deutero-Zecharia* is too obscure to be the basis of chronology. In 1 *Ch.* 9, 3, there is an obscure reference to people of Ephraim and Manasse resident in Jerusalem, a family of Shilonites being specified, v. 5. These were doubtless northern Israelites who persisted in devotion to the Jewish sanctuary. To the Chronicler the northern territory is never Samaria, but always the land of Ephraim, ii, 25, 7, or of Ephraim and Manasse, ii, 30, 1. If such Psalms as *Ps.* 80 are to be attributed to the Post-exilic age, some interesting problems present themselves. Cheyne has interpreted the " libations of blood " in *Ps.* 16 of the superstitious practices of the Samaritans, but there is no proof for this against them (see his *Jewish Religious Life,* 29). In *Ps.* 60, 8–14 (*Ps.* 108, 8–14) scholars from Theodore of Mopsuestia down to Cheyne and Duhm have found a reference to John Hyrcanus's capture of Shechem in the words: " I will divide Shechem, mete out the valley of Succoth "; but the friendly reference to Manasse and Ephraim in the following verse militates against this historical interpretation. I may take opportunity here to note the excellent characterization of the Samaritan schism in Stade's most recent work, *Biblische Theologie des Alten Testaments,* § 147.

CHAPTER V.

THE SAMARITANS UNDER THE HELLENIC EMPIRE.[1]

At the end of the last Chapter probable references to the relations between the Jews and the Samaritans in the Hellenic age have been anticipated. When we turn now to the political history of Samaria under Hellenism, we find few further data concerning the sect until the age of the Maccabees. It is true that the land of Samaria figures constantly in the wars of Alexander and of the Diadochi. Its capital Samaria rebelled against the conqueror and received exemplary punishment;[2] Eusebius also reports that the city was rebuilt by Perdiccas and subsequently, in 296–5, was again destroyed by Demetrius Poliorcetes.[3] But these facts throw no light upon the Samaritan sect, although it may be presumed that it sorely suffered under the harryings of the land, and that its members, men of the hardy Hebrew blood, were often found among the rebels.

Josephus describes the calamities brought upon Syria and upon Juda in particular by the wars of the first Ptolemy, and records that this monarch carried off many captives from the hill-country of Juda, and the places about Jerusalem, and Mount Gerizim.[4] The result of these Ptolemaic

---

[1] See Juynboll, *Hist. Sam.* 93; Schürer, *GJV* i; Appel, *Quæstiones de rebus Samaritanorum,* c. i.

[2] Quintus Curtius, *Hist.* iv, 5, 8; Eusebius, *Chron.* ed. Schoene, ii, 114. The statement is rejected by Niese, *Griechische Geschichte,* i, 88, n. 3.

[3] Niese also denies this latter datum; *op. cit.* i, 355, n. 6. It may belong, however, to the famous Syrian campaign of 311.

[4] *AJ* xii, 1. Despite the doubts of Mahaffy, *Empire of the Ptolemies,* 43, Josephus is corroborated by Diodorus, *Hist.* xix, 86, who reports

wars and conquests was the connection made between Egypt
and the Jews and Samaritans, which brought many of both
sects, partly as captives, partly as willing immigrants, to
the flourishing land of the Ptolemies and its new metropolis,
Alexandria. Josephus also reports that Alexander levied
Samaritan troops for service in Egypt.[5]   We have thus to
date from this period the beginning of the Samaritan Diaspora in Egypt, which enjoyed in the new home a like history, on a minor scale, to that of the great Jewish colony.
The historical data for this Samaritan Disapora are given
in a subsequent Chapter.[6]   Both Jewish and Samaritan records contain accounts of the quarrels which arose in Egypt
between the two sects. Josephus, after describing their
common emigration to that land,[7] narrates the contentions
arising between them as to the proper destination of the
sacrifices, whether Jerusalem or Gerizim; probably the re-
mittance of the royal temple-gifts was the cause of dispute.
Josephus also gives a legend concerning a disputation between the rival sects held before Ptolemy Philometor (182–
146).[8]   The spokesman for the Jews was Andronicus ben-
Meshullam, the advocates of the Samaritans Sabbæus and
Theodosius.[9]   The former, who spoke first, argued so convincingly that the king accepted the Jewish plea, and put
the Samaritan orators to death.   A similar story, evidently
borrowed from the Jewish legend, only with fortunes of

that after the battle of Gaza (312) the Egyptian ruler captured the
strongholds of South Syria. Abu'l Fath, p. 93, tells of this Ptolemy
that he sent one Urudus to seize the temple treasures at Shechem, but
that he desisted upon being shown a charter from Alexander the Great
ordering those funds to be expended for the priests, widows and or-
phans. Juynboll, *Hist. Sam.* 98, has rightly identified Urudus with
Alexander's brother, Arrhidæus; see further Clermont-Ganneau, in
Journal des Savants, 1904, Jan., p. 37.
 [5] *AJ* xi, 8, 7.
 [6] Chapter VIII, § 2.
 [7] *AJ* xii, 1.
 [8] *AJ* xiii, 3, 4.
 [9] Traditional heresiarchs of the Samaritans; see Chapter XIII, § 1.

course reversed, is told by the Samaritan writers.[10] Doubtless such theological disputes were frequently carried on in Egypt, and at times, as when property rights were concerned, the secular courts must have been appealed to.

As for their native land, the Samaritan sect did not possess the numbers and influence enjoyed by the Jews in Juda, and were little able to oppose the Hellenization of Samaria. This tendency was working rapidly enough in Juda, but must have been far more extensive in the North. Hence it is especially necessary from this time on to draw the distinction between the religious sect of the Samaritans, a comparatively small and scattered body, and the citizens of the land, mostly Pagan, those who were civilly Samaritans. The term Samaritan does not necessarily refer to the subject of our present study.

The Samaritan sect at last comes forth into the clear light of day in the Maccabæan period, for which we possess the abundant Jewish sources. The Samaritans played no part in the brilliant war for liberty fought by their Jewish brothers against Antiochus Epiphanes. But of their position toward this struggle we have no certain knowledge. That the mad passion of Antiochus, " the Evident God," affected the northern sect appears from the statement of 2 *Mac.* 6, 2 that the tyrant established not only the cult of Zeus Olympios in Jerusalem, but also that of Zeus Xenios, the Hospitable Zeus, on Mount Gerizim.[11] Josephus gives

[10] *Abu'l Fath,* 94; *Chron. Adler,* 38. Here the Ptolemy is a composition of Philadelphus and Philometer, as Lévi points out, *ad loc.;* he procured translations into the Greek from the learned men of both sects, Eleazar (he of the Aristeas-legend) representing the' Jews, and Aaron with Symmachus and Theodotion (the authors of the Greek versions!), the Samaritans; the king's observation of the discrepancies between the two texts of the Law causes him to inquire further, and the Samaritans succeed in convincing him that they are the legitimate body.

[11] According to the usual rendering this epithet was given because of the hospitable character of the natives. (Could the epithet have been suggested by the first syllable of Gerizim, *ger, i. e.,* stranger?)

a much more extensive story.[12]   He relates that the Shechemites, i.e., the Samaritan sect, under the name of Sidonians,[13] sent a petition to Antiochus, in which, after denying
all relationship with the Jews except in the matter of the
observance of certain religious customs of the land, they
asked the king to allow them to name their temple, " which
at present has no name," after Zeus Hellenios.   This boon
the king granted.   On the other hand an obscure statement of 2 *Mac.* 5, 23 relates that Antiochus placed a governor " in Gerizim," the fact being recorded in connection
with the account of the officials sent to suppress the Jews.[14]
From this it would appear that the king expected resistance
from the Samaritans, so that Josephus's story appears somewhat gratuitous.[15]   That the Samaritans took no part in
the immortal struggle of the Maccabees is without doubt a
fact; probably they bowed before the storm in silence if
not with acquiescence.   It must be borne in mind that the
trouble which came upon the Jews was contributed to by
their own factions, and that Antiochus's innovations were
a response to the Hellenizing party which had control in
Judæa.   Nor could we expect that the northern sect would
have gone to the assistance of the Jews.   But this point is
clear that the Samaritans preserved their faith through these
troublous times.

But Willrich, *Judaica,* 139, comparing Josephus's narrative, is probably
right in translating ἐτύγχανον by " they obtained their request."
   [12] *AJ* xii, 5, 5.
   [13] See Additional Note B.
   [14] It is uncertain whether " in Gerizim " refers to a citadel on the
mountain, in which case it would be the predecessor of the fortifications constructed there by Christian emperors; or whether it means
the district of Shechem in general.
   [15] On Josephus's attitude towards the Samaritans, see Chapter IX.
De Sacy correctly remarks, *N. et E.* 3: " Il est même certain que si
le culte des idoles eût été établi alors parmi les Samaritains, ils n'auroient en rien à appréhender de la fureur d'Antiochus, et n'auroient pas
craint de se voir confondus avec les Juifs." That the Samaritans were
in opposition to Epiphanes is the view also of the Jewish scholar
Appel, *op. cit.* 38.

In the early part of the Maccabæan wars for independence the land of Samaria appears to have been generally avoided by the Jewish armies; it contained the Gentile stronghold of Samaria, while all the classes of the population were antagonistic. Only in the southern districts, where the Jews seem to have settled in the course of their notable expansion, was any part of the land favorable to the new Jewish state. Finally after the conclusion of terms with the Syrian king Demetrius II, three cantons of Samaritan territory were formally annexed to Judæa, Ephraim, Lydda and Ramathaim, *circa* 145. This considerable acquisition pushed the boundary of Judæa far into the interior of Samaria, the limit of Borkeos, which Josephus describes as the boundary in his day, marking probably the extent of the annexation.[16]

With Judæa's outposts now thrust far up into the ancient territory of Joseph, the second generation of the Hasmonæan house found itself strong enough to invade the remainder of Samaritan soil, and not only to pay off old scores with the degenerate Syrian kingdom, but also to take vengeance on the weakened Samaritan sect. In the year 128 John Hyrcanus captured Shechem and Mount Gerizim, and subdued the Kuthæan sect,— so Josephus relates,[17] adding the comment that now their temple was devastated after an existence of 200 years. "The Day of Gerizim" commemorated in the Jewish Fast-Roll, the date being Kislew 21, is to be connected with this signal triumph of militant Judaism over its competitor.[18] This success

[16] For the limits between Judæa and Samaria, see Chapter VIII, § 1, and for the annexation of the three cantons, see below, p. 144. To this event is due the legend of Pseudo-Hecatæus, quoted by Josephus, *C. Ap.* ii, 4, that Alexander gave the Jews the land of Samaria free of tribute.

[17] *AJ* xiii, 9, 1; *BJ* i, 2, 6.

[18] The Fast-Roll, or *Megillat Taanit*, is given by Derenbourg, *Histoire de la Palestine*, 439; Dalman, *Aramäische Dialektproben*, 1. The former scholar, pp. 41, 72, hesitates concerning the reference of the

against the Samaritan sect was later followed up by the conquest of the Pagan capital. An expedition under Hyrcanus's sons Antigonus and Aristobulus captured the city of Samaria after a year's siege, and attempted to obliterate even the traces of the city's existence; this happened not long before 107.[19] The conquest was completed by the capture of Scythopolis, which dominated the northern border of Samaria.[20]

Once again the drama of Jewish history operated on Samaritan soil. About the year 88 Alexander Jannæus met the forces of Demetrius III, supported by the rebellious Pharisaic party, in the neighborhood of Shechem, and was there routed.[21] In Josephus's narrative of Alexander's later conquests, after the abatement of the civil strife, the land of Samaria is omitted, so that it is to be inferred that the district still lay under Jewish control. This supposition is confirmed by the fact that when Pompey subjugated the Jews, in the year 63, he greatly reduced their territory; the city of Samaria was specifically detached and annexed

celebration; the glossator to the *Megillat* refers the anniversary to the visit of Alexander to the Jews and Samaritans.

[19] *AJ* xiii, 10, 1–3; *BJ* i, 2, 7; Schürer, *GJV* i, 267.

[20] Abu'l Fath gives more than usual information about this period, p. 102. He relates Hyrcanus's capture of Samaria, but denies that he took Shechem. There is also a confused recollection of the attempted interference in the war by Ptolemy Lathyrus, which was opposed by his mother, Cleopatra, as Josephus relates; but she is confused with the last Cleopatra. (See Vilmar, *Abul Fath,* p. lxiii; Juynboll, *Hist. Sam.* 110.) But the chronicle's most original contribution to the history is that Hyrcanus at the end of his life became persuaded of the legitimacy of the Samaritan cult, and sent to Gerizim tithes and sacrifice, p. 105. This is an evident allusion to the desertion of Hyrcanus by the Pharisaic party and his alliance with the Sadducees. The legend bears a correct recollection of the ancient affinity between the latter party and the Samaritans, and it is a plausible hypothesis that the preservation of the northern sect during this period of absolute Jewish control of Samaria was due to the liberalistic policy of the Hasmonæans to use the Samaritans as a counterweight to the Pharisaic rigorists. Thus it may be inferred that the despised northerners played their part in the fatal internecine strife which now began to rage in the south to Juda's undoing.

[21] *AJ* xiii, 14, 1–2; *BJ* i, 4, 4.

to the new Syrian province.[22]   This liberation of Samaria, which, it appears, had arisen from its ashes, involved the release of the greater part of the district from the Jewish usurpation.   From this time forth the Samaritan sect is forever free of the hated domination of the sister-sect.

[22] *AJ* xiv, 4, 4; *BJ* i, 7, 7.

6

CHAPTER VI.

THE SAMARITANS UNDER THE ROMAN EMPIRE.

§ 1. TO THE DESTRUCTION OF JERUSALEM, A. D. 70.[1]

The resuscitation of the district of Samaria came with the strong arm of Roman force and law. The ravages of the contending Hellenistic armies now ceased, and the ambitions of the Jewish state were brought under control; the inhabitants of the land enjoyed the fruits of an unknown peace, and those who clung to the faith of Gerizim could pursue the liberties of Roman subjects in the matter of religion without fear of molestation from the fanaticism of the stronger sect in the South. The ancient rivalry was still maintained, and when Jews and Samaritans met in town or on country road it blazed out in acts of violence, wherein either party gave and took. But the political value of Samaria was appreciated by Rome, and especially by the astute Herod, for it offered a sure foothold against the turbulence of the Jews; its majority of pagan citizens despised the Jews, while the Shechemites hated them.

Most of the history of this period revolves around the capital city Samaria, whose ancient glories were once more restored. Rebuilt by an early governor of Syria, Gabinius (57–55),[2] it became the favorite seat of king Herod. His interest in the fair land to the north seems to have been early excited, for Josephus informs us that upon his father's

---

[1] See the authorities named at the beginning of the previous Chapter.
[2] *AJ* xiv, 5, 3; *BJ* i, 8, 4. For the name " Gabinians " assumed by the citizens, see *Cedrenus,* i, 323, ed. Bekker.

death that diplomatic politician "cheered up Samaria and stopped its factions,"[3] and so we are not surprised that in his contest with the Hasmonæan Antigonus the city of Samaria was arrayed on his side.[4] His cunning handling of Augustus after the battle of Actium brought him, along with the recognition of his monarchy, the boon of Samaria,[5] and thus that district fell once more under the sway of a king of the Jews. But the circumstances of the new relation were now favorable to the North. Herod proceeded to rebuild and beautify the capital, paying homage to Cæsar by calling it Sebaste, i.e. Augusta, at the same time erecting a temple in the emperor's honor.[6] But Herod's purpose was not merely an æsthetic one, although he enjoyed himself in the gay city of his creation as he never did in sombre Jerusalem. Josephus correctly gives the reason for this new and elaborate foundation, that "it should be a stronghold to keep the land and Jerusalem in awe, from which latter place Samaria was but a day's journey." With this city of his choice much of the tragedy of his life was enacted. Here he married Mariamne, in its neighborhood after her execution he tried to drown his grief in the pleasures of the chase, and here at the end of his life his and Mariamne's sons, Alexander and Aristobulus, were executed. A Samaritan lady was one of his wives. If then it was a king of Jerusalem who reigned over the district, he was nevertheless a king in Samaria, and his favor and presence must have contributed not a little to the well-being of his Samaritan subjects, Israelites as well as Pagans.[7]

In the disturbances which broke out after Herod's death,

---

[3] *AJ* xiv, 11, 14.
[4] *AJ* xiv, 15, 12; *BJ* i, 17, 5.
[5] *AJ* xv, 7, 3; *BJ* i, 20, 3.
[6] *AJ* xv, 8, 5; *BJ* i, 21, 2; Strabo, *Geog.* ed Kramer, xvi, 2, 34.
[7] Abu'l Fath, 116, records that he slew many Samaritans as well as Jews. For the Samaritan tradition of the Samaritan wife, see below, Chap. VI, note 39.

Samaria remained loyal to the interests of the empire; Varus is said to have spared it,[8] and subsequently upon the division of the kingdom among Herod's sons, the district, which now fell along with Judæa to the tetrarchy of Archelaus, met its reward in having one-quarter of its taxes remitted.[9] Finally when Archelaus was dispossessed (A. D. 6), Judæa and Samaria were united in a province of the third class, subordinate to the proconsulate province of Syria.[10]   The seat of the new procuratorship was Cæsarea, itself one of Herod's foundations, so that now the political centre lay to the extreme northwest, a condition favorable to the Samaritans.   Notwithstanding the union of the lands of Juda and Samaria, the distinction between their boundaries was still preserved, the Jews having recovered, probably in Herod's time, the Samaritan cantons that were cut off by Pompey.[11]

King Herod, only half Jew as he was, had been a buffer between the mighty empire and the Judæan state with its acute sensibilities.   But with the passing of his diplomatic management, the index of doom now began to point towards the well-nigh inevitable catastrophe of the great Jewish revolt, the threatening clouds being only for a short while riven by the reign of Herod Agrippa (41–44).   One manifestation of these symptoms was the recrudescence of the hostility of Jew and Samaritan, in which conflict the weaker sect, probably encouraged by the favor of the political masters, even appears as the aggressor.   Josephus narrates two ugly incidents of this perpetual quarrel.   In the administration of the first procurator Coponius (6–9), the Samaritans gained access on a certain Passover to the porches of the temple in Jerusalem, and scattered about dead men's

[8] *AJ* xvii, 10, 9; *BJ* ii, 5, 1.
[9] *AJ* xvii, 11, 4; *BJ* ii, 6, 3; cf. *Nicolaus Dam.,* in Müller, *Fragm. hist. Græc.* iii, 351.
[10] Schürer, *GJV* i, 454.   This province included the land of Samaria, for Pilate governed the latter land as well.
[11] For Josephus's description of these boundaries, see below, p. 145.

bones; since this outrage, Josephus adds, the Jews forbade that sect admission to their feasts, from which they had not hitherto been excluded.[12]   But a far more serious disturbance occurred in the days of the procurator Cumanus (A. D. 52).[13]   At one of the festal seasons the Samaritans attacked and slaughtered a troop of Galilæan pilgrims at En-gannim, on the border between Galilee and Samaria. In consequence, the Galilæans armed themselves, and in conjunction with robber bands raided many Samaritan villages, which forced Cumanus to appear in the field with a large body of troops and repress the disturbers of the peace with a strong hand.   The Samaritans, as the injured party, further appealed their case to Quadratus, governor of Syria, who came and held hearings both at Samaria and Lydda, the adjudication being in favor of the plaintiffs.   Finally he ordered the chiefs of the two parties to go to Rome and lay the case before the emperor Claudius.   Here the Samaritans had the influence of Cumanus, whom Josephus charges with having been corrupted by the Samaritans; but the Jews were backed by the still more powerful influence of the younger Agrippa, who gained Queen Agrippina's ear, and thus procured the emperor's verdict in favor of the Jews; he condemned the Samaritans to death, along with Celer a Roman knight who was involved, and banished Cumanus.

One other occurrence affecting the Samaritans is narrated by Josephus.[14]   A certain Samaritan fanatic summoned his coreligionists to assemble on Mount Gerizim, where he would show them the sacred vessels which lay hidden there. The crowd gathered armed at a place called Tirathana;[15]

---

[12] *AJ* xviii, 2, 2. For this religious fellowship between the two sects, cf. Chapter X. A like story is told by the Samaritans, how two Samaritans in the reign of Hadrian (is Herod meant, the two names being confused in other places?) substituted mice for the doves a Jewish pilgrim was bringing up to the temple; *Lib. Jos.* xlvii; *Abu'l Fath*, 113.
[13] *AJ* xx, 6; *BJ* ii, 12, 3.
[14] *AJ* xviii, 4, 1–2.
[15] For its location, see p. 146.

but the governor Pilate prevented their ascending the holy mountain by dispatching a large force, which slew many, capturing some who were subsequently executed, and dispersing the rest. The Samaritan magistracy thereupon appealed to Vitellius the governor of Syria against this uncalled-for barbarity, and the upshot of the complaint was the recall of Pilate (A. D. 36).[16] These several instances prove that the Samaritan sect possessed considerable influence with the imperial administration.

The tragedy which terminated the life of the Jewish state involved as well the northern sect. The land of Samaria suffered equally with the other districts adjacent to Judæa from the raids of maddened Jewish bands which swarmed throughout Palestine to take the last reckoning with the heathen world. At the beginning of the Jewish war (A. D. 66), Samaria-Sebaste shared the fate of many a neighboring city, and was burnt to the ground,[17] and in general we have to suppose that the fires which raged in Judæa, Peræa and Galilee seared the valleys of Samaria, and involved its inhabitants, however involuntarily, in the horrors of that war of Armageddon.

There is one incident of this calamitous time which is significant of the Samaritan spirit in that age. The mad fury of the Jews infected the Samaritans with its contagion, and dragged a large body of them, deceived by apocalyptic frenzy, to a like destruction with the Jews. The abstract of Josephus's narrative is as follows:[18] A large number of Samaritans assembled on Gerizim, despising the successes of the Romans, and ready for a fray with them. Vespasian found it necessary to nip this uprising in the bud, and sent his captain Cerealis with 600 horse and 3,000 infantry to dislodge the rebels. So strong were the latter

---

[16] For the legend of the hidden vessels, and for Samaritan Messianism, of which this event was a manifestation, see Chap. XII, §§ 6, 7.
[17] BJ ii, 18, 1.
[18] BJ iii, 7, 32. It is recorded amidst the events of the year 67.

and so well intrenched in their superior position, that the Romans could not attack them. But nature came to the former's aid; there is no water on the mountain, and it being midsummer, thirst destroyed some of the besieged rebels, and drove others to yield themselves, so that Cerealis felt able to make assault. Surrounding them, he first offered amnesty; but the horde was animated by the stiffnecked obstinacy of ancient Israel, and Cerealis proceeded to the slaughter, mowing down 11,600 people. No further information is had concerning this unique uprising; that it did not involve the whole Samaritan sect, is certain, because there was no necessity for the Romans to proceed against any of the Samaritan towns. We must suppose that the more fanatical ones of the sect, filled with Messianic enthusiasm, were infected with the madness of the Jewish coreligionists; fortunately the community as a whole was saved from the destruction which befell political Judaism.

The round century between the beginning of Herod's grace to the land of Samaria down to the fall of the Judæan state was the happiest age, we may assume, that the Samaritan sect has experienced in its long history. The land enjoyed the favor first of Herod and then, in general, of his official successors; its value was recognized, from the days of Herod to those of Vespasian, as affording a sure foothold against the tumultuous Jews. For the one time in history since the Persian period, when the enemies of Juda in Samaria persecuted the renascent Jewish state, the Samaritan community played a prominent and influential part in politics, often turning to its advantage the favorable prepossessions of the administration. Accordingly we greatly desiderate more exact information concerning the sect in this auspicious age. We learn of a Council (βουλή) of the Samaritans,[19] doubtless of the same pattern as the

---

[19] *AJ* xviii, 4, 2. But Schürer, *GJV* ii, 152, interprets this of the council of the district. For the functions of the Boule, see *ibid.*, p. 176.

Jewish Sanhedrin, and accorded much the same rights over the spiritual and social life of its community. The retention of the ancient boundaries between Juda and Samaria indicates the perpetuation of an ecclesiastical territorial jurisdiction for the Samaritans. The Talmud makes provision for Jews living in Samaria who had to pay tithes to the Samaritan hierarchy.[20] As for the political administration, Josephus asserts that there were garrisons placed throughout the land,[21] and that also upon extraordinary occasions the government called out the native element and armed them as a militia, as in the case of the conflict between the Samaritans and the Jews under Cumanus.[22] The franchises of the Samaritans may not have been as extensive as those of the Jews, but it would appear that while the empire made no confusion between the two sects, their privileges were much the same. Samaritanism was without doubt a *religio licita,* with a recognized ecclesiastical territory.

No answer can be given to the query concerning the condition of the cult upon Gerizim; the historical evidence has only the negative result that since Hyrcanus's destruction of the Samaritan temple there is no testimony to its rebuilding. Juynboll argues [23] that Herod could not have rebuilt the temple for fear of the Jews; that no record exists of any such bounty on his part would support this theory. Yet it seems strange that the Samaritans in this Age of Favor did not resume their cult with fitting surroundings. We may well think that when the Samaritan woman argued with Jesus concerning the sanctity of " this mountain," she pointed to some edifice crowning the summit (*Jn.* 4).[24]

[20] See below, p. 183.
[21] *BJ* iii, 7, 32.
[22] *AJ* xx, 6, 1.
[23] *Hist. Sam.* 113.
[24] There is little later evidence for the reconstruction of the Samari-

A COIN OF "FLAVIA NEAPOLIS."
Of the reign of Volusian, whose head appears on the reverse.
Through courtesy of the British Museum.

A MEDAL OF "FLAVIA NEAPOLIS OF PALESTINIAN SYRIA."

The reverse bears the legend, in Greek, "Antoninus, Augustus, Pius, Emperor, Cæsar." Gerizim is here represented, and in the foreground probably the temple of Jupiter with the stairs leading down to Neapolis (referred to by the Bordeaux Pilgrim: ibi ascenduntur usque ad summum montem gradus num. CCC). In the background above appears probably the Pagan sanctuary which once crowned Gerizim's top. This medal is in the Museum of the Royal Library, Paris, and is reproduced from a cut in Bargès, Les Samaritains.

§2. FROM THE DESTRUCTION OF JERUSALEM TO THE CHRIS-
TIANIZATION OF THE EMPIRE.[25]

One permanent result of interest to the sect of the Samaritans came from Vespasian's presence in the land. It is reasonably certain that this emperor built the modern Shechem,
the elder city having lain farther to the east; his foundation
he called Neapolis, " New-City," or more fully and as it appears on the coins, Flavia Neapolis, after the conqueror's
family-name.[26] From its calamity in the Jewish War the
city of Samaria never recovered; in the IVth Century it
was no longer one of the important cities of Palestine, and
soon fell to the rank of a village.[27] Neapolis rapidly
forged ahead of the old capital, and is spoken of in the IVth
Century as one of the greatest cities in Palestine.[28] This
new creation brought wealth and prestige to the centre
of the Samaritan sect, which by the IVth Century seems to
have entirely abandoned the elder Shechem; but the change
was fraught with danger to that community, for the colonization of a Pagan metropolis in their midst contributed
to the fanatical exasperation of the Samaritans against the
Romans, which ultimately brought upon them the same ruin
that had befallen Jerusalem.

After the age of the great Jewish War there exists a

tan temple; see note 102. For the Samaritan traditions concerning its
site, see Chap. III. Epiphanius, *Hæres,* lxxx, 1 (Migne, xlii, 757), describes a synagogue (Proseuche) at Shechem that was open to the
heavens. This may have been the House of God in which the Samaritans performed their sacrifices when restrained from Gerizim. For
the passage, see Schürer, *GJV* ii, 447. On the temple, cf. Chap. VI,
note 102.

[25] Add to authorities previously mentioned, Grätz, *Geschichte der
Juden,* iv.

[26] For the original location of Shechem, see above, p. 19. The fact
that Vespasian founded Neapolis is not directly affirmed by ancient
authorities, but is now generally accepted. See Valesius to Eusebius,
Hist. eccles. iv, 12; Juynboll, *Hist. Sam.* 118; Schürer, *GJV* i, 650.

[27] *GJV* ii, 153.

[28] *Ammianus Marcellinus,* xiv, 8, 11 (*GJV* i, 650). For the coins of
the city, see Eckhel, *Doctrina nummorum,* iii, 434; Mionnet, *Descrip-*

long lacuna in Samaritan history, extending to the reign
of Hadrian, (117–138). When the sect reappears it, too,
is involved in the great conflict between State and Church
which began with the fall of Jerusalem and terminated in
the triumph of Christianity. According to Spartianus the
outbreak of the war of Bar-Kokeba (132–135) was due to
Hadrian's prohibition of circumcision to the Jews.[29] The
worth of this statement has been much disputed; it is certain, however that Hadrian interdicted castration, under
which head circumcision might be included, while there is
some slight evidence that circumcision was prohibited to the
Arabians. If now, with Schürer,[30] the motive assigned to
the outbreak by Spartianus is to be accepted, we are in a position to explain how it is that from this time on the Samaritans were involved in the disasters of the Jews. Practising Jewish rites which now fell under the ban of the empire, the former came to suffer under the legal penalties
which fell upon the latter. And so it is that Hadrian's
memory is bitterly preserved by the Samaritan chronicles as
the first Pagan ruler who persecuted the Samaritan religion.

Nevertheless reliable Samaritan data concerning the Hadrianic period are most scanty, and at the same time intoler-
ably mixed up with prosaic romancings.[31] In the first place
there is a recollection of the siege of Jerusalem by Hadrian;

tion des médailles antiques, v, 500, 515; Supplém. viii, 346. Head,
Historia numorum, 678, thus briefly describes the coinage: "There
are two principal types — (a) representation of Mount Gerizim with
two summits, on one of which is the temple of Zeus, approached by a
flight of steps,— and on the other a small edifice or altar of somewhat
uncertain form; (β) simulacrum of a goddess resembling the Ephesian
Artemis standing between two humped bulls; she usually holds in one
hand a whip, and in the other ears of corn. Among the other types
are Serapis, Asklepios, Apollo, etc." The coins of the imperial city
are found from Titus to Maximinus, and of the imperial colony from
Philip I. to Volusian, the colony having been established by Septimius
Severus.

[29] Vita Hadriani, 14.
[30] GJV i, 674, where a full discussion of the question is to be found.
[31] Lib. Jos. c. xlvii; Abu'l Fath, 113–117; Chron. Adler, 44–48.

in this the Samaritan chronicles are opposed to the view
which now largely prevails that Bar-Kokeba did not hold
Jerusalem.[32] Subsequently, according to the Samaritan
chronicles, Hadrian appeared at Neapolis. He brought
thither the great bronze gates of the Jerusalem temple, and
affixed them to the temple he built upon Gerizim.[33] After
his departure, the Samaritans purified with fire the places
he had defiled,[34] which action gave opportunity to the Jews
to bring malicious accusation against them; thereupon he
gave orders to " kill every circumcised man," and also interdicted " ablutions and sabbaths and feasts." In these
traditions of the imperial visit to Shechem there is considerable historic deposit, especially in regard to Hadrian's
application of his prohibition of circumcision to the Samaritans. It is also on record that this emperor built a temple
to the Most High Jupiter on Gerizim above Neapolis.[35]

[32] See Schürer, *GJV* i, 685. The Samaritan chronicles introduce a
long story concerning two Samaritan youths, Ephraim and Manasse
(notice the artificial names!), who, having been imprisoned in Jerusalem for playing a sacrilegious trick upon a Jew (see above, note 12),
assisted Hadrian to capture the city. With this story may be compared the Jewish tradition that the Samaritans acted hostilely towards
the Jews in their desire to rebuild the temple at this time (*Bereshit
Rabba.* lxiv; text and translation given in Derenbourg, *Histoire de la
Palestine,* 416). But it may be questioned whether this reference to
a siege of Jerusalem and the hostility evinced by the Samaritans to
the Jews do not rather refer to the siege by Vespasian and Titus,
which later tradition has confounded with Hadrian's operations. The
Samaritan legend has also the malicious story that after his capture
of the city, Hadrian pressed into the Temple and there found images,
whereupon he convicted the highpriest of practising idolatry. This
doubtless has reference to the cherubim, etc., and probably the Samaritans, with their far plainer cult, often found fault with the Jews for
their more ornate ritual. The legend is the counterblast, of course, to
that of the Jews that the Samaritans worshipped a bird, and what not,
on Mount Gerizim. There is also a Rabbinic tradition concerning the
part played by the Samaritans in the fall of Bar-Kokeba's fortress of
Bettar; see Derenbourg, *op. cit.* 433.
[33] For a further reference to these gates, see below, p. 108.
[34] For this practice, see Additional Note C.
[35] *Dio Cassius,* xv, 12; the Neapolitan Marinus, quoted by Damascius, in Photius, *Bibliotheca,* Geneva, 1611, 1055f. The coins of Neapolis represent this temple.

The erection of this new Pagan fane excited the passions of the Samaritans, and the consequent excesses brought upon them the emperor's chastisement. The *Chronicle Adler* ascribes the outrage only to "some foolish people of the Samaritans."[36]

One other grievous calamity is ascribed to the days of Hadrian, the destruction of the sacred books of the Samaritans.[37] From this catastrophe, it is stated, were saved only the book of the Law and that of the succession of the priests. It is true that Abu'l Fath[38] ascribes a like calamity to the reign of Commodus, fifty years later, and because of the chronological distortion of the Samaritan data it is impossible to make sure of the exact date. That however some such calamity occurred in this century is corroborated by the fact that only since then do we find in the Samaritan chronicles anything like independent data. That before this period Samaritan culture possessed its literature is indubitable, so that we can best ascribe the almost utter absence of original knowledge of the history before Hadrian to the destruction wrought by the Romans for the rebelliousness of the sect.[39]

[36] Clermont-Ganneau, in a review of Adler and Séligsohn's *Une Nouvelle Chronique Samaritaine* (*Journal des Savants*, ii, 34), has made some interesting archæological notes upon the Samaritan chronicles, some of which may be pertinently referred to here. He would hold it possible that the bronze gates carried off to Samaria by Hadrian are the gates of Nicanor (cf. his *Recueil d'Archéologie orientale*, v, 334). Clermont-Ganneau also maintains that the object of the cult established by Hadrian on Gerizim was Serapis, Jupiter Serapis appearing frequently on the coins of Neapolis; in this view he opposes that of Adler and Séligsohn, who think of Jupiter *Sospes* (compare above, p. 77), and Juynboll (*Lib. Jos.* 334), who would correct the text to make it read *Cæsar*. The Samaritan reading is uncertain: *Lib Jos.* saqaras, *Abu'l Fath,* sapis, sipas; *Chron. Adler,* sapis. In comment upon the prohibition of lustral baths, it is to be noted that a similar interdict was issued by the emperor Verus in the same century against the purifications of Jewish women; see Grätz, *op. cit.* iv, 208.

[37] *Lib. Jos.* xlvii, end.

[38] P. 120, 10; cf. p. 118, 17.

[39] The Samaritan chronicles state that Hadrian had a Samaritan wife on whose account he made an edict that no Jew should dwell in

For the Antonines, Abu'l Fath records an Antoninus, who was "a friend of the Samaritans, and studied the Law both Hebrew and Targum, and acted according to its prescriptions; he lavished his generosity upon the world, and gave gold and silver to the poor, and never ceased reading the Law night and day. And the Samaritans were in his time in the same condition as they enjoyed in the days of Joshua." [40] Now it was Antoninus Pius (138–161) who gained the gratitude of the Jews for removing the imperial ban that lay against their practice of circumcision.[41] But if a statement made by Origen applies to this earlier period as well, then the Samaritans were not included in the franchise of the Jews. That Father in rebutting Celsus's argument that the Samaritans were persecuted as well as the Christians remarks:[42] "But it is said that Samaritans as well are persecuted for their religion. To this we answer as follows: As murderers, [sicarii, i.e. with reference to the Cornelian law *De sicariis,* which punished those who practised castration or circumcision with death], on account of circumcision, because they mutilate contrary to the established laws which allow it to the Jews alone,— therefore they are put to death." The Samaritan tradition therefore appears to be but a replica of the Jewish cycle of legend which made Antoninus not only a friend of Jewish rabbis but even a convert and a diligent student of the Law.[43]

The next reign recorded by the chronicles is that of Com-

Shechem: *Abu'l Fath,* 118, 5; *Chron. Neub.,* 439; *Chron. Adler,* 48; the latter draws the inference that "Hadrian greatly loved the Samaritans"! Evidently there exists a confusion in the Samaritan reminiscence between the similar names of Hadrian and Herod, the latter of which kings married a Samaritan, though doubtless Gentile, lady; see Josephus, *AJ* xvii, 1, 3; *BJ* i, 28, 4.

[40] *Abu'l Fath,* 117; *Chron. Adler,* 48.

[41] The new law is given by Modestinus, *Digest,* xlviii, 8, 11, pr. (quoted by Schürer, *GJV* i, 677).

[42] *C. Celsum,* ii, 13.

[43] For the Jewish romance concerning Antoninos ben Severos, or Severos ben Antoninos, see Ginzberg in *JE, s. v. Antoninus in the Talmud.*

modus (180–92), of whom a lively and bitter memory is cherished. It is chronicled that in his day the Samaritans were worse off than under Hadrian; he instituted bitter persecutions, forbidding the reading of the Law, closing the schools, destroying the scholars, compelling the use of pork, so that the knowledge of the Law well-nigh perished.[44] But although Commodus's cruel nature is notorious, yet nothing is known of any ill treatment on his part of the Israelites, so that the reference may rather belong to the successor of Marcus Aurelius, Verus Commodus.[45]

For the reign of Commodus's first permanent successor, Septimius Severus (193–211), secular history offers a few data bearing upon our investigation. Syria, including Palestine, took part with Severus's rival, Niger Pescennius, upon whose overthrow the conqueror meted out special punishment to Neapolis; " he took away the right of citizenship from the people of Neapolis in Palestine, because they had for a long time been in arms for Niger's cause."[46] Subsequently he established the city as a colony, a change which may have involved the banishment of many of the original citizens.[47] Jerome also notes in his chronology for the fifth year of this emperor a war between the Jews and the Samaritans (Judaicum et Samaritanum bellum motum); Abu'l Faraj, who places the event in the first year of the reign, describes it as a great war, a battle being fought in which many were killed on both sides.[48] Subsequently however the emperor " remitted the penalties which the Palestinians had incurred on account of Niger," and he established " many laws for the Palestinians." But apart

[44] Abu'l Fath, 118–122; Chron. Adler, 80.
[45] For his treatment of the Jews, see Grätz, op. cit. iv, 207.
[46] Spartianus, Severus, 9.
[47] Ulpian, Corp. juris digest 1, 15, 1, § 7. Grätz has " Sebaste," op. cit. iv, 226.
[48] Abu'l Faraj (Gregory Bar-Hebræus), Historia dynastiarum, ed. Pococke, p. 125 (tr. 79). Dio Cassius, lxxiv, 2, tells a romantic story of one " Claudius, a bandit, who had overrun Judæa and Palestine."

from this restoration to civil rights, the emperor took action in 202 toward repressing the Jews and the Christians, the rapid growth of the latter dismaying the administration.[49] As the proof of Jewish membership and conversion was circumcision, the Samaritans must have been included under the same proscription.

Abu'l Fath preserves a fairly accurate reflection of this reign.[50] Severus is described as offering the highpriest Akbun official honor if he will worship the idols and the imperial statute; Akbun refusing, the emperor's advisers demand the destruction of the community. To this Severus objects on the ground that they worship the greatest God of all, and that it will do no good to force them. The officials then obtain the right of espionage over the Samaritans to hinder them from circumcision and purifications,[51] and also to refuse the privilege to rear altars in their midst. There is added the note that the emperor laid upon the community a tax for the observance of the Sabbath; this may have been nothing else than some case of local official extortion.

The next reign recorded by the Samaritan chroniclers is that of Alexander Severus (222–235).[52] But the local historians seem to have utterly missed the mark concerning this ruler. He is depicted as worse than Commodus; he placed a price upon the heads of Samaritans,[53] synagogues and schools were destroyed, doctors of the Law and youths were slain. Yet above all the emperors Alexander Severus is noted for his humanity and liberality.[54] We are accordingly forced to look for some other object of the

---

[49] Spartianus, *Severus*, cc. 14, 17.
[50] P. 123.
[51] Cf. above, note 36.
[52] *Abu'l Fath*, 124; *Chron. Adler*, 50.
[53] This appears to be the meaning of *Abu'l Fath*, 124, line 12, and the parallel in *Chron. Adler;* see the editor's note to latter.
[54] He introduced both Abraham and Jesus into his pantheon, and was accustomed often to quote the Golden Rule of Hillel (not the form

Samaritan denunciation. Juynboll suggests Heliogabulus (218–222) ;[55] yet this blasphemous monarch had an eclectic interest in all cults, while his concubine Severina was favorably disposed to Christianity. But there may be suggested the identification with Caracalla (211–217), who styled himself Alexander in admiration of the great conqueror, by which name he was known upon medals.[56] He spent much of his time in the Orient, where his chosen surname may have come into common use, and then later have been confused with that of the noble and far more famous Alexander Severus.

One important event of the reign of Alexander Severus is recorded by the Samaritan chroniclers, the rise of the Sassanide kingdom of Persia.[57] To this occurrence is attached the story of an embassy sent to the new Persian king to supplicate favor for the Samaritans; by their witty wisdom they gain his favor. This story has its parallel in a later incident ;[58] in general the Samaritans appear as abettors cf the Sassanian attacks against the empire.

For the remainder of the Pagan empire the Samaritans record but three emperors. Of these it is stated that Gordianus (238-244) gave permission to the Jews to rebuild the temple at Jerusalem, but that their efforts were frustrated by a mighty storm,[59]— a replica of the Christian legend assigned to Julian's reign. Philip the Arab (244–

given by Christ, as often erroneously repeated): Quod tibi fieri non vis, alteri ne feceris; Lampridius, *Alexander Severus*, cc. 29, 51. He is also said to have been a patron of Origen.

[55] *Op. cit.* 139. According to Lampridius, *Heliogabalus*, 3, this emperor desired to centralize the cults of the Jews and Samaritans and also of the Christians at his temple on the Palatine.

[56] See Gibbon, *Decline and Fall of the Roman Empire*, ed. Bury, i, 138.

[57] *Abu'l Fath*, 122; *Chron. Adler*, 50. These place the event in the 10th year of Commodus, but the former (122, line 8) also dates it at 545 years from Alexander the Great, which is correct within two years.

[58] See p. 117.

[59] *Abu'l Fath*, 139.

249) is mentioned.[60] Finally Decius (249–252), is recorded as even worse than Severus, and a story is told of the cruel martyrdom by his deputy Rakus of a Samaritan woman who refused to worship the idols.[61]

This deficiency of information in the Samaritan sources is eked out by one datum from Jewish tradition. A Talmudic passage relates that " when Diocletian the king came hither, he decreed that all the peoples should offer libation, except the Jews; and the Samaritans offered libations."[61a] This statement, so far as we can judge, must be a libel, but it is doubtless true that while the Jews, through their influence and ancient prestige, obtained exemption from the drastic laws of revived heathenism, which were especially directed against the Christians, the Samaritans did not share the like good fortune.[62]

Such is an enumeration of the data of Samaritan history for the age between 70 and 323 A. C. Further than this we can only picture in imagination the calamities which racked the falling empire, and which in particular brought havoc and desolation to Palestine; rival emperors, insurgent governors, the wars with Parthians and Sassanians, all heaped their evils upon the devoted land, while within its borders the general civic disorder gave scope, under the cover of repressive laws, to the exactions of wilful and covetous officials, who treated the Samaritan sect, so outlandish to Pagan eyes, with even more despite than they did the rest of their unfortunate subjects. The community was more than decimated, its riches looted, its culture almost

---

[60] *Abu'l Fath*, 145; *Chron. Adler*, 61. For the rigor of the law against Samaritan circumcision, in this reign, as we saw above, Origen is witness *C. Celsum* ii, 13, which was composed under this monarch; Eusebius, *Hist. eccles.* vi, cc. 34, 36.

[61] *Abu'l Fath* 148; *Chron. Adler*, 63.

[61a] *Ab. Zara Jer.* 44d. Cf. Grätz, *op. cit.* iv, 302.

[62] Is Decius in the Samaritan chronicles an error (simple enough in the Arabic script) for Diocletian? At the same time Decius, who was the first systematic persecutor of the Christians, may have included the Samaritans in his proscriptions.

7

exterminated, as indeed the Samaritans record. It possessed no friends in the outside world apart from the members of scattered synagogues and banking-houses, but these never seem to have been able to give much support to the home-church; Judaism could survive even if not a Jew was left in the Holy Land, for the vast and well-organized Diaspora in Mesopotamia gave that church a powerful backing in trouble and a sure place of refuge. But the Samaritans possessed no like material and political advantages. Only the obstinacy of their religion saved them through these and the succeeding centuries of chaos, and in view of this persistence we dare not deny them credit for a true religious faith. With the Christianization of the empire, when at last the related church of the Nazarenes, with whom they had shared the Pagan persecutions, came to the ascendancy, we might expect the Shechemites to find respite under the rule of the followers of the Prince of Peace. But a worse fate pursued them under Christian dominion than under Pagan. Whatever rights had been theirs, the bequest of the ancient humanity of Rome, were now withdrawn to satisfy the persecuting spirit of triumphant Christendom, which had absorbed from Paganism the lesson, opposite to its Master's, to treat like with like, and to bruise the broken reed.

§3. FROM THE REIGN OF CONSTANTINE TO THE RISE OF
ISLAM.[63]

For this period we possess, in comparison with the meagre records of other ages, an extensive amount of information for the Samaritan sect. Except for the last three generations of the Pagan empire, which were marked by religious persecutions, Rome in general had troubled herself little, except on political grounds, over the religion of her subjects.

[63] Cf. especially the works of Juynboll, Grätz, and Appel, as above.

Pal. Ex Fund.   AN OLD CHURCH IN SHECHEM.

But with the ascendancy of the Christian Church, religion became one of the chief factors in the politics and history of the empire. Christian fanaticism at once began to exhibit itself, partly in the mutual persecutions of Christian sects, partly in the persecution and legal ostracism of all who did not bear the name of Christ. Among these the Pagans were the chief objects of the jealousy of militant Christendom, but the sects so nearly related to Christianity, the Jews and the Samaritans, who worshipped the same One God, suffered the more intense spite of the Church. Moreover, as the conscious successors of the Jewish Church, the malevolence of the Christians followed the traditions of Judaism in the despite of the Samaritans, so that the latter suffered a twofold share of persecution. Accordingly we find many laws which, for the first time in Roman jurisprudence, name the Samaritans, while the Christian annalists have abundant occasion to mention the sect. On the other hand, the Samaritan records are fuller and more correct for this than any other period; the race has preserved the bitter memory that its undoing came at the hands not of Pagan or Arab but of the Christian. On a small scale the story of the fanatical desperation which centuries earlier had destroyed the Jewish nation was now re-enacted in Samaria, and the Christian dominion in Palestine stands branded with cruel oppressions of the despised sect and with the responsibility for ruthless and brutal revolts raised by the latter. For these three centuries Samaritan history shares in the horrors of the fall of the Roman empire in the Orient, and the only relief in the cruel story is found in the brief renascence of the sect which occurred in the IVth Century.

The age of Constantine (d. 337) was one of true toleration. That great statesman cared more for the unity of his empire than for the strife of sects which only involved civil commotion and ruin. Several of his laws give privileges to the Jews, in which the Samaritans may have been included. Thus the patriarchs and elders of the former, like the Christian clergy, were exempted from all public functions.[64] At the same time the emperor found it necessary to repress the aggressive violence of the Jews against perverts, and an early law " gives notice to the Jews and their elders and patriarchs that in case anyone escapes from their barbarous sect and reverences the Religion of God, if any Jew dare, after the promulgation of this law, to attack such a one with stones or by any other kind of mad violence,— a proceeding which has come to our cognizance — he is to be promptly burnt to death, being cremated along with his abettors. If any from the people attaches himself to their nefarious sect and attends their conventicles, he with them is to pay the fitting penalty."[65] Another law more explicitly confiscates the property of converts to Judaism;[66] another forbids Jews taking slaves from other cults under penalty of the emancipation of the slave, and if a Jewish master circumcise a slave, he is to be put to death.[67] These restrictive prescriptions seem to be renewals of the earlier ban against Judaism, and without doubt included the Samaritans in their implication.

But the sectarian strife which broke out upon the council of Nicæa (325), as well as the exasperation of Paganism, so sharpened Christian fanaticism that persecution became more and more the order of the day. Constantius (d. 361), who had his hands full enough with the quarrels of Catholics and Arians, promulgated an edict forbidding on peril of death the marriage of Christian women with Jews.[68] For this reign there is also evidence concerning the relations of

[64] *Codex Theodosianus, Lib.* xvi, *Tit.* 8, c. 2, *anno* 330; in the edition of Ritter-Gothofred, Leipzig, 1736–1743, vol. vi, 240. This important Title is called *De Judæis, Samaritanis, et Cælicolis* (*ib.* p. 234).
[65] *Ibid.,* c. 1; *an.* 315.
[66] *Ibid.,* c. 7.
[67] *Ibid.,* xvi, 9, c. 2 (Ritter, vi, 271).
[68] *Ibid.,* xvi, 8, c. 6.

Samaritans with the Jews. In 339 the latter raised a revolt at Sepphoris in Galilee, whence they are said to have " destroyed many Greeks and Samaritans "; that is, the raids were carried into Samaria, or the outlying settlements of Samaritans on the coast or in Peræa.[69]

To the reign of Constantius, the ruler of the eastern portion of the empire (337–361), in association with his brother, the emperor Constans, is to be assigned one anecdote in the Samaritan chronicles. According to this tradition[70] the emperor Decius was followed by Tahus, who prohibited the reading of the Law and the observance of the rites, his prefect in Samaria being a certain Garman. The anecdote proceeds to relate that the highpriest Nathanael was in a quandary how to circumcise his eldest son, the later famous Baba Rabba, for the Samaritans seem to have had the custom of performing the rite before the community. At last he resolved to have it performed in a cave outside of the town, and so gave the child to a servant to carry him thither in a basket, while the party was to follow immediately. The servant was met by the prefect and accosted with the words: " Do what thou intendest and fear not," and upon her return, he again addressed her: " Bring him up in peace, my child." The highpriest learned that the prefect was aware of his illegal action, and full of fear plucked up the courage to approach him with a bribe. The latter refused it, and promised on oath to make no report to the emperor. In consequence of this benevolence it became the custom of the Samaritans, whenever they had occasion to circumcise a child in a cave, to pray that " God have mercy on Garman, the Roman prefect! "

Now there was a bishop of Neapolis by the name of Germanus, who was present at the councils of Ancyra and Neo-

---

[69] Socrates, *Hist. eccles.*, ii, 33; Theophanes, *Chronographia*, 61; *Cedrenus*, 524 (the two latter in the *Corpus scriptorum historiæ Byzantinæ*).
[70] *Lib. Jos.* xlix; *Abu'l Fath*, 150; *Chron. Adler*, 63.

Cæsarea (314), and of Nicæa (325).[71] The title given
the governor, qasîs, means, in both Arabic and Syriac
(qashshîs), an ecclesiastical dignitary, as well as governor.
The official in the Samaritan tradition is therefore no other
than Germanus, the Christian bishop of Neapolis, and the
emperor Tahus doubtless Constantius. We may assume
that the stringency of official measures against the Samaritan religion depended much upon the zeal of the ecclesiastics; in this case we have a rare and noble instance of the
Christian charity of a bishop of that age to the enemies of
his Church. The story also states that watchers were
appointed to keep the Samaritans from circumcision; that is,
the old law of Hadrian was now again set in force against
the Samaritans.[72]

This anecdote is of important chronological value, for it
serves to give the date for an episode which the Samaritans
look back upon as one of the most glorious in their history.
This is the story of their great hero, Baba Rabba, who when
a child was the unconscious object of the clemency of good
bishop Germanus. Despite the arrangement of the Samaritan chronicles, which assign Baba Rabba to the IIId Century, specifically to the reigns of Severus and Philip, all the
sure data refer his life to the mddle of the IVth Century;
probably he flourished under the eastern co-emperor Constantius.[73]

It is unnecessary to enter into the details of the largely

[71] See Reland, Palæstina, 1009.
[72] To Juynboll, Lib. Jos. 151, belongs the credit of recognizing the
historic circumstances of this anecdote.
[73] The history is given at greatest length in Abu'l Fath, 129–146; in
briefer abstract in Chron. Adler, 51–62; also in Chron. Neub. 440–442;
Lib. Jos. xlviii–l. The chronology is fixed by the references to Germanus and Constantius (Tahus), while the exact date is given according to several eras in Chron. Adler, 57f, according to which Baba
" appeared " in the 655th year from Alexander, i. e., A. D. 319, and in
the 308th year after Jesus Christ. His activity is said to have begun
in his 40th year. The name Baba Rabba, " the Great Gate," was doubtless a title of religious significance.

exuberant and absurd story of the hero. The residuum of solid facts seems to be as follows: Baba Rabba was the eldest son of the highpriest, and instituted a great religious revival and reformation. His supporters seem to have been the laity, for he favored the laymen to the prejudice of the priests, establishing a college of Seven Wise Men, only three of whom were priests, while laymen seem to have been set in charge of the synagogues. He reconstituted the priestly line, whose pedigree had been lost. He recovered what he could of the holy books, and restored the worship of the community, also building eight stone synagogues. The land was divided for administrative purposes into twelve districts.[74] The oldest stratum of the story reports that Baba Rabba announced that he did not intend any political revolution in his reformation;[75] but the story develops into extravagant accounts of his successes against the enemies of the Samaritans, in which figures are used in truly oriental style. To give credit to the annalist, Abu'l Fath declares that he is not responsible for part of the impossible story.[76] There is an account of a successful fray with the Roman tax-gatherers, and also of an encounter with Arab invaders, who seem to have been coöperating with the Persian king. At the end of his life the hero was compelled to go to Constantinople, where he was held in most honorable captivity until his death. In connection with this heroic story we also learn that Marka the great theologian of the Samaritans flourished about the same time, a generation or two later than Baba Rabba, and this connection gives us further valuable corroboration of the fact that in this century Samaritanism enjoyed a renascence.[77]

There is no external reference to this episode of Baba Rabba, but without doubt place can be found for it in the

[74] For these districts, see below, p. 150.
[75] Abu'l Fath, 133.
[76] P. 139.
[77] See below, p. 294.

history of the IVth Century. The period of sectarian strife under the sons of Constantine offered an opportunity for the recrudescence of the oriental sects. The follower of those princes, the Pagan but infinitely nobler Julian, in his conflict with the Church showed his favors to the Jews, and the Samaritans may be considered to have shared in his grace. Valens (364–368), the co-emperor with Valentinian I. in the Orient, caused a reaction not only of the Arians but also of the other religions of the empire, and Cedrenus mentions that in his eighth year he conferred honors on the Jews.[78] There is a Samaritan reminiscence of this emperor in the story of an appeal made by the children of a highpriest concerning their patrimony to the " king Balsamis." [79] These reigns accordingly gave a welcome breathing-space to the eastern sects, and in this period we find a place for the Samaritan memories of the glorious age of Baba Rabba. Yet another corroboration may be established in Abu'l Fath's report of the war waged between " the king of Mosul," i. e., Persia, and Rome at this time, referring perhaps to the Persian invasion in 353,[80] and again in the note of the Ishmaelite invasion of Palestine, which is affirmed by external authorities.[81] We possess therefore in the Samaritan annals some fairly correct historical traditions for this period. To the stimulus of the reform and rejuvenation of the sect under Baba Rabba we have to ascribe much of the self-assertive and pugnacious patriotism which the Samaritans displayed during the remainder of the Byzantine age.

Despite his partizan zeal, the empire gained in Theodosius I. (379–395) a ruler filled with the spirit of Roman law.

[78] *Cedrenus*, 544.
[79] *Abu'l Fath*, 164. The Arabic form comes through the Greek, Bales.
[80] *Ammianus*, xiv, 3; so Appel suggests, p. 74. Or is it a reference to Julian's disastrous campaign?
[81] *Abu'l Fath*, 136f; cf. *Sozomenus*, vi, 38; *Socrates*, iv, 36; *Theophanes*, i, 92, 100.

Accordingly his attention was frequently drawn to the Jews in regard both to their peculiar afflictions at the hand of officials and populace, and also to their exceptional rights over against the common law of the empire. He stoutly defended the Jews against the oppression of governors, as in the case of the capital condemnation of a certain Hesychius of consular rank, who had seized the papers of the Jewish patriarch,[82] and gave strict injunctions to restrain the interference of mobs with the rights and property of that race, also disallowing the inequitable municipal exactions often levied upon them, for instance, in the regulation of the prices of their wares.[83] In a certain particular he maintained their ecclesiastical autonomy and discipline by protecting their right of excommunication.[84] In one of his edicts Theodosius includes by name the Samaritans — the first mention of them in Roman edicts that has been preserved. The law reads thus: " It is recognized that the community of the Jews and of the Samaritans cannot be summoned for navicular duty [i. e., the obligation of furnishing ships for the state], for the duty which appears to be enjoined on the whole body can obligate no person in particular; hence on the one hand those who are poor and engaged in petty business ought not to have to perform the duty of contributing ships to the state, so on the other hand, those, who having the means can be chosen from these bodies, ought not to be immune to the aforesaid function."[85] The intent of the edict is evidently this, to relieve

[82] Jerome, *De optimo genere interpretandi, ad Pamachium;* ed Migne, xxii, 570. This letter may not be genuine.
[83] *Cod. Theodos.* xvi, 8, cc. 9, 10, 12 (Ritter, vi, 245ff).
[84] *Ibid.,* c. 8.
[85] *Ibid.,* xiii, 5, c. 18, *an.* 390 (Ritter, v, 84): Judæorum corpus ac Samaritanorum ad naviculariam functionem non jure vocari cognoscitur; quidquid enim universo corpori videtur indici, nullam specialiter potest obligare personam; unde sicut inopes vilibusque commerciis occupati naviculariæ translationis munus obire non debent, ita idoneos facultatibus, qui ex his corporibus deligi poterunt, ad prædictam functionem haberi non oportet immunes.

synagogal communities of the navicular duty, which otherwise would lie upon the poor as well as the rich of those
bodies, and to require that duty of those individual members whose wealth rendered them liable. We observe here
the effort of the imperial lawyer to ignore the semi-
autonomous ecclesiastical communities with their ancient
separate privileges and responsibilities, and, on the other
hand, to place all their members on the same footing with
other citizens.[86] This law is of peculiar interest because of
its explicit reference to the Samaritans; we have also to infer that all the legislation applying to the Jews was generally construed as covering the smaller sect. The law in
question is addressed to the governor of Alexandria, where
there was an extensive Samaritan community.

Of Theodosius's equitable disposition Abu'l Fath reports
what is doubtless a true reminiscence.[87] The Romans came
to Neapolis to keep the Samaritans from worshipping on
Gerizim, but God put it in the heart of king Theodosius
(Tahadis) to drive off the disturbers. The anecdote is
placed in the midst of accounts of frays between Samaritans
and Christians, which seem therefore to have been checked
by the strong hand of the government.

But a far more grievous difficulty now assailed the
Samaritans than any which arose from the law. Samaria
had now become holy ground to the Christians as well as
to the Shechemites, and with the advent of the Church to
empire there arose the fanatical question as to the possession of the sacred sites, most of which the Christians proceeded to claim. On one memorable occasion the land had
been trodden by the feet of Christ, and Christian devotion
promptly addressed itself to the well by Sychar, where Jesus
taught the Samaritan woman, and which was also hoary

[86] Grätz, *op. cit.* iv, 387, has misunderstood the implication of this
law, and is uncertain whether it is favorable or otherwise to the communities concerned.
[87] P. 169.

JOSEPH'S TOMB.

with patriarchal tradition as Jacob's Well — one of the few spots in Palestine which we can exactly identify with Christ's movements. In the IVth Century the sacred Well came into Christian possession, and Jerome, writing about 404, records how the venerable lady Paula visited the church that was built about Jacob's Well; this possession was maintained by the Christians down into Muslim times.[88]

There was yet another holy site not far off from the Well which also claimed the interest of Christians. This was the Tomb of Joseph, which, according to Jewish tradition, attested for the Ist Century A. C., was the sepulchre of the Twelve Patriarchs or Sons of Jacob.[89] Jerome reports that Paula, after visiting Jacob's Well, "turned aside and saw the tombs of the Twelve Patriarchs." Of the conflicts which broke out over the possessions of this site the Samaritan chronicles preserve some interesting reminiscences,[90] these annals being only acquainted with the tradition concerning Joseph, not with that of the Twelve. They report, in *Abu'l Fath,* just before the mention of Theodosius, that the Christians came and attempted to carry off Joseph's bones in order to transport them to their own cities. Their undertaking was frustrated by miracles, including a wondrous light and cloud, and finally they contented themselves with building over the spot a church. This was destroyed by the Samaritans, and the community bought itself off from punishment only through payment of a fine. Thereupon they made the tomb inaccessible for all time. In matter of fact no ancient remains are found on the spot,

---

[88] Jerome, *Epitaphium Paulæ,* ed. Migne, xxii, 888. The pilgrims Antoninus Martyr (of Plaisance), Arnulf, Willibald, mention the church. The Samaritans appear now to have lost all sense of the sanctity of the spot, although acquainted with the tradition. For these references see Reland, *op. cit.* 1008; Robinson, *BR* iii, 110; and Guérin, *op. cit.* i, 380, who gives the references in full.
[89] *Acts,* 7, 16; see J. Lightfoot, *ad loc.,* and commentaries.
[90] *Abu'l Fath,* 169; *Chron. Adler.* 74.

the present structure covering the site being quite modern.[91]

In this connection may be mentioned yet another anecdote which may be placed in the IVth Century.[92] The highpriest built a large synagogue, and furnished it with the gates which had decorated Hadrian's temple on Gerizim, and which that monarch had brought from Jerusalem.[93] For this theft he was called into account by "king Saqafatus," with whom he finally settled by a heavy payment. What is meant by the barbarous name has not been made out.[94] It may be conjectured that this event took place shortly after the fall of Paganism, when the Samaritans ventured to spoil the heathen shrines for their own advantage.[95]

The evil conditions of the Israelite sects increased in the Vth Century. For the bloody persecutions of the Jews, which were led by the clergy and followed with desperate uprisings on the part of the victims, reference may be made to the general histories.[96] The western emperor Honorius (395–423) had occasion to include the Samaritans in an edict concerning the Jews: "The Jews and Samaritans, who flatter themselves to have the privileges of being royal agents [informers], are to be deprived of all such service."[97] Equally with Honorius his second colleague in the East,

---

[91] *Baedeker*, 225.

[92] *Abu'l Fath*, 166; *Chron. Adler*, 72. For a discussion see Clermont-Ganneau, *Journal des Savants*, ii, 43.

[93] See above, p. 91.

[94] Vilmar, *Abu'l Fath*, p. lxxiii, thinks of ἐπίσκοπος. Clermont-Ganneau rejects this identification. I would suggest συκοφάντης, i. e., the imperial informer, the role which was taken by the *Agens in rebus*. The word occurs in Rabbinic; see Jastrow, *Dictionary*, s. v. קטפ.

[95] The Samaritan building is said to have been a synagogue, but this may have been an attempt to rebuild the Samaritan temple.

[96] *E. g.* Grätz, *op. cit.* iv, 389.

[97] *Cod. Theodos.* xvi, 8, c. 16, *an.* 404 (Ritter vi, 254): Iudæos et Samaritanos, qui sibi agentium in rebus privilegio blandiuntur, omni militia privandos esse censemus. However the administration of Arcadius, the co-emperor in the East was very favorable to the Jews; Grätz, *op. cit.* iv, 387.

Theodosius II. (408–450), was intent upon the Christian-ization of the empire. It is significant that in his reign the patriarchate of the Jews, which in the person of the last Gamaliel had received high honors from the imperial court, being given the dignity of a prefecture, was finally abol-ished.[98] But passing over the legislation which names only the Jews, we will notice those edicts in which the Sa-maritans are specified.

For the year 426 a law is preserved which guards the interests of the Jewish and Samaritan converts to the Chris-tian faith; in such cases " no child of Jews or Samaritans is to be disinherited by parents or grandparents, or receive less by testament than if the testator had died intestate."[99] A still more severe edict followed thirteen years later, in which all former disabilities of the opponents of the Catholic faith are reaffirmed, peculiar advantages abolished, and new disabilities imposed. In the first chapter of the IIId Novella to the Theodosian Code (439), addressed against " Jews, Samaritans, Pagans, and all kinds of Here-tics,"[100] the emperor abrogates all earlier laws admitting Jews and Samaritans to civic honors, and prohibits spe-cifically their receiving the function of Defensor, a kind of gentlemanly office with the power of restraining the rapaci-ties of governors in the larger cities. The reason assigned is the fear lest these sectarians might injure or insult the Christians and their clergy. It is further forbidden to con-

[98] See Grätz, op. cit. iv, 389, and Note 22. This patriarch lost his honors through arrogance (415), and the empire terminated the succes-sion upon his death, circa 425. The emperor's wife Eudoxia was an especially zealous patroness of the sacred sites of Palestine.

[99] Cod. Theodos. xvi, 8, c. 28 (Ritter, vi, 267).

[100] See Ritter's edition of the Novellæ of Theodosius, at end of vol. vi, p. 9. The form of this phrase still survives in the Third Collect of the Anglican Church for Good Friday, " Jews, Turks, Infidels, and Heretics." The same phrase appears in the first section: Iudæos Sa-maritas Paganos et cetera hæreticorum genera portentorum. For the last word, cf. Jerome's expression portenta nomina, used of certain sects; Ad Gal. ii, pref. (Migne xxvi, 382).

struct new synagogues, or rebuild old ones, except that dilapidated edifices might be propped up. The conversion of slave or freeman is made a capital crime and entails confiscation of all property, while attempts upon the faith of Christians may involve the same penalty. Those who have honors may no longer enjoy them, any further building of synagogues will inure to the profit of the Church, and all the members of the sects shall relapse into the condition of the meanest inhabitants of the empire. Withal they are not to be released from any of the burdens of the state, as in the matter of all imposts or military duty, lest such exemption should be to their advantage. Only they may not be employed as apparitors or jailors, lest they have opportunities to ill-treat Christian prisoners. This is the fullest imperial law we possess concerning the Jews and Samaritans, and its provisions implied the repression of those sects; later laws could only advance to complete outlawry.

The great conflict that was brewing between the empire and the Samaritans first came to a head under the emperor Zeno (474–491). The oppression of this cruel and degraded ruler fanned the flames of revolt in the provinces, and the civil war started by Illus (484) produced a bloody revolt which particularly devastated Palestine. In 486 there was an uprising of the Jews in Antioch, which was suppressed by their almost entire extermination within that city. After the overthrow of Illus's army, the Samaritans themselves arose and proceeded to a bloody massacre of the Christians (484), some exact details of which are preserved in the Greek chronicles.[101] While the Christians of Neapolis were celebrating Whitsun, the Samaritans attacked them, and cut off the fingers of the bishop Terebinthus, who was officiating at the altar. The Samaritans thereupon named

[101] *Chronicon Paschale,* to year 484; Procopius, *De ædificiis,* v, 7 (placing the event in the year 490).

as king a certain Justa, or Justasa, a Samaritan leader of the banditti that infested the land. The successful rebels with their king then proceeded to Cæsarea, which itself was the seat of a large Samaritan community; here they destroyed many Christians and burnt down the church of St. Procopius, while Justa celebrated a triumph in correct style with the games of the circus. But the governor of Palestine, Asclepiades, and Rheges, an imperial general, advanced against him and overthrew him. Meanwhile the unfortunate Terebinthus had fled to the emperor Zeno and persuaded him to vengeance against the Samaritans. The latter were expelled from Gerizim, and on its summit a church was built in honor of the Virgin, the first Christian sanctuary on that site. About the old Samaritan temple a stockade was established, and a strong guard placed in Neapolis.[102] Procopius adds that the people, though sorely angered and distressed, had to submit.

For these events the Samaritan chronicles have unusually full information, although the chronology is confused, the affair of Justa being assigned to Marcian's reign.[103] The outbreak, it is reported, was due to the attempt of the Christians to remove the bones of the highpriests Eleazar, Ithamar and Phineas, a case like that earlier enacted about Joseph's tomb. The governor of Cæsarea took part with the Christians, but wishing to avoid too much bloodshed, proposed a duel of champions. On the Christian side was a great giant accompanied by a dog of demon-like powers, but the Samaritan champion, Justia, slew the beast, and the Christians were routed. From that time none has at-

[102] This reference to the temple on Gerizim is, in addition to the parallel reference of the Samaritan chronicle, given immediately below, the only testimony to the rebuilding of the temple destroyed by John Hyrcanus. But on the other side is to be placed the testimony of Procopius, in the following century: "They never built any temple there, but revered in their worship its summit as the holiest place of all"; *De ædificiis*, v, 7.
[103] *Abu'l Fath*, 169–172; *Chron. Adler*, 74–76.

tempted to enter the tombs of the patriarchs. Then upon Zeno's arrival in the land, he brought the Samaritans under the jurisdiction of the Christian courts.[104] He forbade their burning, charring, or destroying anything with fire; this prescription must have reference in part to the peculiar fire-purifications prevalent amongst the Samaritans.[105] He then attempted their conversion, ordering them to adore the cross, and killed seventy of their chiefs at the "Colonnade." The holy places of the community were confiscated, the synagogue of Akbun he turned into a monastery.[106] Upon his visit to the synagogue of Baba Rabba he was surprised at the absence of images. Next he demanded the sale of the holy mount, but the Samaritans, while politely acknowledging his power, refused to enter into a bargain; thereupon he seized the temple, its precincts, and the pools of water alongside. The temple he enlarged and turned into a Christian church, surmounted with a large white dome, wherein a light burned at night — which could be seen as far as Constantinople and Rome! He also constructed a tomb in front of the temple, so that when the Samaritans turned towards Gerizim, they would have to face the tomb. As for the body which it contained, Abu'l Fath records two versions of the story: one that he buried there a child of his, the other that he himself was buried there.

In addition to these independent data, there are several interesting correspondences between the Byzantine historians and the Samaritan chronicles, as in the name of the Samaritan leader, the connection of Cæsarea with the his-

[104] This statement is important for our knowledge of the legal status of the community at Neapolis.

[105] See Additional Note C.

[106] *Chron. Adler* has: "he made it a house for the saints, קדושים; *Abu'l Fath:* "he put in it a clergy-house, and made in front of it a place for unveiled (i. e. shameless) women." I suggest that this remarkable allusion is to a nunnery, with an obscene play upon the sense of *qedoshim* according to the primitive technical meaning of *qedesha* as a religious prostitute, e. g. Dt. 23, 18.

tory, the confiscation of the synagogues in the town and of the holy site on Gerizim, and the replacement of the Samaritan temple there with a Christian church.[107]

The loss of their holy places, the abrogation of their peculiar rights, the contumely of the Christians, and the exactions of the corrupt imperial administration, only the more exasperated the wretched Samaritan community, but to its miserable undoing. In the troublous days of Anastasius (491–518), the same kind of fanaticism that exhibited itself in the days of Pilate was repeated by a mob of Samaritans, who, headed by a woman, scaled the sacred hill, surprised and massacred the garrison, and seized the church of St. Mary. But Procopius, governor of Palestine, was soon able to suppress the uprising, and its leaders were slain.[108]

The reign of the most orthodox Justinian (527–565) brought renewed and final disaster upon the Samaritan sect. The memory of the catastrophe seems to have been obliterated in the mind of the latter by the frightful disorders of a bloody uprising and the well-nigh complete extermination of the local sect by the imperial reprisals; at all events no information of this period is to be gained from the Samaritan chronicles. On the other hand the Byzantine annalists and Cyril of Scythopolis have preserved various data, which afford a general view of the events, while the laws of Justinian reflect the brutal history in a passionless legal code.

The tragedy seems to have received its impulse from an edict of Justinian found under the title *De Hæreticis et*

---

[107] The evidence of the Samaritan records concerning the site of the temple and of the church of St. Mary which replaced it has not been appreciated by students. There are several points of archæological interest in Abu'l Fath's story, as in the reference to the dome of the church, and the pools confiscated by Zeno, the locality of which can still be identified. See Guérin, *op. cit.* i, c. xxv, who, however, makes no use of the Samaritan evidence.

[108] Procopius, *De ædificiis,* v, 7.

8

Manichœis et Samaritis, issued in 527.[109]   In this law all the earlier disabilities of Pagans ("Greeks"), Jews, and Samaritans were confirmed. This edict was immediately followed by a new law,[110] providing that Orthodox children of members of those sects may not be cut off by testament, while the next law [111] prohibits the same classes from holding councils, elections, or ecclesiastical offices, and from possessing directly or indirectly any real estate. It is to be noticed that in these edicts the Samaritans still appear on the same footing with the Jews.

The Samaritans were in noble company; in 529 the university of Athens was closed by imperial order, such was the logical consequence of the laws *de Hœreticis.* But the fanatical sects of the empire did not submit to suppression as tamely as did the philosophers of Greece, for Procopius, the contemporary historian and one time governor of Syria, tells how, upon the enactment of these repressive edicts, immediately "the whole Roman dominion was filled with murder and flying fugitives," and the same narrator then proceeds to detail the story of the Samaritan rebellion which was thus incited.[112]

The great uprising took place in the middle of the year 529.[113]   It extended over the whole of Samaria, from

[109] *Codex Justinianus,* i, 5, c. 12. Reference for these edicts is made to Krüger, *Codex Justinianus,* Berlin, 1877.
[110] *Ibid.,* c. 13.
[111] *Ibid.,* c. 14.
[112] For the history of this revolt reference has been made for most of the authorities to the *Corpus scriptorum historiæ Byzantinæ,* Bonn; viz. Procopius, *Historia arcana,* c. 11; *De ædificiis Justiniani,* v, 7; John Malalas, 445; Cedrenus, i, 646; *Theophanes,* 274; *Chronicon Paschale,* 619. The account given by Cyrillus Scythopolitanus in his *Life of St. Saba* is quoted in part by Reland, *op. cit.* 674, and is to be found in Cotelerius, *Ecclesiæ Græcæ monumenta,* iii, 340. Eutychius, *Annales,* ed. Migne, cxi, 1070, assigns the details of this uprising to that of "the 21st year," referring to the one in 556; see below. Cf. also Abu'l Faraj, *Historia dynastiarum,* ed. Pococke, p. 147 (tr. 92); *Chronicum Syriacum,* ed. Bruns-Kirsch, 83.
[113] The month is variously given: May, by Cyril; June by Malalas and Theophanes. The former date may refer to events at Scythopolis, the latter to those at Cæsarea. For the date see Appel, *op. cit.* 84.

Scythopolis in the east to Cæsarea on the coast. Many places were burnt in the neighborhood of the former city, according to Malalas, while Procopius, who is interested in " his city," reports the indignation excited amongst the Samaritans of Cæsarea by the repressive legislation directed against heretics. By reason of an obscure statement of Malalas, it has been argued that the Jews took part in the uprising against the Christians: ταραχῆς γενομένης ἐθνικῆς συμβαλόντων γὰρ τῶν Σαμαρειτῶν μεταξὺ Χριστιάνων καὶ Ἰου-δαίων; with this understanding of the history Theophanes and Cedrenus, who are subsequent to the genuine Malalas at least,[114] agree, stating that it was an uprising of " Jews and Samaritans." But as Grätz points out,[115] the obscure Greek of Malalas indicates that the Samaritans attacked both Christians and Jews. At all events, as from this moment the legislation of Justinian begins sharply to distinguish between the two Israelitish sects, it cannot well be held that the Jews participated in the desperate attempt of their rivals. Procopius adds that the indignation of the Samaritans caused the majority to pervert to the Manichæans and " Polytheists "— an obscure statement, as both the Manichæans and Samaritans were in the same boat. Probably the underlying fact is that the two sects made common cause in this rebellion.

But the center of Samaritan resistance lay naturally in the highlands of Samaria, and here " the rustics " elevated a certain Samaritan bandit, Julian, son of Sabar, as their emperor.[116] At Neapolis, according to Cyril, the bishop

[114] See below, Note 133.
[115] Op. cit. iv, Note 6.
[116] This action repeats the history of Justa, as above, p. 111. Malalas adds here the anecdote that Julian entered Neapolis escorted by a crowd of followers and attended the games; the victor in the first event, Niceas, proving to be a Christian, the upstart king had him slain to avoid the evil omen. But, in the first place there was no theatre at Neapolis, whereas that of Herod at Cæsarea, with its quinquennial games in honor of Cæsar, was famous; and further the story is suspiciously like the anecdote concerning Justa. It is also most

Sammon (or Ammon) was slain along with many presbyters, and the rebels prevailed to the extent of making the highways impassable to Christians. It became imperatively necessary that the administration should interfere; the emperor punished with death the governor Bassus, who had not forestalled the insurrection (so Malalas), and sent duke Theodore to suppress it; he was accompanied, according to Procopius, by the (new) governor of Palestine, whose name is given by Cyril as John.[117] With the forces was associated the Saracenic phylarch. The rebels maintained themselves "for a long time" (so Procopius), but were finally routed and dispersed, losing, the same historian asserts, 100,000 men, which figure is reduced by Malalas to 20,000. Julian was captured, and his head sent to the emperor (Malalas and Cedrenus). The fugitives hid themselves in the hills and caves, especially on Gerizim, or fled into the Trachonitis. The Arab phylarch obtained for his spoil 20,000 captives, who were sold to distant parts of the world.

Cyril tells how the aged and holy Saba of Scythopolis proceeded to Constantinople to obtain satisfaction and protection for the Christians. He found opposition at court however. The Samaritan atrocities at Scythopolis had been repaid in kind by the Christians, who had murdered along with other victims a gentleman named Sylvanus, a protector of the Samaritans. The latter's son, Count Arsenius, accordingly laid a counter-petition before the emperor, and even gained the favor of the empress Theodora. But Saba finally prevailed. The taxes were remitted because of the depredations that had been wrought, the churches were ordered to be rebuilt, and reference is made to edicts of

unlikely that the bandit entered Cæsarea in view of Procopius's silence concerning such an event. The tale is evidently a reminiscence of the earlier history.

[117] But the *Paschal Chronicle* here names Irenæus the Pentadian, who also appears in *Malalas* as the new governor.

outlawry against the Samaritans, which will be noticed below. The new governor then pursued a severe persecution of the Samaritans.

Procopius, in *De ædificiis*, v, 7, gives an account of Justinian's building operations on Gerizim and in Shechem. The emperor reared outside of the old stockade erected by Zeno an impregnable wall.[118] He also rebuilt five churches which had been destroyed on Gerizim.[119]

Theophanes and Malalas recount an interesting sequel to the story of this desperate uprising.[120] A deputation was sent to the Persian king from the Samaritans offering to deliver to him the land of Palestine, and to furnish him the aid of 50,000 Samaritan and Jewish troops;[121] thereupon the monarch rejected the terms of peace which had been brought at that time by a Roman embassy, his covetousness for the rich spoils of Jerusalem being excited by the Samaritan offer.[122] But the plot was discovered by the arrest of the deputation, consisting of five Samaritans, upon their return from the east. The incident has its counterpart in the assistance actually given by the Jews to Chosroes II. in his conquest of Palestine in the early part. of the next century. The Samaritan story of the relations between the Sassanide dynasty and the Samaritans in the IIId Century, is probably a reminiscence of frequent conspiracies with the Persians, in which all non-Christian inhabitants of Syria took part.[123]

[118] The remains of this wall are still to be seen; Guérin, *op. cit.* i, 426.

[119] So the context, and not as Robinson, *BR* iii, 124, "in the city itself."

[120] *Theophanes*, 274; *Malalas*, 455. Malalas, however, narrates the incident in connection with the later uprising of the Samaritans in Justinian's reign, for which see below, p. 121. According to Malalas, the Persian monarch concerned is Choades, *i. e.,* Chobad: according to Theophanes, Chosroes I. The change of throne from the former to the latter monarch occurred in 531.

[121] Malalas has it that 50,000 fled into Persia.

[122] The embassy was led by Hermogenes, according to Theophanes; by Rufinus, according to Malalas.

[123] See above, p. 96.

The new legislation provoked by the desperation of the Samaritans is amply revealed in fresh laws of Justinian. The 17th Chapter of the Title *De Hæreticis et Manichæis et Samaritis,* " Concerning the Samaritans,"[124] belongs to the year of the Samaritan uprising, 529.[125] In it the imperial legislation took prompt steps toward the outlawry of the obnoxious sect. This Chapter provides, for the first time, that their synagogues are to be destroyed, while their rebuilding is penalized; the Samaritans may have no heirs but Orthodox persons; nor may they donate property, which in such a case is to be confiscated, the bishops as well as the governors being charged with the execution of this provision. The next edict[126] repeats the former provisions concerning synagogues, testaments, and civic honors, and further inquires into the pretensions made by Samaritans of conversion to Christianity, the genuineness of which is to be ascertained by examining whether they educate their wives and children in the Christian faith. The children of mixed marriages must be brought up in Orthodoxy. This edict includes with the Samaritans the Manichæans, Borborites, Montanists, Taskogrudi, Ophites, and Pagans in general, but the Jews are not mentioned. With the desperate revolt of 529 the Jews and the Samaritans had finally parted company in the eyes of the imperial legislation.

The inquisition into the genuineness of Samaritan conversions is illustrated by a statement of the *Paschal Chronicle,*[127] which shows that vigilance had to be exercised over the cowed but pertinacious sect. " Some of them in fright attached themselves under stress to Christianity, and were accepted and baptized. And to this day they play a double part. On the one hand in the case of severity on the part of the governors, making a false appearance with secret

---

124 *Cod. Justinian,* i, 5, c. 17 (ed. Krüger, p. 82).
125 Cf. the date of the parallel Latin edict, *ibid.* c. 19.
126 *Ibid.,* c. 18.
127 *Chron. Pasch.* 619.

purpose and of evil intention, they declare themselves to be Christians; but in the case where governors are avaricious, the Samaritans act as hating Christianity and as ignorant of it, persuading the governors to let them *Samaritize* by bribes."[128]

The repressive legislation was continued in an edict of 531, by which Heretics and Jews may not bear witness in cases where Orthodox persons are concerned. Amongst themselves however that right is allowed, exception being made however against " the Manichæans, Borborites, Pagans, and the Samaritans, and those who are not unlike the latter, namely Montanists, Taskodrugi, and Ophites." To these sects all judicial rights whatsoever are interdicted, the only exception being in the matter of wills, contracts, etc., where the public good might be hampered by this strict provision.[129] This law is interesting for its assimilation of the Samaritans with the extreme Christian sects.[130]

In a Novella of 537 Justinian again repeats the provisions of the edict of Theodosius II., to the effect that Jews, Samaritans and Pagans are not free from curial responsibility, although they may enjoy no curial privileges.[131]

But the crushing blows which the law and the arm of the state had inflicted upon the Samaritans produced the desired results. Procopius testifies[132] that a majority of the Samaritans became Christian converts, although that their ready-made faith was often hypocritical has been already

---

[128] Procopius, *Hist. arcana*, c. 27, *sub. fin.*, tells of a certain Faustina, who, forced into Christianity and becoming proconsul of Palestine, nevertheless used his powers to oppress the Christians; he was convicted upon the charges brought against him by ecclesiastics, but bribed the emperor Justinian, and so avoided the penalty.

[129] *Cod. Justinian*, i, 5, c. 21.

[130] The term, "Manichæans and Samaritans" was used as a byword of reproach between the factions of Constantinople in Justinian's reign; *Theophanes*, i, 280.

[131] *Novella*, xlv; cf. above, p. 110. Reference for the Novellæ is made to Osenbrüggen's edition of the *Corpus juris civilis*, Leipzig, 1854, vol. iii.

[132] *Historia arcana*, c. 11.

noticed.   The backbone of revolt now seemed broken, and
Justinian was doubtless too acute a statesman to enjoy
the presence in his realm of a race of absolute outlaws, so
that when an appeal for clemency was made to him by
Sergius, bishop of Cæsarea, in which city the Samaritans
had been both numerous and financially potent, he retracted
some of the extreme prescriptions against the sect.   His
new regulations and the reasons therefor are set forth in
full in the CXXIXth Novella, *De Samaritis,* and are in abstract as follows:

In the Preface he magnanimously asserts that " there is
no delinquency of his subjects which his clemency cannot
heal," and that he follows the principle of tempering " the
justice of wrath with the reasons of mercy."   He refers
to the unique arrogance of the Samaritans in their rebellion, and sums up the earlier edicts outlawing them from
all rights of testament and alienation of property.   Nevertheless, he observes, the keenness of the law has not been
carried out in practice, for he has not permitted the state-
treasury to derive any advantage from those penal statutes.
He then proceeds, in Chapter 1, to relate how Sergius,
pleading that the Samaritans had greatly improved, and
vouching for their future loyalty, had induced him to make
changes in their legal status.   He extends to them the
usual testamentary rights and the laws applying to intes-
tates, and also the powers of contract and donation.   But
in Chapter 2, he asserts he will not put Christian heirs upon
the same footing as those who have remained Samaritans;
in case of intestate property, it can be claimed only by
Orthodox Christians.   Nevertheless, according to the 3d
Chapter, to offer chance of repentance, if any who have been
excluded from inheritance turn to the true faith, they shall
receive their due share, though without the usufruct of the
time elapsed.   But a testator may not devise more than a
sixth of his property to unbelievers, and yet the like chance

of repentance and resulting profit shall be open to these latter. The 4th Chapter prohibits the treasury receiving any advantage from the older laws, and makes the present law retroactive in this respect. But Justinian's earlier severity rather than the clemency of his later days was approved by the results. The sore of the race had advanced too far for "his clemency to heal." The desperate sect arose in yet another insurrection, recorded for the year 556.[133] To condense our authorities, in July of that year, the Samaritans of Cæsarea revolted, attacked and killed many of the Christians, and burnt churches. They slew the eparch Stephen in the prætorium, and plundered his property; his wife fled and appealed to the emperor, who sent as governor Amantius (Theophanes), or Adamantius (Cedrenus), and summary vengeance was taken upon the Samaritans.

There is yet further evidence for the obstinate unruliness of the Samaritans, which again brought upon them the vengeance of the empire. In a letter of a certain Simeon, the author complained to the emperor Justin II. (565–578) concerning the outrages committed by a settlement of Samaritans at the foot of Mt. Carmel upon the Christian churches and especially upon the holy images.[134] The rebelliousness

[133] The authorities are *Malalas,* 455; *Cedrenus,* i, 675; *Theophanes,* i, 355. As the scene is Cæsarea, Robinson holds, *BR* iii, 125, that probably the story belongs to the events of 529. (As we have seen, Malalas and Eutychius are confused between the two uprisings.) But as Juynboll remarks, *Hist. Sam.,* 162, the details of this fresh insurrection differ from those of the earlier date, to which argument it may be added that it is strange that Procopius did not relate these outrages in connection with the history of the events of 529. There are to be sure some cases of confusion in the story of Malalas, as in placing the narrative of the conspiracy with the Persian king in connection with the second insurrection, and in his entanglement of the stories of Justa and Julian. Malalas should be, as a contemporary, a first rate witness, but in matter of fact the xviiith book of his history, bearing on Justinian's reign, is of doubtful authenticity; see Bury in Gibbon, *op. cit.* iv, 518.

[134] This letter is a document laid before the Second Council of Nicæa (787), in the Iconoclastic controversy, and is contained in Har-

of the Samaritans, instanced in such outrages, seems to have been the cause of the reversal of the former imperial clemency, and Justin II. issued an edict, the CXLIVth Novella (572), in which he indignantly deprives them of all privileges, and except in one particular wholly outlaws them.

In the Preface the emperor refers to his father's benevolence, which has been so ill rewarded by the sect. In the 1st Chapter he deprives them of all testamentary and contractual rights, confiscating to the public treasury all property for which there are no Orthodox heirs. In the 2d Chapter he makes an exception in the case of peasant holdings. The rustics may make testamentary and other disposition of their property to their coreligionists, in order that the taxable value of the land may not be decreased through the outlawry of the farming population. In case of failure of heirs to the farmer-tenant the proprietor of the land must take it up and satisfy the public treasury for its taxes.[135] The law then forbids to the Samaritans all military and civil service, the rights of legal advocacy, of legal education, and of the instruction of youth. If upon simulated conversion the Samaritans are found to be keeping the Sabbath or other like institutions, their property is to be confiscated, and themselves exiled. Also to insure genuine conversion, none is to be received to baptism except after a two years' catechumenate under good teachers and with a course of Bible instruction. Children however may be admitted without this preparation. The Samaritans may not possess Christian slaves, and if they hold any,

douin, *Acta Conciliorum*, iv, 290 (cf. p. 781) ; see Juynboll, *op. cit.* 163. The author has been confused with Simon Stylites. The sentiment of the Council was that the Samaritans were the worst kind of heretics because they destroyed images !

[135] This provision is illustrated by a statement of Procopius, *Hist. arcana*, c. 11, to the effect that the Christian proprietors in Samaria suffered great losses upon the rebellion of 529 through the obligation laid on them of making good the taxes, when the peasant tenants had been so largely exterminated and the value of the estates correspondingly diminished.

these become *ipso facto* free; a Samaritan slave obtains his freedom if he accepts Christianity.

Thus, with the avoidance of actual extermination, the imperial legislation had reached the extreme in the outlawry of the Samaritan sect. But one legal right was preserved to a portion of the race; to avoid the impoverishment of the land, the rustic population still maintained some property rights. But every inducement, even of bribery and torture, was offered for perversion to Christianity; all offices of honor, all opportunities of culture, were closed to the wretched people. It is a credit to the firmness of the sect that it alone out of the innumerable petty " heresies " of the Roman empire has survived to the present day, while the cause of its intellectual degeneracy is to be ascribed to the Christian empire, unable as the latter was to blot it out. According to Procopius's remark, only a minority remained true to the ancestral faith; many must have fled to the Persian kingdom, which was now threatening the eastern borders, and we have seen how these sectarians assisted in further embroiling Rome with its oriental rival. As for those who remained at home, only the peasant life was legally open to them.

For the half century succeeding Justin II. down to the Arabic conquest of Palestine, the imperial chronicles report nothing about the Samaritans; the latter have preserved but one reminiscence of the age when Syria was the debatable ground between the Greek empire and Persia. The *Chronicle Neubauer* states[136] that twenty years before the Arabic conquest " Chosroes king of Assyria crucified a great number of Samaritans," and that two years later *Arqali,* king of Rome, seized the land of Canaan. The former event is to be connected with Chosroes II.'s conquest of Palestine in 614; as the Jews gave him hearty assistance, it may be supposed that the Samaritans were

[136] *Chron. Neub.,* 445; cf. *Chron. Adler,* 79.

found in the opposition, and so suffered the ill-treatment recorded. *Arqali* is the emperor Heraclius, who reconquered Syria in 622. With this fragment of information our knowledge of the Roman dominion over the Samaritans comes to an end.

CHAPTER VII.

THE SAMARITANS UNDER ISLAM.

For this period of Samaritan history we have as native sources the *Chronicle Neubauer*, the supplements to *Abu'l Fath*, and the *Chronicle Adler*. The first-named chronicle contains for the most part genealogical material offering but few connections with general history and chronology. The supplements to *Abu'l Fath* bring the history down only as far as the Xth Century.[1] The *Chronicle Adler*, while containing a fairly good skeleton of imperial history, which it has borrowed from Arabic historians, gives, apart from the matter found in the earlier chronicles and certain details concerning some personalities, almost no independent historical information until the XVIIth Century. The references in the Muslim historians are very few, giving valuable notes on the Samaritan religion, but throwing almost no light on their secular history. For the one period when the western world might have left some record of this Palestinian sect, namely the age of the Crusades, we find that the Christian chronicles absolutely ignore the subject of our study. One or two references sum up the information to be derived from mediæval Judaism. With the re-discovery of the Samaritans by Scaliger at the

[1] See Vilmar, pp. v, lxxxv, and in general, below, Chapter XIV, § 11. A supplement common to Vilmar's codices A and C brings down the history, although in many cases with nothing more than the names of the caliphs, to Harun ar-Rashid, while A contains a list of the high-priests to 1853. A second supplement to C pursues the history to the end of the reign of the caliph Radhi, A. D. 940, but the text of this portion is so corrupt that the editor gives only a synopsis of its contents, p. lxxx *et seq.*

end of the XVIth Century, they emerge again into contemporary notice, and their Epistles and then the inquiries
and actual visits of occidental scholars acquaint us more
and more with their later history, until at last Petermann's
famous sojourn amidst the declining sect in 1853 finally
opened up a thorough acquaintance with them on the part
of the western world. But in these last days we can
hardly speak of a history in connection with that almost
petrified fragment of ancient religion. In the following
brief sketch I confine myself to the data concerning the
Samaritans, without attempting a survey of the history
of Palestine.

Abu'l Fath dramatically concludes his Chronicle with
a story, belonging to a wide cycle of Muslim legend,[2]
narrating how three astrologers, a Jew, a Christian, and
a Samaritan — a certain Zohar Sarmasa — became sensi-
ble through their art of the passing of the world-empire
into Mohammed's hands. They simultaneously visited him,
and the Samaritan was able to show how his sacred books
foretold the new prophet. The Jew and the Christian per-
verted to the new faith, but the Samaritan remained faithful, and Mohammed finally granted him a charter bestow-
ing complete immunity in faith and possessions upon the
Samaritans,[3] a legend which is immediately belied by the
subsequent history. The Samaritans received for their obstinate rejection of Islam the same bitter persecutions that
befell the Jews, and we can hardly doubt that the major
part of the sect fell away under the iron hand and the attractive advantages of the new faith, so that the sect was
gradually reduced to a few small fragments scattered over
Syria and Egypt.

With the Muslim victory at Yarmuth, 634, the fate of
Palestine was settled, and the Arabic historians include

[2] See Lidzbarski, *De propheticis quæ dicuntur legendis Arabicis.*
[3] *Abu'l Fath,* 172; *Chron. Neub.,* 443; *Chron. Adler,* 76.

Nablus among the places which soon thereafter fell to the conquerors.[4] Upon this conquest, so the *Chronicle Abu'l Fath* states, the people of the seaboard towns, Cæsarea, Arsuf, Maiumas (the port of Gaza), Joppa, Lydda, Ashkelon, and Gaza, deposited their goods with the highpriest and " fled to the east and never returned hither." This is evidently an authentic account of the flight of the wealthy Samaritans of the coast towns before the certain advance of the Muslims. Where the fugitives found refuge in the east we cannot surmise, but it is to be remembered that they would have had no hope of a welcome in the Byzantine empire which had so bitterly persecuted the sect. The same source also gives an account of the capture of Cæsarea, which fell at last in 640; the Samaritan community in that city must have sadly suffered from the vengeance of the conquerors.

No memories of the age of the Umayyad caliphs are preserved except that of the great earthquake in Marwan II.'s reign.[5] The bloody wars between this dynasty and the Abbasides are noted, and under Mansur (754–775), the second of the new dynasty, occurred the destruction by order of the local governor, Abd al-Wahhab Abu Shindi, of the tomb of Zeno upon Gerizim.[6] Subsequently an assault made by certain people upon the Christian convent in the same locality, involving the murder of the monks, brought upon the Samaritans the wrath of the governor, who put to death the head man of the Samaritans.[7] Under the next caliph Mahdi there was taken a census of the Samaritan community, a function which had been long omitted.[8] The *Chronicle Abu'l Fath* proceeds to give a long account of the various calamities which, in consequence of the civil

[4] Abu'l Fida, *Annales,* ed. Adler, i, 229.
[5] *Abu'l Fath,* 181 ; *Chron. Adler,* 84 (cf. editor's note).
[6] See above, p. 112.
[7] *Abu'l Fath,* 181 ; *Chron. Adler,* 85.
[8] *Abu'l Fath,* 182.

war between Hadi and Harun ar-Rashid (786) afflicted the Samaritans, including a sample of an unnatural crime and a fearful dearth of provisions.[9] But at last God averted his wrath, all the natural disorders, regarded by the chronicler as due to his people's sin, were abated, these happy times coming in under the caliphate of Harun ar-Rashid.[10]

Our authority for the period following this caliph is, as noted above, the supplement peculiar to the codex C of *Abu'l Fath,* as epitomized by Vilmar.[11] The sum of the chronicle is as follows. The wrath of the Abbaside caliphs fell upon all who dissented from Islam, and the Samaritans were so cruelly affected that a great part of them went into exile, while others apostatized. In the war that followed Harun's death (809), between his sons, Palestinian rebels destroyed the Samaritan towns Zaita, Salem, and Arsuf, and variously oppressed the sect. After the death of Amin, the first of the brothers, a governor of Nablus was killed by the Muslims for showing favor to the Samaritans. The land was filled with corpses; a daughter of the highpriest committed fornication, but condemnation was not passed upon her. But at last with the restoration of the divine favor the Samaritans resumed their sacred rites upon Gerizim. Under the caliph Maamun (813–833), his famous general Abdallah ibn Tahir, the governor of Mesopotamia and Syria, brought quiet to the distressed land and gave the Samaritans a breathing space. With Abdallah's departure into Egypt the rebel Ibn Farasa cruelly attempted to force the Samaritans into Islam, and many submitted; at last the caliph suppressed the rebellion. Finally Maamun inaugurated the policy of destroying the castles through the land to prevent them from falling into the hands of rebels, and amongst them the fort constructed

[9] *Ibid.,* 184.
[10] *Ibid.,* 185.
[11] P. lxxx.

by Zeno on Gerizim. The caliph himself oppressed the land with heavy imposts which were cruelly exacted by his governor. In the reign of the succeeding caliph, Mutasim, heretical sects of Islam seized and destroyed Nablus, and burnt the synagogues of the Samaritans and Dositheans. The rebels were finally overwhelmed, but the Samaritans were brought to great straits under the heavy imposts, although none of the people yielded to apostasy. It is also recorded that two of the Samaritan chiefs rebuilt the synagogue which had been destroyed in the wars. At the end of the same caliphate a rebel, Abu Harb (who also captured Jerusalem), took Nablus and scattered the inhabitants, the chief priest being wounded and transported to Hebron where he died. The next caliph Wathik finally allayed the rebellion, and the Samaritans returned to their abodes. But both this monarch and his brother and successor Mutawakkil were so bitterly opposed to all dissenters, that the sufferings of the Samaritans in no wise decreased; under the second of these despots the sacred tomb of a former highpriest Nathanael was destroyed, the law regulating the color of the garments worn in the different religions was introduced, and the Samaritans were prohibited from exercising the offices of their religion.[12] After this Yusuf ibn Dasi, "sultan of Palestine," is recorded as allowing the Samaritans access to Gerizim but forbidding it to the Dositheans. But there followed storms of most frightful evils, and many abandoned their native religion.[13] The last caliph named is Radhi, 934–940, who was helpless to restrain the warring governors of Palestine; a rebel, Abu Tafach, cruelly oppressed the Samaritans. With Radhi's reign the real power passed into the hands of the "Amir of Amirs," or mayor-of-the-palace, and the Abbaside power

[12] This action is parallel to the destruction by the same monarch of the newly built Christian churches in Bagdad.
[13] The reference may be to the Carmathian revolt, which began in the last quarter of the IXth Century.

9

was at end. Such is the conclusion of the last supplement to Codex C of *Abu'l Fath*.

It is evident that some authentic notes have been preserved by this supplement. But it is an unprofitable story except for the almost unintermittent picture it gives of the misfortunes of the miserable sect, persecuted by both orthodox and heretical parties of Islam, and harried by the wars which swept over the debatable land of Palestine.

To take up such scanty data of the Samaritan chronicles as we possess after the failure of the supplements to *Abu'l Fath*, we find some references to the favor shown the Samaritans by the Fatimide caliphs of Egypt, Muizz and Aziz, the former of whom conquered Syria in 970, while the latter (975–996) is said to have shown distinguished honor to a Samaritan ha-Takwi b. Isaac, who was his governor of Palestine, with his seat at Sepphoris.[14] Under the next Fatimide caliph, that magnificent impostor Hakim (996–1020), without doubt the Samaritans suffered under the earlier drastic edicts which renewed the ancient laws against the Christians and Samaritans; but later, we may suppose, the sect enjoyed the liberal terms of the remission of his former severity against dissenters. Juynboll thinks that there are numerous traces of Samaritan polemic against the sect of the Druzes.[15] Shortly after this reign the *Chronicle Neubauer* (*l. c.*) mentions a certain Ab-Chasdiya, a Samaritan, who was an official " inquisitor of all Palestine," with headquarters first at Cæsarea and then at Acco.

For the age of the Crusades, when East and West came to know each other once more, we have most meagre information concerning the Samaritans. Almost all that the

[14] *Chron. Neub.*, 446; *Chron. Adler*, 92. Ha-Takwi's son also served the same monarch in a like capacity at Ramle, *Chron. Neub.*, 448; *Chron. Adler*, 93.
[15] Juynboll, *Lib. Jos.*, 117, with references to de Sacy's studies of the Druzes. *Chron. Neub.*, p. 447, mentions the same Hakim along with an obscure reference to the fate of a governor he sent to rule Palestine.

Chronicle Adler has to say (p. 94 ff) concerning the invasion of the Seljuk Turks and the holy wars which the Europeans waged for the recovery of Palestine, is drawn from foreign sources.[16] On the other hand, the Crusaders, despite the fact that their armies went the length and breadth of the Holy Land and that for extensive terms of years their rule was established on its sacred soil, have left no record of the Samaritans. Nablus played an important part in the internal history of the Kingdom of Jerusalem; it was strongly fortified by the Franks, it became a sort of royal residence for the court, especially for the strong-minded women who troubled the Christian *régime* and found the oriental Naples a convenient locality for their factions.[17] In 1120 a great ecclesiastical council was held at Nablus with the hopeless purpose of reforming the Crusaders.[18] But still there is no mention of the Samaritans, who, if they were noticed at all by the haughty Crusaders, were doubtless reckoned a sect of the Jews. It remains therefore for us only to note the part Nablus played or rather suffered in those troublous times; the chronicle of calamities will contribute to the explanation of the diminution in population and wealth of its ancient sect.

The first reference to Samaria in the Christian chronicles is to the effect that chieftains from the mountains of that land came in to the conquerors of Jerusalem, which fell in

[16] In the Epistle of 1808 the Samaritans record a tradition that 600 years before the Franks carried off with them the Samaritans of Ashkelon and Cæsarea (*N. et E.* 75). Some historical truth may be contained in this notice. It was this tradition which animated the pathetic inquiries of the sect after their coreligionists in Europe. In *Abu'l Fath,* 132, there is reference to a synagogue built by Baba Rabba which lasted until the dominion of the Franks —" God curse them!"

[17] The index to Röhricht, *Geschichte d. Königreichs Jerusalem, s. v.* "Neapolis," exhibits the intimate relations of Nablus with the Crusading kingdom. King Baldwin built a *turris Neapolitana* (*op. cit.,* 120), and later there is mention of two citadels.

[18] *William of Tyre,* xii, 13; the acts are published by Mansi, *Concil.* xxi, 261. It is generally denied that Neapolis became an episcopal see; but see Bargès, *Les Samaritains,* 94.

1099, bringing presents and inviting the invaders to take possession of their territory, an offer which was immediately accepted, as its conquest was already planned.[19] We may incline to the supposition that among these adherents to the new order were hardy Samaritans who welcomed the overthrow of Islam, now that centuries had cast into oblivion the ancient hatred for the Christians. In 1113 Nablus was laid waste by the Saracens.[20] In 1137 Bazawash, a governor of Damascus, surprised and murdered almost all the citizens of Nablus.[21] This event must be identified with one recorded in the Samaritan chronicles,[22] according to which in or before 1137 (as can be calculated from the terms of the highpriests) a certain Bazuga Zeidna (variants exist) took 500 Samaritans captive at Shechem and transported them to Damascus, whence they were redeemed by a generous Samaritan citizen of Acco, and so returned to Gaza.

The Samaritan town, with all its holy places and relics so sacred to the Christians, reverted to Muslim rule under Saladin. In 1184, after the latter's withdrawal from Kerak, it was taken and ravaged by him, with the exception of its two citadels.[23] After the fateful battle of Hattin in 1187, Nablus was again wasted by Saladin's troops.[24] It remained in Muslim hands during the brief triumph of Frederick II. in the Holy Land (1229).[25] In 1242 the

[19] *William of Tyre,* ix, 20; Wilken, *Geschichte d. Kreuzzüge,* ii, 36. According to Sybel. *Geschichte d. ersten Kreuzzuges,* 443, Nablus was one of the few cities which composed Godfrey's actual kingdom. William of Tyre is quoted by Robinson as describing Neapolis as " urbem opulentam."

[20] Foulcher, c. xli (in Guizot, *Collections des mémoires relatifs à l'histoire de France,* xvii, 41) ; Wilken, *op. cit.* 374.

[21] *William of Tyre,* xiv, 27; Röhricht, *op. cit.* 205.

[22] *Chron. Neub.,* 448; *Chron. Adler,* 95.

[23] Baha ad-Din, *Saladini vita,* c. xxviii; Abu'l Fida, *ad an. H.,* 580. The Crusading chronicles seem to deny that the city was injured, Röhricht, *op. cit.* 409.

[24] Baha ad-Din, c. xxxiv; Abu'l Fida, *ad an. H.* 583.

[25] Röhricht, *op. cit.* 786.

city was taken by the Christians, who burnt the city and killed all Muslims who would not pervert to the faith of Christ.[26] In 1244 upon the frightful invasion of the Kharezmians (Khwarizmians) the city was taken by the Egyptian allies of the invaders after the battle of Gaza.[27] With this event we may equate the notice of the Samaritan chronicles to the effect that in the pontificate of the priest who died in 1253, an insolent people came from the east, took the land of Canaan, killed a great number of people at Shechem, and carried off many men, women and children, along with the heir to the priesthood, to Damascus, where they were redeemed by their coreligionists in that city, although only a small number actually returned.[28] Or, disregarding the Samaritan dates, the invasion may be identified with that of Hulagu's Mongols in 1259, when Nablus fell into the hands of those hordes.[29]

We now come to the period of the triumph of the Egyptian Mamluks in Syria, which, beginning with the overthrow of the Mongol hordes at En-Jalut in 1260, reached its zenith in the destruction of the Christian power throughout Syria. Baibars, the fifth Mamluk Sultan (1260–1277), waged a relentless war of many campaigns against the Christians of the Holy Land, and destroyed their sacred places. Along with Nazareth and Tabor, Shechem also fell under his fanatical fury, and we learn of his deportation of the Christian citizens of the city to Damascus in 1261.[30] Under him and his successors the land was frightfully ravaged, brigands were rampant, and all social conditions were destroyed.[31] One after another the Christian strong-

[26] Wilken, *op. cit.* vi, 626; Röhricht, *op. cit.* 854 (on Makrizi's authority).
[27] Wilken, *op. cit.* vi, 646; Röhricht, *op. cit.* 866 (depending upon Makrizi); A. Müller, *Der Islam*, ii, 166ff.
[28] *Chron. Neub.* 451; *Chron. Adler*, 99.
[29] Röhricht, *op. cit.* 910; so Adler in his note.
[30] Röhricht, *op. cit.* 917.
[31] Wilken, *op. cit.* vii, 461, 464.

holds of Cæsarea, Arsuf, Ramle, Joppa, Antioch, fell to Baibars; his great successor, Kalaun, took Tripolis in 1289, and the crowning triumph was gained by the fall of Acco to Ashraf (Khalil) in 1291; this overwhelming calamity for the Christians was followed up by the immediate submission of Beirut, Tyre, Sidon, indeed of all the Christian citadels. We have here to realize that these sieges, followed by awful massacres, and as in the case of Cæsarea, even by the destruction of the cities, involved the wealthy Samaritan colonies settled in them. Probably the original communities were annihilated, subsequent times of peace bringing back for commercial purposes the small colonies which we later find in those places. Only Damascus and Egypt were left as places offering security from the frightful anarchy of the age. The *Chronicle Adler* has some brief notes (p. 99) upon the conquests of these monarchs, naming Baibars, and referring to a sultan of Egypt, who took Antioch, Tripolis, Beirut — who would therefore be a composition of Kalaun and Ashraf. Then the Muslims, the chronicler proceeds to relate, came to Nablus, expelled the Christians and destroyed their churches. Further they took away from the Samaritans their venerable " Synagogue of the Field," the present Chizn Yakub, and demolished all their other edifices, so that the sect was greatly afflicted. No more special information concerning the fortunes of Nablus are preserved for the period of the Mamluk dominion in Egypt (to 1516), except that for the age of Othman I. (*circa* 1300) we read (*Chron. Adler*, 100), of a governor ("caliph") Yarok at Shechem, who was killed by his enemies, whereupon the Samaritans recovered their confiscated synagogue; but the Muslims soon reasserted themselves, and turned the sacred place into a mosque.

Before proceeding to the modern history of the Samaritans, we may observe here the information concerning them given by the mediæval Arabic historians and geographers.

The bulk of the longer sections upon the subject is devoted to legendary history of the sect drawn mostly from Jewish sources, although Makrizi seems to have followed the Samaritan legends; but the Arabs add nothing to our knowledge of the early history. Their notes on the religion of the Samaritans are valuable for purposes of chronology, but do not otherwise substantially enlarge our information; this material, with special reference to the Dosithean sect, is treated elsewhere.[32] In many cases the information seems to have been borrowed with indifferent care, and at times the sect is even ignored in the description of Nablus.

Yakubi (writing in 891) says that Nablus contains Arabs, foreigners and Samaritans.[33] The distinguished historian Masudi, writing in 943, says in his *Meadows of Gold*[34] that " the Samaritans inhabit the districts of Palestine and the Jordan, such as the well-known city ——,[35] which is between Ramle and Tiberias, and other places, and finally the city of Nablus; but the most part of them live in the latter city. They have a mountain called Tur-berik;[36] the Samaritans pray upon this mountain," etc. Istakhri writes (951)[37] that Nablus is the city of the Samaritans and they possess no other cities on the face of the earth. The source of his information is made clear in the next sentence —" the people of Jerusalem say so."[38] Al-Biruni (d.

[32] See Chap. XIII, § 1.
[33] Quoted by Le Strange, *Palestine under the Moslems*, 511. This work gives, pp. 511–514, full quotations from the Arabic geographers who treat of Nablus.
[34] See de Sacy, *Chrestomathie arabe*, i, 342.
[35] De Sacy gives two readings, b'ara, and b'ary, and translates " comme Ara." Can Gaza be intended?
[36] The Samaritan name for Gerizim, now called Jebel et-Tur, "the Mount of the Hill."
[37] Le Strange, *ibid.*
[38] Ibn Chaukal (978) repeats Istakhri, and Mukaddasi, although, or perhaps, because he was Jerusalem-born, ignores the Samaritans in his mention of Nablus. Also Ibn Batuta omits mention of the Samaritans, although he visited Nablus in 1326.

1048) says[39] that most of the Samaritans are found in Nablus, and that most of their synagogues are there.

In the XIIth Century Shahrastani (d. 1153), in his treatment of the Samaritans in his *Book of the Religions*,[40] says that they are people who inhabit al-Mukaddasi (i. e. the name of Jerusalem, which the Samaritans apparently stole), and some cities of Egypt. Idrisi (1154) repeats Istakhri.[41] Ali of Herat (1173) says[42] that the Samaritans are very numerous at Nablus. Yakut, writing in 1225,[43] notes that Nablus is inhabited by the Samaritans, who live in this place alone, and go elsewhere only for the purpose of trade or advantage. He also observes that they call their town *al-Quds* (cf. Shahrastani, above). Dimashki (*circa* 1300) gives an interesting account[44] of Nablus, its beauty and commerce, and describing the sacrifices of the Samaritans he says that " there are the two mountains, Jabal Zaita [the Mount of Olives], to which the Samaritans make their pilgrimage." Further he adds, " In no other city are there as many Samaritans as there are here, for in all the other cities of Palestine together there are not of the Samaritans a thousand souls." This is interesting testimony, coming from a Damascene writer, at a time when we know the Damascus colony existed. Finally Makrizi adds to the notice that most of the Samaritans live in Nablus, the information that they are also found in large numbers in the towns of Syria.[45]

To these Arabic notices is to be added the information gained by a few mediæval Jewish travellers. The first of these is the famous Benjamin of Tudela who visited Pales-

[39] Quoted by Makrizi; see de Sacy *op. cit.* 305.
[40] Cureton's text, i, 170; Haarbrücker's translation, i, 257. Abu'l Fida adds nothing to what he draws from Shahrastani.
[41] Le Strange, *l. c.* But in another place he refers to a Samaritan colony in the Red Sea; see below, p. 151.
[42] Le Strange, *l. c.*
[43] *Ibid.*
[44] *Ibid.*
[45] De Sacy, *op. cit.* i, 304.

tine in 1163. He found at Cæsarea 200 Kuthim; "these are the Jews of Shomron, who are called Samaritans."[46] At Nablus, "where there are no Jews," the Samaritans number about one thousand.[47] At New Ashkelon the same traveller found 300 of the sect, and in Damascus 400, who, he remarks, live in peace with the Karaites there, numbering 100, although the two sects do not intermarry.[48]

An account of the Samaritans in Egypt is given by a Jew, Meshullam b. Menahem, who made a journey to Jerusalem in 1480.[49] According to this traveller he found in Egypt, presumably at Cairo, along with 800 Jewish and 100 Karaite families, 50 Samaritan families ("heads of houses"). He gives a notice of their worship on Gerizim, quite at second-hand, of course, observing that they are idolaters, and set up a golden dove on their holy mount. In Egypt they possessed a synagogue. The whole Israelitish community, he adds, is under the full jurisdiction of a Jewish rabbi. A few years later Obadiah of Bertinoro also found fifty Samaritan families at Cairo, employed in financial business and as agents for the government, so that the community was a rich one.[50]

[46] I cite from M. N. Adler, *The Itinerary of Benjamin of Tudela*, in *JQR*, Oct. 1904, 134f.

[47] Such is the reading adopted by the editor just mentioned upon overwhelming authority of the MSS. The reading that has passed into current use is "one hundred." But this latter figure is much too small, when compared with the information from other contemporary sources, and the new reading relieves a considerable difficulty. Benjamin proceeds to give a brief, accurate account of the Samaritan ritual and practices, and notes their loss of the three gutturals, He, Cheth, Ayin, on which he allegorizes. The same dialecticism is noticed by Isaac Helo in his *Itinerary of Jerusalem*, 1334 (see Carmoly, *Itinéraires de la Terre Sainte*, 252), and also by Makrizi.

[48] *JQR* Jan. 1905, 297, 299.

[49] The pertinent portion of the MS, which is at Florence, is published by Heidenheim, *DVJ* iii, 354.

[50] Neubauer, *Zwei Briefe Obadiah's*, in *Jahrb. f.d. Geschichte d. Juden*, iii (1863), 198, 229, (referred to by Nutt, *Sam. Targ.* 27). This civil combination of Jews and Samaritans has its parallel in Shechem, where Petermann found that the Samaritan highpriest was the responsible chief of the combined communities; *Reisen*, i, 226.

We thus see that the mediæval notices of the Samaritans throw very little light upon their actual condition. In Benjamin of Tudela's day there were about 1000 of the sect in the mother-city, and he enumerates 700 more in other South-Syrian cities. About 1300 Dimashki estimates that there are not more than 1000 Samaritans in Palestine outside of Nablus. Of the number of the community in Egypt for the earlier part of the period, we have no information. We do not know when the colony in Damascus was established, but from 1137 on we learn of violent deportations thither which doubtless swelled the local community, while the literary activity of the Damascene Diaspora from the XIIth Century on is abundant evidence that the Samaritans shared in the prosperity of the city which Nureddin and Saladin raised to an imperial metropolis, and whose glories lasted until the time of Timurlane; in this disaster the Samaritans must have been equally involved, although the colony survived the disaster. Further, in the opulent trading towns of the coast small but commercially influential communities existed, which probably avoided all public display of their religion; but they prospered in worldly affairs, that recompense which fortune so often renders to the small and despised sect. There is every reason to believe that during these troublous times, when Palestine was harried by the wars of the Crusades and by the many invasions which depopulated the land, the settlements of the Diaspora, and especially that at Damascus, fostered in every way the mother community, which otherwise would have perished. We find the direct line of the highpriestly family often living in Damascus. In one case, the heir to the pontificate came up from Damascus to assume his dignity (1205); in

Note may be made here of an early but only recently published Arabic work — that of Ibn Chazm of Spain (994–1064), who wrote *On Jewish Sects,* and treats of the Samaritans. But he gives no data of importance except that "the Samaritans may not go out of Palestine." See Poznanski, *JQR* xvi, 765.

another (1538), a large number of Samaritans returned from Damascus conducting to Nablus the highpriest and his son; and we even find the highpriest remaining in the Syrian capital (1584).[51]

To carry on our story into modern times we find that the Samaritan Chronicles contribute, outside of family annals, nothing to our knowledge of the history between the beginning of the XIVth Century and the XVIIth Century. But in 1623–4 occurred an ominous event in the ecclesiastical life of the sect. The direct succession from Aaron failed, and since that time priests of the tribe of Levi, of the house of Uzziel son of Kohath, have officiated at the sacred rites.[52] The correspondence with the Europeans, which began in 1590, reveals no political details of the sect, except their persecution by the " Ishmaelites " and their poverty, for which they persistently ask the alms of their coreligionists in Europe.

For the first notice of Ottoman rule over the Samaritans we learn of oppressions and confiscations of lands, especially of springs, occurring in the reign of Mohammed IV. (1648–1687).[53] In the following century, under Machmud I. (1730–1754), the Samaritans purchased from the Muslims a piece of ground on Gerizim for their sacred rites;[54] we may assume that this was one incident in the long history

---

[51] *Chron. Neub.* 451, 465, 454.

[52] The exact date is given by *Chron. Neub.* 465, as A. H. 1033. From the Epistles to Scaliger we know that the Aaronic line still existed in 1590. The failure of the succession is indirectly admitted in the Epistle of 1672 (de Sacy, *N. et E.* 179), and directly in the Epistle of 1675 (of which only a fragment is preserved), wherein it is prayed that the Europeans send them a priest of the race of Phineas (*N. et E.* 219). But this fact has been conveniently obliterated in the memory of the modern Samaritans; the Levitical priest who acknowledged his descent from Uzziel to de Sacy in 1820 (*N. et E.* 152), gave a full Aaronic pedigree for himself in his Arabic memorial to the French government in 1842 (Bargès, *Les Samaritains,* 73).

[53] *Chron. Adler,* 106.

[54] *Op. cit.* 108.

of the attempts of the sect to retain its holy ground and of their masters to keep them out of it or to make them pay for the privilege, which in a few years would be annulled, whereupon the struggle began again.   In this case the purchase is said to have been made by a benevolent member of the community, and doubtless the persistence of the sect into modern times is directly due to the charm of gold, which the Samaritans, few as they were, knew how to amass.   A local edict of 1772 enforced several restrictive and shameful regulations against the sect.[55]

It is pitiful to record the fact that the XIXth Century brought upon the Samaritans troubles, along with the threat of violent extinction, such as they had not experienced since the wars of the Crusaders and the Mamluks.   We learn that for 25 years preceding 1810 the sect was restrained from its worship on the holy mount,[56] but it was able to renew its sacred functions by 1820.[57]   For this period we have the graphic memoir of the Samaritan refugee, Jacob esh-Shelaby,[58] who records in detail the wretched plight of the Samaritans.   Because of the notoriously violent character of the Muslim population of Nablus, it has been the custom of the Ottoman government to appoint as Mutesellim or governor only a native Arab, who is nominated from one of four rival families.   In the bloody struggles which now took place among these factions the Samaritans were between the upper and nether millstone, and their sorry condition was aggravated by the Syrian wars of Mohammed Ali of Egypt, with or against whom the rival parties took sides.   That remarkable man's son and general, Ibrahim, took Nablus by the sword in 1832, but found it impossible to repress the defiant Arabs.   According to the *Chronicle Adler,* the Samaritans shared in the relief which Egyptian rule

[55] Mills, *Nablus,* 279.
[56] *N. et E.* 126.
[57] *Ibid.,* 157, 161.
[58] In Rogers, *Notices of the Modern Samaritans,* 1855.

Jacob esh-Shelaby and General Wilson

brought to the inhabitants of Syria, a statement corroborated by Shelaby's notice that in 1832 the sect again renewed its pilgrimage to Gerizim. In 1841 a conspiracy was formed to murder all the Samaritans; their enemies were not appeased with the gift of the Samaritan wealth, and Shelaby gives credit to the chief rabbi of the Jewish community in Jerusalem for issuing a certificate that "the Samaritan people is a branch of the Children of Israel, who acknowledge the truth of the Tora." This generous testimonial satisfied the fanatical Muslims, because it showed that the Samaritans had a right to Islam's protection extended to the "Peoples of the Book."[59] The persecutions induced the community to address an appeal in 1842 to the French government, composed in a Hebrew and an Arabic document; but for purposes of state, Louis Philippe did not even publish the documents, and they were not brought to light until some years later.[60] According to Bargès, who visited Nablus in 1853, the Samaritans said they had been restrained from Gerizim for 80 years; this is of course an exaggeration, though it represented the truth for recent years. Petermann, who visited the Samaritans in the same year, did not receive any such information, and himself attended the Passover on Gerizim. In 1854 the British government was induced by an appeal of the Samaritans to make representations on their behalf to the Porte, and the bearer of this document, the Jacob above-mentioned, brought with him also an appeal to the British public, the result of which was the arousing of the interest of such men as the Earl of Shaftesbury and the collection of funds for the oppressed sect. Through the friendly notice of European governments, especially of England and its consuls at Jerusalem, the Samaritans have been preserved from the

[59] *Ibid.,* 29.
[60] The documents were published in *Les annales de philosophie chrétienne,* 1853, and the Hebrew document by Bargès, *op. cit.* 64; cf. p. 37.

violent annihilation that threatened them. But the wealth they possessed is gone, and they have become a community of alms-seekers, forced to sell their sacred manuscripts for subsistence.[61]

[61] For the bloody commotions which vexed Palestine in the last century, see Macalister and Masterman, *A History of the Doings of the Fellahin,* etc., *PEFQS* 1905, Oct. *et seq.* This work also frequently refers to Finn, *Stirring Times,* which throws much light upon the local troubles.

CHAPTER VIII.

THE GEOGRAPHICAL DISTRIBUTION OF THE SAMARITANS.

§ I. THE SAMARITANS AT HOME.[1]

In Chapter II. we observed that the land of Samaria as a geographical entity was identical with the Highlands of Ephraim. It is bounded on the north by the valley of Esdraelon, to which also belongs the plain of Dothan, with its deep inset into the hill-country. On the east is the Ghor, or valley of the Jordan, the plain of Beth-shean having been distinguished from the land of Ephraim politically as well as geographically from earliest times.[2] On the west the line of the lowlands marked the political boundary, the Phœnicians and Philistines being in possession of the coast, while Mount Carmel, though a spur of the Samaritan hill-country, was cut off politically by the highways which crossed it. Only on the south was there an uncertain border. There a long neck of highland connects Mount Ephraim with Mount Juda, cleft on either side by deep wadies, but withal presenting no one strategic line of boundary. G. A. Smith has graphically discussed this debatable frontier,[3] and points

---

[1] See Juynboll, *Hist. Sam.* 37; Neubauer, *La géographie du Talmud,* 1868, p. 168; Schürer, *GJV*, §§ 23, 24; E. Meyer, *Entstehung des Judenthums,* 1896, p. 105; Smith, *HG* cc. xii, xvii; Hölscher, *Palästina in der persischen und hellenistischen Zeit,* 1903; Conder, *Samaritan Topography, PEFQS* 1876, p. 182 (with extensive treatment of the geographical references in the *Book of Joshua* and the *Chronicle Neubauer*).

[2] See 1 *Sam.* 31, 10. It received a Scythian colony in the VIIth Century, and later became a member of the Decapolis.

[3] *Op. cit.* c. xiii.

out that there were three possible lines, each of which became effective according to the comparative strength of the
two political divisions of Israel. Our present interest in
this question begins with the Post-exilic age.

As Meyer points out, those who worked on the walls of
Jerusalem, according to the list in *Neh.* 3, were not settled
farther north than Gibeon and the uncertain Meronot.[4] According to *Neh.* 11, 25ff the Jews had pushed in the same
age towards Joppa as far as Ono, Hadid, Lydda, a note
disputed by Meyer and Hölscher, who hold that this datum
represents the geography of the Chronicler; at all events
Sanballat hailed from Beth-horon, and Ono in the Shephela
belonged to his sphere of influence (6, 3). Thus in the
first part of the Post-exilic period the district of Samaria
lay close up under Jerusalem. But the powerful Jewish expansion began to drive back this northern boundary, as we
learn from the Chronicler and from the colonization of extensive districts in the south of Samaria, witnessed to in the
IId Century B. C.[5]

In the Maccabæan age the northerly expansion of Judaism received the political endorsement of the Syrian kingdom; the three considerable cantons of Aphairema,— probably the city of Ephraim (*Jn.* 11, 54),— Lydda, and Ramathaim, perhaps the modern Beit Rima, NE of Lydda —
were formally annexed to Judæa.[6] This large acquisition
of territory pushed the Jewish boundary far into the interior
of Samaria, the place of Borkeos which Josephus notes as

---

[4] *Op. cit.* 105; cf. Hölscher, *op. cit.* 26.

[5] Hölscher holds, *op. cit.* 30, that in the late Persian age Juda actually controlled Samaria, adducing the Book of *Judith*, the traditions
of which belong to the age of Ochus, while its action is laid in Samaria. (Cf. Torrey's identification of Bethulia with Shechem, *JAOS*
xx, 160; also such passages as *Zech.* 11, 4ff. Cf. the story of Joseph's
administration as tax-farmer over Samaria, Josephus, *AJ* xii, 4.)

[6] See above, p. 79. For the data, see 1 *Mac.* 11, 20ff: Josephus,
AJ xiii, 4, 9. Cf. Schürer, *GJV* i, 233, and, for the due appreciation
of the extent of the annexed territory, Hölscher, *op. cit.* 74.

the boundary in his day doubtless marking the extent of that annexation.

For the 1st Christian Century we gain more definite details of the boundaries of Samaria, which are described with much exactness by Josephus. Samaria lies, says that historian,[7] " between Judæa and Galilee; it begins at a village that is in the Great Plain, called Ginaia, and ends at the Akrabene toparchy." A little farther on he adds that on the boundary between Samaria and Judæa lies the so-called village Anuath-Borkeos.[8] Now Ginaia is the En-gannim of the Old Testament, the modern Jenin, lying on the southern slope of Esdraelon.[9] Akrabene, or Akrabatta, is the modern Akrabe, 8 mi. SE of Shechem. Borkeos is now generally identified with Berkit to the WSW of Akrabe, in the Wady Ishar; Anuath has not yet been located.[10] These data place the frontier for Josephus's age along the line of the Wady Ishar, which, as Smith observes, is the northernmost of the possible natural boundaries between Judæa and Samaria. The Jewish boundary had thus advanced to within seven miles of Shechem and included the greater part of the ancient land of the tribe of Ephraim.[11] Moreover the western boundary of Samaria was thrust back, as we have seen, by the loss of the canton of Ramathaim, while the Jewish expansion to the northwest included the important cities of Modin, Lydda, Ono, Hadid, and stretched as far as Antipatris.[12]

[7] *BJ* iii, 3, 4–5. It is uncertain just what was the relation of the city of Samaria to this district; Hölscher, *op cit.* 97, following Marquardt, considers it to have been a member of the Decapolis.
[8] Conder has a different translation, *PEFQS* 1876, p. 67.
[9] It also appears as a border town in *Gittin*, vii, 6. The Gemara *ad loc.* also names Kefar Outhenai as on the border. Josephus narrates a bloody fight as occurring here between Samaritans and Jewish pilgrims, *AJ* xx, 6, 1.
[10] The English Survey Map follows Conder's translation in widely separating Anuath and Borkeos.
[11] Mount Sartaba was also in the hands of the Jews; *Rosh-ha-Shana*, ii, 2.
[12] See Neubauer, *op. cit.* 86.
10

Thus by the Ist Century political Samaria had very much shrunk from its original equivalence with the Highlands of Ephraim. Between En-gannim and the Wady Ishar is a distance of 25 miles, between the Jordan and Sharon about 32 miles; but from this limited territory we must exclude the Jordan valley and a considerable Jewish territory in the southwest.

Within this circumscribed region we have no means of ascertaining how numerous or widespread the Samaritans were. There is nothing to show that they were found in the one Hellenistic city of the district, Samaria-Sebaste. Their metropolis was Shechem-Neapolis, and in this city and the villages of its neighborhood must have lain their centre of population. The Talmud throws very little light upon the localities of the Samaritan sect.[13]   We learn from it of two places with the name of Fondeka, i.e. "Inn," namely that of Ammuda, and that of Tibta towards Kefarsaba, i.e. Antipatris. There are still two localities with the same component to be found in Samaria: Fendakumia (Pentacomia), 4 mi. N of Samaria, and Fonduk, 7 mi. SW. We also learn of several Samaritan villages lying on the Jewish border: "The wine of Kador is prohibited because of the proximity of Kefar-Pagesh; that of Borgata because of Birat-Sariqa; that of En-Kushit (i.e. the Samaritan Spring, or Spring of the Samaritaness), because of Kefar-Shalem."[14]   Borgata is doubtless the Borkeos of Josephus; Salem can hardly be the town east of Shechem, but rather the Salem on the Jordan, which Josephus places 8 mi. S of Beth-shean.

The few other places connected with the Samaritans by Josephus and others are Tirathana, near Gerizim;[15] Gittaim,

[13] Ibid., 172.
[14] Aboda Zara Jer. 44d. The Babylonian parallel, Ab. Z. 31a, has the following variants: Ogdor, Parshai, En-Kushi. Cf. Masseket Kutim, 25, which reads Pansha for Pagesh.
[15] AJ xviii, 4, 1: probably the modern Tire, 4 mi. SW of Shechem; Buhl, Geographie, 200, 203.

the birthplace of Simon Magus;[16] and Sychar, *Jn.* 4, 5, generally identified with the modern Askar.[17]

There remains for investigation the abundant geographical material contained in the Samaritan Chronicles, especially that of the *Chronicle Neubauer.* Unfortunately, partly because of the corrupt tradition of the text, and partly because the genealogical lists give no means of identifying the localities, our results must be very incomplete. It will be worth while however, although an exhaustive list is by no means pretended, to learn from some of the places that may be identified the extent of the Samaritan settlements.[18]

In the close neighborhood of Shechem we find mention of Salem, also apparently called Great Salem; Elon More; Askar; 4 mi. N, Tira-luza, i. e. Tulluza; 8 mi. E, Dabarin, if the modern Ain ad-Dabbur; to the south we can recognize Awurta; Bet-porik, i. e. Pherka; Akrabatta; within 10 mi. SW, Yasuf, Marda, Timnat-heres, Zaita (there is another Zaita to the W); Kurawa (to be placed here, and not at foot of Sartaba); to the W, Tul-karam, Kuryat-Hajja (8 mi.), Sarafin (9 mi.), Afra-Piraton,— either the Piraton to the west, or the Ophra-Ferata, 6 mi. SW of Shechem. In Bit-jan we may identify En-gannim. One of Baba Rabba's Wise Men " had his limit from the Great Meadow," i.e. the Great Plain of Josephus, the modern Merj ibn Amir.[19] Taking these data as an average, we find that the Samaritans in their native land were centred about Shechem within

[16] See Chap. XIII, note.

[17] For the discussion of this problem, see above, p. 20. There is nothing to show that the Talmudic En-Socher was a Samaritan locality; but see Neubauer, *op. cit.* 170.

[18] Conder in his article *Samaritan Topography* has treated these geographical references at length. The following identifications, which were worked out before I saw Conder's study, and which I let stand for what they may be worth, concern only the seats of the Samaritans.

[19] *Abu'l Fath,* 130. Kefar-sabbala, *ibid.,* may be Kefar-saba, i. e. Antipatris.

a radius of eight or ten miles; the remainder of their territory was probably largely occupied by Jews and Pagans.

§ 2. THE SAMARITANS IN DIASPORA.[20]

The commercial tendencies of the Samaritans early gave them an impulse westward to the opulent cities of the coast, especially to the metropolis Cæsarea, and to the towns of Philistia; the early rise of the Egyptian colony must have made the latter district a well-used thoroughfare for them. Accordingly we find that in the early centuries of our era the Samaritans pushed southwest into the flourishing region of the one-time territory of Dan; this movement must have been subsequent to the destruction of the Jewish state, which left the Samaritans a free foot in their expansion. Horon is referred to in the Chronicles as a Samaritan locality, and the inscriptions at Emmaus-Nicopolis reveal their presence in that place.[21] We learn of them at Lydda at the time of the Muslim conquest,[22] and later in the Fatimide capital of Palestine, Ramle, they formed an appreciable part of the population, while its suburb, Beit-Dagon, was a Samaritan town.[23] On the coast we find them at Akko; at Cæsarea, where they were numerous enough to carry on bloody feuds with Jews and Christians;[24] at Arsuf; Joppa; Ashkelon; Gaza and its port Maiumas. Gaza remained the chief

[20] Cf. the data from Jewish and Arabian sources given in Chapter VI; also Le Strange, *Palestine Under the Moslems*, 1890.
[21] See Chap. XIV, § 4. A remark of R. Abbahu, in *Yebamot Jer.* 9d: "Thirteen cities reverted to the Samaritans in the days of persecution," may refer to this Samaritan expansion. Frankel, *Einfluss der palästinensischen Exegese*, 245, refers the note to the Hadrianic persecution; but see Appel, *op. cit.* 60; Taglicht, *op. cit.* 19.
[22] See the list of towns in *Abu'l Fath*, 179.
[23] So the early geographers, Yakubi and Mukaddasi; Le Strange, *op. cit.* 403, 405. Clermont Ganneau, in his *Archæological Researches*, ii, 490, notes that the Life of Peter the Iberian (*Petrus der Iberer*, 59, 114), of the Vth Century, records that the town of Yebna, the Biblical Jabneel-Jamnia, was inhabited exclusively by Samaritans.
[24] See Chap. VI, § 3. According to both Samaritan and Byzantine notices Samaritan settlements existed on Mt. Carmel.

coastwise locality of the sect after the destruction of the more northerly cities in the wars of the Crusades.[25] Epistles in the Scaliger and Huntington correspondence were written at Gaza, and the *Chronicle Neubauer* refers to Samaritans settled there in the XVIIIth Century. These colonists, the same chronicle reports, were of the tribe of Benjamin. There is also frequent mention of members of the sect at Gerar.

The narrative of the uprising under Justinian in 529 is witness to the extensive settlement of Samaritans in and about Scythopolis. From that point the Samaritans could easily pass the fords of Jordan into Peræa, and so Eusebius notes, in his *Onomasticon,* a Samaritan town, Thersila, or Tharsila, in this region,[26] which seems to have been a frequent place of refuge for fugitives and the ascetic sects of the community. We have already noted references to the Damascene colony, which was several times fed by forcible deportations, and whose size and wealth are reported by Benjamin Tudela and de la Valle, while as we have seen, it became a second home for the sect.[27] But its members spread still farther north through Syria; at Tyre (at least in the case of the distinguished theologian Abu'l Chasan, " the Tyrian ") ; at Baal-bek,[28] at Kefar Sima (near Beirut),[29] and at Tripoli, Hamath,

[25] Two Samaritan inscriptions have been found at Gaza, along with the probable remains of a synagogue; see Chap. XIV, § 4. The presence of the sect in that city about 300 may be testified to by the prayer made just before his death by the martyr Paul of Gaza at Cæsarea, in behalf of the Samaritans along with other unbelievers; Eusebius, *Mart. Palæst.* viii, 9.

[26] See Thomsen, *ZDPV* xxvi, 97, and for its location the accompanying map by Guthe.

[27] P. 138. See also Chap. XIV, § 4, for the Damascene inscriptions bearing witness to the wealth of the Samaritan colony.

[28] *Chron. Neub.* 461. The Samaritan scholar Muhadhdhib (d. 1227) was vizier to a sultan of Baal-bek; Wüstenfeld, *Gesch. d. arabisch. Aerzte,* 121.

[29] I find I am unable to verify my note on this datum.

and Aleppo.[30]   There is even evidence of their presence in Babylonia, in the IVth Century.[31]

There may be noticed here, for what it is worth, the interesting tradition of a diocesan organization of the Samaritans in Palestine established by Baba Rabba in the IVth Century.[32]   A priest was placed at the head of each of the districts or dioceses, which numbered twelve, if we include the " archdiocese " of Shechem, which belonged to the high-priest.   We may suppose that these were administrative, particularly tithing districts, originating with the intention of incorporating more closely into the community the scattered bodies of Samaritans.   The districts are :

1) From Luza (Telluza) to Galilee on the sea.

2) A district to Tiberias.

3) The country E of Gerizim to the Jordan.

4) From Kefar-Chalul to the Place of Justice (i.e. some governmental centre, not further defined).

5) From Horon to Philistia.

6) From Gaza to the River of Egypt.

7) From " Good-Mountain " to Cæsarea.

8) From the border of Carmel to Akko.

9) From Mount Naker to Tyre.

10) From the river Lita (Litany) to Sidon and the gulf (?).

11) From the mountain country of Galilee to the river (the upper Jordan?), to Lebanon, and all the villages about that mountain.

It will be noticed that these districts are listed according to the points of the compass, beginning with the east.

---

[30] See the Liturgy for the Dead, *DVJ* i, 417, which belongs to the time when the Damascene colony was important.

[31] Gittin, 45a ; see Frankel, *Einfluss* 251.

[32] *Chron. Neub.* 440, and *Abu'l Fath,* 134; the text of the latter is defective and corrupt.   In most cases the Hebrew personal names in the latter have pure Arabic names attached to them, indicating perhaps the purpose of a later scribe to bring the hierarchy up to date. Conder gives the list in *PEFQS* 1876, p. 194.

Proofs for the early origin of this document are found in the presence of only Hebrew names in the earlier text, and in the omission of reference to Damascus. It is to be observed that Peræa and Judæa are not included, so that the scheme is not a merely ideal allotment of the Holy Land among the true Israel. That the Diaspora was found in Galilee is proved by references to the colonies at Safed and Hazor (Hazorim) in the Arabic period.[33]

We have already noted the reports of Josephus and the Samaritan traditions concerning the Diaspora in Egypt.[34] The sect seems to have experienced like fortunes to the Jews in the Hellenic period, being drafted to the Greek cities in the Nile valley by deportation or as mercenaries, and also being attracted thither by the advantages of commerce. There are papyrus references to an Egyptian village named Samaria in the IIId Century B. C.[35] From an Epistle of 1808 we learn that the Samaritans had ceased to exist in Egypt for a hundred years;[36] but the colony must have failed much earlier, for in 1616 de la Valle found at Cairo a synagogue with only seven families, and Huntington, in the latter part of the same century learned on the spot that but one of the sect, an old man, still survived.[37]

A curious note appears in the geographer Idrisi (XIIth Century), who, in describing the islands in the upper part of the Red Sea, says [38] that "the one called Samiri is inhabited by a race of Samaritan Jews. They can be recognized as such because when one wishes to injure another, the latter says to him: ' Do not touch me (*la misas*).' They descend from the Jews who worshipped the golden calf at the time of Moses." This incorporates a frequent

[33] *DVJ* i, 417.
[34] See p. 75.
[35] See Schürer, *GJV* iii, 24.
[36] *N. et E.* 69. For some mediæval references, see above, p. 137.
[37] Juynboll, *Hist. Sam.* 45, referring to the xxxiiid Epistle of Huntington.
[38] *Clima,* ii, § 5; tr. Jaubert, i, 135.

Muslim reference to the Samaritans.[39]   Such an immigration to the far south is not improbable in view of the extensive Jewish Diaspora in Arabia.

There is much significant evidence to the effect that the Samaritans in pursuit of trade were scattered over the western world.   Their inscriptions have been found at Athens.[40] Members of the sect were extensively engaged in banking at Constantinople, where " Samaritan " was synonymous with " accountant."[41]   The repressive edicts of the Christian emperors can best be understood as directed especially against the Samaritans who were spread over the empire engaged in trade and banking, thus provoking the jealousy of fanatical Christians.   Indeed we learn by chance that about A. D. 500 there existed a Samaritan community in Rome.   Cassiodorus Senator has preserved a letter of the emperor Theodoric calling attention to a complaint made by " the people of the Samaritan superstition," who have had the effrontery to declare that the Church had appropriated a building which was once a synagogue of theirs, and to demand their rights.[42]   The capital may not have been the only place in the western world where the hardy sect possessed its synagogue.

But the fearful persecutions the Samaritans have sustained have nearly accomplished their purpose.   According to the Epistle of 1808 the Samaritans were to be found only at Nablus and Joppa, and then numbered 30 families and

[39] E. g. *Koran*, xx. 97.   (The Koranic legend has it that " the Samaritan " made the golden calf.)   The Samaritan fear of contact with aliens is a characteristic of the sect.   Biruni reports that they were called the La-Mesasiyye, " the Touch-me-nots "; de Sacy, *Chrest. arabe*, i, 305, 340.   This scholar also calls attention to the poet Mutanabbi's reference to this Samaritan characteristic; Calcutta ed., 331; de Bohlen, *Comm. de Motenabbio*, 116.

[40] *Corpus inscript. Attic.* nos. 2891–2893.

[41] Edict ix, of Justinian, c. 2; Osenbrügger, *Corpus juris civilis*, iii, 696, and ed. Bekker, Pt. ii, vol. ii, p. 1158: τοῦ γε ὑπογραφέως οὓς Σαμαρείτας καλοῦσι.

[42] Cassiodorus Senator, *Variæ*, iii, 45 (*Migne*, lxix, 600).

about 200 souls, equally divided between the two towns.[43] To-day they are to be found only in their ancient holy city, numbering, as we have seen above,[44] 152 souls of whom nearly two-thirds are males.

To sum up these facts, we may judge that the Samaritans enjoyed their greatest expansion in numbers and importance under the Roman empire. But their fortunes began to diminish through the persecutions of the Christian establishment, and Islam, at first favorable, ultimately only aggravated the downward course of the fortunes of the sect. In the first centuries of the present millennium, according to the few figures we possess, the Samaritans could have numbered only a few thousands in Syria, and in many of the places where we find them located the communities consisted probably of not more than the *personelle* and families of a few banking-houses. With this paucity in numbers for a millennium and more, the existence of the sect stands as an additional proof of the stiff-neckedness, or to use a modern term, of the " staying powers " of the blood of Israel.

[43] *N. et E.* 69.
[44] P. 24.

CHAPTER IX.

THE SAMARITANS IN THE APOCRYPHAL LITERATURE, THE NEW TESTAMENT, AND JOSEPHUS.

In the preceding Chapters we have examined the secular history of the Samaritans; it is a story redolent of friction and conflicts between them and the Jews since the beginning of the schism. The obscurity concerning the origin of the northern sect has been made evident in Chapter IV; however in the Hellenic period the cleft between the two sects had established itself, a fact demonstrated by John Hyrcanus's capture of Shechem as a hostile city. But it remains now, apart from external politics, to investigate the actual spiritual relations between the Jews and the Samaritans in the three or four centuries respectively before and after the beginning of the Christian era. For this study the Samaritan literature is almost absolutely worthless so far as direct references are concerned, for none of it except the Samaritan edition of the Pentateuch can be dated with certainty earlier than the IVth Century A. C. We are therefore thrown back upon the Judaistic literature exclusively, the examination of which will show what the Jews, " the enemies themselves being judges," thought in that period concerning the Samaritans.

There appear to be but two references to that sect in the early non-canonical literature of the Jews.[1] The one is *Ecclus.* 50, 25f: " With two races is my soul vexed; and the third is no nation: with the dwellers of Seir and

---

[1] For reference to certain Hellenistic literature, see Chap. XIV, § 5.

JACOB'S WELL.

Philistia, and with the foolish race that sojourns in She-chem." It is to be noticed that the tone of the writer is one of contempt towards the Samaritans. The identical contemptuous attitude appears in the apocryphal *Testament of Levi*, c. 7: " From this day will Shechem be called the City of Fools " (πόλις ἀσυνέτων).[2] This epithet of fool as applied to the northern sectarian is further witnessed to in the New Testament. In *Jn.* 8, 48 the Jews are repre-sented as saying to Jesus: " Do we not well say, Thou art a Samaritan and hast a devil? " In what sense was Jesus called a Samaritan? The answer has not been satis-factorily given. Commentators variously hold that the epi-thet refers to Jesus' heresy, to his not being a genuine son of Abraham (cf. v. 39ff), or to his hostility to the Jews. But the context leads much rather to the inference that " Samaritan " means here " fool." This comes out clearly in the subsequent conversation, v. 51ff: " Verily, verily I say unto you, if a man keep my saying, he shall never see death. The Jews said to him, Now we know that thou hast a devil. Abraham is dead, and the prophets, and thou sayest," etc. That is, their argument lies against the utter absurdity of Jesus' words. There are thus three distinct references from as many quarters in which the epithet " fool " appears as a byword of common application to the Samaritans. The origin of the epithet is most probably the contempt felt by the Jews for the absurd pretensions of their rivals. That the term was an extreme one, but nevertheless was used by the Jews among themselves, is shown by *Mt.* 5, 22.[3]

[2] See Kautzsch, *Apokryphen*, ii, 467. The date of the Jewish basis of the *Testaments* is uncertain; Schnapp, *ibid.*, 460, inclines to the Ist Century A. C.

[3] It must be left an open question whether there was also a parano-masia between the Hebrew *nabal*, fool, and *nabel*, fading, which oc-curs in the denunciation of Ephraim in *Is.* 28, 1. The same root is used for various other unpleasant connotations, *e. g.* corpse, or that which is morally corrupt. This paranomasia would be parallel to that which has been suggested (first, I believe, by Reland, *Dissertationes*

Before studying the scattered New Testament references to Samaria, it may be convenient to examine the attitude held towards them by the great Jewish historian of the Ist Century, Josephus, who has abundant opportunity to refer to the Samaritans. These appear in his pages under that name, and also as Kuthæans and Shechemites. As Josephus was a well-informed man in contemporary affairs, and also as he had friends in Samaria,[4] he might be taken as a reliable authority. But unfortunately he no more than reflects the current Jewish prejudices of his day, and allows us to perceive some of the truth only through the contradictions in which he involves himself. In his account of the fall of Northern Israel, he adds to the letter of the Biblical narrative that " all " of the people of the Northern kingdom were deported.[5] This must have been the prevailing vulgar opinion in Judaism, and indeed has at least the negative support of the Biblical account. He also draws the inference, so plausible to the reader of *Ezra-Nehemia*, that it was the Samaritan sectarians who interfered throughout with the restoration of Jerusalem and the temple.[6] He charges that the Samaritans affected to be Jews when it suited their advantage, and otherwise claimed to be Sidonians.[7] But an intimation of another side of the question crops out. He tells us in one place that " Shechem is inhabited by apostates of the Jewish nation," and that the Samaritans profess to be Hebrews, although not Jews.[8] And he adds that this apostate community was increased by

miscellaneæ, i, 140) between the *shikkore*, drunkards, of the same passage and Sychar, as an abusive epithet for Shechem, *Jn.* 4, 5. I would suggest that in the epithet " fool " there is a play upon the place More, in the neighborhood of Shechem. The Greek μωρός, " fool ", was adopted by the late Hebrew in the same sense; see Jastrow, *Dictionary,* p. 749, and cf. *Mt.* 5, 22, and commentators *ad loc.*

[4] *Life,* 52.
[5] *AJ* ix, 14, 3; cf. x, 9, 7.
[6] *AJ* xi, cc. 2, 4; c. 5, 8.
[7] See Additional Note B.
[8] *AJ* xi, 8, 6.

Jews who had eaten unclean things, broken the Sabbath, or committed like offences, and who fled to Shechem.[9] Josephus thus admits, however unwillingly and unconsciously that the Samaritans were Israelites, and that they were nearly enough related to the Jews to be an asylum for the discontented or excommunicates of the Jewish Church. The worthy historian is a good example of the ambiguity which affects the whole Jewish attitude toward the sect.

The New Testament has not been sufficiently applied for the understanding of the Jewish treatment of the Samaritans, and the commentators have largely failed in the treatment of the several pertinent passages to apprehend the status of the Samaritans according to the Jewish mind of the Ist Century. But the volume throws considerable light upon our quest. Jesus himself twice met with Samaritan discourtesy, twice used the Samaritans to point a moral, twice referred to the Samaritans in defining the scope of his Gospel, and once had the epithet " Samaritan " coarsely applied to himself.[10] And in the subsequent history, the action of his Church in regard to the evangelization of Samaria is instructive for our study.

In *Jn.* 4 occurs the story of Jesus' conversation with the woman of Sychar by Jacob's Well, a meeting which resulted in his sojourn in the town for two days, when many Samaritans came to believe in him.[11] The scene in which the Samaritan woman at first churlishly refused the wearied

[9] *Ibid.*, § 7. He also knows that Samaritans were up to his own day admitted into the temple precincts; xviii, 2, 2.

[10] See above, p. 155.

[11] The author accepts this story as authentic, and as one of the many instances in which the evangelist appears true to local conditions and color. The mere reference to the Samaritan belief in a Messiah adds corroboration to the anecdote. The city Sychar I take to be Shechem; see above, p. 20. It may be noted here that the Roman martyrology celebrates March 20 as the anniversary of the Samaritan woman " Photina," who is said to have suffered martyrdom along with her sons Joseph and Victor.

Jew a cup of cold water is the classic instance of the mutual hatred of the two sects.

Again, *Luke* 9, 51ff describes a journey Jesus took up to Jerusalem, apparently by the route through Samaria. On this occasion " he sent messengers before him, and they entered into a village of Samaritans, so as to make ready for him; and they would not receive him, because he was evidently going to Jerusalem." This village may have been Ginaia, the ancient En-gannim and modern Jenin, doubtless the scene of frequent conflicts between the Samaritans and Jewish pilgrims, one bloody instance of which is recorded by Josephus.[12] In response to this inhospitality the Jewish feeling of the disciples blazes forth in the spirit of Elija: " Sir, wilt thou that we bid fire to come down from heaven and destroy them? " But Jesus' own mind is revealed by the rebuke he administers to his followers. The party then went into another village where they were more hospitably received.[13]

It is to be observed that in both of these passages narrating the transit of Jews through Samaria, it is taken as a matter of course that Jesus and his disciples lodged in Samaritan villages and purchased Samaritan food. To be sure, the coarse and yet natural inhospitality of the Samaritans toward the Jews broke out on both occasions. With these facts the comment of the Fourth Gospel: " For the Jews have no dealings with ($\sigma\upsilon\gamma\chi\rho\tilde{\omega}\nu\tau\alpha\iota$) the Samaritans " (4, 7), as generally interpreted, disagrees, for in the next breath the evangelist tells how the disciples had gone into the town

---

[12] See above, p. 85.

[13] The possible identification with Ginaia presupposes, with most modern commentators, that Luke gives the story out of historical connection, inasmuch as the last journey of Jesus to Jerusalem, with which the evangelist connects the incident, was by way of the Trans-Jordanic route. If the incident be rightly connected with Jesus' final journey,— so for example by Godet,— then the Samaritan village may have lain in the plain of Scythopolis, or even across Jordan; see Chap. VIII. This would easily explain how the party found " another kind of village ", $\dot{\epsilon}\tau\dot{\epsilon}\rho\alpha\nu$ $\kappa\dot{\omega}\mu\eta\nu$, in the close neighborhood.

to buy food. But there are grave doubts as to the genuineness of the clause, which is omitted in the Alexandrine Codex, the Codex Bezæ, and in the Italic MSS a, b, e; it is rejected by Tischendorf, and bracketed by Westcott-Hort and Nestle. The probabilities favor the view that it is a gloss representing the actual conditions of a later age. If it is to be preserved, then either the author is guilty of an inexact expression, or else the verb requires some different translation than the one generally given to it.[14] But the evangelical narratives show that the Jews in that period exercised considerable liberty in entering Samaritan markets and accepting Samaritan hospitality, a liberty that was the greater when we recall that there were few foods which could not easily be rendered unlawful. Indeed, as the following Chapter will show, this liberty was preserved both in theory and practice well down into the Talmudic age. Also the common statement that the Jews avoided Samaria as an unclean land and therefore preferred the Peræan route, cannot be maintained.[15] For in addition to these Gospel narratives, there is the distinct testimony of Josephus that it was the custom of the Galilæan pilgrims to go through Samaria,[16] a liberty followed into late times by the Jewish rabbis. Finally, there is the explicit Rabbinic dictum that "the land of Samaria is clean."[17] Jesus however seems generally to have gone up to Jerusalem by way of Peræa, and the Fourth Evangelist takes occasion to explain the deviation from his usual custom by the statement

[14] J. Lightfoot, *ad loc.* (*Works*, 1684, ii, 538), seems to be the only commentator who recognizes, quite apart from the textual argument, the difficulty of the clause. The verb συγχρᾶσθαι corresponds to the Talmudic *histappeq*, which is used by R. Abbahu in the IVth Century in admitting that in earlier days the Jews had dealings with the Samaritans; see below, p. 192.

[15] E.g. Smith, *HG* 256; Edersheim, *Life and Times of Jesus the Messiah*, ed. 8, New York, i, 394. In another passage Edersheim corrects himself, p. 400.

[16] *AJ* xx, 6, 1.

[17] See Chap. X, note 27.

that " he had to pass through Samaria," the necessity appearing from the context to be his desire to get quickly away from the hostility of the Judæan authorities.[18] The Jews naturally took the eastern route to avoid the unpleasantness of the journey through Samaria.

The Gospel of Luke, whose interest in " the lost sheep of the house of Israel " is characteristic, also gives the story of the healing of ten lepers, one of whom was a Samaritan, 17, 11-19. Jesus responds to their request that he compassionate them by bidding them go and show themselves to the priests. In thus holding them to the Levitical law, he included the Samaritan with the rest as an Israelite, and the inferred acceptability of the Samaritan as a subject of the Jewish laws of purification at the temple, is in entire accord with the Talmudic spirit; Josephus himself records the permitted participation of Samaritans at the temple feasts.[19] The story proceeds to tell how on the way to the priests the lepers were cleansed, but only one of them turned back to thank his benefactor, and " he was a Samaritan." Jesus responds: " Were there not ten cleansed, but where are the nine? None has returned to give glory to God save this stranger."[20] The gratitude of the Samaritan was made to point a moral to the Jews even as was the faith of a heathen centurion upon another occasion, Mt. 8, 5ff.

From this episode we pass naturally to the Parable of

[18] I cannot enter into the discussion concerning the place of Jesus' baptizing, Jn. 3, 22f. There is no reason to adopt Robinson's suggestion, LBR 333, supported by Stevens, JBL 1883, p. 128, and hypothetically adopted by the map of the Survey of Western Palestine, that Salim and Aenon are in the neighborhood of Shechem; the suggestion contradicts all that we know of the fields of labor of John Baptist and Jesus.

[19] See above, note 9.

[20] Ἀλλογενής. This word is used in the Greek to translate bennekar, e. g. Gen. 17, 27; Ex. 12, 43. In Ecclus. 45, 13, it refers to a member of another tribe within Israel, translating zar. Its sense then is weaker than ἀλλόφυλος, which was used of Gentiles alone, especially of the Philistines. As will be shown below, Jesus maintained the actual distinction between Jew and Samaritan.

the Good Samaritan, *Luke,* 10, 25ff, which in its fame is equalled only by the Parable of the Prodigal Son. The parable has been somewhat stretched by exegetes so as to make it appear that Jesus allowed no difference between Jew and Samaritan, and was indeed inclined to find Samaritans better people than the Jews. This is a fallacy of modern interpretation which would make out of Jesus nothing else than a modern liberal. But the story is merely an answer to the lawyer's question, " Who is my neighbor? " A good Pagan would have served as an example, but the Samaritan was nearer home, while the motive of religious disgust at the bloody and unclean body of the man who fell among thieves could only come into play if an Israelite were the hero. It has been generally overlooked that Jesus' postulate of the possibility of high virtue in the Samaritans is paralleled by the saying of Rabbi Simon ben Gamaliel, frequently quoted and allowed by the Talmud: " Every law which the Samaritans have accepted, they are more punctilious in observing than the Jews."[21] The Talmud also gives an anecdote of an act of courtesy towards a Jewish rabbi on the part of the Samaritans.[22] In fact the argument of Jesus was all the stronger to his hearers because of their recognition of the possible virtues of the Samaritans; they could not retort to him that he was inventing an imaginary good Samaritan.

The dogmatic position of Jesus toward the Samaritans is positively stated in his conversation with the Samaritan woman. The latter enters into a theological argument with the mysterious stranger: " Sir, I perceive that thou art a prophet. Our fathers worshipped on this mountain, and thou sayest that the place to worship is in Jerusalem. Jesus says to her: Woman, believe me that the time is coming when neither on this mountain nor in Jerusalem shall ye

[21] See below, p. 170.
[22] See below, p. 193.

11

worship the Father. Ye worship what ye know not, we worship what we know; for salvation is of the Jews." This theological depreciation of the Samaritans is exactly that of the Jewish Church, although deprived of all malice. The assertion of the peculiar privilege of the Jews was also the doctrine of the Christian Church, which followed its Master, being abundantly expressed by the broadest-minded apostle, Paul, e.g. *Rom.* 3, 1ff. Nor did Jesus respect the institutions of Samaritanism; the cleansed Samaritan he bade go with his Jewish fellows to the priests at Jerusalem. Further, throughout his ministry Jesus carefully distinguished between Jew and Samaritan. In his commission to his disciples he commanded them: " Go not into the way of Gentiles, and enter no city of Samaritans, but go rather to the lost sheep of the house of Israel," *Mt.* 10, 5f. And this restriction against that sect he himself carefully observed; only in the case of the favorable reception accidentally accorded him at Shechem did he give himself out to the Samaritans; but this is as evident an exception to his custom as was the healing of the Phœnician woman's daughter on the borders of Tyre, *Mk.* 7, 24ff; *Mt.* 15, 21ff.[22a]

To the present writer's understanding of Jesus' character and purpose, the limitation of his work to orthodox Judaism was with the deliberate practical intention of devoting himself exclusively in his lifetime to the community which he regarded as the one true Church. But it would be erroneous to gather from *Mt.* 10, 5f, that Jesus put the Samaritans on the same plane with the Gentiles; if so, he would have stood below the level of Judaism, which recognized the Israelitish character of that sect. His mind concerning the Samaritans appears in one of his final instructions to his

---

[22a] There is absolutely no reason to hold with Godet that in *Lu.* 9, 51ff Jesus was attempting a mission in northern Samaria so as to exercise his disciples in the more catholic ideas of his Gospel.

disciples. In *Acts,* 1, 8, he is recorded as saying to them: "Ye shall be my witnesses both in Jerusalem and all Judæa and Samaria and to the end of the earth." Here Samaria is distinguished as apart from Jewry, but equally apart from the rest of the world. Its Lord's injunction the Apostolic Church followed as soon as the opportunity came. According to *Acts,* 8, 1, upon the persecution following Stephen's death "all were scattered into the lands of Judæa and Samaria, except the Apostles." Then in v. 5ff is given the history of the deacon Philip's evangelistic labors in a city of Samaria, doubtless Shechem;[23] he was well received by the people because of his miracles and teachings. Thereupon the Apostles in Jerusalem sent down Peter and John as their commissioners to the Samaritan city, who laid their hands upon the converts that they might receive the Holy Spirit. It appears that according to this history the admission of the Samaritans was regarded as a step forward, and so required the formal cognizance of the mother-church. But in general this action of the Church in freely and easily admitting the Samaritans to fellowship in the Gospel was in full accord with the better Jewish view, which never was able to deny that the Samaritans were Israelites. It is to be noticed that no outpouring of the Spirit in advance is recorded, as in the case of the admission of Cornelius and his family, to give divine endorsement to an extraordinary innovation. The history includes the story of Simon Magus and closes with a reference to the evangelization of

---

[23] Gr: εἰς (τὴν) πόλιν τῆς Σαμαρίας. The article τήν appears in Cod. Sin., A, B, 31, 40, and is adopted by Tischendorf, Westcott-Hort, Nestle. On its face "the city of Samaria" can only mean, as Wendt says *ad loc.,* the chief city of the land, which would be Samaria-Sebaste. But as the whole narrative evidently deals with the Samaritan sect, with which Sebaste had no connection, being a thoroughly Gentile city, doubtless the original tradition meant Shechem, which was the only Polis of the sect. The Syriac has therefore "the city of the Samaritans." In general, the author of Acts seems ignorant of the place referred to, and may have indulged in the confusion, which appears in later literature, between Sebaste and Shechem.

many Samaritan villages.[24] Of these new converts *Acts* offers but little further information; the Church in Samaria is referred to again in 9, 31 and 15, 3.

To sum up the witness of the New Testament: the Samaritan appears as an Israelite, but one whose religion is in the condition of ignorance and whose institutions are irregular. But there is no question over his right as an Israelite to admission to the Kingdom of Heaven. This witness, which is also that of the earlier strata of the Talmud, is truer than the prejudiced opinion of Josephus. As evidence for the Ist Century the New Testament is thus a valuable auxiliary to the testimony of the Talmud, to the consideration of which we shall proceed in the next Chapter.

In Chapters XII. and XIII. the most important of the Patristic references to the Samaritans will be reviewed. Those authorities correctly regard the race as a Jewish sect, or rather as one of the initial heresies of the True Religion. Here may be noticed a passage from Justin Martyr (IId Century), a Neapolitan by birth, in which he closely associates the Jews and Samaritans as branches of the Chosen People. The reference is as follows:[25] " All the other human races are called Gentiles by the Spirit of prophecy; but the Jewish and Samaritan races are called the tribe of Israel and the house of Jacob. And the prophecy in which it was predicted that there should be more believers from the Gentiles than from the Jews and the Samaritans, we will produce."

[24] For Simon, see Chap. XIII, § 2.
[25] *First Apology*, c. 53. Justin does not display any exact information concerning the Samaritan sect. His references to them belong almost entirely to his reports of the Simonian heresy, into which he asserts almost the whole community fell — an erroneous statement, doubtless based on *Acts* 8, 10.

CHAPTER X.

THE SAMARITANS IN THE TALMUDS AND OTHER RABBINIC LITERATURE.[1]

Our chief sources for this Chapter are the Talmuds .of Babylon and Jerusalem and their auxiliary collections of Toseftas (i.e. Additions). Foremost in this material stands the *Masseket Kutim,* or Tractate on the Samaritans, of which a description and translation with notes appear in the next Chapter. Also the Midrashim, especially the great commentary on Genesis, *Bereshit Rabba,* present much Haggadic material. The mediæval Jewish literature contains almost no first-hand information on the subject.

Indeed so hazy did this later Jewish mind become over the Samaritans that provisions concerning the Gentiles came to include as a matter of course the Samaritans. Later, upon the arbitrary exercise of the Christian censor's power over the printed editions of the Talmud, " Kuthim " was easily

[1] The most convenient survey of this subject is the article of Hamburger in his *REJud.* ii, *s. v. Samaritaner.* An abundant and critical collection of material is found in Kirchheim *Septem libri Talmudici parvi Hierosolymitani,* and *Introductio in librum Talmudicum " de Samaritanis "* (*Karme Shomeron*) ; both Frankfurt, 1851 (in Hebrew). Taglicht has given a brief dissertation, *Die Kuthäer als Beobachter des Gesetzes nach talmudischen Quellen,* Berlin, 1888. See also Geiger, *Urschrift, passim;* Frankel, *Ueber den Einfluss der palästinensichen Exegese,* 244; Nutt, *Samaritan Targum;* Edersheim, *Jesus the Messiah,* vol. i, bk. iii, c. vii. Wreschner, in *Samaritanische Traditionen,* Berlin, 1888, treats especially of points of comparison with the Karaites. *The Works of John Lightfoot,* London, 1684, is a thesaurus of references on the present subject. For the Tosefta I refer to M. S. Zuckermandel, *Tosefta,* 1881. The references to the Jerusalem Talmud are made according to the Krotoschin edition, 1866. For references to *Masseket Kutim,* cf. Chapter XI.

used as a substitute for "Goyim," Gentiles, or the sharper expression, "Worshippers of stars and constellations," terms which often included the Christians. Hence in any Talmudic mention of the Kuthim it is necessary to scrutinize both text and context to ascertain whether the word is used in its primary or secondary sense. Elder MSS often show that the reading "Kuthim" is not original.[2]

Our investigation of the political relations between the Samaritans and the Jews has revealed to us the lay mind of the latter concerning the former as exhibited in the New Testament and Josephus. We now proceed to ascertain the status of the Samaritans before the law of the Jewish Church; our special field of investigation is therefore the Corpus of that law, the Talmud. Fortunately this great wilderness of material submits itself in large part to chronological discrimination. It is now generally recognized that its basis, the Mishna, was completed by the end of the IId Century A. C., while the commentary thereon, the Gemara, was not finally redacted, at least in the case of the Babylonian Talmud, until the VIth Century. Moreover as the decisions of the rabbis are generally referred to their authors, whose dates are in most cases well known, we are able to follow the development of Jewish opinion on the Samaritans for the first four centuries of the Christian era. It may be here noted that it is proper to take up this discussion before approaching the subject of the Samaritan

---

[2] The following is a list of the Mishnaic passages in which "Kutim" refers to the Samaritans: *Berakot,* vii, 1; viii, 8; *Demai,* iii, 4; v, 9; vi, 1; vii, 4; *Shebiit,* viii, 10; *Teruma,* iii, 9; *Shekalim,* i, 5; *Rosh ha-Shana,* ii, 2; *Ketubot,* iii, 1; *Nedarim,* iii, 10; *Gittin,* i, 5; *Kiddushin,* iv, 3; *Ohalot,* xvii, 3; *Tohorot,* v, 8; *Nidda,* iv, 1, 2; vii, 3, 4, 5. Schürer's list, *GJV* ii, 15, note 43, includes *Pea,* ii, 7, where *nokrim,* "foreigners," is to be read, and *Challa,* v, 7, where *Kushim,* "Egyptians," is to be read. To his list *Shebiit,* viii, 10, is to be added. See Rabbinovicz, *Variæ lectiones in Mischnam et in Talmud Babylonicum,* 1867, and the critical text of L. Goldschmidt, *Der babylonische Talmud,* 1896. Taglicht notices some of the textual uncertainties concerning "Kutim", *op. cit.* 7.

theology, because sure data in the Samaritan literature do not go back of the IVth Century.

At the same time many uncertainties remain after the most exhaustive criticism. Contemporary doctors of the Law hotly dispute over the status of the Samaritans, and changes of opinions on the part of rabbis are recorded. In many cases there are contradictory reports of the same Halakot, or decisions. Further, at least for any student who is not a thorough-going Talmudist, it is often difficult to interpret the opinions and decisions reported, from lack of a full knowledge of the circumstances and legal questions in which they are involved. But one fact stands out clear and sure: we have to do in the Talmudic treatment of the Samaritans with a historic process. Far down into the period of the Amoraim (i.e. the formulators of the Gemara), Judaism was still making up its mind concerning the adverse sect. We can, most fortunately, follow the growth of opinion from the discussions of Akiba and Meir, Simon b. Gamaliel and Eliezer, in the first half of the IId Century, when the Samaritans were a lively subject of debate, down to the days of Rabbis Ame and Assi, about 300 A. C., when those scholars finally decreed the excommunication of the sectarians, after which time we find only sporadic opinions in variance with the position of the great majority. Accordingly it is advisable to pursue the subject as closely as possible upon chronological lines, and it is first in place to ascertain those points wherein the Jewish doctors were of one mind concerning the Samaritans, at least for the period of the Tannaim, whose decisions finally fixed the Mishna at the end of the IId Century.

We have already observed the unneighborly and frequently hostile attitude obtaining between the Jews and the Samaritans throughout the age of their common existence upon Palestinian soil. It may then cause surprise that to the testimony for this popular attitude of the Jews toward the Samaritans — repaid by the latter in kind — the letter of the Talmud is often flatly contradictory. This phenomenon is not due to a spirit of charity, for ecclesiastical law is never charitable. But the reason for the fact is simple; law is conservative, based on the precedents of past history. It is the easy business of Christian preacher or Jewish Haggadist to stir up the prejudices of the people against the adversaries of the church; but the law assumes a different position even towards the object of its hostile animadversion. The schismatic or heretic, though outlawed, may still possess some rights according to the constitutional law of the mother-church. Hence it is that the Talmudic opinions and decisions, far more than popular tradition and vulgar brawls, bear witness to the actual historical relations originally existing between Jews and Samaritans. When we find the doctors of the IId Century wrestling over this problem, we have good evidence, otherwise almost wholly absent, that in the preceding centuries the Samaritan had a *quasi*-standing within the Jewish Church, which only the widening of the breach and the slow development of law could at last annul. Accordingly Talmudic authority throws desiderated light upon the most obscure ages of Samaritan history.

To approach now the Talmudic appreciation of Samaritanism, we find that no fault was found in the earlier ages with respect to the cardinal tenet of the soleness and spirituality of the God of Israel. The one early exception, for the end of the IId Century, is the anecdote concerning R. Ishmael b. Joseph, who, falling into dispute with a Samaritan at Shechem on his way towards Jerusalem, accused the Samaritans of worshipping the idols hidden under Gerizim by Jacob on his return from Haran (*Gen.* 35, 4).[3] But, as Taglicht remarks, this was only " eine neckische Ant-

---

[3] *Aboda Zara Jer.* 44d; also *Bereshit Rabba*, c. 81; *Debarim Rabba*, c. 3. The rabbi escaped death only by flight.

wort."[4]   The first instance known to me of the Jewish aspersion of the Samaritans for the dove-cult belongs to the middle of the IVth Century.[5]   But against these calumnies we possess the positive, if genuine, utterance of a Tosefta :[6] " One may rent his house to a Samaritan, and have no fear that the latter will bring idols into it."

Again, the Samaritans are never denied entire devotion to the Law of Moses. The many slight textual differences in their edition were generally unnoticed, and even the falsifications introduced in the Pentateuch do not appear to have been a prime source of strife. I know of but one case of reference to such a falsification, and this is of an unimportant nature, while it is doubtless a materially correct gloss.[7]   The Samaritan rejection of the rest of the Jewish canon nowhere appears charged against the sect as a heresy. To be sure, Judaism assigned an infinite superiority to the Law over against the rest of the Old Testament, the latter being for long recognized as Kabbala or tradition.

Moreover the Samaritans possessed not only the letter of the Law but also the Jewish spirit of its practical application.   The Pentateuch was to them as to the Jews the book of life, the all-sufficient code of right living. Their faithfulness in this respect called forth the generous applause of one of the IId Century patriarchs, R. Simon b.

[4] *Op. cit.* 22.

[5] R. Nachman b. Isaac, in *Cholin,* 6a. See Additional Note D. Observe the Samaritan reproach against the Jews for their imagery in the temple; Chapter VI, note 32.

[6] *Tos. Ab. Z.* 2, 9; but Zuckermandel places this clause in his marginal apparatus.

[7] This is the case of the introduction of " Shechem " after " the oaks of More " in *Dt.* 11, 30. In *Sifre* to the passage, this addition is reprobated, according to a Jewish view that another Ebal and Gerizim were meant, a view adopted by Jerome in his *Onomasticon, s. vv. Gebal, Golgol* (*Migne,* xxiii, 946). Yet in *Sota,* 33b, it is allowed that the addition makes no difference. See Frankel, *op. cit.* 243; Geiger, *op. cit.* 81. In one case the grammar of the Samaritan exegesis is condemned, namely in their ignoring of the *he locale,* as in their interpretation of החצה, in *Dt.* 25, 5, which they translated as " the one without "; *Yebam. Jer.* 3a; *Kiddushin,* 76a.

Gamaliel (d. *circa* 165), the father of Juda ha-Nasi, who was the editor of the Mishna. His dictum is: " Every command the Samaritans keep, they are more scrupulous in observing than Israel."[8]   A parallel to this catholic-minded assertion is another to the effect that " a Samaritan is like a full Jew."[9]   Another prescription found in the Mishna, of more restrictive character and negative in expression, reads: " This is the rule: Whatever they are suspected in, they are not to be believed in."[10]

In regard to the two great institutes of Israel which are its most evident marks of differentiation from the rest of the world, namely circumcision and the Sabbath, there is no question in the Jewish law concerning the scrupulousness of the Samaritans.[11]   Indeed in these two respects the latter held more strictly to the letter of the Law, rigorously observing circumcision on the eighth day, and avoiding such sabbatic legal fictions as the Erub.[12]   The latter omission was a heresy in the eyes of the Pharisees, but it may have been just this literalism of practice which provoked the laudatory opinion expressed by Simon b. Gamaliel.   As for circumcision, there is a Boraita (i.e. an extraneous Mishna not found amongst the received Mishnas) of R. Juda, a contemporary of R. Meir, in the middle of the IId Century, which forbids the circumcision of a Jew by a Samaritan on the ground that the latter circumcised " in the name of Mount Gerizim," which seems to mean simply, " with the

----

[8] This saying is frequently quoted, *e. g. Kidd.* 76a; *Berakot,* 47b; *Gittin,* 10a. This Patriarch was very conservative in his opinions; see Grätz, *Geschichte der Juden,* iv, 187.

[9] *Ketubot Jer.* 27a; *Demai Jer.* 9.

[10] *Nidda,* vii, 4; *Mass. Kut.* 16.   In the Gemara, 57a, the principle is applied to sabbatic limits and libation wine.

[11] *Mass. Kut.* 10. A Mishna, *Nedarim,* iii, 10, reads: " He who vows not to derive any benefit from those who keep the Sabbath, has no benefit from Israelites or Samaritans."

[12] *I. e.* the constitution of extended artificial precincts, whereby several houses could be considered as one, and their inmates as of the same household.

intention of attaching the person to the community of Gerizim."[13]   But R. Meir opposed R. Juda, on the ground that
the Samaritan was a genuine convert, and it is this favorable
opinion of Meir's which is preserved in *Masseket Kutim*.[14]
Juda in fact preferred a Gentile as the officiant.   The rise
of this narrower opinion was evidently due to practical reasons.   The Samaritan might easily boast that the child he
circumcised was thereby initiated into his own community.
It was an incongruity that a member of the rival sect could
perform the rite of admission into the community, whereas
the Gentile would not pretend to more than the physical
function.   We may compare the theoretically inconsistent
yet practically logical requirement by the Roman Catholic
Church of the re-baptism of Protestants.

As for the feasts and fasts and other occasions of worship,
the Talmud has in general no condemnation of the Samaritans; that in an earlier age they were once admitted to the
precincts of the temple in Jerusalem without much question
is evident from Josephus.[15]   The Passover, with its scrupulous concern over the removal of leaven well before the
opening of the sacred week, offered a severe criterion of the
straitness of all who claimed to be of Israel.   Yet the prevailing dictum concerning Samaritan usage in this respect
is expressed in the following Boraita: " The unleaven of
the Samaritans is allowed, and one discharges his duty with
it at the Passover."[16]   On the other hand — and this illustrates the difference of opinion — that maxim was contradicted by R. Eliezer, Akiba's opponent upon the Samaritan
problem, in a dictum which accompanies the one just cited:
the Samaritans " are not scrupulous over the fine points of
the Law."   Also in the prayer of Benediction after a com-

---

[13] Cf. the use of " the Name " in the Christian baptismal formula.
[14] *Ab. Z.* 26b–27a; *Menachot*, 42a; *Mass. Kut.* 12.   For Meir's position see further below.
[15] See Chap. IX, note 9.
[16] *Kidd.* 76a; *Chol.* 4a; *Gitt.* 10a; *Mass. Kut.* 24; etc.

mon meal, which required the presence of at least three of the faithful, the slave and the Samaritan could be included, the Samaritan being thus distinguished from the Am-ha-areç, or unlearned man.[17] Also the pronouncing of the Benediction by a Samaritan was so far acknowledged that a Jew could say Amen to it, however with the condition that the former should be heard throughout — evidently from fear lest out of malice or ignorance he might invalidate the worship.[18]

As to the ethics of the Samaritans, the very few Talmudic references are most honorable to their memory. They were acquitted of practising incest,[19] which included all unions within the prohibited degrees, and also of the bestiality ascribed to the Gentiles.[20] But leaving the ethical field, which rarely divides religious sects, we pass to the sphere of technical cleanliness in food and hygiene and habitat. In the first of these articles, we observe that the Samaritan slaughter of meat was regarded as *kosher,* i.e. ritually correct, except that, lest the Jew be deceived by a malicious Samaritan, the seller is required to put into his mouth an olive-quantum of the meat, or the string of birds which he has to sell.[21] Indeed in some respects the Samaritans were stricter than the Jews, for the latter permitted the eating of *koskos,* i.e. flesh of an animal mortally ill when slain, or a fœtus, both of which were forsworn by the Samaritans; accordingly, the Jews forbade the sale of such articles to the other sect.[22] Their wine appears to have been accepted without scruple, except in the case of its origin from cer-

[17] *Berak.* vii, 1. But there was further discussion on the eligibility of the Samaritan in the Gemara, 47b; see below, p. 179.
[18] *Berak.* viii, 8. In the reference in the same Mishna to the spices of the Kuthim, Goldschmidt reads *goyim,* "Gentiles."
[19] *Gitt. Jer.* 43c.
[20] *Ab. Z.* 15b; *Mass. Kut.* 4; 13.
[21] *Chol.* 3b *seq.; Mass. Kut.* 17.
[22] *Mass. Kut.* 15. See there the reason why the Jews did not purchase such things from the Samaritans.

tain localities, down to R. Meir's time. This freedom was finally changed by Meir's decree against all Samaritan wine except that which was sealed and so escaped defilement.[23]

In the matter of hygiene and cleanliness of habitation and soil, the Samaritan usage was in general acceptable to the Jews. Thus the Samaritans were careful with regard to the laws of menstruation, according to a majority opinion recorded in a Mishna.[24] They were to be trusted concerning the burial of abortions,[25] and concerning the marking of graves, although the corollary of the Bet-peras was not observed by them.[26] Hence we find the explicit statement that " the land of the Kuthim is clean, the gatherings of their waters are clean, their dwellings are clean, their roads are clean."[27] As was observed in the preceding Chapter, this point has been generally overlooked in the question concerning Samaria as a land of thoroughfare for Jewish travellers, and illustrates more than one passage in the New Testament.

The Samaritans were considered rightly to observe the Mosaic provisions concerning the consecration of the first-born of beasts, and the state of " uncircumcision " of a tree in its first three years.[28] Also they practised Chalisa and divorce in correct form.[29] Likewise they had the proper

[23] *Ab. Z.* 31b; *Mass. Kut.* 25. For the proscribed localities, see above, p. 146.

[24] *Nidda,* vii, 3; R. Meir expressed a contrary opinion. But according to *Baba Kamma,* 38b, this was the opinion of R. Juda, Meir's opponent.

[25] For primitive Palestinian use in this matter see the note in *PEFQS* 1906, p. 64.

[26] *Nidda,* vii, 5; *Mass. Kut.* 16 (see note there).

[27] *Ab. Z. Jer.* 44d; cf. *Tos. Mikwaot,* 6, 1. Taglicht notes to the latter reference, *op. cit.* 7, that the passage in *Chagiga,* 25a, where wine brought from Galilee is declared unclean because it has touched the district of the Kuthim, should read for this word, according to the MSS, " Persians ", i. e. with reference to the Gentiles of Galilee. For the idea of the purity of the Holy Land see Bertholet, *Die Stellung der Israeliten zu den Fremden,* 304.

[28] *Nidda,* vii, 5.

[29] *Mass. Kut.* 14. Chalisa is the custom of " loosing the shoe ", *Dt.* 25, 5ff.

observance of the gleaning laws, the tithe for the poor in its year, while their poor were to be trusted in their statements on these matters.[30]

The earlier rules concerning intercourse with the Samaritans were most liberal. In utter contrast to dealings with the Gentiles, the Jew might " go in private with them," i.e. he need not be afraid of having his throat cut, and might also commit a child to them to learn letters for a trade.[31] Also according to a Tosefta, contradicted however by *Masseket Kutim*, " an Israelitess might deliver a Samaritaness and suckle her son," and *vice versa*.[32] We thus learn that in those places where both sects were found, there existed very intimate intercourse between them in many most important matters of life. With reference to affairs of ordinary commerce, the relevant dictum, *Masseket Kutim*, 7, says that " we lend and borrow with them on usury," but there is some argument for turning this into a negative, in which case the Samaritans would be in the category of brothers.[33] Also the prohibition of *Aboda Zara*, i, 5, against selling weapons to the Gentiles is applied in the Gemara, 15b, to the Samaritans, but on the ground lest these may sell them again to the Gentiles. It seems strange that, with all the hostility between the two sects, the Samaritans were not reckoned as enemies of Israel by formal legislation, this passage showing that they came to be legally included among the classes hostile to society only by a process of indirection.

With regard to the status of the Samaritan before the law of torts, we possess this Halaka of *Masseket Kutim*, 18: " The Samaritan is on the same footing with the Israelite in respect to all damages laid down in the Law." It would seem that this is an undoubtedly ancient Tosefta. The

[30] *Tos. Pea*, 4, 1; *Mass. Kut.* 8.
[31] *Ab. Z.* 15b; *Mass. Kut.* 13 (which see *ad loc.*).
[32] *Tos. Ab. Z.* 3, 1; *Mass. Kut.* 11.
[33] See *ad loc.*

same Halaka proceeds, quoting from the Mishna,[34] and prescribes the same penalties against members of either sect for manslaughter committed upon one another. It is to be observed that in the Mishnaic passage the Ger-toshab, or alien resident,[35] is not included in this prescription of equality. The Talmud however states one exception to this equality before the criminal law. If an Israelite's ox gore a Samaritan's ox, it goes clear, while an offending Samaritan ox, if that is its first offence, renders the owner liable for half the damage, but if the second offence, obligates him for the full value. This was the opinion of the majority, but R. Meir held that the Samaritan ox was in either case chargeable for the damage at the highest appraisement.[36] Comparing the opinion of the majority with the Mishna to this Gemara,[37] we find that the guiltlessness of the Jewish beast was the same as in the case of the damage done to a Gentile's ox, while the offending Samaritan beast incurred the liability of only half the damage instead of the full cost, for which the Gentile ox would be liable. In this respect therefore the Jewish law of torts gave the Samaritan a midway position between Jew and Gentile. There is no evident reason for this exception; perhaps the law for beasts underwent change easier than that for persons. R. Meir's harsher opinion is not intelligible, except on the ground of his change of opinion toward the Samaritans, which is otherwise testified to. The Gemara proceeds to discuss why that rabbi, who regarded the Samaritans as genuine converts, placed them under this disability.

We turn now to the consideration of the major differences between the two sects. These *differentia* are briefly summed up in the last Halaka of *Masseket Kutim:* "When shall we take them back? When they renounce Mount Gerizim and

---

[34] *Makkot,* ii, 4. See note to *Mass. Kut.* 18.
[35] For this definition, see Schürer *GJV* iii, 126; Bertholet, *op. cit.* 325.
[36] *Baba Kamma,* 38b; *Mass. Kut.* 19.
[37] *B. Kam.* iii, 2.

confess Jerusalem and the resurrection of the dead," — as a modern would put it, one difference in cult, and one in theology. The latter difference testifies to the position of the Samaritans in eschatology, wherein they but preserved the original Jewish doctrine. But the contradiction with respect to the proper place of the cult is the *origo mali,* the chief article of the Samaritan heresy. These people had formed a separate community which worshipped elsewhere than in Jerusalem. In a word, if we may use the terms of Christian theology, the fault of the Samaritan sect was not that of heresy but rather of schism. And all who know ecclesiastical history recognize that the latter is practically regarded by ecclesiastics as almost worse than the former, for it strikes at the idea of the church. In a word, the most important prescriptions laid down by the Jewish Church against the Samaritans proceed from the judgment of them as schismatics rather than as heretics.

That not heresy but schism was the fault of the Samaritans in the mind of the Jewish Church comes out in the great discussions held in the IId Century concerning their status as converts to the religion of Israel. It was hotly debated whether they were "genuine converts" (*gere emet*), or "lion-converts" (*gere ariyot*). The latter expression arose from the story in 2 *Ki.* 17, 25ff, according to which the Samaritans might be placed in the category of those who through fear, force, or unworthy inducements, were persuaded to enter Israel.[38] An extended discussion upon the true character of the Kuthite converts — they are never otherwise regarded than as aliens in blood — is found in *Kiddushin,* 75a—76a. Here R. Ishmael, who in general appears as an antagonist of Akiba (belonging to the "generation" preceding him), held that the Samaritans were

[38] See Weber, *Jüdische Theologie,* 74; Bertholet, *op. cit.* 341. Other references to lion-converts, apart from the one given in the text, are *B. Kam.* 38b; *Sanhedrin,* 85b; *Chol.* 3b; *Nidda,* 56b.

lion-converts, Akiba that they were genuine converts; R. Eliezer agreed with Ishmael. Also, according to *Baba Kamma,* 38b, R. Meir, although as we shall see, his mind underwent a change in another respect and he was equal to drawing nice distinctions against the Samaritans, nevertheless held with Akiba. The dispute was not allayed till at least the IVth Century. The composition between the two views was probably obtained by charging the change to the Samaritans themselves; in the words of R. Simon b. Eleazar, *circa* 200, " the Samaritans have long since become corrupted."[39]

Doubtless the discussion as between " lion-converts " and " genuine converts " was an ancient one. At the same time we are not to think that the latter opinion was suddenly invented by Akiba; in all probability it had good standing long before his day. For while the reproach of being converts from fear must be as ancient as the Biblical tradition in *2 Ki.* 17, we have to remember that enforced conversion was by no means despised in early Judaism. The Hasmonæan princes practiced the proselytism of neighboring races by force of arms, and slaves seem to have been bought with the purpose of circumcising them.[40] That the Samaritans were recognized as converts in some sense of the word was an honored tradition which the Jewish law only slowly surrendered. It was not therefore as heretics, or false Israelites, except in minor points, that the Samaritans were condemned, but rather as schismatics, who held themselves aloof from the institute of God's Kingdom.

Accordingly we have to regard the Samaritans as a separatist sect of Judaism, holding an ambiguous position in the eyes of the latter church, and one which had to be nicely balanced by the lawyers. The existence of such sectarian-

---

[39] *Ab. Z. Jer.* 44d. I confess here that as between the Eleazar and the Eliezer who were Akiba's contemporaries the Talmudic text appears to me indefinite.
[40] Josephus, *AJ* xiii, 9, 1; Bertholet, *op. cit.* 238, 254.

12

ism partly within and partly without the borders of Judaism, while subsequently rendered almost impossible by Talmudic law, has nevertheless more than one parallel in the earlier and far more catholic Judaism. We may think of the Essenes; of Jewish Hellenism, with its variant Canon,— not to speak of the extreme development in the temple at Leontopolis; of the Sadducees, who were gradually pressed to the wall by the Pharisees for observances resembling those of the Samaritans; and then there was the Am-ha-areç the Boor, who was the Pariah of Judaism, standing in the lowest rank of all. But when Essenes and Pharisees had disappeared, and the Hellenizers had gone over into Christianity or else been driven back into Pharisaic rigor, precedent for the peculiar status of the Samaritans failed, and the law was finally forced to excommunicate them in full.

In practice, far down in the Talmudic age, the sect was regarded as a sort of *Mittelding* between Gentiles and Jews; the world was divided into " Jews, Samaritans and Gentiles."[41] The distinction would be somewhat like that which is made in modern Christendom. A Christian map of the religions of the world distinguishes by its colors between the Catholic and the Protestant faiths as well as between these and the other religions. And yet the Christian mind would always place the great divisions of Christendom in one category as over against all the other religious systems.

A word may here be said as to the comparative worth of the Samaritan and the Am-ha-areç before the Talmudic law. In general, and as we saw above in the case of the saying of the Amen after the Benediction, the Samaritan stands above the Am-ha-areç.[42] The distinction is dis-

[41] Cf. *Acts*, i, 8; *Demai*, vi, 1; *Tohorot*, v, 8.
[42] In *Demai*, iii, 4, the presumption concerning the millers of the Samaritans and of the Am-ha-areç is the same, and opposite to the presumption against the Gentile miller.

cussed in the Gemara of *Berakot*.[43]   Here R. Abaye (*c.*
300) holds that the Samaritan so privileged must be a Chaber, i.e. a " Fellow " in the Law, and so opposed to the
Boor; this position seems to recognize that there were some
of the sect who were learned in the Law.[44]   But R. Raba
held that the privilege obtained even if the Samaritan were
an Am-ha-areç, a position which would in general rate all
Samaritans above the Jewish Am-ha-areç.

To take up now the discussion of the principal points in
which Judaism condemned the Samaritans, there is none
more important and significant than its attitude towards
their women.   In general the latter are looked upon as foul
in all sexual matters.   A Mishna teaches:[45] " The Samaritan women are menstruous from the cradle.   And the
Samaritans defile a bed both below and above, because they
have connection with menstruous women, and the latter sit
upon every kind of blood."   And another Mishna recites:
" The dwelling of the unclean women of the Samaritans defile after the manner of an Ohel, because they bury there
their abortions."[46]   (At the same time, as noted above, the
Samaritans were regarded as scrupulous in certain cognate
matters.[47])   Consequently we are not surprised to find that
marriages with Samaritan women were forbidden, a prohibition which *Masseket Kutim* extends against the men.[48]

This treatment of Samaritan women is strange in more
than one respect.   Whatever direct knowledge we possess of
the Samaritans shows that they were peculiarly scrupulous
about the laws of defilement.   Again it seems like a most

[43] 47b.
[44] The Samaritan Liturgy shows the use of the word Chaber in this
sense; e. g. *BS* ii, 72, bottom.
[45] *Nidda*, iv, 1.
[46] *Nidda*, vii, 4.   An Ohel is a precinct which is unclean and so
renders anyone entering it unclean.   The same Mishna also contains
an opinion of R. Juda (*c.* 150) to the effect that "they do not bury,"
etc.
[47] P. 173.   Cf. *Mass. Kut.* 11.
[48] *Kidd*, 75a; *Mass. Kut.* 6; 27 (where see the reasons advanced).

anomalous ban of outlawry against these " converts " that intermarriage with them was prohibited, and their social habits condemned. But we have to remember that from the beginnings of Judaism there existed two opposing views concerning marriage with proselytes.[49] On the one hand there were the classic examples of intermarriage with foreigners, as in the case of Moses and David's own ancestor Boaz.[50] Along with this position went the Jewish propaganda, which, taking its cue from *Deutero-Isaia,* bade fair to break down the ties of blood.[51] On the other hand was the rigorous position, which appears after the Return in the scrupulousness concerning the family registers. There was precedent therefore for the Samaritans to be treated as converts in one of two opposite ways.

Moreover we must recognize another fact, largely overlooked in the consideration of ancient Judaism; that is, the existence of recognized castes, between which marriage was prohibited. We have observed how the Am-ha-areç was the Pariah; but there were also several other grades, which are thus listed in a Talmudic passage:[52] " The priest is before the Levite, the Levite before the layman, the layman before the Mamzer [i. e. a bastard, or one of uncertain parentage], the Mamzer before the Nethin [the descendant of the ancient temple-slaves or hierodules], the Nethin before the proselyte, the proselyte before the freedman." As all these distinctions were perpetuated by blood, it was a matter of *morale* to avoid breaking down their barriers through intermarriage.

Now the Samaritans, even if admitted to be " genuine

[49] For this interesting question, see Weber, *op. cit.* 77, 294; Bertholet, *op. cit.* 255, and §§ 7, 8.
[50] Whether or not, as many now hold, *Ruth* is a tractate of the Vth Century supporting the liberal idea of marriage, at all events its incorporation in the Canon is witness to the power of liberal ideas at a late date.
[51] *Yebamot,* 47b: " The proselyte is like the Israelite in all things."
[52] *Horayot,* iii, 7.

converts," are treated by the Talmud as an Israelite caste of much the same nature as the Mamzerim; they are of uncertain origin. The reason for this attitude toward the sect appears in full in the argument given in *Kiddushin, 75a,*[53] where they are treated in the same way as the Mamzerim. In like terms a Mishna fixes the status of the Samaritans in respect to Jewish marriage: " These are the people of uncertain condition [i. e. with whom one may not marry] : those of unknown parentage, foundlings, and Samaritans."[54] The Gemara likewise classes the sect amongst those peoples intermarriage with whom is forbidden to the priesthood, namely, the Ammonites, Moabites, Egyptians, Edomites and Nethinim.[55] If the regulation of *Dt.* 23, 3ff were followed, the Samaritans could not hope for *connubium* with the Jews until the tenth generation, or practically indefinitely, and this application is actually made in *Kiddushin, 75a.*

Now it suited the policy of the Jewish Church to deny *connubium* with the Samaritans, for, that policy governed such regulations, is shown by the distinctions made in *Dt.* 23, 3ff. The Samaritans were sinful schismatics; social relationship with them meant the infection of their sin in the body politic. Intermarriage with Gentile proselytes was far less dangerous, for the Gentile became wholly a Jew, whereas the Samaritan in his pride would feel he had no spiritual benefit to receive from the alliance. It is, I believe, on account of this policy, which was based on most practical grounds, that the Jewish law aspersed the Samaritan women; by rendering these odious to the religious sense they attempted an effective barrier against intermarriage with that schismatic and Pariah-like sect.

In regard to matters of the sanctuary and the priesthood,

---

[53] Cf. *Mass. Kut.* 27.
[54] *Kidd.* iv, 3; *B. Kam.* 38b.
[55] *Nidda,* 74b. Also in the criminal law concerning seduction the Samaritaness is placed in the same class with the bastard or Nethin woman; *Ketub.* iii, 1; *B. Kam.* 38b.

so far as participation in the Jewish institutions would have given the Samaritans any prescriptive claim thereon, the general rule was their exclusion; they were placed on the same footing with the Gentiles. The most extensive regulation on the subject is found in *Shekalim*,[56] in the prescription concerning those who had the privilege of paying the ecclesiastical poll-tax of the shekel. This Mishna orders: " Although they say, the shekel poll-tax is not to be levied upon women and slaves and children, yet if they pay, it is to be received from them. If idolaters or Samaritans pay, we do not accept it from them. Nor do we accept from them bird-offerings of men or women affected with gonorrhœa, or those of women in childbirth, or of women who are in the condition of sin or under ritual penalty. But vows and offerings may be accepted from them. This is the rule: All that is vowed and freely offered is to be accepted from the givers; all that does not come through vow or freewill offering is not to be accepted from them. And so it is laid down according to Ezra, as it is said [*Ezra* 4, 3]: There is nothing in common between you and us in the building of a house to our God." The temple-tax was the privilege of the faithful alone, and to allow its payment by the Samaritans would have been an acknowledgment of their full rights in the community; it was essential to exclude them from any legal claim upon the privileges of Jerusalem.

But this exclusion from the payment of the temple-tax did not prohibit them from rendering the voluntary gifts of " vows " and " freewill offerings " (Nedarim, Nedabot), which were readily accepted from them even as from Gentiles, according to the Mishna above quoted. Also they could, like the Gentiles, present the tithes and priest's offering (Teruma), and make " dedications." (Kaddishin).[57] As

<hr>

[56] i, 5; *Mass. Kut.* 2.
[57] *Teruma,* iii, 9.

for tithes, they are said to offer them rightly.[58]   The contribution of tithes and the priest's offering may be understood as of Samaritans dwelling upon Jewish soil, where these taxes were regarded as civil taxes, levied on all land-owners alike.   In this connection we may also recall Josephus's note that down into his century the Samaritans frequented the temple feasts.[59]

Concerning the legitimacy of the tithes raised by the Samaritans in their own territory and applied to their own priesthood, contradiction exists in the Jewish regulations. According to *Masseket Kutim*, 9, " their produce is forbidden, as in the case of Gentiles," — i. e. it was not tithed, and was therefore forbidden to the Israelite.   This is illustrated by *Demai*, vii, 4, where there is a prescription for the proper tithing of wine purchased from the Samaritans.   But a Tosefta[60] holds that while merchandise in any place is uncertain (*demai*) as to its tithing, yet the produce brought in by the Samaritans is undisputed.   This opposition seems to be a contradiction between earlier and later views.   The latter would be the logical position of Judaism, as tithes applied to an outlaw clergy would not suit any strict sacerdotal theory. On the other hand, especially in earlier ages, when the Jews and the Samaritans were often closely intermingled on Palestinian soil, it may have been argued that the tithes having been rightly set aside, the food would not be affected by the actual destination of the tithes, while there are also patent practical reasons why a purchaser would not wish to pay a double tax.   Indeed in another case we find a letting down of rigorous barriers for expediency's sake; according to *Masseket Kutim*, 22, " the priests of Israel may share the tithes with Samaritan priests in the territory of the latter, because they are thus, as it were, rescuing the Samaritans

[58] *Berak*, 47b.
[59] See above, Chap. IX, note 9.
[60] *Tos. Demai*, 3, 3.

from their own priests." The same reason expressed in practical terms would be, " Half a loaf is better than none at all." But the same Halaka continues: " But not on Israelitish territory, lest the Samaritans should have a presumption on our priesthood." Naturally on Jewish soil the full tithes would be demanded for Jerusalem; it would be a private matter for alien residents if they sent a further tithe to Gerizim. It also appears from another dictum of *Masseket Kutim*, 23, that the intention in tithing, quite apart from the ultimate destination, was respected by Jewish law; an Israelite was forbidden to eat the food of a Samaritan priest, except when the latter was unclean, and so could not eat of the sacred offerings. The corollary is that the tithes and other sacerdotal dues of the Samaritans were taboo to the Jewish layman, i. e. they were proper tithes. This earlier attitude of Judaism helps to explain the Gospel narratives, in which the Jews appear as freely buying in the Samaritan markets. We thus see that Jewish sacerdotal principles were not drawn absolutely against the sect.

It is not difficult to understand a provision of *Masseket Kutim*, 5, which proceeds to apply to the Samaritans certain Talmudic inhibitions directed by the Talmud against the Gentiles:[61] " We do not give them possession of immovable property; we do not sell them sheep for shearing, nor crops that are to be harvested, nor standing timber; but we may sell them cattle for slaughter." It was the policy of the Jewish Church to prevent the alienation of any part of the Holy Land in its control, and to bar to others any shadow of a claim thereto; yet the application to the Samaritans was only slowly made.

There remain to be noted some miscellaneous variations in the observance of the Law for which the Talmud condemns the Samaritans. The most important of these is the practice of levirate marriage, *Dt.* 25, 5ff, in which point the sect had

[61] *Ab. Z.* i, 7; 20b.

certainly abandoned the letter of Moses. In modern times they understand by the brother a co-religionist who lives in the same house,[62] but in Talmudic days they appear to have explained the brother's widow as referring to the woman whose betrothed had died, not of the widowed wife. This aberration is announced as the chief ground for the excommunication of the Samaritans in the lengthy argument concerning them in *Kiddushin, 75a, seq.*: If the Samaritans be genuine converts, nevertheless they have been excluded because they practice Yibbam only with the betrothed.

In the matter of legal papers the Samaritans seem to have had a different, perhaps a simpler usage than the Jews, and so were excluded as witnesses; the exceptions were in the matter of divorce-writs and emancipation-papers. The relevant Mishna reads:[63] " Every legal paper which is subscribed to by a Samaritan witness is rejected, except papers of divorce and emancipation. There was a case which was brought before R. Gamaliel at Kefar-outhenai; he declared as valid a woman's divorce-paper, whose witnesses were Samaritans." The Gemara following contains a discussion over this precedent, whether it is lawful for all the witnesses to be Samaritans. Also *Masseket Kutim,* 14, admits their legal nicety in divorce by stating that " the Samaritan practices the Get, and may be trusted to bring a Get from a foreign city to an Israelite." This latter permission therefore classes the Samaritans with the Jews, as heathens and slaves were excluded from that function.[64] To be sure there were reasons of public utility in allowing the Samaritans to be witnesses in such necessary legal matters, just as the Roman government upon its outlawry of the Samaritans permitted

[62] See above, p. 43.
[63] *Gitt.* i, 5.
[64] For the reasons and the law on this general point, see Amram, *The Jewish Law of Divorce* 177 (Philadelphia, 1896). The Get is the divorce-writ.

them to act as witnesses so that the public business might not be impeded.[65]

Under this head may be included the charge that the Samaritans were not scrupulous in the matter of betrothal.[66] We may presume that the Samaritan form or use of the marriage contract, the Ketuba, was different from that of the Jews. The whole marriage law of the Jews, especially in respect to betrothal and marriage, was in so great a flux in the Talmudic age, that it is not strange if the Samaritans had variant usages. Further, these people, in company with Sadducees, Gentiles, slaves, women, children and apostates, are excluded from the preparation of Bible manuscripts, Tephillin and Mezuzot.[67] It is patent why they might not prepare copies of the Scriptures; as for the other articles, they, like the Sadducees, have never accepted the literal interpretation of *Dt*. 6, 8f.[68]

Finally, there remains one cardinal point of doctrine, already referred to, wherein the Samaritans differed from Pharisaism. The sect did not believe in the resurrection of the dead. The specific authorities on the Jewish side for this fact of early Samaritanism are *Siphre* to *Num*. 15, 31; *Sanhedrin*, 90b; *Masseket Kutim*, 28; it is also witnessed to by many Christian writers.[69]

But this last difference is one which distinguished not only Jew and Samaritan, but also within Judaism itself Pharisee and Sadducee. Moreover the difference is but one of several in which we find Sadducee and Samaritan agreeing as against the Pharisee. It is pertinent therefore to take up here the question of the agreements between the great conservative party of Judaism and the northern sect.[70]

[65] See above, p. 119.
[66] *Kidd*, 76a, which also condemns their conduct of divorce.
[67] *Menachot*, 42b.
[68] See above, p. 32.
[69] See below, p. 250. For the passage in *Siphre*, see Geiger, *op. cit*. 128.
[70] Cf. Nutt, *op. cit*. 31; Wreschner, *op. cit*. p. vii. The latter work

Both Sadducees and Samaritans denied the resurrection of the body, — not, it must be noted, the immortality of the soul.[71] It is not true, as alleged by Patristic writers, that the Sadducees, like the Samaritans, denied the later portions of the Canon;[72] but they appear to have assumed a depreciating position towards the later strata, which contain proofs for the resurrection of the dead, and it is to be noticed that Jesus in his argument with them appealed to a Pentateuchal passage. Both Sadducees and Samaritans clung to the literal interpretation of the Sabbath observance, denying the fiction of the Erub, and so invalidating it. Both agreed as against the Pharisees in the rigorous fulfillment of the law concerning the use of a carcase, *Lev.* 7, 24.[73] Neither believed in, and therefore were forbidden to prepare, Tephillin and Mezuzot.[74] In one point the Sadducees may have agreed with the Samaritans in annulling a doubtless Biblical prescription, that of the levirate marriage; at least this may appear from the sarcastic question put to Jesus concerning the future possession of the woman whom seven brothers took to wife, *Mt.* 22, 23ff.[75]

is concerned at length with the relations of Samaritans, Sadducees and Karaites. For elder literature, especially Geiger, see Wreschner, p. vii, note 4. I have not attempted to enter upon the recondite problem of the relation of the Samaritans and Karaites, which latter sect preserved or restored many elements of original Sadduceeism. Jewish scholars differ upon this point. Against Geiger, Wreschner would find Samaritanism largely dependent upon Karaitism; his arguments seem to be based mostly upon minute points of ritual. For a return to Geiger's position, see S. Rappoport, *La liturgie samaritaine.*

[71] For the Sadducees, e. g. *Sanh.* 90b; *Mt.* 22, 23ff.

[72] See Schürer, *GJV* ii, 411, who gives full quotations.

[73] For the Sadducæan use, e. g. *Chol.* 44b. The Samaritans required that the animal should have been slaughtered.

[74] See above, p. 186.

[75] This heresy was really not of much account. In the Mishnaic age the old law was largely abridged, and the Jewish lawyers confessed it to be more honored in the breach than the observance, *Bekorot,* i, 7. The question later arose, which was the more honorable, the assumption of such a marriage, or the suffering of the shameful rite of Chalisa. See Hamburger, *op. cit.* i, 928; Edersheim, *op. cit.* ii, 400. Modern Judaism has completely abrogated this survival of primitive marriage.

The Talmudic thought concerning the likeness of the Samaritans to the Sadducees is strikingly expressed in a Mishna:[76] "As for Sadducee women, when they undertake to walk in the ways of their fathers, then they are like the Samaritan women; if they separate themselves to walk in the way of Israel, then they are like Israelites. R. Jose said: They are always like women of Israel, until they separate themselves to walk in the way of their fathers." Thus is expressed for the Sadducees much the same accusation that was brought against the Samaritans, that their women are unclean from the cradle. And equally in both cases, no serious specification of uncleanliness is charged against either party; indeed the Sadducees stuck closer to the scriptural text in this matter than did the Pharisees.[77] But the above opinion must have been due to the Pharisaic desire to prevent social intercourse and especially *connubium* with the Sadducees, even as in like terms the Samaritans were ostracized. This close relationship of Sadducees and Samaritans in doctrine and practice, and the Pharisaic assignment of both to much the same category, arouse interesting questions concerning the historical connections that may once have existed between the two bodies. At all events we recognize that the Samaritans largely preserved more primitive beliefs and usages than the Pharisees, and so give valuable testimony to the character of early Judaism.[78]

We come now to the difficult question of the final drawing of proscriptive lines against the Samaritans, a process which began in the middle of the IId Century and which came to its rigorous conclusion about A. D. 300 with the complete excommunication of the sect. It has been held that the Hadri-

---

[76] *Nidda,* iv, 2.
[77] Gemara to above Mishna; cf. Hamburger, *op. cit.* ii, 1047.
[78] It should be noted that by the Mishnaic age the problems of the law concerning both Sadducees and Samaritans had become largely theoretical, and this condition only increased in. the subsequent centuries.

anic persecutions drove the Samaritans into the denial of
their faith, and that " the corruption of their ways " which
ensued compelled Judaism to outlaw them. On the other
hand the favor shown to the Samaritans by such influential
men as Akiba, Meir, and Simon b. Gamaliel, in the IId
Century has induced scholars to postulate for this age a
closer rapprochement between the two communities;[79] according to this view the Samaritans would have taken part
with the Jews in their rising against Rome. The subsequent
excommunication would then be a return to the earlier position. But I believe that the discussions of the IId Century
were not so much due to any historical events as to the logical working out of the principles of Pharisaism. After the
fall of Jerusalem, and still more after the destruction of the
political hopes of the Jews in Hadrian's reign, Pharisaism
won its final victory by being enabled to pursue its course
undisturbed. Judaism now became a close religious community. The worldly party of the Sadducees had disappeared. There was no room any longer for castes like the
Am-ha-areç. Proselytes, if any dared the terrors of the
imperial laws, became Jews wholly. The old discussions
about the different strata of the church still remained, but
these were largely theoretical, even as were the laws concerning sacrifice. Judaism came more and more to be centred in
Babylonia, and the problems of Palestinian soil were relieved. Hence with respect to the Samaritans, we find the
law drawing its logical conclusions; this schismatic sect
could no longer be tolerated. Some Jewish leaders like
Akiba may, on liberal political grounds, have favored the
Samaritans; but this tendency was suppressed by the fatal
result of Bar-Kokeba's insurrection, as a result of which even
that hero lost caste in later tradition.[80] Conservative lawyers, on principle like Meir, or from sluggishness like Simon

[79] E. g. Hamburger, *op. cit.* ii, 1069.
[80] He was known later as Bar-Koziba, the Deceiver.

b. Gamaliel, held by earlier precedents, or only slowly changed their minds. But this change of attitude developed very cautiously, and it is a wonder that so much law that is favorable to the Samaritans is preserved not only in the Mishna but also in the Gemara. That many earlier Halakot were excluded from the Talmud, being preserved in the Tosefta or deposited in *Masseket Kutim,* shows that while a severe criticism of the Samaritans had already set in by the IId Century, it was not able to enforce itself throughout.

We have noted above Akiba's liberal attitude toward the Samaritans; his opinion is given that " the Samaritans are genuine converts, and the priests with whom they are defiled are legal priests."[81] There is also a Mishna which relates the following anecdote:[82] "Again they said to him [R. Akiba]: R. Eliezer used to say: He who eats of a morsel of the Samaritans is like one who eats swine's flesh. He said to them: Be silent; I will not say to you what R. Eliezer said in this matter." This curt reply is an irritated denial of Eliezer's aspersion on the Samaritans.[83]

The position of R. Meir, the younger contemporary of Akiba is contradictorily given in the Talmudic discussions; according to some he held that the Samaritans were genuine converts, according to others that they were not.[84] But the composition of these two views is doubtless to be found in the postulation of a change of opinion on Meir's part. Thus it is stated in *Masseket Kutim,* 25, that " R. Meir said: All their wine is allowed except that which is open in the market." But the following Talmudic anecdote shows how the

[81] *Kidd.* 75b; cf. above, p. 177.
[82] *Shebiit,* viii, 10.
[83] Eliezer's position is much mitigated, if with Kirchheim (*Introductio,* 22; *Septem libri,* 35), on the authority of parallel passages (Gemara to *Sheb. Jer.* 19; *Tos. Pea,* 2) "leaven" is to be read in place of "morsel." The reference is then to the Samaritan lack of scrupulosity concerning leaven, not all foods.
[84] Cf. *Chol.* 6a and *B. Kam.* 38b.

same teacher came to change his opinion.[85] " R. Meir sent a disciple, R. Simon b. Eleazar, to buy wine of Samaritans. A certain old man met him, who said to him: Put a knife to thy throat, if thou art a man given to appetite [*Pr. 23, 2*]. R. Simon b. Gamaliel went and reported these words to R. Meir, and he uttered an opinion against the Samaritans." A similar anecdote is told of the much later R. Abbahu (*c.* 300), whose disciple being sent to buy Samaritan wine, was accosted by an old man with the words, " There are no keepers of the Law here! " In consequence RR. Ame and Assi persisted until they placed the Samaritans in the full status of Gentiles.[86] " The old man " of these anecdotes is a frequent figure in the Talmud; he is a sort of oracle, probably representing popular opinion, which was often accepted by the learned. The reason given for Meir's position is that " he took into consideration the possibility of the rarer cases," i. e. he laid a general embargo on the wine, although it might be unclean only in the minority of instances. This decision affected only exposed wine, and so the use of all Samaritan wine was not interdicted until a much later period. Meir's more rigorous opinion is also expressed in his judgment concerning the goring Samaritan ox,[87] and the prohibition of Samaritan circumcision of a Jew.[88] Juda ha-Nasi, the compiler of the Mishna, followed suit to this rigorism, and even gave vent to the dictum that " the Samaritans are like Gentiles," an opinion not in agreement with his great work.[89]

---

[85] *Chol.* 6a; cf. *Ab. Z. Jer.* 44d.

[86] *Chol.* 6a. For the law concerning Samaritan wine, see *Mass. Kut.* 25.

[87] See above, p. 175.

[88] *Ab. Z.* 26b, *seq.* (*Menach.* 42a). At least such is Hamburger's interpretation of this difficult passage, *op. cit.* ii, 1070. But according to *Mass. Kut.* 12, it is Meir who holds the liberal opinion against R. Juda. For Meir in general on this subject, see Hamburger, *l. c.,* and Appel, *op. cit.* 65.

[89] *Ketub. Jer.* 27a; *Berak. Jer.* 11b; *Demai Jer.* 25d.

These arguments concerning Samaritan wine are parallelled by the long discussion concerning the lawfulness of Samaritan slaughter in *Cholin,* 3b-6a. As we saw above,[90] the earlier view allowed the meat if the purchaser tested the good faith of the Samaritan vendor. But the question was taken up again in the school of the patriarch Gamaliel III. (*c.* 250), and the majority forbade Samaritan meat, for the same reason as that which influenced Meir in his treatment of wine. But a strong minority seems to have stood by the earlier tolerance; it is reported that R. Yochanan (*c.* 275), who is regarded by many as the founder of the Palestinian Talmud, and R. Assi (*c.* 300), who later excommunicated the Samaritans, ate their meat. It must be remembered that these discussions over the lawfulness of foods were of serious import, for their results affected the social relations of the two sects.

Such are the discussions and decisions of the Tannaim of the IId Century, and their followers in the IIId. The crisis resulted about the close of the latter century. The Talmud charges the Samaritans with having offered libations to heathen deities in Diocletian's reign.[91] In the same period, in connection with the anecdote concerning Abbahu and Samaritan wine, above narrated, RR. Ame and Assi did not cease their efforts until they had excommunicated the sect.[92] Of the same Abbahu, who at his home in Cæsarea must have had considerable intimacy with the Samaritans, an anecdote is told which closes the drama of excommunication with a touch of pathos. The Samaritans said to Abbahu: " Your fathers had intercourse with us; why do ye not do the same? " He said to them: " Your fathers did not corrupt their ways, but ye have corrupted your ways." [93]

[90] P. 172.
[91] *Ab. Z. Jer.* 44d.
[92] *Chol.* 6a.
[93] *Megilla,* 28a; cf. *Ab. Z. Jer.* 44d. Taglicht, *op. cit.* 23, referring to *Ab. Z. Jer.* 44d, shows that the position of Abbahu was not as pro-

The Samaritans had not in matter of fact corrupted their ways, but the schism had hopelessly deepened, and Pharisaism proceeded to its logical verdict against the hated sect. It will be of interest to note here some further examples taken from Rabbinic literature of the Jewish attitude toward the Samaritans as exhibited in maxims and anecdotes. There are indeed some exceptions to the general story of mutual unkindness; thus R. Abaye lost an ass, and asked it back, and the Samaritans returned it out of respect for him.[94] But popular life and language were generally harsher than the law. The term " Samaritan " was a term of contempt, as it had been in Jesus' day; this is exemplified in the following saying : " It is the tradition : Whoever teaches Scripture and Mishna only and does not minister to the disciples of the wise men, him R. Eleazar holds for an Am-ha-areç, R. Samuel b. Nachmani for a Boor, R. Yannai for a Samaritan."[95] Again : " Three things make a man transgress against his own mind and the mind of God ; these are, an evil spirit, the Samaritans, and the rules of poverty."[96]

History recounts the constant feuds between the two sects, which seem to have been ever ready for mutual friction. A Mishna relates [97] how in former times fire-signals were used for conveying notice of the new-moon to Babylonia by way of the Mount of Olives, Mount Sartaba, Agruppina, and the Hauran, but that the Samaritans made mischief through in-

nounced as that of RR. Ame and Assi; that rabbi refused to follow certain deductions, whose corollary would be the prohibition of Samaritan wine and water.

[94] *Gitt.* 45a. The same passage contains a parallel story of R. Chasda, whose slave ran away to Samaritans, but the latter refused to return him, appealing to *Dt.* 23, 16.

[95] *Sota,* 22b. Cf. the saying of Jesus, *Mt.* 18, 17.

[96] At least this is the reading given by Lightfoot, *op. cit.* i, 600, for a dictum in *Erubin,* 41b. But I can find no authority for " Samaritans," in place of which all accessible texts read " Gentiles " or " Worshippers of Stars." Lightfoot's reading, however, is plausible.

[97] *Rosh ha-Shana,* ii, 2.

13

terfering by false signals, so that messengers had to be substituted. While we generally hear only of Samaritan violence, the Jews could retort in kind, as when in a certain year of Release they plundered a Samaritan market.[98] Numerous are the wordy debates which are narrated, often occurring at Shechem itself, through which the rabbis passed on their way to Jerusalem, and sometimes the bold stranger barely escaped with his life for aspersions on the Kuthite religion.[99]   The Samaritans retorted with the ugly epithet of Bet Kilkalta, Cursed House, for Jerusalem, while Gerizim was the House of God, the Blessed Mount (*tur berik*). The " stupid " Samaritans seem not always to have been equal to the sharp wit of their opponents. " R. Meir once asked a Samaritan what his origin was. He replied, From Joseph. Not so, Meir replied, but from Issachar, because it is written [*Gen.* 46, 13] : The sons of Issachar, Tola, Phuwa, Job, Shimron,— from whom the Samaritans are derived! The Samaritan went to the patriarch, and repeated the strange saying of Meir. By thy life, said the patriarch, he has counted thee out of Joseph, but has not advanced thee to descent from Issachar! "[100]

Finally, the excommunication of the Samaritans was thrown back by Haggadic lore into the authoritative age of Ezra and the Great Congregation :[101]   " Ezra, Zerubbabel and Joshua gathered together the whole congregation into the temple of the Lord, with 300 priests, 300 trumpets, 300 scrolls of the Law, and 300 children, and they blew the trumpets and the Levites were singing. And they anathematized, outlawed and excommunicated the Samaritans in the name of the Lord, by a writing written upon tablets,

[98] *Tos. Ohalot,* 18, 16. So Taglicht, p. 24, but Zuckermandel reads *Goyim.*
[99] *Bereshit Rabba,* cc. 81, 32, etc.
[100] *Bereshit R.* c. 94.
[101] *Tanchuma,* § *Wayyesheb,* 2 (Lublin, 1893 — not in Buber's edition) ; *Pirke R. Eliezer,* c. 38.

and with an anathema both of the Upper and Lower Court [i. e., of heaven and earth] as follows: Let no Israelite eat of one morsel of anything that is a Samaritan's; let no Samaritan become a proselyte, and allow them not to have part in the resurrection of the dead. And they sent this curse to all Israel that were in Babylon, who also themselves added their anathema."

The great Maimonides set his seal upon this verdict for later Judaism: "By reason of idolatry, separation from them was established, and their slaughter was prohibited." [102]

[102] Quoted by Taglicht, *op. cit.* 25. The Samaritans retorted by cursing Maimonides; *VJD* iv, 191.

CHAPTER XI.

THE TALMUDIC BOOKLET, MASSEKET KUTIM.

At the end of the IVth Seder, or Series, of the Babylonian Talmud, along with a number of extra-Talmudical tractates, are found the " Seven Jerusalemite Booklets," the sixth of which is entitled *Masseket Kutim*, i. e., *De Samaritanis*. The classic edition of these seven tractates is that of Raphael Kirchheim, *Septem libri Talmudici Hierosolymitani*, Frankfurt, 1851 (in Hebrew), edited from the MS. of Eliakim Carmoly, and provided with a sagacious commentary.[1] The sixth tractate is an interesting collection of dicta, some of which are found in the Talmudic literature, some of which are independent Boraitas, and some Talmudic opinions referring to the Gentiles, but now applied to the Samaritans.

The translation herewith appended is intended to afford an easy oversight of the strata of the treatise. In plain type are given such dicta as are not found in the Talmudic literature. Small capitals indicate identity with Talmudic passages; this type is used also where the exact wording of the source does not appear. In italics are given those Talmudic dicta which in their original meaning referred to the Gentiles alone; most of these come from *Aboda Zara*.

This critical discrimination offers an insight into the process of the Jewish legislation concerning the Samaritans. Most of the independent Halakot are favorable to them, e.g.

---

[1] An excellent English translation, with some notes, is given in Nutt, *Samaritan Targum*, p. 168. In general, see Hamburger, *REJud.* Supplementband, 95; Strack, *RE* xviii, 328, and *Einleitung in den Talmud*, 1900, p. 46; Schürer, *GJV* i, 137.

Nos. 1, 5, 8, 28, and so may be presumed to be discarded Boraitas. On the other hand, the Halakot which have been bodily applied to the Samaritans from the law concerning the Gentiles, testify to the later practical identification of the two classes.

The supplementary notes are to be credited almost entirely to the full apparatus of Kirchheim. Where he corrects the received text, I have indicated such corrections with quotation marks. I have further carefully digested the Halakot with the material given in the preceding Chapter. The numbering of the Halakot is my own.

MASSEKET KUTIM.

SECTION I.

1. The usages of the Samaritans are in part like those of the Gentiles, in part like those of Israel, but mostly like Israel.

2. WE DO NOT ACCEPT FROM THEM THE BIRD-OFFERINGS OF MEN OR WOMEN HAVING ISSUES, NOR THE BIRD-OFFERINGS OF WOMEN AFTER CHILD-BIRTH, NOR SIN-OFFERINGS OR GUILT-OFFERINGS. BUT WE ACCEPT FROM THEM " VOWS AND FREEWILL-OFFERINGS."
Shek. i, 5. The quoted words are restored from the Mishna. See above, p. 182. Cf. *Lev.* 12; 15.

3. *We do not give them possession of immovable property, we do not sell them sheep for shearing, or crops that are to be harvested, or standing timber; but we may sell them " cattle " for slaughter.*
The first clause is from the Mishna, *Ab. Z.* i, 7, those following are the gist of the discussion in the Gemara, 20b. See above, p. 184.

4. *We do not sell them large cattle, even if they are maimed, nor ass-foals, nor calves; but we may*

*sell them that which is maimed so it cannot be
healed.*

Ab. Z. i, 5. This Mishna is directed against the unnatural
crimes charged to the Gentiles, of which the discussion in the
Gemara, 15b, fully acquits the Samaritans. The transference
of this prohibition to the Samaritans is contradicted in 15b,
where it is forbidden to sell only a maimed beast to the Samaritans.

5. WE DO NOT SELL THEM WEAPONS, NOR ANYTHING
   THAT CAN DO DAMAGE TO PEOPLE.

   Ab. Z. i, 5, applied in 15b to the Samaritans because they
   might sell to the Gentiles. The same rule includes all Jews
   who might make misuse of weapons. See above, p. 174.

6. We do not give them wives, NOR DO WE TAKE WIVES
   FROM THEM.

   Kidd. 75a. See above, p. 179.

7. But we (do not?) lend or borrow on usury with them.

   The text places the Samaritans on the same footing with
   Gentiles. But Kirchheim, following Geiger, argues that "not"
   should be inserted, referring to the exception made against the
   Samaritans of Cæsarea, with whom, because of their perversion, the laws of usury obtained; *Ab. Z. Jer.* 44d. N. B. the
   adversative "but." See above, p. 174.

8. We give them the gleanings and the forgotten sheaf
   and the corner of the field; and they have the custom
   of the forgotten sheaf and the corner, and so may be
   relied upon concerning the gleanings and the forgotten sheaf and the corner in the proper time, and
   also concerning the tithe for the poor in its year.

   Cf. *Lev.* 23, 22: *Dt.* 24, 19: 26, 12. The "reliability" of the
   Samaritans was of importance, because the gleanings were not
   tithable. Hence *Tosefta Pea,* 4, 1, has it: "The poor of the
   Samaritans are like the poor of Israel."

9. But their produce is forbidden as untithed, as in the
   case of the Gentiles.

   For the contradiction of this dictum with *Tos. Demai,* 3, 3,
   see above, p. 183.

10. They invalidate the Erub even as the Gentiles.

    See above, pp. 170, 187.

11. *A Jewess may not deliver a Samaritaness, nor suckle her son; but a Samaritaness may deliver a Jewess and suckle her son in her* [the Jewish woman's] *quarters.*

   Ab. Z. ii, 2. As Kirchheim's note shows, the application of this prohibition to the Samaritans brings the Jewish commentators much trouble, because not only was private intercourse with the Samaritans allowed, but also *Tos. Ab. Z.* 3, 1, contains just the opposite dictum. See above, p. 174.

12. AN ISRAELITE MAY CIRCUMCISE A SAMARITAN, AND A SAMARITAN AN ISRAELITE. R. JUDA SAYS: A SAMARITAN IS NOT TO CIRCUMCISE AN ISRAELITE BECAUSE HE CIRCUMCISES HIM IN NOTHING ELSE THAN THE NAME OF MOUNT GERIZIM.

   Ab. Z. 26b–27a. For this vexed question see above, pp. 170, 191.

13. WE MAY LODGE A BEAST IN A SAMARITAN INN, OR HIRE A SAMARITAN TO GO BEHIND OUR CATTLE, OR HAND OVER OUR CATTLE TO A SAMARITAN HERDSMAN. WE COMMIT A BOY TO A SAMARITAN TO TEACH HIM A TRADE. WE ASSOCIATE and converse WITH THEM ANYWHERE, which is not the case with the Gentiles.

   Ab. Z. 15b. See above, p. 174. Kirchheim approves a suggestion that for *mesapperim,* "converse," "*mishtapperim,*" "have one's hair cut," should be read, comparing *Ab. Z. Jer.* 7b: "An Israelite who has his hair cut by a Gentile must look in a mirror, but if by a Samaritan he need not look into a mirror." The innuendo of the precaution is to the effect that the barber may cut his throat!

14. A Samaritan suffers the Chalisa from his sister-in-law, and gives a divorce-writ to his wife. He may be relied upon to bring a divorce-writ from a foreign city to an Israelite.

   See above, pp. 173, 185.

15. These are the things we may not sell them: carcasses not ritually slaughtered, or animals with organic dis-

ease; unclean animals and reptiles; the abortion of an
animal; oil into which a mouse has fallen; an animal
that is mortally ill, " or a fœtus," although Israelites
eat them both, lest the sale lead them into error.
And as we do not sell these things to them, so we do
not buy them from them, as it is written [*Dt.* 14,
21]: For thou shalt be a holy people to the Lord
thy God. As thou art holy, thou shalt not make another people holier than thyself.

Kirchheim reads for the unintelligible *shemen* שנמופו, *shemen shel seripha, i. e.,* the (holy) illuminating oil, which if defiled could be used by the Jews (*Teruma*, xi, 10), though apparently not by the Samaritans. For the principle at the end,
cf. *Pesachim*, 50b–51a: "As for things which are allowed but
which are prohibited by others, thou mayest not permit them
in the presence of such people." In this passage the Samaritans
are adduced as an example, the reason given for their scrupulosity being that "they confound one thing with another"; see
the correct reading in Jastrow, *Dictionary*, 1028a.

16. A SAMARITAN MAY BE RELIED UPON TO SAY WHETHER
OR NOT THERE IS A TOMB [in a field], OR WHETHER
AN ANIMAL HAS HAD ITS FIRSTBORN OR NOT. THE
SAMARITAN IS TO BE RELIED UPON concerning a tree
whether it is four years old or is still unclean, and
CONCERNING GRAVESTONES, BUT NOT WITH REGARD
TO THE CLEANLINESS OF OVERHANGING BOUGHS OR
PROTRUDING BOUGHS; nor concerning the land of
Gentiles, NOR CONCERNING THE BET-PERAS, BECAUSE
THEY ARE OPEN TO SUSPICION IN ALL THESE THINGS.
THIS IS THE PRINCIPLE: THEY ARE NOT TO BE BE-
LIEVED IN ANY MATTER IN WHICH THEY ARE OPEN
TO SUSPICION.

See *Nidda*, vii, 4, and the Gemara following, 57a. For the
uncircumcised tree, cf. *Lev.* 19, 23. "Overhanging boughs," etc.,
make precincts that can harbor uncleanliness. Bet-peras is an
area of land rendered unclean by the presence of bones.

Section II.

17. We do not buy meat from a Samaritan except that of which he himself eats, nor strings of birds unless he first puts them into his mouth. We do not buy offhand what he would give to Israelites, for they have been suspected of giving Israelites flesh of ritually unclean carcasses.
Chol. 3b *seq.* See above, p. 172.

18. The Samaritan is on the same footing with the Israelite in respect to all damages laid down in the law. The Israelite who slays a Samaritan, or a Samaritan who slays an Israelite, if unintentionally, is to go into exile [i. e., to a city of refuge]; if intentionally, he is to be slain.
Makkot, ii, 4, reads: " Everyone is to go to a city of refuge for slaying an Israelite, and an Israelite is to go to a city of refuge for slaying anyone. The alien resident (Ger-toshab) is excepted; he does not go to a city of refuge except for slaying an alien resident." A following Boraita, 8b, has it that " a slave or a Gentile goes to a city of refuge or receives lashes on account of an Israelite, and an Israelite the same on account of a Gentile or slave." But with Kirchheim, for " Gentile " in this Boraita should be read " Samaritan," inasmuch as the Mishna and its Gemara treat the Gentile separately under the head of the Ger-toshab.

19. If the ox of an Israelite gore the ox of a Samaritan, it goes free. But in the case of the ox of a Samaritan, if it is its first offence, it is to pay half the damage; if a subsequent offence, the full damage. R. Meir says: The ox of a Samaritan which gores the ox of an Israelite, whether it be the first offence or the second, is to pay the full damage and at the highest appraisement.
B. Kamma, 38b; see above, p. 175.

20. Their cheeses are allowed. R. Simon b. Eleazar says: To wit, the cheeses of householders, but those of dealers are forbidden.

For "dealers" Kirchheim would read, on the strength of his MS, "villagers," *kepharim.*

21. THEIR POTS AND PRESSES IN WHICH THEY ARE ACCUSTOMED TO MAKE WINE AND VINEGAR ARE FORBIDDEN. This law applies to the Gentiles in *Ab. Z.* ii, 6. But *Ab. Z. Jer.* 44d, expands it so as to include the Samaritans: "The cooked foods of the Samaritans are allowed. This law he (R. Eleazar) announced concerning a food which they do not prepare with wine or vinegar."

22. The priests of Israel may share the priestly dues with the Samaritan priests in the territory of the latter, because they are thus, as it were, rescuing the Samaritans from their priests; but not on Israelite territory, lest they should have a presumption on our priesthood.

See above, p. 183.

23. If a Samaritan priest, when he is unclean, eats and gives of his food to an Israelite, it is permitted; if he is clean, the Israelite is forbidden to eat of his food.

See above, p. 184.

24. WE DO NOT BUY " BREAD " FROM A SAMARITAN BAKER AT THE END OF THE PASSOVER UNTIL AFTER THREE BAKINGS, NOR FROM HOUSEHOLDERS UNTIL AFTER THREE SABBATHS, NOR FROM VILLAGERS UNTIL AFTER THREE MAKINGS. When does this apply? When they have not celebrated the Feast of Unleaven at the same time with Israel, or have anticipated it by a day; but if they celebrate the feast with Israel, or are a day later, their leaven is permitted. R. Simon forbids it [in general], because they do not know how to observe the feast like Israel.

Kirchheim compares *Tos. Pesach.* 2, and *Orla Jer. sub.,* ii, 6, which, with other variations, read "leaven." For the Samaritan observance of the laws of leaven, see above, p. 171. Observe that the restrictions announced here against Samaritan leaven are dependent upon the variation of the Samaritan calendar from the Jewish.

25. FORMERLY THEY SAID: THE WINE OF KADOR IS FORBIDDEN BECAUSE OF [the proximity of] KEPHAR PANSHA. THIS THEY CHANGED TO THE EFFECT THAT WHEREVER THE PEOPLE ARE SUSPECTED OF MINGLING WITH THE GENTILES, WINE THAT IS OPEN IS FORBIDDEN, THAT WHICH IS SEALED IS ALLOWED. R. Meir said: All their wine is allowed except that which is open, if it is in the market. BUT THE WISE MEN SAID: THAT WHICH IS OPEN IN ANY PLACE IS PROHIBITED, THAT WHICH IS SEALED IS ALLOWED; THAT WHICH IS BORED INTO AND THEN SEALED IS AS THOUGH SEALED.

Ab. Z. 31b; *Ab Zar. Jer.* 44d. (For the places see Chapter VIII, § 1.) The opinion of R. Meir is in contradiction of that assigned to him in *Chol.* 6a. See for the general subject and the ambiguity of Meir's position, p. 190.

26. *Their jars if new are permitted, if old are prohibited.*
Ab. Z. ii, 4; 33a.

27. Why are the Samaritans forbidden to marry into Israel? Because they are mingled with the priests of the high places. R. Ishmael said: They were genuine converts at first. WHEREFORE WERE THEY FORBIDDEN? BECAUSE OF THEIR BASTARDS, AND BECAUSE THEY DO NOT MARRY THE BROTHER'S WIDOW.

Kidd. 75b, where Ishmael appears only with the opinion that the Samaritans are lion-converts. See above, p. 176.

28. When shall we take them back? When they renounce Mount Gerizim, and confess Jerusalem and the resurrection of the dead. From this time forth he that robs a Samaritan shall be as he who robs an Israelite.

For the Jewish condemnation of Samaritan eschatology, see above, p. 186.

CHAPTER XII.

THE THEOLOGY OF THE SAMARITANS.[1]

§ 1. INTRODUCTORY.

It is proposed in the present Chapter to give a digest of the Samaritan theology. Such a presentation is exposed to the scientific criticism that it avoids the historical processes of the development of doctrines. But the writer would meet this criticism by his intention to note carefully the more important changes in the theology, while withal he submits that to do full chronological justice to the subject a whole volume based upon many exhaustive investigations would be required. However, he has reached the opinion that Samaritanism had practically attained its ripeness by the IVth Century A. C., when, in the teachings of its great theologian Marka, all the elements of its doctrine are found at hand. Karaitism may subsequently have influenced practice, and Islam has largely affected theological expression, while it cast the doctrine of God into a more Deistic mould and affected especially the eschatology. But in general we are not doing violence to historic method in regarding Samaritan theology from its first literary monuments in the

---

[1] For the literature, besides the works of the earlier scholars, as Reland and Cellarius (consult Bibliography), see especially Gesenius, *De Samaritanorum theologia;* de Sacy in the introduction to his edition of the Epistles in *N. et É.;* Petermann, *Reisen im Orient,* i, 269; *RE* ed. 1, s. v. *Samaritaner;* Kautzsch in the 2d and 3d editions of the same; Heidenheim, in introductions to his *Bibliotheca Samaritana,* and numerous articles in *DVJ;* Nutt, *Samaritan Targum;* Hamburger, in *REJud.* ii, *s. v. Samaritaner;* Cowley, *Some Remarks on Samaritan Literature and Religion, JQR* viii, 562.

IVth Century down to our own time as a whole which may be systematically digested.

Also we can, from external if not sure internal evidence, trace Samaritan doctrine farther back than the IVth Century. The Jewish notices of the sect, which have been studied in the three preceding Chapters, throw invaluable light upon its theology. So far as we can learn from these extraneous sources the general outlines of Samaritanism were already fixed in the Ist and IId Centuries. Therefore while we possess, apart from the Pentateuch and some few Hellenistic fragments, no literature that can be surely assigned to an earlier date than Marka, we must infer that the greater part of the theology as we have it is the precipitate of the age at or before the beginning of the Christian era. The chief exception would lie in eschatology. And if the contention, now generally accepted even by Jewish scholars be correct, that the Samaritans are but a Jewish sect, then we must hold that their theology has developed in a straight and consistent course ever since the schism from Judaism. This development has gone along on the whole *pari passu* with the theology of the latter religion. No intellectual independence is to be found in our sect; it was content to draw its teachings and stimulus from the Jews, even long after the rupture was final. Nevertheless, it possessed a certain patriotic hardiness which enabled it to preserve its own characteristic, and in many cases to maintain the elder and more conservative position as against progressive Pharisaism. And that Samaritanism is a witness to earlier phases of Jewish thought than later Jewish orthodoxy is evident in several points, but most of all in the eschatology. While the doctrine of this department is voiced in liturgical pieces which may all or in large part date from the Islamic period, nevertheless in great part it represents the fluctuating eschatological notions which were in the air in the centuries just before and after the beginning of our era. Our subject therefore takes us back to the original womb of Judaism from which the sect sprang.

To make a rough historic division of Samaritan theology, we may divide it into the age before Marka (the IVth Century), and that subsequent to him. The latter again may be subdivided by the point where Islamic influences begin to evince themselves; this epoch may be dated about the end of the Ist Millennium.[2] With Marka and his age, celebrated in the traditions concerning Baba Rabba, we have evidence of a positive intellectual development of theology. There is the sudden appearance of extensive Haggadic literature, while a certain manifestation of Rabbinism comes to the front, testified to by Baba Rabba's appointment of lay doctors to the despite of the priests. This development is the reflex of the processes in Judaism which were finding immortal expression in Talmud and Haggada. The influence of Islam does not, as already observed, contribute much materially to Samaritan theology, but nevertheless it gives a turning-point which is valuable at least for purposes of chronology.

In the following exposition I have made use chiefly of the Samaritan Epistles to European scholars, and of the Liturgy. In any sect it is the prayers and hymns which most truly represent its actual religion. The later works, the theological treatises and commentaries, do not add much to the general knowledge of our subject. With reference to the subsequent development of theology, it may be said that the bloom of Haggadic thought which is most exuberant in Marka does not maintain its hold on the sect. The Samaritans fell back into the prosaic type characteristic of them, so that their theology has become a hard and dry product with little imagination and spiritual afflatus. I trust the full apparatus of references will give credence to my statements and also that they may be of use to scholarly readers.

[2] See Chapter XIV on the literature of the Samaritans.

§ 2. THE SAMARITAN CREED.

WE SAY: MY FAITH IS IN THEE, YHWH; AND IN MOSES SON OF AMRAM, THY SERVANT; AND IN THE HOLY LAW; AND IN MOUNT GERIZIM BETH-EL; AND IN THE DAY OF VENGEANCE AND RECOMPENSE.[3] Such is the Samaritan confession of faith, constantly appearing in the literature. It takes its place alongside of the Christian Creed, and of Islam's confession, "There is no God but God, and Mohammed is his prophet." The statement is parallel to the latter religion's six articles of faith, which consist in belief in God, in his angels, his scriptures, his prophets, the resurrection and Day of Judgment, and in God's absolute decree.[4] The first three points of the Samaritan creed are identical with the cardinal beliefs of Judaism, while the fourth is the cause of schism between the two communities. These first four points sometimes appear by themselves,[5] the fifth article concerning the Latter Things being a later addition to the Samaritan theology. In the discussion of our theme we cannot do better than follow the formal scheme of this creed.

§ 3. THE BELIEF IN GOD; ANGELS, CREATION, ETC.

(1.) THE ONE GOD.

The doctrine of the oneness, the uniqueness, and the spirituality of God is the supreme theme of Samaritan theology, and he is the sole object of all worship. The character of the Samaritan notion of God may be appreciated from the following passage of a hymn:[6]

---

[3] *Ep. to the Brethren in England,* 1672, *N. et E.* 173 (tr. 181) ; 1 *Ep. to Ludolf,* Ludolf, *Ep. Sam.* 8; *Epistle of Mashalma, DVJ* i, 100; *BS* ii, No. xxiv.
[4] Sale, *Koran, Prelim. Disc.* § 4.
[5] *BS* ii, No. xl; *N. et E.* 179, 223.
[6] Gesenius, *CS* 100.

There is nothing like him or as he is;
There is neither likeness nor body.
None knows who he is but he himself,
None is his creator or his fellow.
He fills the whole world,
Yet there is no chancing upon him.
He appears from every side and quarter,
But no place contains him.
Hidden yet withal manifest, he sees
And knows everything hidden.
Hidden nor appearing to sight,
Nothing is before him and after him nothing.

The doctrine of the unity of God is based upon the formula of the Shema, " Hear, O Israel, Yhwh thy God is one Yhwh,"[7] but it is generally expressed in the terms of Islam, " There is no God but God." This is the beginning and end, the constant refrain of all piety. The doctrine appears aggressively in the polemic against the Christian belief in distinctions within the Godhead, and Gnostic ideas of emanation. The polemic is constantly expressed in such language as the following: " O Being of unity, who hast no fellow, no second, nor colleague." The last term, *shateph* corresponds to the Arabic *sharik,* which with its collateral forms is frequently used in the Koran in the prohibitions against " associating " anything with God.[8] In another hymn the opening stanzas evidently antagonize Christian Trinitarianism:[9] " God is the one without plurality, the first before all that was made in plurality, the Head so that naught arose from plurality. He is found for what he is, another comes not in the count. There is no place sufficient

[7] There is evidence of the use of the Shema, *BS* ii, 191, bott.
[8] *CS* No. ii, 10. *Shoteph* is used in Talmudic literature in like way. The Arabic equivalent appears in *Lib. Jos.*
[9] *BS* ii, No. xxiii.

for him that plurality may be comprehended therein. He is YHWH, and is not to be inwardly distinguished (יִמְדֹד).
. . . There is known no second who has wrought with him. . . . He has no instruments and no hands, no equal and hypostatization (מֶדָּה). "

The latter term is evidently the hypostatized Midda, or Attribute, of Jewish Gnosticism. The Samaritan literature is fairly free of such Gnostic notions; however Marka made extensive excursions in that direction, while there are later echoes of his language. Thus Marka represents God's Grace and Goodness as standing at the right and left of Moses.[10] The idea of the Glory, Kabod, of God, does appear constantly as a hypostatization, especially in connection with the theophany on Sinai. It is identified by Marka with the Angel which was to lead Israel through the desert.[11] This notion of the Kabod comes from primitive Judaism, appearing first in Ezekiel.[12] There is also constant reference to the Shekina, or manifest Residing of God over Gerizim; this has been withdrawn from mortal eye during the Age of Disfavor.[13] The Word of YHWH appears a few times in the Samaritan Pentateuch after the example of the Jewish Targum, e. g. *Num.* 22, 20; 23, 4, 5, 16; but the hypostatized Memra appears scantily or never in the literature. God is said to have spoken and created by his Word, but it is especially taught that this Word has no existence by itself. There is no development of a Logos-doctrine. An echo of Jewish Wisdom literature is found when it is said that " God created the heavens by his wisdom,"[14] but no further development of this notion appears.

[10] *Marka,* 15a.
[11] *BS* iii, 101.
[12] *Eze.* 1, *seq.;* Weber, *Jüdische Theologie,* 161.
[13] *BS* ii, 124, bott.; *N. et E.* 212.
[14] *BS* ii, No. xiv, Beth. Cf. *Prov.* 3, 19.

14

The Spirit of God receives scant attention, the references to it being based almost entirely on *Num.* 11, 28ff.[15] We thus find some interesting points of connection with early Jewish Gnosticism, but withal little positive development in the way of hypostatization; Marka's trend, doubtless dependent upon incipient Kabbalism, was not pursued by the unimaginative Samaritan mind, which was influenced much more by the hard Deism of Islam. Despite the traditions and opinions concerning Simon Magus, there is little to show that Samaritanism was ever Gnostically minded.[16] Later theology, as we have noticed, denied all hypostatization, while even such Scriptural passages as suggested this notion were often emended. Thus the four places in the Pentateuch where *Elohim,* God, is construed with a plural verb are corrected in the Samaritan to the singular number: *Gen.* 20, 13; 31, 53; 35, 7; *Ex.* 22, 9. The rendering of " the Sons of God " in the Targum of *Gen.* 6, 4 follows the Targum Onkelos in offering " sons of rulers." In *Gen.* 48, 16 of the Samaritan Hebrew, *Mal'ak,* the Angel, is turned into Melek, the King, so as to give all glory to God.

God's essence is pure spirit. Contrary to much Old Testament phraseology, and especially to apocalyptic Judaism, which located God in the highest,— the third or seventh heaven,— the Samaritan generally can find no local place for him. This spiritual notion receives noble expression in a verse published by Gesenius:[17] " The abode which I shall have is the place of thy power; no ocean is there, nor sea [cf. *Rev.* 21,1], nor the very heavens themselves." In his relation to creation, God " fills the world."[18] Most particularly does the Samaritan theology dwell upon the

[15] E.g. *BS* ii, 116; No. xcviii, stanzas, ii, iii. In *Marka,* 38a, the Holy Spirit is classed with the Cloud and Fire, but in 73a the Glory takes its place.
[16] See Chap. XIII, § 2.
[17] *CS* iii, 13.
[18] *Ibid.* iv, 5. But according to a hymn, quoted by Heidenheim, *DVJ* iv, 549, God built his temple in the highest heaven.

incorporeality and impassibility of God, surpassing Judaism in this respect. The earliest evidence of this tendency is the Samaritan Pentateuch with its Targum, which latter exceeds even the Jewish Targumists in the avoidance of original anthropomorphisms. A comparison of the Samaritan Targum with both Onkelos and the Greek in the *locus classicus, Ex.* 24, 10f, shows how far the former went in this direction. In v. 10 by a slight textual change the seeing of God becomes "they feared God," and in v. 11 the having the vision of God becomes " they were assembled with God." This quite outdoes Onkelos, who has it that " they saw God's glory," and the Greek, " they saw the place where God was." This anti-anthropomorphic tendency is carried to a still greater extreme in Abu Said's Arabic translation, in which some 600 cases of such revision are found.[19]

But in the extra-Biblical literature this trend of doctrine becomes absolute. It is continuously taught that God perceives and acts without the aid of parts or senses. " He sees with the eye of wisdom, but he sees not with eyes; seeing what is in the world, seeing but he sees not."[20] And so he hears without ears,[21] he made and sustains the world without a hand.[22] He speaks without mouth or voice, and there is no more body to the utterance than in the line of writing which may be rubbed off a tablet.[23] Even the mystic " Be " of creation is uttered without a word. He suffered no toil in his work of creation, for " he worked without fatigue and rested without weariness."[24] This has reference to the divine Sabbath, and is of course good Jewish doctrine since Philo. Finally " he never grows old for

---

[19] Gesenius, *De Pentateuchi Samaritani origine*, 59. Further for the Targumic use, see Kohn, *Zur Sprache*, etc., 179.
[20] *BS* ii, No. xvii, st. 1.
[21] *Ibid*. No. xxii, st. 2.
[22] *CS* ii, 9.
[23] *Ibid*. ii, 5; 7.
[24] Petermann, *Gramm. Sam. App.* 23; *CS* i, 6.

he has no want.[25]   The one standing exception to this rule is the constant reference to the writing of the Tables of the Law by the finger of God; here the effective anthropomorphism of Scripture and the reverence for the Law are too strong for the otherwise spiritualizing Samaritan theology.

In respect to God's moral nature, he is absolutely holy and pure and righteous; the latter quality is especially taught in connection with the doctrine of the Day of Judgment, which shall be a time of awful apprehensions on the part of saints as well as of sinners.   But the quality that receives the crowning emphasis is that of God's love to his people; he appears pre-eminently as the Gracious and Merciful God, in terms taken from *Ex.* 34, 6ff, and after the fashion of the standing title in the opening of the Suras of the Koran. To give one example of this characterization of God, he is " the treasury of love." [26]   It is pathetic to observe how in its litanies and hymns the petty, persecuted sect has cherished its faith in the mercy of God, a love which seemed the more intense because of its limitation to that small community; it is marvellous how that wretched people has clung so passionately to this faith, which history has but little confirmed.

On the other hand, quite in line with the severe avoidance of everything approaching anthropomorphism, the doctrine of the Fatherhood of God, which was first developed in Judaism and later made the cornerstone of religion by Jesus, is ignored and even contradicted by the Samaritan faith.   God appears as Father only in the few passages of the Pentateuch where his paternity for Israel is asserted,

---

[25] *BS* ii, No. xxii, st. 2. *Per contra,* "the Ancient of Days," *Dan.* 7, 13, and the current Kabbalistic terms, "the Ancient," "the Most Hoary"; see Hamburger, *REJud.* ii. s. v. *Kabbala.* The expression, "the Ancient," however, appears in a XIVth Century Midrash, *DVJ* iv, 209.

[26] *BS* ii, 174, v. 5.

e.g., *Ex.* 4, 22. In this matter Samaritanism adheres to the
elder Sadducæan theology, a stage which was overcome by
the more intense personal religion of the Pharisees. Under
the influence of Islam this tendency went still farther to the
extreme. Abu Said paraphrases all such Biblical passages;
for example in the one just cited he translates " my first-
born son " as " my own people."[27]

As for the divine names, God is generally expressed by
El, Ela, the Biblical Elohim appearing more rarely, as a
rule for the sake of rhyme,— either through Islamic influence or from caution against its plural significance. But
the great name of revelation, YHWH, appears constantly
throughout the literature, without any trace of that fear at
even the writing of it which characterizes Judaism. The
pronunciation of the name has come to be avoided by utter-
ing in its stead שמא (pronounced Shémma), " the Name,"
corresponding to the Jewish use of השם, e. g., *Lev.* 24,
11.[28] Yet the pronunciation itself has survived in
Samaritanism, whereas long lost in the Jewish Church.[29]
It appears from the Liturgy that the name was still used in
the priestly blessing till a late date.[30] As is well known,
Theodoret, of the Vth Century, gives the Samaritan pronunciation as Ἰαβε, or Ἰαβαι.[31] In another place I have
shown that the tradition of the right pronunciation has survived amongst the Samaritans to our own day, namely as
Yahwa.[32]

As for the Jews so also for the Samaritans, YHWH is
the grand mystery of revelation, and the revelation of mys-

[27] See Gesenius, *Pent. Sam.* 59, n. 202.
[28] This fact gave rise to Aben Ezra's statement (Introduction to
Commentary on Esther) that the Samaritans taught that Ashima
(2 *Ki.* 17, 30) made the world.
[29] According to tradition, since the days of the highpriest Simon the
Just, *Yoma,* 39b.
[30] *BS* ii, 117, v. 26.
[31] *Quæst. in Exodum,* xv (ed. Migne, lxxx, 244) : Ἰαβε; *Hæreticarum
fabularum compendium,* v, 3 (Migne, lxxxiii, 460) : Ἰαβαι.
[32] *Notes from the Samaritan, JBL* 1906, p. 49.

tery, the clue to all the secrets of God. It is the great, the glorious, the hidden Name,[33] and there has been no day like that on which it was revealed to Moses.[34] It becomes then the duty of the illuminated to penetrate the mystery of the Name, which is accordingly subjected to processes of Gematria.[35] However, there is no attempt to make any magical use of the formula, such as appears in certain phases of Judaism.[36]

Of the other Biblical names, Adonai and Shaddai are in frequent use. But especially favorite is the employment of the " I am that I am," or simply, " I am." With this may be compared the use of the same phrases in the Kabbala; however, the Samaritans do not appear to have indulged in the developed Gnostic and metaphysical interpretations found in the Kabbalistic literature.

The frigid monotheism of the Samaritan theology is relieved and enriched by an exceedingly large vocabulary of epithets describing the uniqueness of God. In his nature he is the absolutely Existent, the First, and the Endless, and the Unlimited, the One before the world and the creatures. He is the infinite God, and Tohu-wa-Bohu (*Gen.* 1, 2), i. e., the original essence or source of all things, by which idea the Samaritan doctrine overcame the notion, latent in the Scriptural verse, of the independent existence of matter; elsewhere he is also called the Creator of Tohu-wa-Bohu. He is frequently termed the Root, as the origin of all. He is Creator, King, King of kings, King of the worlds; God of gods, and Lord of lords; King of our spirits, God of the spirits. He is Might, the Mighty One—an exceedingly frequent epithet; he is Great, Strong, Able, Enduring; Victor, Redeemer, the Rock and Stone of Israel, the Living One and the Wise. But the epithets manipulated by Sa-

[33] *E.g. BS* ii, p. 57, v. 4; No. xvi, Beth; p. 117 v. 26.
[34] *BS* ii, No. xvii, st. 1.
[35] *E.g. ibid.*
[36] See Dalman, *Der Gottesname Adonai,* 49.

maritan piety would be more than tiresome in their full enumeration; it may suffice to refer the curious to two Hymns published by Heidenheim, each consisting of twenty-two verses, in alphabetic acrostic, and each verse containing four epithets beginning with the cue-letter of the verse.[37]

The Existent One, קעימה, a most constant epithet. Heidenheim, *BS* ii, p. xxxvii, would find in this expression the influence of Simon Magus, who called himself ἑστώς, the Standing One, which equals the Hebrew word, a participle of קום· But the term appears of God in Philo, e. g. *De nom. mut.* 1052, and rather bears witness to the influence of Hellenism upon the Samaritan theology. The same adjective is also used of the finite creation as that which "is."— The First, קמאי; Endless, בלא סוף; Limitless, דלא לו תחום· — Before the world, the creatures, קמי עלמה, קמאי בריות· — The Infinite God, אל אפס, *BS* ii, p. 208, v. 15,=ὁ ἀπέραντος. Cf. the Kabbalistic אין, nonexistence, the Greek τὸ μὴ ὄν. But the Samaritans did not go as far as the Kabbala in attempting to express the Absolute One, and confined themselves to Scriptural language.— Tohu wa-Bohu, *BS* ii, p. 21, v. 22. Creator of Tohu wa-Bohu, *Marka,* 23b.—The Root, עיקר, אקר, e. g. *BS* ii, 208, v. 15; *Marka,* 6b, to which see Heidenheim's note. The Simonians spoke of God as ῥίζωμα τῶν ὅλων.— — God of Gods, Lord of Lords, *Lib. Jos.* xxix; cf. 1 *Tim.* 6, 15; *Rev.* 17, 14. Also Judge of Gods, *CS* v, 4; cf. *Ps.* 82.—King, God of the Spirits, *CS* iv, 13; *BS* ii. p. 212, v. 12; cf. *Nu.* 16, 22; *Enoch,* 39, 12.—The Might, חילה; cf. *Mk.* 14, 62; *Vita Adami,* 28; *Acts,* 8, 10, where Simon Magus uses it of himself. Cf. Bousset, *Religion des Judenthums,* 310.— The Mighty One, etc., גדול, חיולה, יכולה, גבור· —Victor, נצועה, Redeemer, גאל· —God also appears, in agreement with Rabbinic use, as אלה, מעונה, *BS* ii, No. lxx, 11; cf. אל מעון הקודש, *ibid.* No. xcviii, part 5, l. 3.

(2.) THE ANGELS.

Reland, the great archæologist of the XVIIth Century, vigorously maintained the thesis that the Samaritans possessed no belief in angels.[38] Some external references and

---

[37] *BS* ii, Nos. ci, cii.

[38] Reland, *De Samaritanis,* 7, 9; cf. Hottinger, *Smegma orientale,* 1658, p. 491; *Enneas dissertationum philol. theol.* 1662, p. 18. See on the other side, Juynboll, *Lib. Jos.* 122.

the denial of the doctrine by the party of the Sadducees (e.g., *Acts*, 23, 8), supported this contention. But the far wider range of literature at the command of modern scholarship has effectually disposed of this thesis, except so far as it may hold for earlier Samaritanism,[39] and an account of Samaritan angelology might make a considerable chapter.

In the Samaritan Hebrew literature the prevailing name for the angels is the Pentateuchal term Mal'akim, as an equivalent for which Sheliach, "deputy," is found. There is frequent use of "Host," or "Hosts"; the "Spirits" are rarely mentioned. In the Aramaic literature the most common term is "Powers," which also appear as "Potencies," "Exalted Ones," and "the Celestial Folk," or "the Church Above"; also as "Foundations," and the "Plenitude of Deity." These beings are numberless.

שליח, deputy, *BS* ii, p. 164, v. 19 (also Rabbinic).— צוה (=צבא) השמים, *ibid.* p. 77, He 5.— רוחות, spirits, in "God of the Spirits," *ibid.* p. 212, v. 12; cf. *Enoch, 15,* 4ff, and Greek to *Num.* 16, 22; so *Heb.* 1, 14.—Cherubim, *BS* ii, p. 66, v. 21.— Powers, חילן, as in *Dan.* 4, 32, חיל שמיא, = δυνάμεις, e. g. *Eph.* 1, 21.— Potencies, גבורן· —The two Cherubim, i. e. of the Ark, *BS* ii, p. 66, Lamed, v. 21.— Exalted Ones, גבאי, *ibid.* p. 191, v. 23.— Celestial Folk, עם עלאי, *ibid.* 191, v. 11; cf. *Berak,* 16b, פמליה של מעלה· Cf. Koran, 37, 8; 38, 69.— The Church Above, כנשה דקעם לעל, *BS* ii, p. 138, st. 7. Cf. *Heb.* 12, 22f.— Foundations, יסדיה, *BS* ii, p. 138, st. 10.— "Plenitude," עתרה דאלותך, *CS* iii, 8; see Gesenius's note comparing the Mandaic use of אותרה for angels.— Angels without number, *CS* iii, 8; so the Jewish doctrine, Weber, *op. cit.* 169.

The Angels or Powers hold an intermediate place between God and man. With reference to their relation to Deity, the figure of the Angel in the Pentateuch offered a theological difficulty, yet also a means of escape from the anthropomorphic dilemma. We have seen above, that to avoid the former obstacle, Mal'ak was changed to Melek.[40]

---

[39] Epiphanius witnesses to the denial of the belief, *Hæres.* ix, 13.
[40] P. 210. In *Marka,* 29a, 33b, "the Ruler," or "the Glory" is substituted.

On the other hand "angels" is used in place of the Biblical *Elohim,* where it has a polytheistic flavor. Thus in the Targum to *Gen.* 3, 5, the Serpent says, "Ye shall be like angels," a paraphrase like that in *Targum Onkelos,* and probably in this sense the expression "God of gods and Lord of lords" was used. In the hymns the exchange is sometimes deliberately made, as in the phrase, "a sweet-smelling savor to YHWH," where in place of "God" "Spirits" is substituted.[41]

In regard to the origin of the heavenly spirits, our literature is in general indefinite. In reply to de Sacy's question whether the Samaritans believed in angels, the curt reply was: "We believe in the holy angels who are in the heavens."[42] Indeed the modern Samaritans appear to have fallen into indifference towards this theologumenon. From a frequently recurring phrase, "Powers and creatures,"[43] it might appear that the former were regarded as uncreated; de Sacy is inclined to think that the Samaritans regarded them as emanations of Deity.[44] This is indeed a view which appeared in early Christianity, and in general it is to be observed that except in formal theology the question of the origin of the angels is naturally ignored. However, a passage in a hymn shows that the angels were regarded as created beings. The reference reads as follows:[45] "O God, our God, who wast before every creature, who made and began and finished the world by himself; in Bereshit [i. e., at the very beginning] mighty creatures he created; in wisdom they grew up, in perfection and with no defect." Further, in a passage already cited,[46] "creatures" is doubtless used of one kind of celestial beings, as the extract tells

[41] *BS* ii, 116, v. 27.
[42] *N. et E.* 106 (121).
[43] *E.g. CS* iv, 8; *BS* ii, 138, st. 10.
[44] *Sam. Theol.* 21.
[45] *BS* ii, 181, v. 1ff.
[46] *BS* ii, 138, v. 10.

how they and the " Foundations " came down upon Mount
Sinai. St. Paul also uses κτίσις in the same way, of
spiritual beings, *Rom.* 8, 39. From the passage quoted
above, it would appear that angels were created on the
first,[47] not the second day, as the Rabbinic theology came
to teach, while of the later Jewish doctrine that the angels
were an emanation from the fire under the throne of God
there is scarcely a trace.[48]

As in the earlier Jewish theology, the angels are conceived of as closely related to or identified with the stars;
so in the expression, " the heavens and their powers."[49]
Thus at the revelation on Sinai, along with the angels appear " the winds and the waters and the fires and the
material elements," as spiritual existences.[50]

There are a few references to a hierarchy amongst the
angels. These are represented as sitting in ranks at the
theophany upon Sinai,[51] and Heidenheim has published a
hymn in which the angels who wait upon God in his heavenly temple are divided into classes, some of whom attend
to the morning and evening oblations, while others of
higher rank perform the divine commissions in the universe,
receiving their orders through an angelic porter.[52] Four

[47] So *Marka*, 148b.
[48] *Bereshit Rabba*, c. 78, Weber, *op. cit.* § 34, Bousset, *op. cit.* 316.
According to Heidenheim (*BS* iii, pp. xviii, xxv) the doctrine of emanation appears in *Marka*, 105, 106,—a passage which he has not published. The earlier Jewish doctrine taught that the angels were created
on the first day; see *Jubilees*, ii, 2. Judaism subsequently transferred
their creation to the second day so as to avoid the idea that they
assisted God in his work. But Samaritanism retained the elder notion.
[49] *BS* ii, 19, st. 11. It is not clear whether in the description of the
stars of the seventh heaven, *ibid.* No. xiv, Beth, they are regarded as
animate.
[50] The identification of the angels with the stars, as in the interpretation of " the Lord of Hosts," is very ancient in Israel. The elemental
spirits, belonging to the four elements, and even to every kind of creature, appear constantly from the *Benedicite* and the *Book of Enoch*
down; cf. *Enoch*, 60, 11ff; *Jub.* 2, 2; *Gal.* 4, 3, 9; *Col.* 2, 8, 20. See
Bousset, *op. cit.* 317.
[51] *BS* ii, No. xix, He.
[52] *DVJ* iv, 551.

angels are given names and special functions, to wit, those who attended the ark of the child Moses, Kabbala, Penuel, Anusa and Zilpa, the first two also appearing as " Helpers " of Moses.[53] With the exception of the historical references to the Serpent in Eden,[54] there are but few allusions to evil spirits in the literature.[55] But Petermann learned orally that the Samaritans considered as devils Azazel, Belial, Jasara (the hornet, *Ex.* 23, 28), and also ranked in the same class the Cainites and the Nephilim.[56] We thus observe that Samaritanism by no means followed the extreme Jewish development of angelology and diabolology, and has been able to withstand the doctrines of Islam in this field.

> Kabbala, כבלע is represented as God's minister, in the ninth heaven, *BS* ii, p. 26, v. 20f. This being has some mystical connection with Deity: " K is the secret of his Name," p. 85, v. 13. (According to Heidenheim, *BS* iii, p. xxv, he appears in *Marka,* vi, 260b [unpublished] as identical with God.) His function seems to be like that of the Rabbinic Metatron; see Weber, *op. cit.* § 37. The etymology of the word is entirely obscure. May it be a personification of Qabbala, the secret doctrine of God? Such a theory supposes a confusion between initial Kaph and Qoph, which is possible if the word were borrowed orally.— Penuel, פנואל (cf. *Gen.* 32, 30), is the Angel of the Presence, *Jub.* i, 27, 29; *Test. Levi,* 3, 18; *T. Juda,* 25 (*Is.* 63, 9). His place is generally taken in Judaism by Gabriel, *Lu.* 1, 19.— Anusa, אנוסה, appears in the Kabbalistic literature as a form of Enoch (Enosh), who was the Demiurge, the Prince of the Presence, and even identified with God himself.— Zilpa, זלפה, I cannot trace further.— According to Petermann, *l. c.,* the priest gave him as the names of the four great angels, Fanuel, Anusa, Kabbala, Nasi, whom the priest assumed to find in *Gen.* 32, 31, *Ex.* 14, 25, *Nu.* 4, 20, and *Ex.* 17, 15, respectively.

[53] *BS* ii, 29, v. 6; p. 205, v. 18.

[54] *E.g. ibid.* 112, Samek, v. 21.

[55] Cf. *Lib. Jos.* c. xxiii, according to which the reading of the Law has a magical effect against the spirits.

[56] *Reisen,* i, 283. Also Cowley notes, without further reference, that " there is a destroying angel Mehablah, who corresponds somewhat to Satan "; *JQR* viii, 571.

As for the functions of the angels, they are such as usually appear in Jewish and Christian theology. In general they are spoken of as " the Hidden Powers," [57] but their manifestation has been vouchsafed to the Patriarchs and at the great moments of revelation. The principle is laid down that " they are present only at the times of temptation." [58]   But the supreme moment of the revelation of the heavenly powers was the awful scene on Mount Sinai. According to almost every one of the Midrashic hymns which repeat the story of that momentous event, all spiritual essences appear as summoned to witness and add dignity to the scene, all Powers and Creatures, the spirits of all the elements, the lightnings and thunders, the stars and their constellations; in serried ranks this Church Above assembles, while below gather the tribes of Israel, the angels themselves glorying in the giving of the Law.

> The passage summarized is found in BS ii, No. xix, p. 77, He. Cf. p. 45, Mem, Samek; p. 111, Nun; No. xxxiv; CS iii, 8; iv, 8; etc. This Midrashic treatment, based on Dt. 33, 2, is parallel to that of the Jewish literature (see Weber, op. cit. § 57; cf. Heb. 12, 18ff), with some original details. Moses appears more exalted than in the Jewish Midrash, for here the angels do him reverence. The Samaritan doctrine also holds an independent position in one important point; it does not allow that the angels had anything to do with the mediation of the law to Moses. " God spoke with all Israel, speaking without an interpreter (repeater)," מתני (BS ii, 139, st. 16). Samaritanism insists on the immediate gift of the Law written by God's finger to Moses, in contrast to the Jewish dogma that angels were the mediators, Jub. 1, 27–c. 2; Philo, De Somniis, 642 M; Josephus, AJ xv, 5, 3; Gal. 3, 19; etc.

This revelation of the Hidden Powers is unique, but nevertheless the heavenly spirits still have communion with the Faithful on earth, and will take their part in the deter-

[57] E.g. CS iv, 11.
[58] BS ii, 7, No. v. Marka, 2a, has a like phrase, but uses it in a different sense. The former passage proceeds to enumerate their appearances to the saints down to the giving of the Law.

mination of the future fate of men. Like the saints, they will possess at the Last Day some intercessory power with God, but the wicked need expect no favor from them.[59] Gerizim is "the tabernacle of God's angels," [60] where they "taste and kiss" the sacrifices,[61] and at the Passover the two Cherubim and the angels are present, hovering about.[62] The Hosts attend the priestly blessing, and they attend the faithful in their prayers.[63] At the Day of Judgment when the scales are set, they shall appear as assessors, and acquit each one of the righteous, as they ask concerning every event of the latter's lives.[64] In all these notions of the angels we find concepts that are rooted in the Old Testament and which flowered richly in Judaism and Christianity. But on the whole the Samaritan conception has remained simpler and soberer; in this the earlier Sadduceeism is evident. There is no trace of a belief in guardian angels.

(3.) CREATION.

According to Samaritan dogma God has revealed himself in two grand acts, namely the creation of the universe and the giving of the Law. Hence most of the Midrashic hymns begin with an extensive description of the creation, based upon the narrative in *Gen.* I.[65] The Samaritan doctrine teaches strictly that God was the creator of all things. This absolute theology represents an earlier stage of Jewish doctrine, before oriental dualism and the Greek distinction

[59] *BS* ii, 191, v. 12. Cf *Job,* 33, 23.
[60] *N. et E.* 63 (77).
[61] *BS* ii, 116, v. 27.
[62] *Ibid.* 66, Lamed. Cf. the Christian idea in connection with the Eucharist.
[63] *Ibid.* 117, v. 27; no. lii.
[64] *BS* ii, 94. The idea of the Scales is taken from Islam; *e. g.* *Koran*, xxi, 48; see Tisdall, *The Sources of the Qur'an,* 198.
[65] Comparison may be made with the great ancient Eucharistic Prayer, which relates the drama of human redemption, beginning with creation.

between matter and spirit had rendered possible even in Jewish monotheism the notion that anything could have independent existence apart from God. It is in contradiction to such dubious theology that the Samaritan doctrines hold that God created the Tohu-wa-Bohu, and even that he is Tohu-wa-Bohu.[66]

> A frequent expression is that God created "from that which is not," *e. g. BS* ii, 164, v. 3; *CS* i, 4; *Sam. Theol.* 19. (Gesenius renders the phrase, ex eo ubi nihil, but האן is the pronoun "that.") For the earlier Jewish doctrine of absolute creation see 2 *Mac.* 7, 28; for the later notion of independence of things in origin and condition, see Weber, *op. cit.* § 43, and for like philosophy, *Wisdom*, 11, 17.

Marka almost alone, as we have seen, enters into Gnostic speculations; according to him the angels were emanations from the Glory. The same theologian teaches that "the Law came forth from the fire" of God, and that the two Tables " were separated from the lamp (face?) of his knowledge."[67] One might find in this theologian almost a pantheistic conception; he describes God as one " from whom all is and to whom all returns;"[68] also a Hymn speaks of God "making all things go forth from himself."[69] But we may not push such a criticism too far; Paul also taught that "of him and through him and unto him are all things," *Rom.* 11, 36, while the return of all to Deity is a common doctrine of the Koran. Samaritan theology in general draws the sharpest line between God and his creatures.[70]

[66] See above, p. 215.
[67] *Marka,* 68b; cf. Weber, *op. cit.* § 42. Also Moses' staff and the four Caves were created in the Six Days, 5b, 77b; cf. *Pirke Abot,* v, 9, and Taylor, *ad loc.* Cf. above, note 48.
[68] 144a.
[69] *CS* iii, 16.
[70] There is no notion of the opposition to his purposes on the part of the angels as held by some Rabbinic literature; see Weber, *op. cit.* § 43.

The mystic means of creation was the command, "Be," which is the object of adoring wonder to the devout Samaritan. In dependence upon Jewish exegesis, ten creative words were spoken, the first of which was found in *Gen.* 1, 1, when Tohu-wa-Bohu and the angels were created.[71] Marka also holds the later Jewish notion of the "renewal" of the worlds, i. e., of several creations (Toledot) before the present world was made.[72] The universe is divided, as in the simpler Jewish conception, into two worlds, the upper and the lower, or, more frequently, into the Things Concealed and the Things Manifested.

As for the heavenly regions, references are found to both seven heavens and to nine. In a passage giving the former number, the sun is assigned to the highest heaven.[73] In the passage describing the nine heavens, each of the first eight possesses its own firmament and stars, while in the ninth is "the Holy Abode, and Kabbala its minister."[74] This number, which approximates the ten heavens of Kabbalism, appears also in the *Acts of St. Thomas,* where Paradise is placed in the eighth.[75] The hymns give lengthy descriptions of the heavenly bodies, in long discourses compounded of pseudo-science and mysticism; of course, astronomical observations played a large part in ecclesiastical thought because of their importance in regulating the ecclesiastical calendar, being created indeed "for omens and seasons" (*Gen.* 1, 14).[76] The day of creation was the first Nisan.[77] The knowledge of the elements of matter went no further than the four principles of fire, wind, water, and earth.[78]

---

[71] *Pirke Abot,* v, 1; see pp. 218, 274.
[72] *Marka,* 151b; cf. Weber, *l. c.*
[73] *BS* ii, No. xviii, Waw; *DVJ* iv, 552.
[74] *BS* ii, No. xiv, Beth.
[75] Thilo, *Acta S. Thomæ,* 27; 47 (cited by Heidenheim). For ten heavens, cf. also *JE* i, 591.
[76] For the calendar, see Chap. XIV, § 12.
[77] *Marka,* 30a. The Jewish doctors disagreed as between Nisan and Tishri.
[78] *E.g. Marka,* 43b.

Great interest is displayed in Adam, who in his original estate appears as the ideal man. He was made out of the dust of Gerizim, differing from the beasts by walking upright. Marka tells how he was formed of fire and water, or fire and dust, by God's own hand, being also compounded of the Holy Spirit and soul. A fine passage tells how he came to adore the one creator of all things. He was placed in the Garden of Eden, where he remained a year in felicity. After his fall, he went off by himself for a hundred years, in which time " he begat children without form or shape," i. e., the demons or Jinn of the corresponding Jewish and Islamic legends. But then he repented and God took him back into favor, so that he came to rank as one of the heroes of the true religion, being, along with Abel, Enosh, Enoch and Noah, one of the original worshippers of God on Gerizim. There is, however, an entire absence of all Kabbalistic lore concerning Adam Kadmon. Comparatively little is made of the fall of Adam in the hymns, somewhat more in Marka. The Biblical text is closely adhered to, and there is no development of diabolology in connection with the Serpent.

See especially the opening stanzas of *BS* ii, Nos. xxi, c. For Marka, see 58b, 68b.— For the antediluvian patriarchs as true worshippers, *ibid.* 69b, 70b, 180b.— Almost no legendary lore appears concerning Enoch, except a reference to the flight of his sons, which is drawn from the legend of the *Wars of Enoch*, *ibid.* 157a, and cf. Heidenheim's note.— For Enosh, compare the reference above to the angel Anusa, p. 219. An extensive apocryphal literature ascribed to the patriarchs seems to have been known to the Samaritans,— *e. g.* a *Book of Adam,* or *Book of Signs,* a *Book of Wars,* but there is no reference to the *Book of Enoch,* although Enoch legends are found; see Heidenheim, *DVJ* iv, 213, 350, 189.— The absence of expansion of doctrine concerning the Fall represents the earlier Jewish position; cf. Baldensperger, *Die messian.apokalyptischen Hoffnungen d. Judenthums,* i, 220.— Gesenius quotes a verse alluding to man as the Microcosm, *CS* 100.

§ 4. MOSES; THE PATRIARCHS, PRIESTS, PROPHETS.

The Samaritan Bible is the Pentateuch; this means to Samaritan belief that Moses was the sole medium of God's revelation. Accordingly the absoluteness of the Law and the Lawgiver is never tempered as it is with the Jews, who range alongside of the Tora, although on an inferior plane, the Prophets and Hagiographa. It was impossible for the Samaritan to look forward with a Jeremia to a time when a new Law should be written in men's hearts, or with a Joel to an outpouring of the Spirit which should discount the revelation of the past. In the Samaritan sect Moses takes a place parallel to that enjoyed by Mohammed in Islam: " Moses is the Prophet of God," and there is none other like him. But the Samaritan doctrine even surpasses Islam in reverence for its prophet. For while Muslim orthodoxy thinks of the Arabian prophet with rational soberness, the Samaritan advances the great Lawgiver to a position where he becomes an object of faith. He is rather like the Christ of Christianity, one whose origin is often held to be mysterious, who now lives to make intercession for his brethren, who will appear effectually for the saints at the last day; the Messiah himself will be but an inferior replica of that absolute Prophet.

It would take well-nigh as long to enumerate the epithets accumulated in Moses' honor as those applied to Deity. As it is true that almost every hymn begins with the praise of the Creator, so it is likewise true that the hero of the second act of the Midrashic drama is always and at great length Moses. He is, according to Biblical terms, the Confidant of God, the Son of his House, with whom God talked face to face; he is also the end, the limit of all revelation, a very ocean of divine utterance.[79] In language which has

---

[79] See Gesenius's discussion of these epithets, *Sam. Theol.* 24. " The son of his house," properly " slave," is used honorably, and seems to antagonize such an argument as appears in *Heb.* 3.

15

doubtless been affected by Christianity, he is God's Evangelist,[80] the Pure One, the Light on earth,[81] the Light of the world,[82] and all others are liars.[83]   As in Christian dogma he undid the work of the Devil,[84] and the saint dies in the faith of Moses.[85]   His name alone may be associated with that of God; " We begin our discourse," says an Epistle, " with the name of God and conclude with the mention of Moses."[86]   No prophet has ever arisen like Moses, or ever will arise.[87]   He is the absolute prophet, for all things hidden and revealed were shown him on the holy mount, so that other prophets are superfluous.[88]   On his account the world was made,[89] prayer is offered through the merits of Moses,[90] his prayers for the faithful will be granted by God in the Day of Judgment.[91]

The Midrashic treatment of the history of Moses is very extensive, particularly with regard to his experiences beginning at the Burning Bush.   For his earlier life there is not as much of amplification of the story as appears in the Jewish Haggada, which glorifies Moses as the greatest and most learned among the Egyptians.[92]   There is given

[80] *BS* ii, 93, v. 37.
[81] *Marka,* 75b, *seq.*
[82] *BS* ii, No. xiv, Dalet; Kaph.
[83] *Ibid.* No. xiv, Lamed.
[84] *Ibid.* No. lxix, v. 17.   The same notion appears in Judaism; see Weber, *op. cit.* 273.
[85] *BS* ii, No. cxxi, v. 17.
[86] *N. et E.* 52 (64).
[87] This despite *Dt.* 18, 18ff, but the doctrine is based on the Samaritan reading, Hebrew and Targum, of *Dt.* 34, 8: "no prophet shall arise"; cf. *SC* vii, 1; *Marka,* 143a.
[88] *E. g. BS* ii, No. xv, Samek; *Marka,* 143b: "He knows Bereshit and the Day of Vengeance," *i. e.* the beginning and end of things.
[89] *Marka,* 67b; a like notion exists in Judaism.
[90] See below, p. 231.
[91] *CS* vii, 30.
[92] His birth on the 7th day of the 7th month is asserted in correspondence with Jewish legend, *BS* ii, No. xv, He. His staff was handed him out of the fire of God, *Marka,* 5b; cf. the Jewish legend, *Pirke Abot,* v, 9. For his wisdom (cf. *Acts,* 7, 22) an ampler treatment is found in the *Legends of Moses,* published by Leitner in *DVJ* iv, 184.

a pretty infancy legend which speaks of the four guardian angels in charge of the child Moses, when he lay in the ark.[93] But the Samaritan imagination follows the Jewish lead in letting itself out in the glorification of the experiences of Moses upon the holy mount. Not satisfied with the Biblical accounts of the visions vouchsafed to him, there is grandiose enlargement upon the prophet's fellowship with the angels. He entered into heaven itself, and there sat on a great white throne, while he wrote the Scriptures; by the glory of the angels was he nourished, of their food he ate, at their table he sat, with their bread he satisfied his hunger, in their bath he bathed, and in their tent he dwelt.[94] In heaven he figures as greater than the angels, for these all sing the praises of the Lawgiver, as they call upon him to read the Law: " O Priest, begin and read! . . . . Each says to the other: See and hear, O comrade! What is this but the voice of the Glory? Opened to him is heaven's door. And every constellation and its stars listen, and the two stars [sun and moon] are in vision to Moses, while each says to him, O Lord and Master! "[95] One Scriptural passage referring to God is even applied to Moses: " He (Moses) ascended into the firmament of Levi, and appeared, and came forth from Sinai, and lightened from Seir, whose appearance was like sapphireenamel."[96] There is constant reference to the transfiguration of Moses' face, after *Ex.* 34, and especially to the horn of light with which he was clad, v. 29; this is the same exegesis as appears in Aquila and the Vulgate (*cornuta*).[97]

But the most interesting development of dogma concerning Moses is found in the doctrine of his pre-existence.

[93] *BS* ii, No. xiv, Chet; see above, p. 219.
[94] *Marka,* 156b.
[95] *BS* ii, No. xix, He.
[96] *BS* ii, 205, v. 15; cf. *Dt.* 33, 2; *Ex.* 24, 10.
[97] Horn of Light, *BS* ii, No. xi, 14; No. c, v. 15; etc. It appeared in Egypt, *ibid.* p. 107, v. 27.

This theologumenon, which however is infrequent, appears in the various phases common to such conceptions. At times the pre-existence is only ideal or deterministic;[98] Moses was the end of creation, therefore he possessed an ideal being before his historical manifestation: " We had been expecting his advent since the ages that are past."[99] His prophethood had ideal pre-existence, and in the fulness of time clothed him like a garment; so in a stanza quoted by Gesenius:[100] " Prophecy was his, a crown from the days of creation; the prophethood of Moses, which was worthy of him, clothed him." Moreover the doctrine approaches that of a real pre-existence; he is " the man in whom the Spirit of God was established since creation; the eyes of God were upon him with the generations of the days and years."[101] Further, the connection between the pre-existent state and that in the flesh was mediated by a species of metempsychosis, the sacred germ of divine light being transmitted through his forbears until it fully incarnated itself in the prophet. " He walked in the knowledge of YHWH; from the day of the creation of Adam his spirituality was in this child, and his grandeur was in the world. And he set him as a drop of light, passing from generation to generation [distillation to distillation], and then he descended into Jochebed's womb, and was placed within her."[102] This doctrine is nothing else than a replica of the Islamic legend of " the Light of Mohammed."[103] It is in accordance with this notion that Moses is called, in Christian terms, " Light from Light."[104] His pre-existence is more definitely stated in the epithet used of him, " the Star of Creation whom God created from the Six

[98] Cf. Baldensperger, op. cit. 86.
[99] BS ii, No. xv, Yod; this is a reminiscence, or parallel, of Mi. 5, 1.
[100] Sam. Theol. 27.
[101] BS ii, No. xcviii, st. ii.
[102] BS ii, No. xv, He; cf. DVJ iv, 547.
[103] Tisdall, op. cit. 246.
[104] DVJ ii, 99.

Days." However despite this divine emanation of the germ of Moses, he appears as a created being, and is frequently spoken of as "the quintessence of creation."[105] In one passage, as read by Heidenheim,[106] Moses is thus addressed: "Art thou not, O Moses, Prince of the (divine) Form, Tabernacle of the Shekina of God?" Here Moses appears in the form of the Prince of the Presence, and the embodiment of God's glory, much like the Jewish Metatron. But this is most exceptional, while the text is uncertain; in general even Moses' pre-existence originated in the Days of Creation. A lengthy Midrash describes the death of Moses, but his decease is a natural one, although attended by glorious circumstances; there is no doctrine of the assumption of Moses.[107]

Logically therefore Samaritanism has no room for other prophets than Moses; the fortunate canonization of the Prophets allowed Judaism to cherish Moses as the first of a long line of successors, but to the Samaritans he was also the end of prophecy. Frequent reference is made to prophets, but the thought seems to be confined to the incident in *Num.* 11, where Eldad, Medad and the Seventy Elders are seized with the Spirit of God; these inspired men are much honored by the Samaritans, who profess to have their tombs. Also in one passage the author of a hymn asserts that he himself is "a scion of the prophets and cannot lie,"[108] but this assumption of inspiration is unique, at least in the literature.

Aaron also takes a very subordinate position. He is only the moon to Moses' sun, while the latter is Priest as well

[105] *E. g. BS* ii, No. xv, Chet, v. 10. So, in connection with the Biblical דמעה, Gesenius, *CS* 68, understands דמע, a word often used of Moses and Israel. I would suggest that it may mean "first fruits," like the Talmudic *dema'*; cf. *Jer.* 2, 3; *Ja.* 1, 18.
[106] *DVJ* ii, 88; *Zur Logoslehre der Samaritaner, ibid.* iv. 126.
[107] See Munk, *Des Samaritaners Marqah Erzählung über den Tod Moses'*, and his remarks, p. 3.
[108] *BS* ii, No. xx, Chet.

as Prophet.[109]   Aaron appears at length in the Midrashic treatment of the first chapters of Exodus, but he fades away in the light of Moses' glory upon the mount.   His successors, Eleazar and Phineas, receive frequent notice, the latter especially, because of the Biblical statement concerning his inheritance in the land of Samaria, *Jos.* 24, 33. These three priests are counted among the Meritorious Ones.   Extreme care was taken with the preservation of the priestly line, and the chronicles are arranged under the successive highpriests whose line is given from the beginning.[110]   Their sacerdotal rights were fully preserved, and only when the highpriestly line failed in the XVIIth Century, did others of the tribe of Levi dare to assume their functions.   In general the control of the community has lain in the hands of the priesthood, has not been usurped by lay doctors.   Despite this fact, Moses has triumphed over Aaron, probably because of the enforced spiritualization of the Samaritan religion during its long sufferings of persecution since the days of John Hyrcanus.   The Samaritan theology is not interested in the treatment of the sacrificial laws of the Pentateuch, as Judaism has been, which expounded those ordinances long after they were obsolete.   To the contrary, we find in Samaritanism a greater stress laid upon the moral side of the Law, which is treated more after the way of Haggada than of Halaka. Hence a certain tone of spirituality, however ethically genuine it may be, marks Samaritan theology, so that it appears in a way as one of those numerous developments of Old Testament religion which were forerunners of the spiritual worship of synagogue and of Christianity.   This stage may have been reached earlier than in Judaism, for the glory of Gerizim fell two centuries before that of Jerusalem.

[109] *Ibid.* No. xix, He.
[110] But the frequently incomplete and often contradictory genealogies allow us no dependence upon the authenticity of the lists for earlier times, at least before the age of Baba Rabba.

It is in consequence of this rigor of doctrine concerning Moses that the other great hero of revelation, Abraham, enjoys no such elevation as is given him in Jewish Haggada. In this literature that patriarch becomes a close second to Moses, so that like the latter, " for his sake the world was created," while the spiritual superiority assigned to Abraham by Paul as the type of true believers had its close anticipations in the Jewish apocryphal literature.[111] There are traces of the Jewish legends of Nimrod's enmity towards Abraham;[112] Marka enlarges upon the sacrifice of Isaac, which according to Samaritan tradition occurred on Gerizim. We have already in the preceding Section touched upon the antediluvian patriarchs, whose histories are also all connected with Gerizim.

The patriarchs and other early saints play a considerable part in Samaritanism through the doctrine of their merits. They are the Guiltless Ones, or with reference to the notion of *zekut,* the Meritorious Ones.[113] These are primarily Abraham, Isaac and Jacob.[114] This number is also enlarged so as to obtain the mystical seven, but the list varies. Sometimes it includes with those three Joseph, Aaron, Eleazar and Phineas, to whom Moses may also be added.[115] This doctrine of the merits of the Fathers takes the same place in Samaritan doctrines as the corresponding teachings in Judaism, and the later extravagant development of the merits of the saints in Christianity. Thus a hymn for Kippur reads:[116] " Let us stand in prayer be-

[111] *Bereshit R.* c. 2; cf. cc. 48, 12. See in general, Weber, *op. cit.* § 56; Bousset, *op. cit.* 178.
[112] *E.g. BS* ii, 191, v. 17; *Marka,* 47b. According to *BS* ii, No. xcviii, st. i, " Abraham's merits gained for him Paradise." The *Legends of Moses,* cited above, contains a mass of patriarchal traditions.
[113] See Rappoport, *Liturgie samaritaine,* 20.
[114] *E.g. BS* ii, No. ii: " our Fathers."
[115] *BS* ii, No. xcviii, st. vi, p. 190, middle. Judaism likewise singled out three or seven saints,— the three patriarchs, with Moses, Aaron Miriam, Benjamin; see Hamburger, *REJud* i, 38.
[116] *BS* ii, No. xvi, p. 52, st. 16. Cf. *N. et E.* 181. Here and generally

fore Yhwh the Giver, and pray and say: O Lord
Yhwh, turn from thy hot anger, and be appeased for the
sake of Abraham and Isaac and Jacob, and for the merit
of thy servant Moses." This notion is also connected with
the Scriptural passages referring to Abraham's and Moses'
intercessory powers with God; the prayers they offered still
have virtue for Israel. They are also present intercessors;
thus it is prayed that the son of Terah " may intercede for
us,"[117] and Moses' prayers will be efficacious at the Day of
Judgment.[118]

There may also be noticed here the doctrine of the Seven
Covenants, frequently referred to in the Epistles. These
are respectively: the covenant with Noah in the bow; with
Abraham in circumcision; with Moses in the Sabbath; the
Tables; the Passover; the Covenant of Salt, based on *Num.*
18, 19; and the Covenant of Priesthood with Phineas, *Num.*
25, 12f.[119]

§ 5. THE LAW.

We have already observed the absolute uniqueness which
Samaritanism ascribes to the Tora. On the whole the doctrine in details goes *pari passu* with that of Judaism.

In general it is taught that the Law came forth from
the very essence of God, was detached from the fire of
deity. Here, if anywhere, we come upon a clear notion of
emanation; no origin is too divine for the Law. " The
Tables had lain hidden in the midst of the fire "; " they
shone like gleaming lightning "; " they were inscribed with
a finger of devouring fire."[120] " They are a fragment of
the hidden world, increasing wisdom for all genera-

'amal, opus, equals the Jewish *zekut,* " merit." Also *segila* is used of
the " treasury " of merits, *e.g. BS* ii, No. xv, Waw. For the Jewish
doctrine, see Weber, *op. cit.* § 63.
[117] *BS* ii, p. 98, top.
[118] *CS* vii, 30.
[119] *N. et E.* 119; cf. p. 74. On p. 159 only six are named.
[120] *Sam. Theol.* 28.

tions;"[121] "the Law is a spark from God's vesture."[122] And thus Marka:[123] " The Law came out of the fire; " " the Tables were sundered from the divine essence." The Tables are not however from eternity, for " they contain the will of God which he decreed in those Six Days."[124] That is, they were separated from the divine glory in the creative week, and remained hidden in the divine fire until the day of revelation. The same was widespread Jewish doctrine, according to which the Tables were of divinely mystical substance, fiery and translucent.[125] Only it is to be observed that there is none of the indefinitely long and so practically eternal pre-existence claimed for the Law which is found in some Jewish teaching; nor is there any of the personification of the Law which early developed in connection with the Jewish ideas of Wisdom and the Word.[126]

Samaritanism does not halt at anthropomorphism in its description of the giving of the Tables, and here it has the authority of the Scriptures. God himself wrote the Tables and gave them to Moses with his own hand; [127] in this may be contained a protest against the Jewish doctrine of the mediation of the Law by the hands of angels.[128] The scene of the divine legislation is depicted with all the solemnities and terrors which appear in the Jewish Midrashim. All things seen' and unseen were present; all angels in their ranks, the stars and the constellations, even

[121] *CS* iv, 17.
[122] *CS* iii, 4.
[123] 68b.
[124] *CS* iv, 18.
[125] *E.g. Pseudo-Jonathan* and *Targum Jer.* to *Ex.* 19, 16ff; 20, 2ff; Rashi to *Dt.* 33, 3. Cf. Gesenius, *Sam. Theol.* 28; *CS* 80.
[126] See Weber, *op. cit.* § 4.
[127] *E. g. BS* ii, 112, v. 23, at top; p. 138, v. 1; No. xxxii, v. 4: " thy autograph."
[128] See above, p. 220.

the dead with the living; the whole universe trembled before this divine revelation.

In another place is given a description of the sanctity the Samaritans ascribe to the rolls of Scripture, and especially to the archetypal copy of Abishua;[129] no wonder then that they prostrate themselves at its exhibition and sing a Gloria.[130] By the Samaritans the Law has been found to be " the Book of Life," or even " Life " itself,[131] even as the Old Testament has been to the Jews and both Testaments to Christendom.[132]

§ 6. GERIZIM.

The fourth article of faith of the Samaritans, the one which differentiated them *toto cœlo* from the Jews, is based upon what must be acknowledged to be the root falsehood of the Samaritan religion. It is true that for neither sect did the common authority of the Pentateuch offer any determination of God's sanctuary in the Promised Land. The Samaritans had the advantage in the fact that the early centres of Israel's religion were in the Highlands of Ephraim, at Bethel or Shilo, while *Dt.* 27 provided for a solemn covenant to be enacted on the two mountains of Shechem. But Shechem seems to have early lost its prestige, and Bethel became the chief sanctuary of the Northern Kingdom. Yet in the matter of true ritual succession the South had the advantage in at last securing the Ark of the Covenant and in consecrating therewith the new high-place at Jerusalem. And, if our understanding of the history be correct, after the Exile the remnant of Northern Israel

[129] See Chap. XIV, § 6.
[130] *BS* ii, p. xxxvi, *seq;* see above, p. 41.
[131] *BS* ii, No. xxx; No. xxxvi, v. 7.
[132] According to *Lib. Jos.* xxiii, the reading of the Law possesses a magical influence against evil spirits, the evil-eye, incantations, etc. But in general Samaritanism is remarkably free from such superstitious notions.

largely gave in its adherence to the sanctity of Zion. It was the northern schism after the Exile which again turned the mind of the Samaritans to the choice of a local sanctuary, and they chose Gerizim for reasons which have already been specified in the IVth Chapter. But this was in the nature of an afterthought; the succession of sanctity had for centuries been broken. And the Samaritans in their choice of Gerizim confessed the weakness of their position by taking recourse to the natural weapon of the weaker party, namely the lie. They felt themselves compelled to falsify the Biblical text. This theological emendation was simply made by changing the " Ebal " of *Dt.* 27, 4, to " Gerizim "; it was then on Gerizim that the first altar of God for the Twelve Tribes was built.[133]

The Samaritans having thus invented Mosaic authority for the sanctity of Gerizim, proceeded to dignify the mountain with every epithet of honor, and to identify it with every possible transaction of sacred history. For them Gerizim is the Blessed Mount, the Eternal Hill.[134] It is

[133] The great critic Kennicott was among the defenders of the Samaritan reading, in his *Second Dissertation*. But Verschuir, *Dissertationes philol-exegeticæ*, No. iii (1773), demonstrated at length the falsity of the Samaritan position. The points of the argument would include: (1) the unanimous witness of the versions to the Massoretic text; (2) the point of the great ceremony is the curse, the altar therefore should be connected with the place of cursing; (3) the Jews would have no reason to alter the text, as Ebal and Gerizim are indifferent to them, and they allowed that the latter was the mount of blessing. As against Lightfoot, who argues that the absence of Talmudic reference to this corruption proves the late origin of the change, Gesenius rightly holds that the details of textual comparison were of little concern to the Jews, *Pent. Sam.* 61. The modern Samaritans deny the report that they offer sacrifices on Ebal, *N. et E.* 122. In this connection the Samaritans also make the following changes in the text. At the end of *Dt.* 11, 30, " before Shechem " is added; this against an early view which attempted to find a Gerizim and Ebal near the Jordanic Gilgal, although the Jewish disputant in *Sota*, 33b admitted that by " the oaks of More " Shechem was meant. And then to make self-assurance doubly sure, the Samaritan adds after *Ex.* 20, 17, and *Dt.* 5, 21, a long pericope, consisting substantially of *Dt.* 27, 2–8, and 11, 30.

[134] *Tur berik; e. g. Lib. Jos.* xxi,— with reference to *Dt.* 27, 12. The

"the House of God (Beth-el), the Mount of Inheritance and of the Abode (Shekina), the great and chosen Place;"[135] "the House of the powerful God, the Tabernacle of his angels, the Place of the presence of his majesty, the Place destined for sacrifices."[136] Like Jerusalem for the ancient Jew and Mecca for the Muslim, Gerizim is the Kibla of the Samaritan, the place toward which he prays.[137]

The standing name of the holy mount is "Gerizim-Bethel-Luza." The first epithet is used in the sense that Gerizim is the veritable Bethel of patriarchal history. Hence we find no reference to the historical Bethel. According to Samaritan tradition, upon the schism under Eli the renegades set up their worship at Shilo,[138] and the calf-cult of Jeroboam, also an apostate from the true Israel, was located at Samaria.[139] While the geography of this identification is sadly in error, nevertheless the use of *beth-el* is the retention of a primitive term for a sanctuary, used by the Jews also of Jerusalem. A corroboration for this identification was the existence of a town upon Gerizim named Luza, which accounts for the second epithet above, and was naturally identified with the Luz-Bethel of *Gen.* 28, 19.[140]

Eternal Hill, *e. g. N. et E.* 165 (177); *BS* ii, 66, top; based on the Samaritan reading of the singular in *Dt.* 33, 15. But Mills, who gives a list of thirteen epithets for Gerizim taken down from the highpriest with their interpretations (*Nablus,* 268), gives as the present explanation of the term, "mountain of the world" (*har 'olam*). This is an interesting survival of a very ancient idea, appearing in connection with the Babylonian temples and also in Biblical ideas concerning Jerusalem, *e. g. Is.* 2, 1ff.

[135] *N. et E.* 212 (217); cf. *BS* ii, No. xxiv.

[136] *N. et E.* 63 (77).

[137] *Ibid.* 164 (176); see Chap. III.

[138] *Lib. Jos.* xliii.

[139] *Abu'l Fath,* 53.

[140] Where the Samaritan Hebrew reads "Luza." This place Luza is testified to by Jerome in his *Onomasticon* (Migne, xiii, 954). For the ruins of Luza, see Guérin, *Samarie,* i, 433; Conder, *Tent Work in Palestine,* 63, identifying the place with the present spot of sacrifice. But in *PEFQS* 1876, p. 191, Conder is by no means certain as to the

But the connection of the Patriarchs with Gerizim was not confined to the history of Jacob. As the Jews identified the Mount Moria of the sacrifice of Isaac with Zion, so the Samaritan tradition connected it with Gerizim through the etymological correspondence of Moria with More in the neighborhood of Shechem; this identification is then corroborated by making Melchizedek king of the Salem which is to the east of Shechem. The Samaritans still point out the place where Isaac was offered.[141]

At the end of the 3d Section we referred to the traditions connecting the worship of the antediluvian Patriarchs with Gerizim. But further, it was the sanctuary of God from the beginning; it is the holy place which God " chose " at the very first.[142] Hence it is given the name Har Qadim, the First Mount, by which Marka understands its appearance, along with the Garden of Eden, before the rest of the dry ground, although in another place it implies for him Gerizim's pre-existence before the rest of creation.[143] Here Adam was made, " created out of the dust of Mount Safra."[144] The latter name for Gerizim is very common,[145] and Gesenius is right in connecting the tradi-

identification. Dean Stanley held that this locality was the Luz of *Ju.* 1, 26.

[141] This identification for Moria appears in the Samaritan Hebrew of *Gen.* 22, 2, where מרה stands for המריה The place Salem, to the east of Shechem, is also the Samaritan interpretation of שלם in *Gen.* 33, 18 (cf. Septuagint, Syriac, Vulgate), and this was further identified with Melchizedek's city, so that yet another notable episode of Abraham's life was located in the neighborhood of Gerizim; see *VJD* iv, 187. Stanley (*Sinai and Palestine,* note to chap. vi.) accepted the Samaritan identification of Moria, but he has not been generally followed by other scholars. However, there has been recently a revival of Stanley's position; see Wellhausen, *Comp. d. Hex.*³, 19; v. Gall, *Altisr. Kultusstätten,* 111; E. Meyer, *Die Israeliten,* 260.

[142] *BS* ii, No. xcix, st. vi; *Marka,* 72b. The Sam.-Hebrew reads the perfect *bachar,* " chose," for the imperfect in *Dt.* 12, 14.

[143] *Marka,* 68a; 71b. He also associates it with *miqqedem,* " on the east," *Gen.* 12, 8, where Abraham built an altar.

[144] *CS* xii, 18.

[145] *E.g. BS* ii, No. xxiii, Chet: " the congregation of S."

tion with the similar one of Islam concerning Mount Çafra in the neighborhood of Mecca. But here again their peculiar geographical exegesis comes to the help of the Samaritans. The Har Qadim (or Qedem) is "the mount of the east," Har Haqqedem, which is named Sephar in *Gen.* x, 30.[146] Thus the Muslim legend is adapted to Samaritan geography — unless we may hold that the reverse process has actually taken place.

It also appears that the Samaritans made Gerizim, as the Mount of the World, the site of the Garden of Eden, an identification which has its roots in the antique idea set forth in *Eze.* 28, 13ff, where the Mount of God and Eden are identical. There is a legend in the *Book of Joshua,* xxi, *s. fin.,* of a river descending out of Gerizim in the Age of Grace, while Marka speaks of "the concealed river Euphrates."[147] This notion of a mystical river connected with the sanctuary mount has also its antique parallel in the Old Testament, in regard to Jerusalem, *Eze.* 47; *Zech.* 14; *Ps.* 46. The river is "concealed" against the future, when it and the Garden of Eden will be restored to view. Here again local geography comes to the aid of exegesis. The Wady Fara descends east from Gerizim, and this name in its original form was probably identical with the Biblical word for Euphrates, Perat.[148] Also, as is instanced by a Jewish Midrashic passage, the Samaritans held that Gerizim was not overflowed by the waters of the flood.[149] Again in the latter days it is to be the site of Paradise; when all other things shall have been destroyed, "the Eternal Hill shall be left in the midst of the Garden."[150] But even in the present unhappy age the Presence of God

---

146 Cf. Mills, *op. cit.* 270.
147 *Marka*, 76a.
148 Cf. the probable confusion of a local stream Perat with the Euphrates in the exegesis of *Jer.* 13; see Giesebrecht, *ad loc.*
149 *Bereshit R.* c. xxxii.
150 *BS* ii, 93, v. 21.

and the angels still dwell upon Gerizim, although unseen. The holy Tabernacle has disappeared, but it is only " exalted,"[151] existing in some mystical fashion above the mount; but it will return with the Ark and all the sacred paraphernalia of worship to perfect the ritual of the saints in the Age of Grace.[152] A somewhat different form of the legend, and one which has its Jewish counterpart, is that the Ark is preserved in a cave on Mount Gerizim;[153] this doctrine can be traced back to the Ist Century, for Josephus records the enthusiast who led the Samaritans up the mountain, promising to reveal to them the holy vessels.[154]

§ 7. ESCHATOLOGY.[155]

It has been observed above in connection with the Samaritan Creed that the eschatological tenets of the faith are of later and secondary origin. The elder Samaritans doubtless held to the primitive notion, exhibited almost throughout the Jewish Scriptures, that the dead went to Sheol, herein agreeing with Sadducæan doctrine as against Pharisaism. However the dogma of the resurrection appears already in full bloom in Marka in the IVth Century. Also in the development of Messianism the Samaritans lagged behind and largely imitated Judaism, nor did their

[151] *N. et E.* 114 (126) : " we weep over the tabernacle and its exaltation."
[152] *E. g. BS* ii, No. xxiii Pe *seqq.*
[153] *Marka,* 77b. For the Jewish legend, see 2 *Mac.* 2. According to Marka there were four graves or caves preserved since the third day of creation: those of Machpela, Gerizim, Hor and Nebo. (Cf. *Pirke Abot,* v, 9.) The sacred cave on Gerizim has been referred to above, p. 36.
[154] *AJ* xviii, 4, 1–2. The tombs of many of the patriarchal worthies are to be found, according to Samaritan tradition, on or near Gerizim.
[155] In addition to the bibliography given at the beginning of the Chapter, see Friedrich, *De Christologia Samaritanorum,* 1821 ; Cowley, *The Samaritan Doctrine of the Messiah,* in *Expositor,* 1895, p. 161. The present Section was practically completed before the author saw the last-named article, which has, however, given him some important suggestions.

Messianic ideas ever play the same capital part as in the other faith. The references to this doctrine are comparatively few and generally vague, and it comes ultimately to be more a pious belief than a positive dogma. In general, Samaritan eschatology represents the primitive stages of Jewish doctrine.

The first development in the doctrine of the Latter Things sprang out of the ancient Israelitish theologumenon of the Day of Yahwe, which appears as early as Amos. The like and even sadder experiences of the Samaritan sect required that they should develop, after the pattern of Judaism, the doctrine of an ultimate theodicy, when at last the sufferings of the church should be compensated. Hence the Samaritans look forward with eager hopes to what they generally term the Day of Vengeance, or the Day of Vengeance and Recompense, יום נקם ושלם. It is also called the Last Day, and the Great Day.[156] This doctrine was anterior to that of the resurrection; the community was to be vindicated, not the individual, according to earlier thought. As for the home of the future justified and glorious community, this is universally found on Gerizim, a belief parallel to the early Jewish notions, which made Jerusalem the centre of all eschatological expectations. When subsequently the doctrine of the resurrection was added to this more ancient dogma, the notion of the earthly Paradise does not seem to have been much disturbed. The resurrection would restore the blessed dead to transfigured Gerizim; hence it is the pious belief that burial on Gerizim is especially efficacious for an easy transit into the new condition. The Samaritans appear not to have advanced as a body to notions of a Paradise in some mystical portion of the earth or in a celestial region, as in the apocalyptic developments of Jewish thought. Here

---

[156] The Last Day, BS ii, 65, Kaph, v. 3; the Great Day, BS ii, 92, v. 30. Cf. Joel, 2, 31; Mal. 4, 5.

again we find them retaining the position held by earlier Judaism.

The Day of Vengeance and Recompense is the grand objective of the Samaritan philosophy of history which lies at the base of all the chronicles. According to this interpretation of human events, the world's whole history is divided into four ages. Preceding these æons there was the age of Adam's perfection, when all things were good as God had made them. But with Adam's fall began the rotation of certain cycles of God's providence. First there came the days of Panuta, an Age of Disfavor, which lasted till the revelation on Mount Sinai. With Moses the world was regenerated, so far at least as the holy people were concerned, and the Age of Grace, the days of Ridhwan, was ushered in. This continued for 260 years, during which time the theocracy was duly and rightly governed by God's vice-gerents, the kings and priests, the two classes working harmoniously together. But this happy age was terminated by the evil priest Eli, Samson being the last king of the old order. Then originated the schism of the Jews, while the working of the evil continued in the further schism of Jeroboam, whom with his cult the Samaritans disown. God's presence was no longer visible on Gerizim, the holy vessels were hidden away, the enemies of Israel interrupted the sacred cult, and the calamities began under which the church has ever since suffered. This is the second Age of Disfavor, the present Panuta, in which God has *turned away* his face from his people. However communion with God is still maintained through the succession of the true highpriesthood and the sacrifices on Gerizim, and the people's hope looks forward to the early return of God's favor. Then at last the second and great Ridhwan is to come, and in it God's Israel shall enjoy perpetual peace and felicity, while their enemies are suppressed. This happy age will be introduced

16

by the advent of the Messiah upon the 6000th year from creation, beginning the last day of the divine week of human history. The fortunes to be expected in that last millennium will be treated below in connection with the doctrine of the Messiah. But we may observe here that the dates which appear in the Samaritan chronicles possess more than mundane significance; they are the figures of the divine chronology, and the faithful can calculate thereby the days to the end. But the irony of millennial belief has befallen the Samaritans even as it has pursued every eschatological speculation since the Book of *Daniel*. In the XVIth Century the Samaritans confessed in the Ist Epistle to Scaliger that God alone knows the day of Messiah. In the year 1808 the Samaritan correspondents of the Europeans dated their letter with the year of creation 6246. With the Samaritans then as with Jew and Christian, millenarian doctrine has had its bloom; only the words of the old faith are kept, ghosts of what once was really believed in.

For the above philosophy of history, see *Lib. Jos.* and *Abu'l Fath.* For the Ages and their calculation, see especially Vilmar, *Abu'l Fathi annales,* p. xxx, and the chronological table, p. lxxxiv. The Messiah's reign is to last 110 years from A. M. 6000, so that the date of the second Panuta, which is 3050, is midway between creation and the end of Messiah's kingdom. The epochs of Alexander's death and of the Hegira also have cardinal places in this scheme, the former being placed 1050 years after the date of Panuta, the latter just 2000 years from the same period. The three days of Panuta are those, respectively, of schism and strife, of the Greek dominion, and of Islam (*op. cit.* p. lii).—"The Age of Grace": the day of רחותה, refreshment, or רצון, favor; in Arabic: the days of *ridhâ,* or *ridhwân,* favor.—"The Age of Disfavor": *panuta,* from the Hebrew root *pana,* means the turning away of God's face, inclusive probably of the thought of Israel's defection. See Juynboll, *Lib. Jos.* 126; Vilmar, *l. c.;* Kohn, *Zur Sprache,* 47ff; Cowley, *op. cit.* 169. Also "the Days of Wrath and Error."—For the Jewish doctrine of 6000 years before Messiah's advent, see Bousset, *op. cit.* 234; Schürer, *GJV* ii, 530. The Samaritan division of the period is different from the Jewish, which follows the fortunes of the temple.— Up to a late period the millennial hope appears to have assigned exact dates for the Messianic advent. According to Petermann, *Reisen,* i, 283, the year 1858 had been fixed upon.

While doubtless the Samaritan notion of the Messiah is a borrowed accretion of faith, nevertheless we can trace it back to a fairly early period. For the IId Century A. C. Justin Martyr bears witness to it.[157] For the Ist Century we have as probable testimony the anecdote of the enthusiast who asserted the power to discover the hidden vessels, perhaps a Messianic claimant himself; also possibly the story of Simon Magus (*Acts* 8), who claimed to be " the Great Power of God," although this assumption outbids all we know of Samaritan Messianism. But most instructive for this century is the remark of the Samaritan woman to Jesus: " I know that Messiah is coming; when he comes he will tell us all things " (*Jn.* 4, 25). This whole narrative is, to the present writer's mind, a witness to the acquaintance of the Fourth Gospel with Palestinian conditions. The Samaritan notion, as it appears in the literature, makes of the Messiah only a second Moses, one whose function it will be to reveal what is hidden; he is primarily the prophet that shall come like Moses (*Dt.* 18), and so we can understand the comparatively ready acceptance of Jesus by the woman's coreligionists, because he appeared to them as a " prophet " (v. 19).[158]

With this Samaritan Messiah it is natural to attempt to find some connection in the enigmatic Messiah-ben-Joseph, or M.-ben-Ephraim, who appears in later Jewish literature. His function was to be that of precursor of the Messiah-ben-David, and his particular duty to collect and lead home the scattered Ten Tribes. He will captain the hosts of Israel against the forces of Gog and Magog in their onslaught upon the Holy Land, and will fall in battle against

[157] *I. Apol.* 53.
[158] See also for the same position, Cowley, *op. cit.* 171.

them; then will appear the victorious Messiah of David's seed.[159] Bousset is inclined to hold that this doctrine is an adaptation by Judaism of the Samaritan Messiah. But certainly this could not have been done of intention; to the contrary the latter would have been ranked in the category of Anti-Christ. Rather, with Dalman and Schürer, this Jewish figure must be regarded as an artifice of exegesis to explain such passages as Dt. 33, 17; Zech. 12, 17, and in general to meet the Christian doctrine of the suffering Messiah. On the other hand, as we shall see, the Samaritan Messiah dies, but by natural death, in accordance with the primary stage of Jewish Messianism.[160]

The Samaritan doctrine of the Messiah was doubtless stimulated by the Jewish theology at an early period, being subsequently corroborated to the mind of the sect by its adaptable exegesis of the Pentateuch and its interpretation of the history of the age of the Judges. Hence we find Joshua given the title of " the King " in the Book of Joshua, passim, while the Judges are also all kings.[161] Accordingly the regal function of the Messiah has its prototype in that earlier royal succession. Proof texts for this kingly line may have been found in Dt. 33, 17 and especially v. 5: " There was a king in Jeshurun." However these Pentateuchal allusions to the regency of the House of Joseph, from which indeed the Messiah was to descend, are too scanty and indefinite to have provided a sufficient foothold for an original notion of the Messiah on Samaritan soil; the kingly quality of their Christ was but a faint reflection of the Jewish expectations of the glories of the Son of David. A prophet after the manner of Moses (Dt. 18) was what the Samaritans desired in

---

[159] See Hamburger, REJud ii, s. v. Messias Sohn Joseph; Dalman, Der leidende und sterbende Messias der Synagoge, 1; Schürer, GJV ii, 535, note (with extensive bibliography); Bousset, op. cit. 211, 218.
[160] E. g. Jer. 33, 17; Ps. 45.
[161] Lib. Jos. xxxix.

their Messiah; this notion accordingly limited the Samaritan ideas. He was to be a Revealer of hidden or lost truths like the one the Samaritan woman had in mind, and inasmuch as there could be no greater prophet than Moses nor one equal to him, the Messiah is an entirely inferior personage.[162] Accordingly, in contrast with the developed Jewish doctrine of the Messiah, such as was abroad since the Danielic prophecy of the Son of Man,[163] the Samaritan Messiah never attains the character of a divine personality. He always remains human and the thought concerning him moves in a prosaic plane.

Inquiry concerning the Messiah has been one of the chief points of the European correspondence with the Samaritans. The Epistles show that the word Messiah was known; thus the IIId Epistle to Ludolf says: "The Messiah has not yet arisen." In the Epistle to the Brethren in England, 1675, the correspondents content themselves with the remark: "the first name of that prophet will be M." Also in another passage of the Epistle it is said: "We know his name in accord with what the rabbis say."[164]

But the Samaritans, while acquainted with "Messiah," have their own peculiar term for that personage, and herein

[162] Cowley, op. cit. 165, rightly corrects the theory held by Juynboll, Merx, Hilgenfeld (the one which I had adopted), that one form of the Messianic expectation looked for the re-incarnation of Moses (Merx: of Moses or Joshua). But there is no proof for this theory. Only the bishop Eulogius (in Photius, Bibliotheca, Geneva, 1591, col. 883) states that some of the Samaritans expected the Messiah to be Joshua son of Nun. But it may be questioned if the bishop was not mistaken in understanding the likeness of the Messiah to King Joshua as an identity. The Samaritan name for the Messiah, the Restorer (see below), might, after the analogy of Elija who appears in the same role in Malachi, have suggested the return of the great prophet, a fairly common notion in Judaism. Still no evidence of this notion appears in Samaritanism.

[163] E.g. Jn. 7, 27.

[164] N. et E. 115 (127). A Samaritan guide told Robinson that the Messiah was known by the Arabic title el-Muhdi, i. e. the Mahdi, BR iii, 100.

exhibit an independence of Judaism, or at least the survival of a more primitive strain of thought. His proper
title is Ta'eb, used with or without the article ha-. Nothing in Samaritan literature has produced a greater variety
of explanations than this same term. Cellarius says:
" There is need of an Œdipus for the interpretation of this
name," and he has been justified by the labors scholars
have spent thereupon. For the history of its interpretation, which includes suggestions of Arabic and Persian
origin, reference may be made to a note by Gesenius.[165]
It is this scholar who is now generally credited with having
reached the proper solution, which is as follows:[166]

The word is the participle of the root תוב, the Samaritan Aramaic equivalent of the Hebrew שוב, " return," " do
again," " restore," the latter form also appearing rarely
in the Epistles as שהב. Through the Samaritan indifference in the use of gutturals, the participle also appears
spelt תהב but without influencing the pronunciation.[167]
The root is used, as in the Hebrew religious language, of
the change of heart, or repentance, of man or God;[168]
hence Taeb has been interpreted by some as the Penitent
One, who vicariously meets God's demand. But, with
Gesenius, it is to be understood in the active voice, as in the
Biblical שוב שבות, " make restoration," so that the Samaritan Messiah is the Restorer. And this is in fact the interpretation that is given by the Samaritans themselves, as
thus in one of their most recent Epistles, that to
Kautzsch:[169] " This word תהב means the one who con-

[165] Sam Theol. 43, n. 105.
[166] Ibid. 44; adopted by de Sacy, N. et E. 29; Cowley, op. cit. 164;
etc.
[167] Cf. Petermann, Gramm. Sam. 44. It appears that the word is
vulgarly pronounced ha-Tab, or ha-Shab.
[168] E.g. BS ii, No. xiv, Taw; CS iii, 22 (here correct Gesenius's interpretation according to de Sacy, N. et E. 29).
[169] ZDPV viii, 152f. The highpriest defined the word to Bargès as
" le Restaurateur "; Les Samaritains de Naplouse, 91.

verts the people." Heidenheim connects the connotation
of the term with the Panuta: the Restorer is to counteract
the turning away of God's favor.[170] But a more historical
and substantial suggestion has been made by Bousset,[171]
who aligns the term with an early Jewish notion of the
Messiah, which makes of him the Restorer. This idea appears, at least verbally, concerning Elija in *Mal.* 4,5f, according to which passage this Messianic personage is to
"turn the heart of the fathers to the children, and the
heart of the children to their fathers," i.e. restore the per-
verted relations of society. With this may also be compared the Messianic "times of restoration," *Acts, 3,* 21.[172]
In this idea of a Restorer we have a characteristic mark
of Samaritanism, whose genius harked back to the past
far more than that of Judaism, for the larger hope of the
Canon of the Prophets led the way for the Jewish belief
that the future could be more glorious and even of another
character than the past. Doubtless the term Taeb also included the connotations of the divine and human repentance.[173]

As the Samaritans were shut up to the Pentateuch, they
were forced to find therein their Messianic proof-texts. A
Samaritan Epistle[174] gives a collection of such texts,
namely: *Gen.* 15, 17: "a smoking and a burning lamp";
Gen. 40, 10: "to him shall the people submit themselves"
(with appropriation of Juda's blessing!); *Num.* 24, 17:
"He shall destroy all the children of Seth;" *Dt.* 18, 17:
"Thy God shall raise up to thee a prophet like unto me,

[170] *BS* iii, p. xxviii.
[171] *Op. cit.* 219.
[172] Bousset also adduces *Testament Levi,* 18. The notion is very
ancient; cf. *Is.* 11, 1ff.
[173] In *BS* ii, 89, v. 33, *Nu.* 24, 5, is rendered: "How goodly are
thy tents, O Taeb" (for "Jacob"). This is evidently a play upon the
root of "Jacob."
[174] Of year 1675; *N. et E.* No. xxi. Compare Cowley, *op. cit.* 167,
for a larger list of proofs from a hymn of the XVth Century.

unto him shall ye hearken." To these references may be added, besides *Num.* 24, 5, already cited, *ibid.* v. 7: "His king shall be higher than Gog" (following a Rabbinic interpretation), while "the star out of Jacob," v. 17, is also adduced as a Messianic symbol.[175]

As for the identity of the Taeb, he was to come of the house of Joseph, the first "king" of Israel, and inherit that leader's royal qualities.[176] For the doctrine of the manifestation and work of the Taeb we may refer to the lengthy Midrash on the subject appearing in a hymn published at length by Heidenheim.[177] The outline of the passage is as follows:

The advent of Taeb shall be in peace and his star shall shine in the heavens. When he has reached adult life, YHWH will call him, teach him his laws, give him a scripture, and invest him with prophecy. He shall dwell upon the Holy Hill. Then shall be revealed the Tabernacle with all its furnishings, and the ancient ritual will be restored in the full ministrations of the priesthood. Israel shall dwell in safety and security, and perform its solemn feasts in peace,[178] and the Taeb shall have a perpetual kingdom until the latter day. Confession of his

[175] See *BS* ii, 89, No. xx, vv. 33, 35. For the star (also "star of thy prophet," and "star of grace"), *ibid.* p. 88, He, v. 10; p. 92, v. 17; p. 96, v. 32; p. 72, v. 24. Cf. *Mt.* 2, 2; *Test. Levi,* 18. Moses is called the Star of Creation, *BS* ii, 104, v. 18. It may be observed that the Samaritans have an original exegesis of "Shilo" in *Gen.* 49, 10, interpreting it *in malo sensu* of Solomon; so also Abu Said's Arabic version.

[176] For Eulogius's statement that Messiah is to be Joshua himself, see above, note 162. It would appear from *Marka,* 195a, that Taeb would not be greater than Joseph: "There is no king like Joseph, even as there is no prophet like Moses."

[177] *BS* ii, No. xx, He, *seq.* The passage was published and treated, with ignorance of Heidenheim, by Merx in the Proceedings of the Eighth International Congress of Orientalists, of the year 1889, i, 2, p. 119, and by Hilgenfeld, in the *Zeitschrift für wissenschaftliche Theologie,* xxxvii, 233. A partial translation, based upon an amended text, is given by Cowley, *op. cit.* 162.

[178] Cf. *Jer.* 23, 6; *Nah.* 1, 15.

majesty shall be made, after the fashion and in the language of Balaam, by a representative of the heathen. No worldwide dominion is predicated of the Taeb, his function is solely for Israel. The hymn then (stanza Zayin) briefly refers to his death in peace, when he shall come to his tomb and be gathered to his fathers. (According to Petermann[179] he shall reign 110 years, i.e. the age of Joshua (*Jos.* 34, 29), and less than that of Moses; according to an Epistle [180] he will be buried alongside of Joseph.) But "the star of Taeb" will shine perpetually over his tomb as the continued sign of the divine grace. Israel shall continue to increase most marvellously, and the saints shall enjoy all prosperity.

It is thus the chief function of the Taeb to introduce the Millennium, which, as our Midrash proceeds to relate, is to be disturbed by the grand final conflict between God and the forces of evil. Here we have the replica of the Jewish and Christian notions of Gog and Magog and of Antichrist. The happy condition above described shall last for many days. But at last God's wrath will wax hot against the Gentiles, for the earth will again corrupt itself, as in the days of the Flood. Then will come the Day of Vengeance, the Great Day, accompanied with cosmic cataclysms. " The light of the sun shall grow pale at the beginning of every month, and the moon and the stars shall not give their light. Every high place shall be overthrown, and the valleys and hills, with quaking at the Day of Vengeance, its glory and its majesty." [181] The earth and all its natural features will be overturned. All things will be wiped out (stanza Chet), man and beast, rivers and mountains, and only the Eternal Hill will be left in the midst of the Garden, i.e. Paradise, for the residence of the saints.

[179] *Reisen,* i, 284.
[180] The Arabic Epistle to the English Brethren, 1675; *N. et E.* 209.
[181] I follow Cowley's translation. Cf. *Is.* 2, 7ff; *Joel,* 3. Cowley calls attention to the likeness to *Mt.* 24, 29, 37, 39.

It appears that all die from fear of the righteous God. Then comes the resurrection and the judgment. Among the risen ones appears Moses who acts as an intercessor for his people. God then holds the session of his court, in which the angels act as inquisitors of good and evil, and the merits of the respective souls are weighed in the Scales.[182] Israel will be divided into two classes, the good and the bad, the former passing into the Garden of Eden, the latter into the Fire.— Such is the outline of a formal presentation of the events of the Latter Days. As with all eschatology, so in Samaritanism there were doubtless many various views of the end of the world. Thus Marka makes the advent of the Messiah a time of woe to the Gentiles, and regards his coming as contemporaneous with the resurrection.[183] We also note in correspondence with the assertion of *Jn.* 4, 42 concerning the Samaritan expectation of the Taeb as the Saviour of the world, that an Epistle teaches that all peoples will make submission to the Prophet of the Last Days and believe in him.[184]

We have already touched upon the Samaritan attitude towards the doctrine of the resurrection of the dead; as we have seen above, the sect originally held to the old-fashioned Sadducæan position, and on this score were considered heretics by Rabbinic Judaism. The Church Fathers find frequent occasion to notice this heresy.[185] But such information is only partially exact for the IVth Century and afterwards, being due to tradition or else to the survival of the elder view among some of the Samaritans,[186] for in Marka the doctrine of the resurrection appears in full

---

[182] See above, note 64.
[183] *Marka,* 65a.
[184] *N. et E.* 205.
[185] *E.g.* Origen, *Comm. in Mt* xxii, 23 (Migne, xiii, 1564); *Hom.* xxv, *ad Num.* (M. xii, 763); Epiphanius, *Hæres,* ix, 1; Philastrius, *Hæres,* vii; etc.
[186] A Dosithean sect denied the resurrection; see Chapter XIII, § 1.

force, and we may hold that from his age at least this became an orthodox tenet. In self-defence against the attractive eschatologies of Judaism and Christianity, Samaritanism had to formulate some theology concerning the future; subsequently Islam gave further strength to the dogma. In course of time the idea of the individual resurrection has taken the place of the notion of the resurrection of the community, and on the whole this belief is phrased in just such terms as are used in other religions. Truly ethical notions are connected with the fears and hopes of the life after death; not the Israelite as such but only the good Israelites can attain felicity, and the thought of death is often made the theme of solemn admonition.[187] We also find at times the elder notion adhered to, once common in Judaism and Christianity, that only the good shall experience the resurrection.[188] As we have observed, Paradise is conceived of as earthly, being located on Gerizim, although no further sensuous ideas are connected with it, as in Islam. In one passage at least appears a more spiritual and mystical faith: " My future abode is the seat of thy dominion, where is neither sea nor ocean nor heaven itself."[189] In general Samaritanism is sober in its conceptions of the after life and rarely shares in the exuberant imaginings on the subject which mark Judaism and Christianity; herein we see the ancient Sadducæan strain surviving. This antique heritage is also preserved in the name given to the cemetery by the Samaritans; it is called the House of the Dead, not, as with the Jews, the House of the Living,— a significant contrast.[190]

[187] *E.g. BS* ii, No. cxx, a hymn on death and repentance; No. cxxi, a requiem hymn. Prayers for the dead appear in the latter, v. 20 *seq.*
[188] *CS* vii, 10.
[189] *CS* iii, 13.
[190] Mills, *op. cit.* 206.

CHAPTER XIII.

THE SAMARITAN SECTS; GNOSTICISM.

§ I. THE SAMARITAN SECTS.[1]

Extensive testimony is given by the Samaritan Chronicles, especially by Abu'l Fath, to the existence of sects since an early period; to this information much can be added from Patristic and Muslim sources. It is the more unfortunate that the data concerning these sects are meagre and confused, because these phenomena exhibit the operation of external forces affecting Samaritanism.

The arch-heresy of the Samaritans according to all accounts is that of the Dositheans. But before taking up this sect, it is advisable first of all to look at the others which are grouped along with it by the Christian authorities. First, the Jewish-born Hegesippus, of the IId Century, in a passage quoted by Eusebius, enumerates the Dositheans, the Gorothenians and the Masbothæans, to each of which he assigns an eponymous founder.[2] The Syrian Epiphanius is the next Christian writer to list the Samaritan sects, which he makes four in number, namely the Essenes, the Sebuæans, the Gorothenians, and the Dosi-

[1] For the literature, see *inter al.*, Juynboll, *Lib. Jos.* 110; Nutt, *Samaritan Targum*, 46; Appel, *De rebus Samaritanorum*, 90 (a brief essay: *De Dositheo et Dositheanis*). For the Rabbinic references, see S. Krauss, *Dosithée et les Dosithéens*, REJ xlii, 1901, p. 27; A. Büchler, *Les Dosithéens dans le Midrasch*, REJ xlii, 220; xliii, 50, who considerably criticizes Krauss's credence to the historic reliability of the Rabbinic material.

[2] Eusebius, *Historia ecclesiæ*, iv, 22. "Gorothenians" is variously vocalized, though the tradition of the consonants is fairly certain. Nicetas has Sorothenians, *Thes. orthod. fidei*, i, 35; see Heinichen, *Eusebius, ad loc.*

theans.[3] It would be natural then to identify the Masbothæans with the Sebuæans.[4] Of the Sebuæans Epiphanius reports that out of hostility to the Jews and to
avoid friction with them this sect observed the Passover in
the month Tishri, so that their feast of Tabernacles fell
about the Jewish Passover. The name has been variously
explained, but the best interpretation is that of Juynboll,
who deduces it from the Hebrew שבוע, " hebdomad," and
makes it refer to the Passover celebration in the seventh
month.[5] There is a single reference to this sect in *Abu'l
Fath,* 131, where the Subuaï appear as opposed to Baba
Rabba and as having their own ecclesiastical organization.
Of the Gorothenians nothing further is known than Epiphanius's information that they agreed with the Dositheans
in observing the orthodox calendar as against the Sebuæans.[6] As for the same authority's mention of the Essenes,
all he tells us is that they were orthodox Samaritans, and
in the disputes of the sects sided with the party who happened to be in the neighborhood of their respective communities. Some evidence will appear below of Essene influences in Samaria.

Of the Dositheans we possess much more extensive information, but all of a confused and contradictory character, and coming from every source, Samaritan, Jewish,
Patristic, and Arabic. It is a question whether there is

[3] *Hæres,* i, 10; cf. his *Respons. ad epistol. Acacii et Pauli.* Epiphanius is followed by Theodoret, *Hæres,* i. 1; John of Damascus, in
Cotelerius, *Eccles. Græc. monum.* i, 282; Nicetas, *l. c.*

[4] If the former is an independent sect, we have only the definition
offered by Isidor Hispalensis, *Etymologiæ,* viii, 4, according to whom
they held that Christ ordered them to sabbatize in all things — the sect
thus appearing as a Christian body. Ewald, *Geschichte des Volkes
Israel,* 1868, vii, 135, identifies them with the Basmothæans of the
Apostolic Constitutions, vi, 1, 6.

[5] *Lib. Jos.* 112. This etymology is supported by the Arabic form
given in the next sentence of the text. For other explanations, see
Nutt, *op. cit.* 47.

[6] Heidenheim would find a geographical origin for the name, *BS* ii,
p. xxxviii.

not more than one sectary of the name Dositheus, while the age of the origin of the respective sects is uncertain. The following variant traditions have to be examined. (1) There appear a Dostai and a Sabbai as the priests sent by the Assyrian king to Samaria.[7] (2) Sabbæus and Theodosius appear in the legend reported by Josephus, *AJ* xiii, 3, 4, concerning a dispute carried on before Ptolemy Philometor between the Jews and the Samaritans, the advocates of the latter being those two men.[8] (3) According to Abu'l Fath,[9] there arose in the time of Alexander a sect called Dustan, for which name an obscure etymology is offered.[10] These people held for impure a fountain into which dead vermin had fallen; altered the time for reckoning the purification of women; forbade the eating of eggs except those which were found inside a properly slaughtered fowl; considered dead snakes as unclean, as also cemeteries, and held anyone whose shadow fell upon a grave as impure for seven days. They rejected the formula, " Blessed be our God forever," and substituted " Elohim " for " Yhwh ; " they held that God was to be worshipped in the land Zuwaila (?), until he is worshipped (again) on Gerizim; they altered the calendar by giving thirty days to each month, and rejected the seasons of fast and mortification. Like the Jews, they counted Pentecost from the day after the Passover. A priest might enter an infected house as long as he did not speak; if there was a question whether the impurity of a house extended to the adjoining tenement, the case was decided by watching whether a clean or an unclean bird first lighted upon the latter. On the Sabbath they ate and drank only

---

[7] *Tanchuma*, sect. *Wayyesheb*, § 2; *Yalkut*, ii, 234; *Pirke Eliezer*, c. 38, *sub fin.* A variant for Sabbai is Zecharia.
[8] See above, p. 76. Theodosius and Dositheus are interchangeable forms; cf. the Biblical Jehoiachin and Conia.
[9] P. 82; cf. *Chron. Adler*, 37.
[10] The word is identical with "Dositheans"; for an attempt to explain the Arabic etymology, see de Sacy, *Chrestomathie arabe*, i, 335.

from earthen vessels, not from those of metal — as they might be tempted to purify the latter on the Sabbath, whereas clay vessels cannot be purified; food and water were provided for cattle on the day before the Sabbath so as to last over the latter day. They separated from the Samaritans and had their own synagogues. They had for highpriest a certain Zara, a man of profound learning and son of the Samaritan highpriest, who had been excommunicated for his conduct with a woman of bad character.

(4) Turning now to Patristic authorities, we learn of a Dositheus who was an early Samaritan heresiarch, and, with some authorities, the father of all heresy. Hippolytus, a scholar of Origen, began his *Book of Heresies* with the Dositheans; the same position is taken by the Pseudo-Tertullianic *Adversus omnes hæreses,* 1, which work is probably based upon the lost book of Hippolytus, and which makes Dositheus the root of the Samaritan heresy, "the first to reject the prophets." Philaster also follows suit, saying that Dositheus was a Jew who denied the resurrection, being followed by Sadok, the founder of the Sadducees. The *Clementine Recognitions,* i, 54, gives like priority to Dositheus.[11]

(5) Another class of Patristic references places Dositheus in the Ist Century A. C., and generally in some sort of relation with Simon Magus. Hegesippus puts him immediately after Simon.[12] Origen makes several references to this heretic; he assigns him to the Ist Century, after the time of Christ, and alleges that he made himself out to be the Messiah promised by Moses, thus being in the same category with the pretenders Judas and Theudas. Of this sect Origen reports that only thirty remained in his day. They rejected the Jewish notion of sabbatic limits,

[11] For Hippolytus, see Photius, *Bibliotheca,* cxxi; Philaster, *De hæres,* 4; Jerome, *Adv. Lucifer.* 23, quotes Pseudo-Tertullian.
[12] See note 2.

and required that one should remain in the same condition throughout the Sabbath.[13] Jerome follows Hegesippus in placing Dositheus after Simon.[14] Subsequently this tradition is developed so as to make him the teacher of Simon, as in the Pseudo-Clementine literature, according to which the latter usurped his master's place.[15]

(6) Finally, according to a second report of Abu'l Fath, there is the sect founded by one Dusis in the age of Baba Rabba, the IVth Century, of which sect that chronicler gives a long description.[16] Dusis, son of Fufil (Philip ?), who seems to be assigned an Egyptian origin, came in danger of his life for adultery committed with a Jewess in a Jewish district. He obtained pardon however by undertaking to go to Samaria, there to found a new sect. He arrived at the town Askar, and associated himself with a sage named Yachdu, whom he led into some extreme literal interpretations of the Scriptures. But Dusis played his friend false by conniving at a charge of fornication against him, and so had to flee the land, settling at Shuwaika (the Biblical Soco, SW of Jerusalem). Here he composed many books, and upon leaving the place counselled his landlady that none should read them until he had first washed in the well which was close by. Then he departed, went to Anabata, where he entered a mountain cave; here he died of hunger, and his body was devoured by dogs. Meanwhile search for him was still prosecuted, and the highpriest's nephew Levi, a very pious young man, with a party of men, finally came upon his tracks at Shu-

13 *Adv. Celsum*, i, 57; vi, 11; *In Matt. comm.* c. 33; *Hom.* 25 *in Luc.*; *In Joan* xii, 27; *De princ.* iv, 17; *Philokalia*, i, 17.

14 *Adv. Lucifer.* 8. But for another report, see above, note 11.

15 *Clem. Recog.* ii, 8; cf. *Hom.* ii, 24. Dositheus had a fixed college of thirty disciples.

16 *Abu'l Fath*, 151; cf. *Chron. Neub.* 442, where he is called Dustis, son of Falfuli; also *Chron. Adler*, 64. Abu'l Fath's narrative follows immediately upon that concerning Simon Magus, a connection reminding us of some Patristic arrangements.

waika. The woman told them of Dusis' writings and his injunctions concerning them. Evidently out of fear, the party resolved to descend into the well, with the pretext that it could do no harm. But when the first who bathed emerged from the pool, he cried: "My faith is in thee and in Dusis thy servant!" Each of the men had the like experience, until at last Levi, angered at this manifestation, also dared to make the descent; but on emerging he too uttered the like confession: "My faith is in thee, YHWH, and in Dusis thy prophet!" Then they read the books of Dusis and found he had changed the greater part of the Law. At the following Passover Levi, who was called upon to read, made use of one of Dusis' readings, and upon being rebuked defied the Samaritans for their unbelief, whereupon he met a martyr's death. His followers removed to a city near Jerusalem, where they founded a sect, having as chief objects of its cult the writings of Dusis and palm-leaves stained with Levi's blood, which might be seen only by those who had first fasted seven days and nights. As for their customs, they cut off their hair, and made all their prayers in water, hiding their bodies in the bath by plashing the water over them. They greatly honored the Sabbath, observing feasts on that day only, and if they travelled at all on the Sabbath, they did not take their hands out of their garments. They believed the dead would rise again soon, and when one of their number died, they girded him, and put a stick in his hand and shoes on his feet, for the reason that "when we rise, we shall rise in haste." They also believed that as the dead man rose from the tomb, so should he enter Paradise. From this party of Dusis went forth many sects — which will be noticed below.

With this history the account Epiphanius, *Hæres.* i, 13, gives of the Dositheans largely agrees. According to that authority, the Dositheans confess the resurrection, abstain

17

from animal food, practise either celibacy or else sexual abstinence after the death of the wife,[17] and in general are devoted to ascetic habits. They are also scrupulous in avoiding contact with other people. As for the founder Dositheus, he was a very learned Jew who, disappointed of his ambitions in his own church, went over to the Samaritans and founded his sect among them. Finally he retired to a cave, and there died of voluntary starvation, his body being afterwards eaten by worms and flies. Also the references to the Dositheans left by Origen, as noted under (5), evidently refer to this same sect; he remarks their strictness as to travelling on the Sabbath, *De princ.* iv, 17, their possession of some books of Dositheus, and the belief in certain fables about him, how that he had not tasted death but was still alive, *In Joan.* xiii, 27.

Of the Dosithean sect which denied the resurrection (No. 4) we have evidence late into the Arabic period. Photius has preserved an account of a dispute held by Eulogius, bishop of Alexandria, probably about 600 A.C.,[18] with two parties of Samaritans; one of these followed "a certain Dosthes or Dositheos," and claimed him as the prophet foretold by Moses; he denied the resurrection, held that the world is incorruptible, and had composed many writings. The other party believed in Joshua as the prophet, and, it may be inferred, accepted the resurrection.[19] The bishop delivered a lengthy written argument against the sects, epitomized by Photius, and a council summoned by him passed a decree, which doubtless contributed to the repression of the Samaritans in Egypt.

From the beginning of the Arabic period down to the

---

[17] Either thus, or "after procreating children," the text being uncertain; see Oehler, *Corpus Hæresiologicum, ad. loc.*

[18] Photius, *Bibliotheca,* no ccxxx, ed. Stephan, Geneva, 1611, col. 883. The text places the bishop in reign of emperor Marcian, but there is reason to correct this to the reign of Mauricius, 582–603; see Krauss, *op. cit.* 39.

[19] For this belief in Joshua, see Chap. XII, note 162.

middle of the IXth Century, we have the testimony of the supplements to Codex C of *Abu'l Fath*[20] to violent feuds between the Dositheans and the orthodox Samaritans. Later we possess the evidence of Arabic writers to the Dositheans. First, Masudi (d. 956) speaks of two sects among the Samaritans, the Kushan and the Dustan, " one of which teaches that the world is eternal."[21] The great writer on religions, Shahrastani (d. 1153) is our next informant: the two sects of the Samaritans are the Dustaniya and the Kushaniya, and their chief point of difference is that the former deny a future life, teaching that recompense comes in this world, while the latter believe in a world hereafter.[22] Abu'l Fida (d. 1331) repeats Shahrastani's notice,[23] while Makrizi quotes Masudi.[24] According to the Epistle of 1810 there were then no Dositheans in existence.[25]

The terms given for the two sects by the Arab writers require examination, namely Dustanians and Kushanians, as also the epithet applied to the former, who are called al-Alfaniya, by Shahrastani, or al-Faniya, by Abu'l Fida. The former authority explains Kushaniya as " the truthful ones," and Alfaniya as " the liars." Juynboll's suggestion that the former term is a corruption for " qushtaniya," from the Aramaic קשם," truth," is a happy one, and better than de Sacy's theory that it stands for " Kuthim," for the Samaritans never use that name of themselves. For the other word with its doubtful reading, various etymologies have been offered. Juynboll takes it from the root, *lfy*,

[20] Epitomized by Vilmar, *Abu'l Fath;* see pp. lxxx, lxxxii, lxxxiii.
[21] De Sacy, *Chrestomathie arabe*, i, 342. The dogma specified is that noticed by Eulogius.
[22] Ed. Cureton, i, 170; Haarbrücker's translation, i, 258; see de Sacy, *op. cit.* i, 363.
[23] Fleischer, *Abu'l-fedæ historia ante-Islamitica*, 160; see de Sacy, *op. cit.* i, 344.
[24] De Sacy, *op. cit.* i, 113, 305.
[25] *N. et E.* 127.

" injure one's rights "; Vilmar, accepting *alfaniya,* understands it as " millenarian." As the name is probably an
opprobrious epithet given by the stronger party, Juynboll's
etymology is preferable, unless, as I would suggest, *faniya*
is to be connected with *panuta,* i.e. the Dositheans are the
sect of the Aversion.[26]

As to the origin of the Dosithean sect Shahrastani gives
the following information: " There arose among the Samaritans a man called al-Ilfan, who claimed prophethood
and believed that he was the one Moses had promised,
the star of whom, it is written, should shine with
the light of the moon. His appearance took place about
100 years before Christ." This description agrees very
closely with that of the heresiarch with whose sect Eulogius contended, while the date corresponds to that given
by some Patristic authorities concerning their Dositheus.

With traditions referring wildly to a space of time rang-
ing from Alexander the Great to the IVth Century A.C.,
what definite results as to chronology and personality can
we gain from these contradictory reports concerning a heresiarch Dositheus or Dusis, and a sect of Dositheans or
Dustan? To begin with, we can at once reduce our six
categories to a smaller number. As for (1) and (2),
their traditions of a Sabbai and Dositheus, or Theodosius,
are probably mere reminiscences of two early sects the
Sebuæans and Dositheans. At the utmost there may be
some truth in the tradition that Dositheus opposed the
Jews in Egypt, as Josephus relates. As for Sabbæus, he
may be nothing more than an eponymous invention for
the origin of the Sebuæans.[27] At all events Josephus gives
us a date, the first Christian Century, before which the
rise of the Sebuæans and one Dosithean sect must have

[26] For these various theories, see de Sacy, *op. cit.* i, 341; Juynboll,
Lib. Jos. 112; Vilmar, *op. cit.* p. lxxii; Nutt, *op. cit.* 49.
[27] See the beginning of the Chapter.

taken place. The two categories (1) and (2) may then be identified with (3), the first mention in Abu'l Fath of a Dosithean sect, the one which arose in the age of Alexander.

But Abu'l Fath records at great length another sect of practically the same name (6). The Patristic data in (4) and (5) have then to be aligned with one or the other of the two named by Abu'l Fath, if we would attempt to reduce the six categories to two. This simplifies the case better than the views of Nutt and Krauss, who find three heresiarchs named Dositheus.[28] Can we go further and reduce these two to one? Such is the natural aim of the critical scholar, and it is the argument of Appel.[29] This scholar's reasons would lie in the many general resemblances between the two sects recorded by Abu'l Fath. Similar aspersions are made against the life and character of the respective heresiarchs; both are rigoristic sects, and follow some Jewish usages. The rejection of the formula, " Blessed be God forever," by the first sect, is claimed by Appel to be their denial of the Samaritan-Sadducæan formula, and he assumes their adoption of the Pharisaic form, " Blessed be God forever and ever," which would be a confession of the resurrection.[30] Both sects then would possess the same eschatological tenets.

But plausible as Appel's hypothesis is, I am not able to accept it in the place of the one that I had already reached before reading his essay — namely that there were two Dosithean sects. As we have seen, according to a series of Patristic references one sect of Dositheans denied the resurrection, and so are placed in connection with the Sadducees. The later evidence from Eulogius down to the Islamic authorities knows only of one sect, namely the one

---

[28] Nutt, *op. cit.* 48; Krauss, *op. cit.* 36.
[29] *L. c.*
[30] Referring to *Berakot, Mishna*, c. 9, *sub fin.*, for the Sadducæans.

which rejected that doctrine.[31]   The one argument against this solid line of testimony is the rejection by the first sect, as recorded by Abu'l Fath, of the formula, " Blessed be God forever; " but this omission may have been intended to deny more pronouncedly than before the disbelief in resurrection.   As for the rigorism predicated of the two sects, it is to be observed that this feature is common to all sects, and is not remarkable in Samaritanism, which itself was literalistic and rigorous in an old-fashioned way. That there were two sects would appear from the statement of the well-informed Origen, that of the Dositheans he describes there were only thirty survivors in his day, whereas there is evidence of another Dosithean sect of size and importance far down into the Arabic period, flourishing in Egypt as well as in Palestine.   It may be argued that it is unlikely that there were two sects of the same name; but it is not impossible that two heresiarchs bore the very common Samaritan name of Nathanael-Dositheus.[32]   There is also this distinction evident in the two reports of Abu'l Fath, that the second sect was distinctly an enthusiastic body, possessing apocryphal writings, ascetic customs, etc., thus differing from the first.

The most probable reconstruction of these data will then be the assumption of two sects founded by and named after different Dosithei.   The first of these would have arisen, following the note of Josephus and one line of Patristic tradition, before the Christian era, perhaps in Egypt. It was a reforming sect, harking back to a greater liter-

[31] Appel has not, in his confessedly brief thesis, treated the Arabic evidence.

[32] Beside the many Nathanaels appearing in the highpriestly line, there is the Hellenistic poet Theodotus. Observe also the obscure reference in an Epistle, *N. et E.* 112 (121), to " the Targum of Nathanael " (see below, p. 292.)   A Dustan is also a liturgical composer; Cowley, *JE* x, 673. For the great frequency of the name in Judaism, see Krauss, *op. cit.* 32; Büchler, *op. cit.* xliii, 224. N. B. the probability that the legend of Simon Magus is based upon two historical Simons (Salmond, *Dict. of Christ. Biog., s. v.*).

alism of interpretation, at the same time coming under the influence of Judaism; however it continued the ancient Samaritan doctrine of the denial of the resurrection. Subsequently with the general Samaritan acceptance of that doctrine, by the IVth Century, this faction became the minority and were forced into the condition of a heterodox sect; it survived however into the IId Millennium. But the other sect is very different in spirit and practice. It is to be counted among the many enthusiastic and absurd cults which had their rise about the beginning of our era. It was ascetic and encratitic; the ritual bath was an accompaniment of all devotion; certain mystical books, among them those of " the Sons of the Prophets," were included in their scriptures, while there was the Messianic devotion to the founder of their faith, along with the cult of a martyr of their sect. They were ardent resurrectionists of a very materialistic order of belief, and were awaiting the end of all things with millenarian expectations. We can probably even identify the influences producing this sect. Several points of practice connect them with the mysterious community of the Essenes, namely, not only their frequent baptisms, but also their scrupulousness in hiding their bodies when in the bath, which is to be compared with the Essene rule of wearing a loincloth when bathing, while further the fear of contact with others — amongst the Essenes even with those of a lower caste in the order — is common to both. The vegetarianism of the Dositheans also agrees with Jerome's report of the like practice among the Essenes, although this notice is now generally invalidated by criticism.[33] Some element of truth therefore is found in Epiphanius's statement making the Essenes a Samaritan sect.[34] The rise of this body may then be placed about the

[33] For these practices of the Essenes, see Schürer, *GJV* ii, 567.
[34] Some Morning Hymns open with very poetical apostrophes to the sun; *BS* ii, Nos. xlvi, xciii. May this phenomenon have Essene origin?

beginning of our era, a date which would agree with the Patristic references collocating Dositheus with Simon; Abu'l Fath's assignment of its origin to Baba Rabba's age is a post-dating common to Samaritan chronology. This sect had evidently, from Origen's note, a short-lived existence, as it was already moribund in his day. It doubtless was a product of the influences which induced the Samaritan adoption of the doctrine of the resurrection, and in this respect secured a triumph over its like-named rival.

We may notice here the account Abu'l Fath gives of a number of similar enthusiastic sects which, he says, sprang from the party we have just described.[35] The first was the sect of the Be'unaï, or Ab'unaï, which followed an anchorite life. Of a sect founded by one Ansama, or Antami, nothing particular is told. The next sect, which taught that all laws were abolished, were called the Kilataï or Katitaï. Accepting the latter reading, which has double authority, we may connect the word with *Encratite*, and suppose the sect to have been libertine in character, the contempt of the flesh passing over into license, a phenomenon marked in many Christian sects.[36] Another sect, the Sadukaï, had a "mystic" faith. Yet another took to itself the name of "the Proud and Humble;" they went and lived in the desert across Jordan; we naturally compare the "Afflicted Ones" of the Old Testament, and the Christian Ebionites. The next sectarian recorded is Shalih ibn Tirun ibn Nin, or Sakta ben Tabrin; his Arabic name assigns him to the age of Islam. He was an extremist in departing from the ancient customs, even giving up the ascent of Gerizim, and having Puritanic traits like those of the Karaites. The sect of the Sons of Josadak, or

[35] *Abu'l Fath*, 159. Cf. *Chron. Adler*, 70, which is much briefer and with a different order of sects.
[36] Clement notes a sect of Entychitæ, a branch of the Simonians, *Stromata*, vii, 17. They appear as Eutychetæ in Theodoret, *Hæres.* i, 1.

Sadok, was more orthodox, but made some ritual innovations. A certain Aulian founded a sect which appears to have had a communistic basis. Finally there was the sect of the Faskutaï, which proceeded to the extreme in daring fleshly passion, until at last they all passed over into the worst lasciviousness. May this name be connected with the Greek *physikos,* or *psychikos?* The sect would then be another specimen of encratitic delusion. Samaritanism thus experienced the variegated religious influences of the first centuries of the Christian era, and we have to assume for it in its small sphere a life of inner sectarian turmoil, very unlike the hard and fast orthodoxy into which it has long since settled down.

§ 2. SIMON MAGUS; GNOSTICISM; KABBALISM.

Many of the early Christian writers assert that Simon Magus (*Acts,* 8), was one of the earliest heresiarchs, if not the first, that disturbed the peace of the Church. In fact an extensive romance has been spun about that mysterious personage, appearing especially in the apocryphal Clementine literature. To the student of the New Testament and Patristics the inquiry into the relation of Simon to Samaritanism would appear to be of prime importance. In the following pages the Samaritan data on Simon will be collected and their relation to Christian references noted, along with the consideration of his assumed influence on the Samaritan sect; but the results will prove disappointing to the student who desires more light on that arch-heresiarch.

In *Acts,* 8, Simon appears as a sorcerer and an impostor whom his dupes acknowledge as " the so-called Great Power of God." Justin Martyr, himself a citizen of Neapolis-Shechem, although not a Samaritan, is the next to give details concerning Simon's life and character. He was born at Gittai in Samaria;[37] almost all the Samaritans and many of other nations believed in him, and he was accompanied by a woman, a former prostitute named Helena, whom he declared to be his "first conception," ἔννοια πρωτή. Justin himself says that he had written a special treatise against the Simonian heresy, and it is thought probable that this work is the basis of Irenæus's treatment of the sect. This Father gives an ampler account of Simon's doctrine, which has become a perfect example of full-blown Gnosticism. Other features of the heresy are given in Hippolytus's *Refutation of all Heresies,* with special stress upon its immoral features. Later there is the development of the romance of Simon with its caricature of St. Paul, found in the Pseudo-Clementines, which has been so thoroughly exploited by the school of F. C. Baur.[38]

In the Samaritan Chronicles "Simon the Sorcerer" appears only as a wonder-worker and as an opponent of the Christians.[39] His birthplace was 'Alin (*Abu'l Fath*) or Tablin (*Chron. Adler*). A long anecdote is given recounting how his magic worked the death of an innocent man, whom he later restored to life. He then went to Armiya, or Armina, evidently Rome,— this in correspondence with the Christian tradition, which is as ancient as Justin. He had encounters with the Christians, whom, according to *Chron. Adler,* he overcame with his magic. He then went

[37] The word appears in our Patristic references as Γιτθων, Γιττων. After the analogy of the Greek representation of place-names, this probably stands for the Hebrew Gittaim; cf. *2 Sam.* 4, 3; *Neh.* 11, 33. Place-names compounded with *gath* were common in Palestine, and there is no tradition of the exact location of Simon's birthplace. Robinson may be correct in identifying it with Kuryet-Jit, 7 mi. W. of Nablus, on the road to Joppa; *LBR* 134.

[38] The references in Justin are found in *Apol.* i, 26; 56; ii, 15; *C. Tryph.* 120; in Irenæus, in his *Hæreses,* i, 23. For an admirable discussion of the subject, see Salmond in the *Dict. of Christ. Biog.,* s. v. *Simon Magus.* Justin does not appear to be well acquainted with the Samaritan sect; cf. Chap. IX, *sub fin.*

[39] *Abu'l Fath,* 157; *Chron. Adler,* 67. The MSS give both the Hebrew and the Greek forms of the name, Sim'on and Simon.

to the philosopher Philo of Alexandria, and asked his help to destroy the Christians; but Philo bade him let the thought alone, for " if this thing be from God, none will be able to exterminate it " (cf. *Acts,* 5, 39). Finally Simon returned to his birthplace and died there, being buried " in the valley over against the house of the disciple who first testified to the Messiah, whose name was Stephen."[40] The age of Simon is placed by the chroniclers in the IVth Century; but the story of his connection with Philo evinces a truer chronological tradition. To sum up, the Samaritan version of the Simon legend is very scanty, being based on the Christian romance, and yet embracing some independent details drawn probably from a Palestinian form of the story. It possesses no information concerning Simon's doctrines.

Finally the question arises as to the Samaritan origin of the Gnostic heresies which defiled " the virginity " of the early Church. According to the Fathers and especially the heresiologues, the first heretics, or amongst the first, were Dositheus and Simon, and the latter's disciple Menander,[41] the last two being Gnostics. Palestine had long been the meeting-place and crucible of the religions of East and West, and no region was better fitted to be the peculiar home of syncretism than Samaria. Lying next door to Judæa, it was susceptible to the attractions of the Jewish religion, and likewise had ample opportunity to affect both Judaism and its daughter Christianity. Yet there is little or no proof for the hypothesis that the Samaritan religion was responsible for these processes of amalgamation, or

[40] According to early Christian tradition Stephen was buried by Gamaliel in his own tomb at Kaphar-gamala (or Kaphar-Gamaliel?), 20 miles from Jerusalem, the remains being removed to Jerusalem in 415; see Cave, *Lives of the Fathers,* " Life of St. Stephen."
[41] See the Patristic references in the preceding Section. For Menander, see Justin, *I. Apol.* 26, 56. Another disciple of Simon was Cleobius, *Apostolic Constitutions,* vi, 16.

became the mother of Gnosticism. So far as we have been able to sound the obscure ages of Samaritan religion, even according to the hostile Jewish evidence, we can find no syncretistic features therein, no native tendency to Gnosticism. Simon Magus appears not as a type of Samaritanism, but only as an incident; doubtless there is exaggeration concerning the universality of his influence upon the Samaritans, as recorded in *Acts* and by Justin. From what we learn of his doctrine in these two sources, he probably found his following rather amongst the Hellenistic population of Samaria, than in the Samaritan sect. His claim to be the Great Power of God represents nothing we find in Samaritan doctrine, whose Messianism was of a very primitive type. Further, he left behind no influence, either upon Samaritan religion or upon its historical traditions. Samaritanism was touched by like influences on the circumference, as appears from the sects described above, but the latter seem to have been of small importance and to have separated from the orthodox community, and so were soon lost. Whatever may be the worth of the tradition of the syncretistic origin of the Samaritan sect found in 2 *Ki.* 17, the Samaritans by the Ist Century A.C., had been for centuries nothing else than a Jewish sect.

It is true that, as we saw in the Chapter on Samaritan theology, there are considerable traces of an incipient Gnostic speculation, as in the childish inquiries into the origin of certain mystic things like the Book of the Law, or of such a personage as Moses. But, as abundantly appeared in that Chapter, all these speculations have their parallel in orthodox Judaism. Critical comparison and chronology indicate that in such developments the Samaritans were borrowing from the far stronger-minded Jewish theology; there is no original phenomenon of the kind in the former sect. In fact in these developments of Samaritanism, appearing especially in Marka, we have nothing else than a faint reflex of that process in Judaism which is a form of Gnosticism, and to which the technical name of Kabbalism had best be given. This tendency appeared already in New Testament times, and was serious enough to require the attention of the *Epistle to the Colossians;* it constantly manifests itself in the Talmud, still more in the Midrashim, while the later Kabbala worked out the process into a logical philosophy. Yet Samaritanism, while a debtor in part to Jewish Kabbalism, never went the whole length; for such speculations its dry, unimaginative genius seems to have been unfitted. In a word Samaritanism cannot be held responsible for Simon Magus, or for the Gnostic developments of which the Christian heresiologues have made him the archetype.[42]

[42] The chief advocate of an extensive Gnosticism, even veritable Simonianism, as existing in Samaritan literature, is that assiduous scholar Heidenheim; see especially *BS* ii, p. xxxv. But he advances no proofs for anything but what is found in incipient Jewish Kabbalism. He takes the frequent divine epithet מיעם as representing the Simonian expression ἐστώς, *Clem. Hom.* ii, 22; yet the term is used by Philo, *De nom. mut.* 1052. The Glory is only an ancient Jewish theologumenon, equivalent to the Shekina. We may also cite such Kabbalistic phrases as "the Line," by which God created the world, and "the treasury of knowledge"; *BS* ii, 57, v. 6; 85, v. 12. Some other like instances are given above, Chapter XII, § 3. But no theory of a developed Gnosticism or Kabbalism can be built on these meagre data. Reference may be made to Cowley's pertinent remarks on the subject, *JQR* viii, 571.

CHAPTER XIV.

THE LANGUAGES AND LITERATURE OF THE SAMARITANS.[1]

§ 1. THE HEBREW LANGUAGE.

The native tongue of the Samaritans was the Hebrew, the great monument of their use of this language being their text of the Pentateuch. But Hebrew met with the same fate in Samaria as in the Jewish territories of Palestine; it early succumbed to the predominance of the Aramaic, whose intrusion as the vernacular took place some centuries before the Christian era. Except as a sacred language Hebrew suffered a long eclipse, until, with the passing of the Aramaic before the new tongue of Islam, the use of Hebrew again revived, so that the literature of the IId Christian Millennium, when not written in Arabic, was composed in Hebrew. The latter is the language used, along with the Arabic, in the correspondence with European scholars. Even as in Jewish literature, the Samaritans preserved some classical sense in their use of their sacred tongue; thus the idiom of the *waw*-consecutive appears.[2] But in general the Hebrew has become thoroughly debased under the influences of Aramaic and Arabic.

§ 2. THE ARAMAIC LANGUAGE.

Toward the end of the last pre-Christian Millennium the West-Aramaic became the vernacular in Palestine.

[1] See especially Nutt, *Sam. Targ.* 77; Kautzsch, *RE s. v. Samaritaner;* Cowley, *JE s. v. Samaritans.*
[2] *E. g. BS* ii, § 2.

The form which it adopted in Samaria can hardly be called a distinct dialect, so closely is it related to the neighboring dialectical varieties, especially that of the Jews of Galilee. It shows a somewhat larger use of Hebraisms and Greek words than its neighbors. Its principal monument is the Samaritan Targum, or rather Targums, of the Pentateuch. Unfortunately this Targumic literature has become so debased in its text by transmission for centuries through scribes who were ignorant of Aramaic, that it is no longer a reliable witness to the Samaritan dialect, unless subjected to exhaustive philological criticism. As Kautzsch says, Kohn has convincingly proved that " the usual assumption of peculiar (so-called ' Kuthæan ') roots and words in the Samaritan Aramaic, rests merely upon the wholly untrustworthy corruption of the Targum MSS." Hence the attempts of scholars since Castellus' day to connect the peculiarities of this dialect with the tradition of the origin of the Samaritan sect from Assyrian colonists fall to the ground. No satisfactory lexicon of this Samaritan Aramaic dialect has been compiled, although one is promised by Vollers; the lexical attempts and the grammars are recorded in the foot-note. Aramaic composition lasted as late as the XIth Century, when Hebrew began to supersede it, apparently entirely replacing it by the XIVth Century. The Targums went out of use, although the memory of them is retained in the Epistles. Petermann says:[3] " The Samaritan translation has almost entirely fallen out of use."[4]

[3] *Reisen* i, 285.
[4] See, for the true characterization of the dialect, Kohn, *Zur Sprache, Litteratur und Dogmatik der Samaritaner,* 99; cf. p. 206; Kautzsch, *Grammatik d. Biblisch-Aramäischen,* 13. *For* a comparative list of forms and words in the Palestinian dialects, see Dalman, *Grammatik der jüdisch-palästinischen Aramäisch,* 33; according to the comparative tables there presented, the Samaritan almost always agrees with the Galilæan dialect as against the Judæan. Grammars have been published by the following scholars: Crinesius, Ravis, Morinus, Hilleger, Cellarius, Otho, Masclef, Stöhr, Uhlemann, Nicholls, Petermann, Rosenberg. Of these, Morinus, Hilleger, Cellarius, Otho, Uhlemann,

§ 3. THE ARABIC LANGUAGE.

With Islam's conquest of Syria in the decade following Mohammed's death, the potent Arabic displaced the local Aramaic dialects, with the exception of remote districts or where the native tongues survived as ecclesiastical languages. In general the Samaritan Arabic is of a provincial, vulgar type, containing many Hebraisms and Aramaisms. The literary elegance of the classical literature of the Arabs had its influence however, and a superior ideal was followed in the Arabic translations of the Pentateuch, and in purpose at least, by the chronicler Abu'l Fath.

§ 4. THE SAMARITAN SCRIPT AND INSCRIPTIONS.

The script employed by the Samaritans not only for Hebrew and Aramaic but also often for Arabic, differs from the Jewish square character, and, as representing a much earlier type of the so-called Phœnician character, is an object of interest to the epigraphist.

Fortunately a few early monuments are preserved which show an alphabet of much more antique form than that used in Samaritan MSS, the great majority of which date from the XIIIth Century and onwards, although a few bear earlier datings.[5] The most considerable of these monu-

Petermann give glossaries. The only lexicon is that of Castellus in his *Lexicon heptaglotton,* published when only the Targum was known. (For the titles of these works, see Bibliography.) In his Grammar Petermann has given most valuable transliterations representing the modern Samaritan pronunciation, and on the same basis attempted a philological study of the Hebrew entitled, *Versuch einer hebräischen Formenlehre nach der Aussprache der heutigen Samaritaner* (criticism by Nöldeke in *Göttinger Gelehrte Nachrichten,* 1868, p. 485). For the Samaritan grammarians' views of the pronunciation, see Nöldeke, *Ueber einige sam.-arab. Schriften.*

[5] The St. Petersburg Codex No. 4 is dated 717 B. C., and the Watson Codex II. (see Bibliography) bears the early date of 655, although this profession of so high an antiquity has aroused general skepticism. The bulk of the great Barberini Triglot has the date 1227. On the dating of Samaritan MSS, see Gottheil, *JBL* 1906, p. 29.

Pal. Ex. Fund.

PLATE 1. THE SHECHEM DECALOGUE INSCRIPTION.

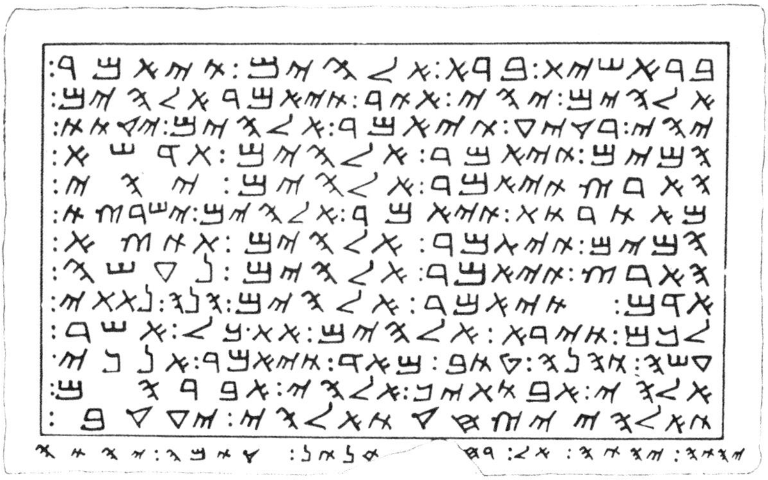

From Lidzbarski.

PLATE 2. THE SHECHEM INSCRIPTION OF THE TEN WORDS OF
CREATION.

PLATE 3. THE LEEDS FRAGMENT OF A DECALOGUE INSCRIPTION.

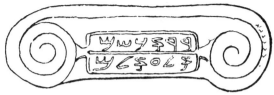

From Lidzbarski.

PLATE 4. THE FIRST EMMAUS INSCRIPTION.

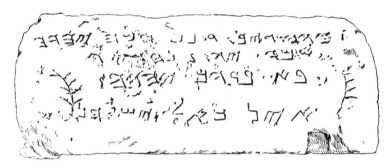

PLATE 5. THE SECOND EMMAUS INSCRIPTION.

PLATE 6. THE THIRD EMMAUS INSCRIPTION.

PLATE 7 (SOBERNHEIM, ABB. 8.)

בשם : יה : דאמר : (non-Biblical) וף : ע :
ו : יה : ב : נ : (*Ex.* 12, 13) ו : יה : על : הף :
ו : י : המ : לב : אל : ב : ל : (*Ex.* 12, 23)

Translations of the text signified by abbreviations: "And I will pass over you and there shall be no plague amongst you. And YHWH will pass over the door and will not allow the destroyer to plague you."

עהמה
יהוה
אין כאל
ישרון
יהוה
אחד

יהוה
גיבור
יהוה
נצחה
יהוה
שמר

PLATE 8. BRONZE TABLET (SOBERNHEIM, ABB. 15, 16).

Obverse: "The Existent (קהמה), YHWH, None Like God, One."
Reverse: "YHWH, Great, Victorious YHWH, his Name" (to be read שמו ?).

ments are two inscriptions which hail from Nablus and from the one-time synagogue of the Samaritans, but which is now the Muslim mosque Chizn Yakub ("the weeping of Jacob," i.e. for Joseph), also called al-Chadhra, "the mosque of the green (tree)," and according to Samaritan tradition "the portion of the field" which Jacob purchased (*Gen.* 33, 18). One of these inscriptions is built in the east wall of the minaret of the present mosque, and contains the Decalogue in abbreviated form.[6] A reproduction from a photograph is herewith given (Plate 1), along with the translation, as follows:

1. ....thy God ......
2. ......Thou shalt not take the name of Yhwh
3. thy God in vain. Keep the day
4. of the Sabbath to sanctify it. Honor thy father
5. and thy mother. Thou shalt not murder. Thou shalt not commit adultery.
6. Thou shalt not steal. Thou shalt not witness against thy brother
7. falsely. Thou shalt not covet the house
8. of thy neighbor. (Thou shalt not covet thy neighbor's wife.)
9. And thou shalt build there (an altar to Yhwh thy God).[7]
10. Arise Yhwh, return Yhwh.[8]

[6] The first transcript of it was made by the German consul Schultz, and his narrative and copy of the inscription were edited by Rödiger in the *Hallesche Allgem. Literatur-Zeitung,* 1845, p. 658. It was treated independently by Blau with notes from another copy by Blau in *ZDMG* xiii, 275, with plate, and with notes by Rödiger, and again by Rosen on the basis of his own far more correct transcript, *ZDMG* xiv, 622, with plate, and with supplementary remarks by Rödiger, p. 632. See Rosen's article for full account of the *provenance* of the inscription. For the Decalogue in the Liturgy, see Heidenheim, *DVJ* iii, 486.

[7] This line from *Dt.* 27, 5, being part of the long pericope introduced by the Sam. Pent. after the Decalogue, which itself was regarded as the Xth Commandment. For a MS thus numbering the X Commandments, see Rosen, *l. c.*

[8] *Num.* 10, 35–36. The above text is conflate from *Ex.* and *Dt.*

18

The second inscription, which is in almost perfect condition, was found in the ruins about the above-named mosque and sold to Jacob esh-Shelaby; it was first published by Rosen.[9] The accompanying Plate (No. 2) reproduces the inscription; the following is the translation, which shows that we have here the Ten Words of Creation.

1. In the beginning God created. And said
2. God, Let there be light. And God said,
3. Let there be a firmament. And God said, Let be collected
4. the waters. And God said, Bring forth (grass)
5. the earth. And God said, Let there be
6. lights. And God said, Let swarm
7. the waters. And God said, Bring forth
8. the earth. And God said, Let us make
9. man. And God said, Behold I have given you.
10. And God saw all that
11. he had made, and behold it was very good. And he said, I
12. am the God of thy father, the God of Abraham
13. and the God of Isaac and the God of Jacob.
14. [margin] Yhwh, Yhwh, a God mer(ciful and) gracious, the Existent, Yhwh.

It may be observed that this grouping of the Ten Words of Creation is very common in Samaritan literature, and also has its Rabbinic parallels.[10]

Yet another inscription, greatly mutilated, is now in the

[9] In the article cited above, *ZDMG* xiv, 622, a plate being given. Transliteration and facsimile may also be found in Lidzbarski, *Handb. d. nordsem. Epigraphik,* 440, and Plate xxi.

[10] See Heidenheim, *DVJ* i, 563. According to *Pirke Abot*, v, 1, "by ten words the world was created." There was a difference of opinion as to which was the tenth word, both the Samaritan and the Rabbinic parallels having "he said" only nine times. The more common opinion was that the first word was contained in the introductory statement of creation. See Taylor, *ad loc.*

Library of the Leeds Philosophical and Literary Society.[11]
The fragment (see Plate 3) is the lower right-hand quarter of a Decalogue inscription, being like that found at
Nablus, but differing in the last line. The last six commandments can be traced; then, in the last line but one,
appears " an altar unto," thus helping us to fill out the
lacuna in line 9 of the Nablus inscription. Of the last
line only משה לנו ה is visible, but it may be supplied
from *Dt.* 33, 4, so that the inscription once read: " Moses
commanded unto us a law, an inheritance for the assembly
of Jacob."

As to the date of these inscriptions we may argue with
Rosen that they are anterior to the disruption of the Samaritan community by Justinian; but epigraphy is not in a
position to be more specific.[12]

But other epigraphic material of an earlier date has
been discovered at al-Amwas, the ancient Emmaus-Nicopolis. The first of these inscriptions, discovered by Clermont-
Ganneau in 1881, contains only nine characters of the
alphabet, and reads: ברוך׳ שם ולעולם: " Blessed be the
Name even (and) forever " (see Plate 4). This is generally spoken of as a Samaritan inscription; it is however
much more archaic than any other Samaritan inscriptions we possess, while the words " and forever " are remi-
niscent of the Pharisaic formula of benediction, " forever
and ever," which was eschewed by the Samaritans.[13]

Two other inscriptions however have been found by Lagrange at Emmaus, which are doubtless of Samaritan
origin as they bear the genuine Samaritan type, while their
collocation of Scripture texts is parallel to the phenomenon

[11] Published by Wright in *PSBA* vi, 1883, Nov. p. 25, with plate.
It was given to the Rev. Joseph Hammond by the Samaritan highpriest in the sixties.

[12] For the XVIIIth Century inscription in the present synagogue,
see Chap. III, note 13.

[13] For this inscription, see the Bibliography under *Clermont-Ganneau.* Lidzbarski gives a copy of it, Plate xxi.

of the Damascus inscriptions to be noticed below. The first of these inscriptions, which we may call the second Emmaus inscription, was found in 1890.[14] A copy of it is here given (Plate 5); it is to be transcribed and translated as follows:

יהוה גיבור במלחמה יהוה
שמו יהוה נחיתו
בא ברוך יהוה
אין כאל ישרון

"YHWH is a hero in war [Ex. 15, 3[15]], YHWH: is his name. YHWH, thou hast conducted him [cf. Ex. 15, 13]: Come thou blessed of YHWH [Gen. 24, 31; cf. Ps. 118, 26; Mk. 11, 9, etc.]: There is none like the God of Jeshurun [Dt. 33, 26]." There appears to be reference to some historic event, the hero of which is addressed in almost Messianic terms.

The third Emmaus inscription was found by Lagrange in 1896.[16] The inscription (Plate 6) is legible enough to allow us to make out the following Biblical text:

ופסח יהוה על הפתח
ולא יתן המשית לבא

which is found in Ex. 12, 23: "YHWH will pass over the door: And will not allow the destroyer to enter."[17]

At the more distant Gaza Clermont-Ganneau has reported that he saw in a private residence in 1874 a Sa-

[14] For Lagrange's first report, see Bibliography. His final readings are found in Revue biblique, ii (1893), 114.
[15] The change from איש , "man," is the reading of the Samaritan Hebrew, ad loc. For the same anti-anthropomorphic tendency, cf. Ps. 24, 8. This was a favorite Samaritan text: see the Damascene inscriptions given by Sobernheim (No. I), and Musil (No. IV).
[16] Reported by him to de Vogüé, who published it with plate and notes in Revue biblique, v (1896), 433; de Vogüé's transcription is given here in Plate 6.
[17] N. B. the loss of the guttural in the next to the last word — in good Samaritan fashion. This Paschal text also appears in the Damascene inscriptions; Sobernheim, No. III, and Musil, No. I.

maritan inscription of nineteen short lines, engraved on a
long marble block; unfortunately he failed to obtain a
transcription or a satisfactory photograph. According to
his recollection it was liturgical in character.[18]

A second Gaza inscription, first reported by Abel,[19] is
also a fragment of the Decalogue, giving the opening words,
Ex. 20, 2–4a (*Dt*. 5, 6–8a), breaking off at " likeness." It
is prefaced with יהוה בשם, which indicates an origin in
the age of Islam.

In this connection reference may be made to the inscriptions found in houses in Damascus, once belonging to
wealthy Samaritan families. Ten such inscriptions from
one house were discovered and published by Sobernheim.[20]
More recently Musil has published, although with ignorance
of Sobernheim's discovery, seven similar inscriptions,
copies of which were forwarded to him from Damascus.[21]
These inscriptions are almost wholly composed of Biblical
quotations combined in a very abbreviated form, the initial
letter of a word being often all that is given. From some
of the texts they appear to have been intended for private
tenements, and with the purpose of fulfilling the command
in *Dt*. 6, 8f. Those published by Sobernheim are executed with great elegance. Some of these inscriptions as
published by Sobernheim and Musil are reproduced here
(Plates 7–12), including a small bronze tablet inscribed
on both sides (Plate 8).

In the accompanying Plate (Plate 13), the Samaritan
alphabet is presented in variant forms, and also in comparison with selected types of its forbears in the Phœnician
alphabet. In Columns II–V, I give various early types of

---

[18] Clermont-Ganneau, *Archæological Researches*, 1896, ii, 430.
[19] Published by Clermont-Ganneau, *Inscription samaritaine de Gaza*,
Revue biblique, 1906, p. 84, with plate.
[20] *Samaritanische Inschriften aus Damascus*, MDPV viii, 70, with
plates of the inscriptions, and plan of the house.
[21] *Sieben samaritanische Inschriften aus Damaskus*, Vienna, 1903.

related alphabets, using the nomenclature of Lidzbarski, on whose Tables I depend for the forms; the Vth Column offers a few Aramaic forms which are suggestive of certain Samaritan developments. In Cols. VI–VIII appear monumental Samaritan types, those respectively of the first Emmaus inscription (if this may be considered Samaritan), of the Nablus inscription of the Ten Words, and of the Leeds inscription, again with dependence upon Lidzbarski's reproductions. In Cols. IX–XIII are found Samaritan manuscriptal types, viz.: No. IX, from the evidently early Targum published by Nutt, the facsimile given by him being made use of; No. X, the majuscule characters of the earlier portion of *Liber Josuae* (dated 1362); Col. XI is drawn from Plate XII of Wright's *Oriental Series,* in the publications of the London Palæographical Society, being a Biblical MS dated 1362; Cols. XII and XIII are cursive types, drawn from the Gotha MSS, whose forms are reproduced by Gesenius in his *Carmina Samaritana,* and from the minuscule types of the latter part of *Liber Josuae,* whose date is 1513. These cursive forms are of interest as they exhibit some primitive and independent characteristics. The type of Col. XI is most representative of the dominating form of Samaritan chirography. In Col. XIV are given the printed types used by Petermann (in freehand reproduction).

The Samaritan alphabet is predominantly of the Early Hebrew type, but with some peculiar developments. The Çade has been made to stand upright on its legs, as is also the case with Yod. Waw and Zayin have developed their own forms, which however can easily be traced back to the Early Hebrew. Similarity to Middle Phœnician appears in Yod and Qoph. For Tet an Aramaic form is the nearest equivalent. Samaritan has gone its own way in developing a box-like figure for Samek out of the original crisscross character, with whorls that are lineally descended

Plate 13. Comparative Table for the Samaritan Alphabet

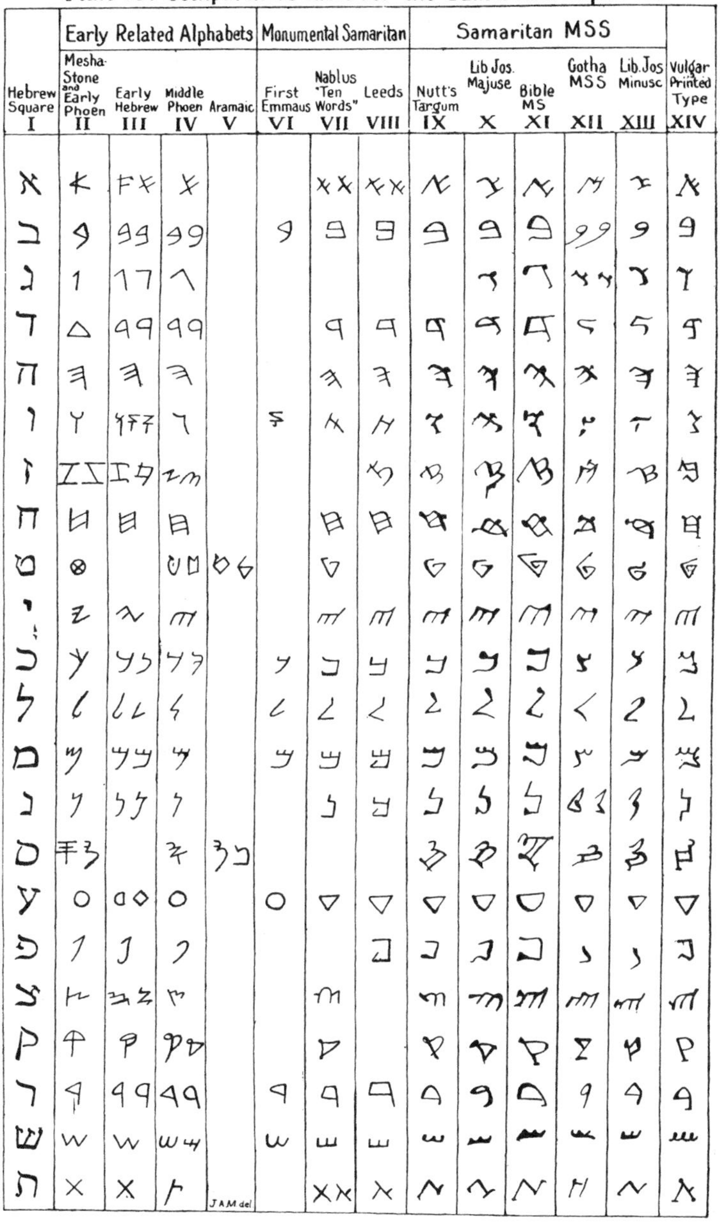
Early Related Alphabets
Monumental Samaritan
Samaritan MSS
Hebrew Square I
Mesha Stone and Early Phoen II
Early Hebrew III
Middle Phoen IV
Aramaic V
First Emmaus VI
Nablus "Ten Words" VII
Leeds VIII
Nutt's Targum IX
Lib Jos. Majuse X
Bible MS XI
Gotha MSS XII
Lib. Jos Minusc XIII
Vulgar Printed Type XIV
J A M del

from early forms. The Early Hebrew type has apparently been affected by Phœnician influence, and also has asserted its independence in retaining many early characteristics. It is to be noticed that the types of the Nablus and Leeds inscriptions in part preserve the ancient inclination to the left, in part have attained a square, upright character; the Hebrew alphabet is also followed or imitated in the turning of the tail of several of the characters square around to the left, i.e. בּ, כּ, מ, נ, פ . The same assimilation between characters has taken place as in the Hebrew square-letter, necessitating the use of diacritical lines, as for instance in ד and ר, כ and פ. In ה one of the cross-pieces has been deliberately broken, and its parts set out of alignment, perhaps in artificial imitation of א . In the cursive script of the MSS we find an eccentric development of whorls and knots, with neither beauty nor usefulness, the result being an exaggerated " Gothic " type, which has arisen from the effort, paralleled in Judaism, to produce a conventional ecclesiastical script. A slight carelessness on the part of the scribes, often unskilled in the language they copied, easily produces great confusion between many pairs of letters, e.g. ד and ר, ה and ר, נ and פ, ע and ק .[22]

A great diversity in the form of the characters exists in the MSS. Unfortunately the conventional European printed type, which came into vogue with the Polyglots and was continued by Petermann, has created an outlandish style of its own, being a caricature rejected by the Samaritans themselves. De Sacy considerably bettered things with the type in his edition of the Samaritan Epistles in *Notes et Extraits,* and this again has been improved upon by the fonts of the *Journal asiatique.* The following remarks by Euting may be of interest for the history of the subject: " Die samaritanischen Schrifttabellen bei Berger, Is. Taylor, The Alphabet, i. 242ff sind werthlos, ebenso die

[22] See Lidzbarski, *Handbuch der nordsemitischen Epigraphik,* 185.

von mir in Gesenius-Kautzsch Grammatik, 25. Auflage.
Brauchbare Alphabettabellen sind nur in Gesenius Carmina
und in der semitischen Schrifttafel von mir, die Bickell's
"Outlines of Hebrew Grammar" (Lpz. 1877) beigegeben
war."[23]

The difference between the Samaritan script and the
Aramaic type adopted by the Jews was claimed by the Samaritans as a proof of their own priority, and became a
serious subject of discussion in the polemics of the two
sects. Both the Jews and the Samaritans speak of the
elder script which the Samaritans preserved as the " Hebrew script." The closeness of the Samaritan to the old
Hebrew writing is shown by an experience which Nach-
manides, of the XIIIth Century reports: " The Lord
blessed me so that I came to Acco, and I found there in the
hands of the elders of the city a silver coin engraved like
a seal; on the one side there was the like of an almond
wand, and on the other the like of a flask (vase). And
on the margin of the two sides there was an engraved writing, very clear indeed. And they showed the writing to the
Kuthim, and they read it at once, for it was the Hebrew
writing which was left to the Kuthim, as it is said in *Sanhedrin*. And they read on the one side, ' The shekel of
shekels,' and on the other, ' Jerusalem the holy.' "[24]

How the change of script was effected in the Jewish
Church is explained in the *locus classicus* of the Babylonian
Talmud, *Sanhedrin,* 21b: " Mar Zutra (early in Vth
Cent.)— according to others Mar Ukba (middle of IIId
Cent.),— said: At first thè law was given to Israel in He-
brew script and in the holy tongue. It was again given to
them in the days of Ezra in the Assyrian (i.e. Syrian)

[23] In his notes, p. 8, to Almkvist, *Ein samaritanischer Brief.*
[24] Quoted by Lidzbarski, *op. cit.* 92, in the Hebrew text from de
Rossi, *Meor Enaim* (Wilna, 1866), p. 450. The coin was a shekel of
the first Jewish revolt. The interpretation of the obverse is wrong;
it reads, " shekel of Israel."

PLATE 9 (SOBERNHEIM, ABB. 11.)

וברך : את : לחמך : ואת : מימיך : והס : מ : מק :

"And he will bless thy food and thy water and will remove disease from thy midst." (*Ex.* 23, 25.)

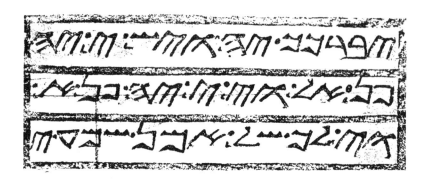

יברכך : יה : ויש : ו : יה :
פנ : אל : וי : י : יה : פנ : א :
וי : לכ : של : אמן : שמע : י

The abbreviation of the priestly blessing, *Num.* 6, 24–26, followed by *Amen,* and the introduction to the Shema: "Hear, Israel."

יְצַוֶּה ׳ יְהוָֹה ׳ אִתְּךָ ׃   יצוה ׳ יה ׃ א ׃

אֶת ׳ הַבְּרָכָה ׃   את ׳ הבר ׃

בַּאֲסָמֶךָ ׳ וּבְכֹל ׃   באם ׃ וב ׃

מִשְׁלַח ׃   משלח ׃

יָדֶיךָ ׃ וּ ׳   יד ׃ ו ׳

בֵּרַכְךָ ׳   בר ׳

כְּ   ב

אֶרֶץ   א

PLATE II (MUSIL, VI).

From the Samaritan-Hebrew text of *Dt.* 28, 8

וְרָאוּ : כָּל : עַמֵּי :   וראו : כל : עמ :

הָאָרֶץ : כִּי : שֵׁם :   הא : כי : שם :

יְהֹוָה : נִקְרָא :   יה : נק :

עָלֶיךָ :   עליכ :

וְיִירְאוּ ˙   ויי ˙ ˙

מִמֶּךָ   ממ

כָּל :   כ :

אָדָם   א

PLATE 12 (MUSIL, VII).

From the Samaritan-Hebrew text of *Dt.* 28, 10, *plus,* at the end,
˙א : כ, *i. e.,* כל אדם, "all men."

script and in the Aramaic tongue. Israel chose for themselves the Assyrian script and the holy tongue, and they
left to the ' Idiots ' the Hebrew script and the Aramaic
tongue. Who are the Idiots? R. Chasda (*c.* 300) said:
The Kuthim. What is the Hebrew script? R. Chasda
said, The " libonaa " (ליבונאה, var. ליבונאי) script."[25]

We need not further pursue the Jewish traditions except so far as they characterize the differences between the
two scripts. In the passage quoted above the Rabbis called
the Samaritan script " Libonæan." Another description is
given in the passages referred to above, by a word variously
vocalized, viz. *ra‘aç, ro‘aç, ra‘uç,,* while the Aruch gives the
variant *da‘aç.* The root רעץ signifies " to break " and
would capitally characterize the " splinter-like," angular
style of the earlier script; this may be the sense of the
passive formations *ra‘uç,* and *ro‘aç,* the term subsequently
coming to be interpreted *in malo sensu,*— " when they
sinned it was changed into breaking," even as אשורית,
" Assyrian," was interpreted *in bono sensu,* as " blessed,"
מאושר . The root of the variant דעץ means " to prick,"
and might be used of the work of an iron stylus operated
upon stone.

As to the choice between the two roots דעץ and רעץ ,
a Patristic passage adduced by Hoffmann appears to cast
the die,[26] viz: Hic igitur Esdras [i.e. the assumed Ezra
who brought the Law to the Samaritans] quem diximus,

---

[25] The same story appears in *Megil. Jer.* i, 71b; *Sota Jer.* vii, 21c.
One opinion was that the Law itself was given in the Syrian script,
so greatly were the Rabbis concerned over their form of the text.
The patristic writers have the same tradition: Origen, ed. Migne, xii,
col. 1104; Jerome, *Prol. galeat.,* M. xxviii, 593; on *Ezek.* 9, 4, M. xxv,
88 (noticing the antique cruciform Taw of the Samaritans) ; Epiphanius, *De XII gemmis,* § 63, M. xliii, 356 (to be quoted below). Bux-
torf (*Diss. de litt. Heb. antiq.*) has collected later Jewish traditions to
the effect that the Samaritan Law and script were obtained through the
Jewish priests sent by the king of Assyria.

[26] Epiphanius, *De XII gemmis,* § 63, Migne, *Patrol. Gr.* xliii, 356
(existing only in a Latin version).

ascendens Hierosolymam, Pentateuchum tantummodo, id est quinque libros Moysi, detulit eis Veteris Testamenti libros scriptos secundum formam quam dedit Dominus in monte Sina; quam formam Hebræi *deession* [var. *dession*] vocant, quod interpretatur insculptum; nunc enim non eadem sunt elementa litterarum quibus Hebræi utuntur, librique eorum non sunt scripti iuxta veterem formam, quæ tunc in tabulis lapideis constat insculpta. Hæc igitur forma, quam nunc tenent Iudæi, vocatur Somahirenus. Samaritani servant *dessenon* quæ forma fuit olim, ut diximus, in tabulis impressa lapideis. At Esdra [the Jewish Ezra] ascendens a Babylone, volensque discernere Israel a reliquis gentibus, ut genus Abrahæ non videretur esse permixtum cum habitatoribus terræ, qui tenent quidem Legem, non tamen et Prophetas, immutavit pristinam formam relinquens *deessenon,* propter quod ea forma a Samaritanis præoccupata iam fuerat, ut per hoc Abrahæ semen distingueretur a nationibus reliquis.

Hoffmann would read *deessenon* in all three instances, understanding the last two syllables as a Greek adjectival ending, -ηνον, equivalent to -ινον. The first two syllables then would represent the Talmudic variant *da'aç*. Accordingly this independent Greek authority corroborates the less attested Rabbinic reading, and must be allowed to decide the question between the two. The *da'aç* character is then the ancient chiselled type, as distinguished from the flowing cursive of the Hebrew square character. The more common variant *ra'aç* arose through an easy confusion of letters, and may have been preferred because of the aspersion which it suggested against the Samaritan script.

Upon the adjective "Libonæan," the final word has not yet been spoken. It has been explained by Geiger as "the well-balanced form of writing," but, as Hoffmann remarks, this would apply far more pertinently to the Hebrew square character. The form is apparently gentilic, and hence it has been explained as " Libanian," i.e. of Lebanon, or as representing the Ephraimitish town Lebona, the modern Lubban,— so Hoffmann, who suggests that this may have been the seat of a Samaritan school. Most recently, and very reasonably, Halévy has argued that it is a corruption for ניבולאה " Neapolitan," i.e. of Shechem-Neapolis.[27]

In *Tanchuma* (*Wayyesheb*, § 2), and *Pirke Eliezer*, c. 38, *sub fin.*, the ancient script preserved by the Samaritans is called נוטריקון, i.e. *notaricum*, a notary's or stenographer's script. The earlier alphabet was much better fitted for rapid writing than the square character, and may have survived in business use comparatively late.

Finally there may be noted here the bit of Jewish humor over the enclosed form of the antique Ayin: " If anyone says the Law was given in *ra'aç*, the letter Ayin was a miracle " — on the basis of the legend that the writing of the Law on both sides of the tables of stone meant that the letters were cut through the tables, in which case the core of the round or triangular Ayin would have been wholly detached from the rest of the stone.[28]

§ 5. THE SAMARITAN HELLENISTIC LITERATURE.

With the spread of Hellenism over the Orient the Greek became, and remained for nearly a millennium, a second language in the mouth of the Samaritans. It was used by them as by the Jews not only for international intercourse, but also as a literary vehicle for placing themselves in a dignified historical and literary light before the

[27] For an excellent apparatus of references to the terms discussed above, see Jastrow, *Dictionary, s. vv.*, and, for extensive quotation from Rabbinic sources, Lightfoot, on Mt. 5, 18. For discussions of the terms, see ·Hupfeld, *Beleuchtung dunkler Stellen alttest. Textgeschichte*, in *Theologische Studien und Kritiken*, i (1830), especially p. 289ff; G. Hoffman, *Lexicalisches*, ZATW i (1881), p. 334; ii, 53; Geiger, *JZW* v, 115; Halévy, *Mélanges de critique et d'histoire*, 1883, No. xv.
[28] *Megil. Jer.* 71c.

eyes of Greek culture, and also doubtless as a means of
polemic against the Jews; this must have been the case
especially in Egypt. Samaria with its thoroughly Pagan
capital Sebaste and through its physical openness to foreign influences, doubtless even more than Judæa accommo-
dated itself to the use of the new tongue.

Only scanty fragments and references throw light upon
the Hellenistic literature of the Samaritans. The few
historical excerpts have been preserved by Josephus, Clement of Alexandria, and especially by Eusebius; they all hail
from the historical work *Concerning the Jews,* composed
by Alexander Polyhistor, a Roman historian who flourished
about 50 B. C.[28a] Of one of these authorities of Alexander, Eupolemus, Eusebius has preserved extensive extracts *(Praep. evang.* ix, 17, 18, 26, 30–34, 39). Of
these, sections 17 and 18 give a Midrash on Abraham's
life, in which Gerizim appears as ὄρος ὑψίστου, " the
Mount of the Most High." Hence it has been argued that
Eupolemus was a Samaritan. But as the other fragments
are distinctly Jewish, while Eupolemus may be identified
with Judas Maccabee's ambassador to Rome (1 *Mac.* 8,
17; 2 *Mac.* 4, 11), it is more reasonable to hold with Freudenthal and Schürer that sections 17 and 18 are from the
hand of an unknown Samaritan writer.[29] Freudenthal also
thinks that the Cleodemus-Malchus, quoted by Josephus
(AJ i, 15), and from him by Eusebius *(Praep. evang.* ix,
20), was a Samaritan; but as Schürer judges, the passage
could easily hail from a Jewish hand.[30]

Fragments amounting to 47 hexameter lines have been
preserved by Eusebius from an epic poem in Homeric style
composed by a certain Theodotus, who, because of his de-

[28a] Schürer, *GJV* iii, 346.
[29] *GJV* iii, 351, 358, and there the literature. The texts of these
Samaritan historians may be found in C. Müller, *Frag. hist. Grₑc.* iii,
207 *seqq.*
[30] *GJV* iii, 357.

scription of the beauty and sacredness of Shechem, which he calls " sacred city," has generally been assumed to be a Samaritan.[31] Of interest to textual criticism is the question whether a Samaritan Greek version of the Pentateuch ever existed, the query being prompted by Origen's references in his Hexapla to τὸ Σαμαρειτικόν. This is generally understood by critics as referring to the Samaritan Hebrew Pentateuch, which, however, is also termed τὸ τῶν Σαμαρειτῶν Ἑβραικόν. But Kohn especially has argued for the existence of an independent Greek version, on the ground of the correspondence of the readings reported by Origen with the Samaritan Targum.[32]

Outside of our sect Samaritan Hellenism produced some notable men. Justin Martyr was a native of Neapolis. According to Epiphanius, Symmachus, one of the Greek translators of the Old Testament, was a Samaritan, who, accepting Jewish circumcision, made his version in antagonism to those current among the Samaritans; but Eusebius and Jerome know of him only as an Ebionite.[33] The philosopher Marinus, who succeeded the Neo-Platonist Proclus at Athens in 485, came from Neapolis, as Da-

[31] The fragments are preserved by Eusebius, *Præp. evang.* ix, 22; see Schürer, *GJV* iii, 372, and add to the bibliography there, Ludwich, *De Theodoti carmine Græco-Iudaico commentatio*, Königsberg, 1899 (a university programme), giving a revised text. Ludwich is not inclined to think that the poem comes from a Samaritan hand; Eusebius says that Theodotus's work was " Concerning the Jews." Ewald, *History of Israel*, v, 262, argues that *Sibylline Oracles*, xi, 239–242, is of Samaritan origin. For extract from Theodotus, see above, p. 13.

[32] For the references to the Samaritikon, see Field, *Origenis Hexapla*, i, p. lxxxii; there are 43 such references, and four more probably from the same source. For Kohn's views, see his *De Pentateucho Samaritano*, 1865; *Samareitikon und Septuaginta*, in *Monatsschrift für Geschichte u. Wissenschaft des Judenthums*, 1893, pp. 1, 49; cf. *ZDMG* xlvii (1893), 650. König approves Kohn's position, *DB* extra vol. 71. Against Kohn, see Geiger, *ZDMG* xix, 611.

[33] Epiphanius, *De mens, et pond.* § 15; see Swete, *Introduction to the Old Testament in Greek*, 49. For a Samaritan reference to Symmachus, see Chap. V, note 10.

mascius records, quoting the philosopher as speaking of Mount Gerizim, on which " there was a most holy temple of Highest Zeus, and there Abraham, the first of the ancient Jews, was consecrated."[34] Also the sophist Siricius hailed from Samaria.[35]

§ 6. THE SAMARITAN HEBREW PENTATEUCH.

Probably the greatest stimulus ever given to the textual criticism of the Old Testament was the discovery, early in the XVIIth Century, of the existence of codices of the Hebrew Pentateuch, belonging to the Samaritans and written in their peculiar script, and in antiquity vying with or excelling the Jewish manuscripts; furthermore they presented a distinctly different text.

The possession by the Samaritans of the Law of Moses is throughout assumed and acknowledged by the Talmud and early Jewish writers, although these authorities claimed that the Samaritan Law contained forgeries, the most important of which references have been cited in Chapter X. The Patristic writers likewise had cognizance of the Samaritan text, and the early Christian critics from Origen down make frequent reference to it, using it without prejudice for the Jewish text, the latest Greek reference to it being found in George Syncellus (*c.* 800).[36] Then with the decay of learning, all remembrance of the Samaritan Pentateuch faded away, the Jews who could best have preserved the tradition being doubtless glad to ignore it.

But in 1616 Pietro della Valle, in his oriental journey, purchased a copy of this unknown text from Samaritans at Damascus, and forwarded it to Europe, where it came

[34] Damascius, in Photius, *Bibliotheca,* 1055.
[35] Reland, *Palæstina,* 1005.
[36] Origen, *Hexapla, ad Num.* 13, 1; Jerome, *Prol. gal.;* on *Gal.* 3, 10; Cyril of Alexandria (adduced by Migne to latter passage of Jerome); George Syncellus, *Chronographia,* 83 (ed. Bonn, p. 156): "the Hebrews acknowledge it to be the earliest" (cf. the same, p. 166).

THE SACRED PENTATEUCH CODEX

into the possession of the library of the Oratorians at Paris. Its publication however was long deferred, until at last it appeared, very badly edited, under the hand of Morinus, in the Paris *Polyglot* (1645). It was published again in the London *Polyglot* (1657) by Walton, "only the most glaring typographical blunders having been corrected, but a much more complete and exact list of variations was appended, the Latin version to some extent amended, and the deviations of the Targum from the Pentateuch noted."[37] Forthwith this text entered into all discussions. Kennicott carefully noted the variants of the Samaritan MSS in his great apparatus to the Hebrew Bible. Strangely enough no satisfactory edition of this text has as yet been published, although two are now promised.[38]

The codices of the Samaritan Pentateuch in European libraries have very much increased over the sixteen copies known to Kennicott, and some are to be found in private hands in America. But the codex that excites the greatest interest is the sacrosanct text preserved by the Samaritans as the palladium of their religion. It claims to have been written by the great-grandson of Aaron, as is set forth in the Tarikh between the columns of *Dt.* 5, 6ff, as follows: " I Abishua, son of Phineas, son of Eleazar, son of Aaron, — may YHWH's favor and glory be theirs — wrote the holy book in the gate of the tabernacle on Mount Gerizim in the 13th year after that the Israelites ruled the land of Canaan in its borders round about. I make known YHWH." The claim is preposterous, but how old the copy is, has not been ascertained, as so far it has been im-

[37] Nutt, *Sam. Targ.* 103.
[38] The text appears in Blayney. *Pentateuchus Samaritanus,* 1790; Lee, *Biblia sacra polyglotta,* 1831, *et seq.* A new edition is projected by the (English) Text and Translation Society, under the editorship of Ginsburg; and another by v. Gall,— see his prospectus, *ZATW* 1906, p. 293. For the MSS in Europe, see *BS* i, p. xix, and v. Gall, *l. c.*

possible for scholars to make a thorough examination of it.[39]

The publication of the Samaritan Pentateuch at once kindled a great strife in European theological circles. The Protestants and Catholics were already arrayed against each other over the question of the authentic text of the Scriptures, the former going almost to the Jewish extreme in upholding the authority of the Massoretic text, the latter taking every occasion to discredit it to the advantage of their ecclesiastically approved versions, the Vulgate and Septuagint. Capellus, who had already taken positions against the Massoretic text, proved that the Samaritan script was older than the Hebrew. Morinus, the French Oratorian, who edited the Samaritan Pentateuch for the Paris *Polyglot,* warmly espoused its text, bringing down upon himself the severe opposition of de Muis and Hottinger. In the middle of the next century the Catholic Houbigant was met by the Protestant Ravius, and Poncet by Michaelis; the great English scholar Kennicott was warmly inclined to the Samaritan readings. Finally Gesenius took up the question in an entirely dispassionate way, and carefully analyzed all the variations between the two rival texts; he believed he could reduce the valid important variants to a very small number, four in fact (*Gen.* 4, 6; 14, 14; 22, 13; 49, 14). The argument has never since been taken up in such extensive detail, students of the Pentateuch

[39] This Tarikh is frequently quoted by the Samaritan literature; e.g. *N. et E.* 169, (179); *DVJ* i, 99. For an account of the codex, first seen and described by Huntington, see Rosen, *Alte Handschriften des samaritanischen Pentateuchs, ZDMG* xviii, 582 (with plates), on the authority of two visitors to Nablus, Levisohn and Kraus, who were so fortunate as to obtain a good view of the ancient codex and to acquire a rough tracing. A photograph of a part has also been secured by the Palestine Exploration Fund. Also see Mills, *Nablus,* 308. A high antiquity is claimed for many other MSS; see Rosen, *l. c.;* but this is often due to a misunderstanding of the cryptogramic way of writing the date; see Cowley, *PEFQS* 1904, p. 344; *JQR* 1904, p. 483; Gottheil, in *JBL,* 1906, p. 29.

A Page of Watson Codex II.

Containing the Samaritan-Hebrew of *Dt.* 2, 22b-32. This MS claims the date 35 of the Hegira.

Through courtesy of the owner, the Rev. W. Scott Watson of West New York, N. J. (See Bibliography.)

since Gesenius spending their energies empirically upon the separate readings. It must be said that present scholarship is inclined to give far greater credence to the Samaritan than Gesenius allowed, and to make its testimony weigh very heavily when in agreement with other versions, especially the Greek.[40] As to the relation of the Samaritan to the Massoretic, and its origin, the most different views have been held, varying all the way from the extreme Catholic position that the Samaritan was to be preferred to that which would make it dependent upon the Septuagint. All mysteries and theological preposessions aside, the simplest hypothesis is that the Samaritan represents an actual early form of the Pentateuchal text. When we recall that the orthodox Jews of Alexandria produced a translation that varies from our present Massoretic text, we cannot be surprised that the heterodox Samaritans, who long before the origin of the Septuagint possessed their own textual tradition, have preserved a variant text. Indeed it is not the disagreement that is remarkable so much as the great similarity of the two texts. Apart from the few falsifications inserted by the Samaritans, there are no material differences, such for instance as would give the historian a different view of the

---

[40] For a review of the earlier discussions, see Wolf, *Bibliotheca Hebraica* (1721), iii, 421. Nutt *op. cit.* 86, gives a lively account, with dependence upon G. W. Meyer, *Gesch. d. Schrifterklärung,* 1804. Of the earlier works we may notice, Morinus, *Exercitationes ecclesiasticæ in utrumque Samaritanorum Pentateuchum,* 1631; Hottinger, *Exercitationes anti-Morinianæ,* 1644; Capellus, *Diatriba de veris et antiquis Hebræorum literis,* 1645; *Critica sacra,* iii, c. 20; Walton, *Prolegomenon xi,* to London *Polyglot;* Simon, *Histoire critique du Vieux Testament,* i, c. 12; Kennicott, *Dissertation the Second.* Gesenius' work is entitled *De Pentateuchi Samaritani origine,* etc., 1815. Frankel, *Einfluss der palästinensichen Exegese,* 237, takes a still more severe position than Gesenius. Further, see Kohn, *De Pentateucho Samaritano,* and most recently König in *DB,* extra vol. *s. v. Samaritan Pentateuch.* Eichhorn, *Einleitung in das alte Testament,* §§ 378–390 (ed. 4) contains an excellent apparatus of material, and Ezra Abbot in his article in Smith's *Bible Dictionary* presents an extensive synopsis of Samaritan variants.

19

age to which the composition belongs, or of the history which it relates; the variations will never be more than of interest to the textual scholar, illustrative to him of the origin and processes of various text-traditions.[41]

§ 7. THE TARGUM.

Samaritanism, like the sister sect, felt the need of rendering its Bible into the Aramaic vernacular, and there arose a Targumic literature, which remains as the most interesting monument of the Samaritan dialect. But the Targumic text exhibits such gross blunders of translation, and has so frightfully suffered through transmission at the hands of uneducated scribes ignorant of the language, that it has been the puzzle of scholars ever since its existence was made known to the western world. To this day no satisfactory edition of the Targum exists.

The first MS to come into the hands of a European was that now in the Vatican library, which was purchased by Pietro della Valle along with copies of the Hebrew Pentateuch; it has the date 1514. A much earlier text is the Barberini Triglot, presented to Cardinal Barberini by de Peiresc, who bought it at Damascus in 1631, and it is still to be found in the Barberini library. The bulk of the MS is dated 1227; the last portion, from *Dt.* 11, 29, hails from the year 1476. Numerous Targumic fragments are also to be found in European libraries, some of which may be of earlier date than the MSS described.

The della Valle MS was used in the Paris and London Polyglots, undergoing some emendations in the latter. This has remained the only published text until our own times. Petermann, whose work was completed by Vollers, has now published a sumptuous edition of the Targum upon

---

[41] For the bearing of the Samaritan Pentateuch upon the question of the date of the Samaritan schism, see above, p. 73.

PAGE OF THE BARBERINI TRIGLOT (A. D. 1227.)

Gen. 47, 1b — 11a in Hebrew, Arabic, Aramaic (from right to left respectively). From *Oriental Series,* Plate lxxxix of Palæographical Society's *Facsimiles.*

the basis of MSS obtained by him at Nablus, collated with the Polyglot texts. But this edition suffers through arbitrary editing and the lack of any critical description of the MSS used. Heidenheim has more recently put forth an edition of *Genesis,* collating for this purpose, for the first time, the Barberini Triglot, which, however, does not come to assistance until *Gen.* 34, 25.[42]

Since the day of the great lexicographer Castellus the Targum has been the basis of the wildest theories concerning the lexical nature of the Samaritan dialect, theories which have their excuse when we take into account the traditions concerning the origin of the Samaritans and also the horrible condition of the texts. All strange words were regarded as " Kuthæan roots," and they were explained from every language under the sun, not only Persian and Coptic, but also from Welsh in the west to Annamese in the

---

[42] For the Barberini MS, see de Peiresc in *Antiquitates ecclesiæ orientalis,* London, 1682, *Ep.* xxxvi, 179. It is described by Hwiid, *Specimen ineditæ versionis Arabico-Samaritanæ Pentateuchi,* Rome, 1780; de Rossi, *Specimen varr. lectionum......Appendix de celeberrimo Samaritano tritaplo,* Rome, 1782; de Sacy, in *Mémoires de l' Académie des Inscriptions,* xlix, 3; and by others — see Heidenheim, introduction to *BS* i. A page, *Gen.* 47, 11, has been beautifully reproduced in the Palæographical Society's *Facsimiles of Manuscripts,* etc., in the vol. *Oriental Series,* edited by W. Wright, London, 1875, Plate lxxxix. (The same volume contains two other plates of Samaritan MSS: Nos. xii and xxviii.) The Barberini Triglot contains the Hebrew, Arabic, and Targum, in parallel columns, all in Samaritan script. The Vatican MS is described by Assemani, *Bibliothecæ Vaticanæ catalogus;* i, 1, p. 464. The published editions of the Targum, or fragments, apart from the Polyglots (in the Paris Polyglot by Morinus, in the London Polyglot by Castellus) are: Petermann-Vollers, *Pentateuchus Samaritanus* (a misleading name!), Berlin, 1872–1891; Nutt, *Fragments of a Samaritan Targum,* 1874 (with facsimile); Brüll, *Das samaritanische Targum,* 1875; Kohn, *Die Petersburger Fragmente des samaritanischen Targum,* 1876; Heidenheim, *Die samaritanische Pentateuch-Version: Die Genesis,* 1884, in *BS* i (cf. Kohn, *Zur neuesten Litteratur über die Samaritaner, ZDMG* xxxix, 165); Kahle, *Fragmente des samaritanischen Pentateuchtargums,* 1902. For criticism of the Petermann edition, see especially Kohn, *Zur Sprache,* part ii.; and his review of the whole work in *ZDMG* xlvii (1893), 626; and in general see Kahle, *Textcritische und lexicalische Bemerkungen,* 1898. For an admirable presentation of the facts, see Nutt, *Sam. Targ.* 107.

east! It has been the merit particularly of Kohn to break down these philological absurdities and at the same time to help demolish the historical tradition.[43] This scholar has reduced the number of obscurities to a minimum, which he thinks may be safely assigned to text corruptions. He has very fully treated the question of the relation of the Targum to the Septuagint, to Onkelos, and to Abu Said, or his predecessors, from the XIth Century on, for there are correspondences with the Greek, Rabbinic, and Arabic versions. For the Greek connection, we find the presence of many Greek words; the dependence upon Onkelos has been supported or considered likely by scholars from Hottinger down to Nöldeke, while Frankel has even maintained an origin in the age of Islam.[44] But Kohn explains all these later correspondences upon the theory of glosses and interpolations entering the text at the hand of wilful or ignorant scribes, the Targum having undergone constant revision, until it fell into desuetude. Its history then would be parallel to that of the Jewish Targums.

As for the age of the origin of the Samaritan Targum we may hold that it was contemporary with the Jewish Targums, which are now supposed to hail from the IIId and IVth Centuries.[45] A Samaritan Epistle contains a reference to " the Targum of Nathanael," as doubtless the text is to be translated.[46] Cowley suggests identifying this Nathanael with the father of Baba Rabba, c. 300;[47] this hypothesis would agree with the probabilities as to the date,

---

[43] See above, § 2.
[44] See Kohn, *Zur Sprache,* 116, 124: Frankel in *Verhandlungen der ersten Versammlung deutscher u. ausländischer Orientalisten,* 10.
[45] *GJV* i, 149.
[46] *N. et E.* 106 (121) : מן חרגום נתן אל (not, " the Targum which God gave "). According to Winer, *De versionis Pent. Sam. indole diss.,* 9, the Samaritan tradition places Nathanael in the Ist Century.
[47] *JE* x, 677. It may be questioned whether, just as Symmachus appears as a Samaritan hero, Nathanael is not a reminiscence of Theodotion, the other Jewish or Ebionite Hellenic translator of the Old Testament.

although the history of "Onkelos" warns us from laying too much stress upon the personal tradition. The Targum then would be a product of that age of literary revival which followed the cessation of Roman persecution of the Hebrew sects and preceded the persecutions by the Christian empire.

§ 8. THE ARABIC TRANSLATIONS OF THE PENTATEUCH.

The Samaritan Arabic versions of the Pentateuch were stimulated by the elegant version of the Jewish Arabist Saadya, who died in 942. These translations have come to bear the name of Abu Said, who lived in the XIIIth Century. But criticism has shown that various translations or recensions have been made, starting possibly from Abu'l Chasan of Tyre, who flourished in the XIth Century, and passing through the hands of a certain Abu'l Barakat. Such are the results arrived at by the recent investigations of Kahle and Bloch. Several problems however remain unsolved, as for instance the relation of the Arabic version to the Targum and Saadya. No complete edition of the Samaritan *textus receptus* has as yet been published, though Kuenen has edited the first three books of the Law. It appears that many important MSS have never yet been collated, such as the Barberini Triglot and the English codices. As has been noticed above in the account of the theology of the Samaritans, the Arabic version is characterized by the painful avoidance of all anthropomorphisms; the translation is said to be "careful, and close to the Hebrew."[48]

---

[48] Hwiid, *Specimen*, etc., describes the Arabic text of the Triglot; cf. also the literature on this codex in note 42 above. The Leyden MS is described, with excerpts, by van Vloten, *Specimen philologicum,* 1803. Juynboll published a *Commentatio de versione Arabico-Samaritana,* in *Orientalia,* ii, 1846, and his pupil Kuenen, upon his suggestion, edited *Genesis, Exodus, Leviticus,* from the Leyden MS and two from the Paris Library, in 1851-4. Bloch has published a portion of *Deuteronomy* in his *Die samaritanisch-arabische Pentateuchübersetzung, Deut.*

§ 9. COMMENTARIES AND OTHER RELIGIOUS TREATISES.

The great theologian of the Samaritans is Marka, who has left behind extensive and important remains. His sect claims that he is the eldest of its writers,[49] but he is now generally identified with the Marka who was son of a certain Amram-Tuta (or Tuta b. Amram), who was deputy of one of the districts into which Baba Rabba divided his land.[50] Accordingly he would have lived in the latter part of the IVth Century. This datum agrees with the probability that the theological development which he led began in that notable period of the revival of Samaritanism. His name is, with Baneth, to be explained as a form of the Latin Marcus, while he seems to have had as his native name Moses, the change of name being explained by the tradition that he was named Moses by an angel at his birth, but that his people refused him the right to use the name, for which Marka was substituted as having the same gematriac value.[51] That an older literature preceded him is shown by his quotation from earlier writers.

His great work is a large Midrashic volume treating of various portions and subjects of the Pentateuch. It is composed of six books, divided into these four parts (so Baneth): (1) " The Book of Miracles," treating of Moses' Song; (2) an explanation of Dt. 27, 9–26; (3) do. of Dt. 31, 30–32, 43, on the death of Moses; (4) " a Book dealing with the 22 Letters, the Elements of the Hebrew Language," being an explanation of the use of the letters in

i–xi, with a valuable description of the MSS; see Kahle's criticism in *Zeitschraft f. heb. Bibliographie*, vi, 1902, p. 6. The latter has edited an extract (*Ex.* 4, 20–26) in his *Arabische Bibelübersetzungen*, 1904. In general see Cowley's summary of the question, *JE* x, 677.

[49] Petermann, *Reisen*, i, 236.

[50] *Chron. Neub.* 441; *Abu'l Fath*, 133; *Chron. Adler*, 63. See above, pp. 103, 150.

[51] Petermann, *l. c.*

the Law,— a Haggadic treatment which has its parallels in Rabbinic literature.

This work is composed in Aramaic, and is rendered most difficult for the modern student by its illogical vaporings as well as by the sad state of the MS. In his theology Marka is the most Kabbalistically inclined of all the Samaritan writers, and he has evidently drawn his Haggadic material from every apocryphal quarter of the Jews and even from more distant religions, as that of the Mandæans. The Samaritan lack of genius and logic is capitally displayed in this writer of whom the sect boasts as its great theologian. A large number of liturgical pieces are also extant under his name, and some which are ascribed to a certain Moses are believed by Baneth to come from his hand.[52]

A fragment of an Arabic commentary, of date of 1053, has been in small part published by Neubauer; the fragment covers *Gen.* 1–28, 10. This editor speaks slightingly of its value, but it is given a higher appreciation by Cowley.[53] It is interesting for its quotations from the Jewish Bible and the Mishna.

The most extensive and most truly exegetical commentary among the Samaritans is that of Ibrahim ibn Yakub. The author lived in the XVth Century, according to Klumel, but Hanover thinks, not before the XVIth. The

---

[52] The MS of Marka's commentary is in the Berlin Library. Three books, with extracts from the others, have been edited by Heidenheim in *BS* iii, along with extensive prefaces, dealing especially with the theology. Baneth has edited the last portion of the work in his *Des Samaritaners Marqah an die 22 Buchstaben......anknüpfende Abhandlung,* 1888, with preface and notes. Munk has published the " Death of Moses," *Des Samaritaners Marqa Erzählung über den Tod Mosis,* 1890; Emmerich, the " Book of Miracles," in *Das Siegeslied,* etc., 1897; and Hildesheimer, the same, *Marqah's Buch der Wunder,* 1898. For the liturgical material of Marka, see *BS* ii, and articles by Heidenheim in *DVJ*. The *Pessach-Haggadah,* published by Kohn, is also a composition by Marka.

[53] Neubauer, *Un commentaire samaritain inconnu,* 1873, giving the text of the preface; Cowley, *JQR* vii, 132.

work treats the first four books of the Pentateuch, and embraces 3288 manuscript quarto pages. It differs from Marka in containing but a minimum of Haggadic material and is predominantly Halachic.[54] An anonymous commentary on Genesis of the XVIIth Century exists in the Bodleian Library.[55] In 1753 Gazal ibn Abu(1) Sarur wrote a commentary on *Genesis* and *Exodus,* called the " The Dissipater of Darkness from the Secrets."

Little is known and very little has been published of the other theological literature of the Samaritans. In 1041 Yusuf ibn Salama composed the *Kitab al-Kafi,* " a kind of Samaritan Shulchan Aruch."[56] The *Kitab at-Tabbach,* " Book of Cooks," by Abu'l Chasan of Tyre, of the XIth Century, is a polemic against the Jews. The same author wrote the *Kitab al-Ma'ad,* on the future life, and the *Kitab at-Tauba,* on repentance. In the XIIth Century Munajja ibn Sadaka composed the *Kitab al-Khilaf,* on the differences between the Jews and the Samaritans.[57] His son Sadaka, a physician in Damascus, and author of medical treatises, also wrote theological books.[58] Gazal ibn Duwaik wrote on the story of Balak and the restoration of the kingdom. Other authors that may be named are Salich ibn Sarur ibn Sadaka, Abu'l Faraj ibn Ischak (an abridgment

---

[54] Small sections of the commentary have been published by Klumel, *Mischpatim. Ein samaritanisch-arabischer Commentar zu Ex.* 21–22, 15 *von Ibrahim Ibn Jakub,* 1902 (the portion concerning the civil law) ; Hanover, *Das Festgesetz der Samaritaner nach Ibrahim ibn Ja'kub* (to *Lev.* 23) ; also, I believe, by Drabkin, *Fragmenta commentarii ad Pentateuchum Samaritani-Arabici sex,* 1875. See these authors' introductions. For other commentaries reference may be made to Steinschneider, *Die arabische Literatur der Juden,* 324.

[55] Schnurrer has edited *Gen.* 49 in Eichhorn's *Repertorium,* xvi, 154.

[56] See Cohn, *Die Zaraath-Gesetze der Bibel nach dem Kitab al-Kafi des Jusuf ibn Salamah,* 1899.

[57] See Wreschner, *Samaritanische Traditionen,* for the author, his other works, and a discussion of his relations to the Karaites, upon whom he reveals a great dependence.

[58] Wreschner, *op. cit.* p. xix ; Nutt, *Sam. Targ.,* 139.

of the laws of Moses), and Ismaʻil ar-Rumaichi (on the praise of Moses). Haggadic material appears in Heidenheim's *Vierteljahrsschrift;* e. g. Leitner, *Legenden Mosis,* iv, 185.[59]

§ 10. THE LITURGY.

Apart from the Samaritan Pentateuch with its textual importance, and the Targum with its philological problems, by far the most interesting field of Samaritan literature is the Liturgy. It is strange that this department of research has been comparatively neglected. The pioneer Gesenius was the first to edit a group of Samaritan hymns; Heidenheim has gained the honorable merit of publishing what is, up to present writing, the largest collection of Samaritan liturgical pieces, some 123 in all; the English scholar Cowley now promises an early volume on this subject, which doubtless will present a text to replace the unreliable editing of Heidenheim, withal providing the much-needed commentary to the material.[60] What has been so far published gives no idea of the character and arrangement of the Liturgy as a whole, and for the following brief review I am indebted to the descriptions given by Heidenheim and especially by Cowley.

The text of the Samaritan Liturgy in the British Museum fills twelve large quarto volumes, of 2000 pages;

[59] I have followed above Nutt, *op. cit.* 131ff; Cowley, *JE* x, 680; comparing also Geiger, *ZDMG* xx, 143, and Steinschneider, *op. cit.* 319ff.

[60] Gesenius, *Carmina Samaritana,* 1824 (he observes, p. 1, the attention paid to this subject by Castellus and Marshall); Heidenheim, several liturgical pieces in his *VJD,* and finally in *BS* ii, 1885; Petermann, texts in *Appendix* to his *Grammatik;* Merx, *Carmina Samaritana,* 1882; also publication of separate hymns by Geiger, Kohn, Rappoport, *et al.* (see Bibliography). For a description of this literature, see Heidenheim *BS* ii, *Einleitung;* Cowley, *The Samaritan Liturgy and Reading of the Law, JQR* vii, 121; *JE* x, 628; Rappoport, *La liturgie samaritaine,* 1900. Also see Margoliouth, *An Ancient MS of the Samaritan Liturgy, ZDMG* li, 499.

much more material is also found in other libraries of Europe. One branch of this material is composed of Biblical *florilegia,* or *catenæ* of verses from the Scriptures, generally bound together by some clue of thought or word; another branch consists of prayers, largely in prose; yet another embraces Shirot, or hymns, which extend from brief ascriptions of praise to God to long-drawn-out Midrashic compilations composed for recital on the great feasts and fasts and the Sabbath. Provision is made for liturgical response between minister and congregation. No sacrificial formulas appear to have been preserved; offices for circumcision and marriage exist, but have not been published.

Cowley, the only scholar who has given a scientific and chronological account of the material, divides the liturgical cycle into five divisions, as follows: (1) the Defter (through the Arabic from διφθέρα, i.e. "the Book"); (2) the services for the first month, Passover, etc.; (3) for the Pentecostal period; (4) for the seventh month, the Day of Atonement, and Booths: (5) for circumcision, marriage and burial. The Defter comprises compositions, prayers and hymns, written by Marka and the contemporaneous Amram Dara, and is the eldest stratum of the Liturgy; this material is composed in the Samaritan Aramaic. Amram's work, making what is called the Durran, is chiefly in prose; Marka gave himself out in poetry, if his hymns in alphabetic acrostic may be so termed. These productions are for a variety of occasions, and the same book also includes some prayers for daily use and for the Sabbath. Altogether this early compilation of IVth Century compositions has set the norm for the whole Samaritan Liturgy.

Cowley establishes two subsequent epochs of liturgical development. The first is the XIth Century when compositions of Abu'l Chasan of Tyre and his son Ab Geluga were added to the Defter. Their language is still Aramaic.

The second liturgical revival occurred in the XIVth Century under the stimulus of the highpriest Phineas b. Joseph, the patron of Abu'l Fath. The liturgical language had now become Hebrew. Composition in this field has continued down to our own age, but with steady debasement.

To consider briefly the published hymns, most of them have their stanzas arranged according to alphabetic acrostic. Those of the later period rhyme the verses of a stanza upon the same syllable, as in Arabic poetry. To fit his Procrustean mould both at the beginning and end of the verse, the writer does not hesitate to distort his words. The theology and general contents of these hymns have been touched upon in Chapter XII. We find litanies and praise-songs, hymns for the Sabbath and the morning; responsive forms used at the exhibition of the law; requiem hymns, meditations over death and the Day of Judgment, warnings to the sinners.

Of greatest interest are the long Midrashic hymns composed for the Passover, Pentecost, Booths, Kippur, the most notable of which for religious feeling and expression are those for the two great seasons in the seventh month. The hymn regularly begins with the story of creation; it may go off into a long astronomical excursus; the lives of the Patriarchs may be touched upon; but it always comes at last to the legislation on Sinai; the final stanzas are then devoted to the encouragement of saints and the rebuke of sinners. In all this material poetic genius is rarely found; there is occasionally a bit of literary imagination, as in " Abishua's Dream "; some of the Morning Hymns seem to be a little kindled with the rising sun. But as the poetical form is borrowed and artificial, so also the idea of writing poetry seems to have been in imitation of the Jewish and Syrian-Christian churches, and the Samaritans simply followed suit by casting their tiresome legends into the moulds of a mechanical poetry, subsequently modelled after the Arabic. One characteristic cannot be denied this literature; it is full of moral earnestness and of sincerity to the principles of the faith, and this genuine religious spirit gives a true dignity to very much that is in itself absurd and trivial.

§ 11.   THE CHRONICLES.

Four Samaritan Chronicles have been published by European scholars; they are as follows:

(1) A Hebrew work called the *Taulida,* the equivalent of the Hebrew *Toledot,* " genealogy," or " history." Its full title is " The History (*taulida*) which has taken place between the Samaritans and the Jews (Rabbanites), and the Memorials of the Samaritans extending down to the Present." The text has been published and translated by Neubauer and by Heidenheim; having been discovered by the former scholar, it may for distinction be called the *Chronicle Neubauer.*[61]

The basis and major part of this composition was a manuscript prepared by Eleazar, a son of the highpriest Amram, written in 1149. It begins with a brief astronomical calculation, and then takes up the history from Adam to the writer's own time. His work has been continued by his descendant Jacob b. Ishmael, who prefaces it with a calculation of the Jubilees which have occurred since the conquest of Canaan, down to the year of the continuator's writing, 1346. He has added a little to the

[61] A. Neubauer, *Chronique samaritaine, JA* 1869, p. 385 ; Heidenheim, *Die samaritanische Chronik des Hohenpriesters Elasar, DVJ* iv, 347. Heidenheim is all unconscious of Neubauer's earlier publication. The MS is in the Bodleian Library, and Neubauer collated it with a private MS which he does not further describe. The references in this work are to the pages of Neubauer's translation. The Hebrew text is accompanied with an Arabic translation, whose readings are frequently cited by Neubauer. According to Conder, *PEFQS,* 1876, p. 187, the original text is at Nablus, and each high priest adds to it the events of his pontificate.

chronicle, which then was expanded by other hands and is brought down to 1856. The work is not much more than a list of the highpriests and of the chief Samaritan families with their locations, some scanty and brief references to external history being introduced.

(2) The *Book of Joshua*. This is an Arabic work written in Samaritan characters; the greater part of the MS (to the middle of c. xlvi) belongs to the date 1362, the balance, written in much poorer script, to 1513. It has been published by Juynboll in text, and translation, along with ample commentary.[62]

The work is actually a Midrash, not a chronicle, and so differs from the curt annalistic form of the other chronicles. It begins (cc. 1–8) with an account of the last days of Moses, including the story of Balaam and the war with Midian. Chap. 9 takes up the proper story of Joshua, which is an extensive Midrash based upon the Hebrew *Joshua*. There follows (cc. 26–37) the apocryphal story of Shaubak, a Persian king, who attacked Israel with the aid of the Giants and with diabolic wiles, which were frustrated by Nabich who had been appointed king of Trans-Jordan (the Nobach of *Num*. 32, 42). There follows a description of the Golden Age of the Divine Favor down to

---

[62] Juynboll, *Chronicum Samaritanum*, ... *cui titulus est Liber Josuæ*, 1846. (This chronicle was earlier treated by Reland in his *Dissertations*, and by Hottinger in *Exerc. anti-Morin.*, and *Smegma orientale*.) The results of Juynboll's exhaustive criticism and commentary for the most part still stand. The MS he used is that of Scaliger, procured by that scholar from Egyptian Samaritans, and now deposited in the Leyden library. Another MS, of date 1502, and in the British Museum, is noted by Nutt, *Sam. Targ*. 119. Also Adler, in his account of his obtaining the chronicle which he has published, speaks of a MS of this work which he attempted to purchase from the Samaritans. But the *Book of Joshua* does not seem to have had wide vogue in Samaria, nor is it mentioned by any early authorities — a fact which induced Hengstenberg to deny that it was an early work (*Authentie d. Pentateuches*, i, 41). Kirchheim has given a Hebrew translation in his *Karme Shomron*, and an English translation has been published by O. T. Crane, *The Samaritan Chronicle or The Book of Joshua*, 1890.

the death of Samson, cc. 38–40. The causes of the Age of Disfavor are then narrated, the ringleaders of the schism from the true Israel being the house of Eli, and Samuel. In c. 45 is given the " history of Nebuchadrezzar, king of Mosul." That king, after destroying Jerusalem (the account in *Kings* is briefly followed), also harries and depopulates Samaria, exiling the Samaritans and replacing them with Persian colonists. But the land loses its power of production; its fruits are fair without but rotten within. The king learns that the cause of this calamity is the failure of the proper rites of the God of the Samaritans, and he allows the whole people to return. The Jews accompany them, but refuse to take part ir the worship on Gerizim, desiring to rebuild Jerusalem. The case is appealed to the king, and the books of the two sects are presented in argument. The Samaritan king Sanballat suggests the ordeal of fire; he casts the Jewish Scriptures, presented in evidence by Zerubbabel, into the flames, and they are destroyed. The latter begs off from thus ill-treating the holy Law of the Samaritans, but submitting to the king, casts it into the flame three times, and it comes forth unharmed.[63] C. 46 is the history of Alexander the Great; it includes a parallel to the Jewish story of the appearance of the highpriest to Alexander in a dream, and the conqueror's subsequent graciousness; Alexander's visit to the land of darkness; the legend of his ascending car; the story of the evasion of his command to erect his statue by the Samaritans naming their children after him. The history of Hadrian, c. 47, containing the story of Ephraim and Manasse, has been referred to in Chap. VI, § 2. CC. 48–50 give the history of Akbun, his son Nathanael, and his grandson Baba Rabba,

[63] The Samaritans professed to have this identical " Fire-tried Manuscript "; see Rosen, *ZDMG* xviii, 586, and for its subsequent fortunes, Conder, *Tent Work*, i, 54.

the data of which have already been made use of in Chapter VI, § 3.

Juynboll's results are in brief as follows: The basis of the work is cc. 9–25, which, as the title to c. 9 shows, is the original *Book of Joshua*. The Egyptian origin of the work is rendered probable by its use of the Septuagint narrative in many places, and as well by the non-use of the Seleucidan era, which appears in native Samaritan writings. The original, according to the statement of the compiler in the opening words of c. 1, was composed in the Hebrew language, by which doubtless is to be understood the Samaritan Aramaic dialect. This early composition belongs then to that extensive class of literature dealing with Moses, the Exodus, and the early history of Israel, which had its beginnings early in the Alexandrian age; Aristobulus of the age of Ptolemy Philometor was a prolific composer of such writings, and in addition there may be recalled the extensive Moses legends, fragments of which have been preserved, and also the dramatic compositions composed by the Jewish poets Philo and Ezekiel, and the Samaritan Theodotus, who has been noticed above.[64]

In addition to this early Hellenistic composition which has been preserved only in free rendering in the present Arabic form, Juynboll assumes three other Arabic sources which have also been used by the compiler, one of these being the basis of the first eight chapters, the other two being used in the last part of the work; the legends incorporated in these documents would also doubtless go back to early Jewish or Hellenistic sources. Thus the Balaam episode in cc. 3, 4 is probably drawn from "the Books of Balaam" mentioned in c. 41, and these compositions are to be connected with the considerable literature which, it would appear, grew up about the false prophet's

[64] Consult in general Schürer, *GJV* iii, esp. pp. 219, 287, 384.

name.[65] The legend of Shaubak, in which the Israelitish hero Nabich appears in a more distinguished light than Joshua, evidently goes back to some early independent source,— we may conjecture from some Trans-Jordanic literature which extolled the local history.[66]

The legends incorporated in the last part of the book, from c. 47 on, are all parallel to, in most cases drawn from, Jewish material. In general it is to be noticed that the legends for the Biblical period are entirely taken from the Old Testament literature, although not at first hand, as appears in the confusion concerning the period of Nebuchadrezzar. Also the official annals of the priesthood have been used, but not in so annalistic a way as in the other chronicles.

Juynboll regards the present *Book of Joshua* as the compilation of one hand. But it is probably preferable to agree with Vilmar in regarding cc. 47 *et seqq.* (beginning with the story of Nebuchadrezzar) as a later supplement. In Abul Fath's reference to our book, [67] he speaks of a manuscript containing "the *Book of Joshua* and other material." That is, this supplementary material was already added to the book, but regarded as distinct; also the same chronicler reports that he drew his story of Baba Rabba's nephew Levi from an old Hebrew narrative, which he gives for what it is worth. It thus appears that this supplement

[65] Juynboll, p. 81; notice the reff. to Origen, *Hom. xiii, in lib. Num;* C. *Cels.* i, 59.

[66] No trace of this story appears independently in the Jewish literature, but Samuel Shullam, the Jewish editor of *Juchasin* (1556), appended an abstract of the Samaritan legend to his edition, remarking: "I happened to see (this) in the annals of the Samaritans, who delivered what they saw in a certain commentary (Midrash) of the Jews." We cannot tell on what authority the latter part of this assertion is made. This would be the only instance where later Judaism has borrowed from Samaritan literature. See Juynboll, 81, 263.

[67] See below, p. 306. The historian Masudi (writing 943) in referring to the Samaritan story of the Exile does not appear to be acquainted with the *Book of Joshua;* de Sacy, *Chrest. arabe,* i, 343.

was not yet added, but was known to Abu'l Fath in its original form.[68] The compilation then is a mass of legends drawn from many sources, much of which material may be traced back to the beginning of the present era and perhaps earlier. As for the age of the compilation, which Juynboll assigns to one hand, that scholar argues with great acuteness that the compiler lived in the first half of the XIIIth Century,[69] and that he was of priestly race and Egyptian habitat. The chronicler Abu'l Fath used the book in the century following, and the Arabic historian Makrizi, in the XVth Century, appears to have been acquainted with it.

(3) *The Chronicle of Abu'l Fath.* This is the most successful attempt among the Samaritans to produce a chronicle with some aim at literary form. The author writes in a vulgar Arabic, is unfitted as a critic, and very disproportionate in his use of his material. Withal there is a pathetic interest in his undertaking, which intended to recover the history of his people in a day when the traditions of the sect seemed in danger of disappearing, and he evidently made an honest effort to procure all reliable written material that was at command. The text has been published by Vilmar, and partly published and translated by Payne Smith.[70] The author belonged to the distinguished Danafite family — to be connected probably with the village Defne, E of Nablus. He gives an interesting introduction telling how he came to write his book; he executed

---

[68] See Vilmar, *Abu'l Fath,* p. lxvii. The reference in *Abu'l Fath* is p. 139, l. 5. Notice that c. 47 is entitled, " The history of Nebuchadrezzar, which is found in books,"— i.e. evidently a supplementary addition.

[69] P. 97.

[70] Vilmar, *Abulfathi annales Samaritani,* 1865; Payne-Smith, *The Samaritan Chronicle of Abu'l Fatch, DVJ* ii, 303, 431 (for the suspension of this work see the Bibliography). *Fath* should properly be transliterated *fatch,* the *ch* to be pronounced independently of the preceding *t.*

20

the work " only for the reason that he was in a certain country, and the ruler of it asked him about their chronicles, and requested him to compile for him this chronicle." This request he bore in mind when he visited the highpriest Phineas in Nablus in 1352, and the latter commanded him to compile such a history. He delayed the work, however, for three years, when he again visited Nablus, and then asked the highpriest to provide him with the materials for his undertaking. He tells us that he omitted much that was wearisome, and honestly followed his authorities; " I have aimed at what was true and sincere, and endeavored to compile an authentic narrative."

He then gives a list of his authorities; they are: (1) the Book of the Province (qit' al-baladî), in Arabic script and language; (2) the Chronicle of the Book of the Province (tarikh, etc.), in Hebrew script but Arabic in language; (3) a chronicle with which is bound up the Book of Joshua, along with other material, in the Arabic script and language; (4) three defective chronicles, " in my own possession," which were brought to him from Damascus; (5) " a genealogy (salsalat) copied by the hand of our lord the highpriest aforesaid, in (from ?) the writing of the highpriest Eleazar aforesaid, wherein is recorded the origin of the Samaritans;" (6) some fasciculi. The chronicle of Sadaka, however, he would not use, because, while he acknowledged its literary excellence, it was not corroborated by genuinely historical authorities.

Abu'l Fath has made large use of the Book of Joshua, and a comparison of his work with the Toleda of Eleazar (Chronicle Neubauer) shows his dependence upon that work as well. It is not apparent which of the sources he names was this earlier chronicle; it may have been the Salsalat which he connects with Eleazar the highpriest.[71]

[71] Payne-Smith has ignored the reference to Eleazar in his translation. I cannot make sense out of the passage except by supposing

Abu'l Fath begins with Adam, and carries down his work as far as the commencement of the Muslim empire, or more exactly to the year 756, with which date he concludes. At least so Vilmar, doubtless rightly, judges, holding that the subsequent additions, which appear in only two of the four MSS, are the work of subsequent composers. The other two MSS jointly continue the story into the time of the first Abbasides. Each of these is further continued with its peculiar supplements, the latest belonging to the year 1853.[72] Abu'l Fath lays special stress in his chronology upon the exposition of the well-known theory of the Samaritans concerning the ages of the world.

(4) Yet another *Toleda* exists which from its discoverer and editor we may call the *Chronicle Adler*.[73] The language is Hebrew, with some Samaritan words, and with two liturgical pieces in the Samaritan dialect, a hymn of Baba Rabba and one of Marka. The work is arranged under the years of the world and according to the succession of the patriarchs and highpriests, coming down to the year 1899. It is much more expansive than the earlier *Toleda,* drawing most largely from *Abu'l Fath,* so far as that goes, and also containing some independent material.[74]

that the contemporary highpriest had made his copy "from" (correcting "in") the writing of Eleazar, who then might be the author of the *Toleda,* although the latter does not appear to have been high-priest, only the younger son of one. Vilmar, p. xxix, thinks that Eleazar the son of Aaron is meant and that the work is the genealogy of the "Book of the Highpriests" mentioned in *Lib. Jos.* c. 47, *sub fin.* We do not know who is the Sadaka, the author of the chronicle Abu'l Fath rejects; he may be the theologian, the son of Munajja, mentioned above. It appears from his phraseology that Abu'l Fath also made direct use of the Jewish Scriptures; see Vilmar, p. xcviii.

[72] See Chap. VII, note 1.

[73] The text appears in Adler and Séligsohn, *Une nouvelle chronique samaritaine, REJ* 1902–3, and in reprint, with some change in the preface, in 1903. A translation accompanies the text, with excellent brief notes, some from the hand of Israel Lévi, especially bearing upon the correspondences with the other chronicles. The editors have used a copy made to order from a Nablus MS.

[74] For some valuable notes on the new data of this chronicle, see

It is evidently later throughout than the other chronicles registered above. The references to foreign events in its history of modern times show that the Samaritans have learned to take an interest in things apart from their own concerns.

From the above brief study of the extant chronicles it is evident that a considerable literature both of annalistic and of Midrashic character stood at the disposal of the Samaritan historians. Abu'l Fath has described the sources which he made use of, and they were of considerable extent. Two of these can be identified with the first *Toleda* and the *Book of Joshua,* but the others are still unknown to us. The two " Books of the Province " are probably nothing else than registers of the families in their respective settlements, the material which largely lies at the base of the first *Toleda.* Another authority was a genealogical list. The *Book of Joshua,* c. 47, *sub. fin.,* mentions in a list of the Samaritan literature, most of which it asserts was lost in the Hadrianic persecution, a Book of the Highpriests; Annals containing the birth-dates and the ages of the priests; and also a book containing the lives of the priests — which was preserved. Among the MSS which Adler tried to purchase at Nablus was a Chronicle, דברי הימים, and a Book of Inheritances, ספר ירושות,[75] probably a domesday book, of the same nature as the " Books of the Province." Further, as to these sources, it is to be remarked that they all must have been in the Hebrew, Aramaic, or Arabic tongues, for by the IId Millennium all knowledge of Greek and Latin had doubtless perished from the Samaritans; whatever sources of Hellenistic origin underlie our chronicles, were

Clermont-Ganneau, *Journal des Savants,* 1904, p. 34. The chronicle was compiled in 1900. A slightly variant text, and older by a few years, of this chronicle is noted by Macler, *Note sur une nouvelle manuscrit d'une chronique samaritaine, REJ* 1905.

[75] In introduction to his *Nouvelle chronique.*

mediated to the authors through versions in the native vernaculars.

For the purpose of a brief analysis of the sources of the chronicles it is logical to divide them into those of native and those of foreign origin. Of the native sources doubtless the most reliable were the official priestly genealogies, which the Samaritans proudly trace back in direct succession to Eleazar son of Aaron. But when we recall that in the far more historically-minded Jewish church the record of their highpriests has been only partially and often contradictorily preserved by Josephus and Christian chronographers, there is no antecedent reason why we should place confidence in the names and successions of the Samaritan genealogy, at least before the IVth Christian Century, since which age the Samaritan chronicles become more trustworthy as to native memorials. That the succession is defective is shown by the long chronological gaps which actually exist between the ages of men who are supposed to have succeeded one another; in some cases it appears that the Jewish lists have been copied.[76] When in later days the priesthood had become the sole school of learning, we find that their official lists assumed more of an annalistic character, noting important events even in foreign history, as we observe in the latter part of the *Chronicle Adler*. But we cannot detect any such native notices of general historical character in the early Toledot; all such information seems to have been worked up by the subsequent compilers, who made use of the genealogies as a skeleton, into which they arbitrarily fitted material drawn from foreign sources.

[76] Since the time of Scaliger these lists have been of interest to historians. But the records in the several chronicles differ; there is discrepancy in *Abu'l Fath* between the list followed in his chronicle and that appended at the end of the work. Heidenheim gives a comparative table of the lists in the first *Toleda* and in *Abu'l Fath* in *VJD* iv, 387. Attention may here be called to the list of highpriests

What has been said concerning the Midrashic compo-
nents of the *Book of Joshua* is sufficient to show the un-
historic character of that material; much of it comes down
from the Hellenistic period, but has no independent authority for the history of the Samaritans, as it is almost
entirely borrowed or imitated from Jewish legends.

As to foreign sources, our chroniclers follow the example of the chronographers in inserting notices of events
of universal history: thus they observe the rise of sects,
like Judaism and Christianity, make mention of contemporary philosophers like Ptolemy. But these references,
as Vilmar judges,[77] do not depend upon original Samaritan chronicles or traditions, but ignorantly and ineptly
borrow from various late chronicles of the Jews, Christians, and Moslems. *Josephus b. Gorion* seems to have
been the medium of much of the Jewish history, and in part
Eutychius was relied upon. Only for the period of the
Samaritan revival in the IVth and Vth Centuries does there
appear to be any genuine native tradition, although even
here the chronology is sadly confused, showing that only
certain brief stretches of history were preserved by tradition. For the ages of Islam in which we no longer have
the guidance of Abu'l Fath, the chronicles are vague and
intermittent, as evinced in the Chapter devoted above to
the Islamic period.

If then the historian comes to the Samaritan chronicles
with any large expectations, he is bound to be disappointed. They throw almost no light on universal history,
add nothing to our scanty knowledge of the beginnings of
the Samaritans and of the first six centuries of their existence, at the best but illuminate the cruel history of the
Byzantine period, and give much insipid gossip on events of

from the time of Mohammed to 1853 in the supplement to Codex
A of *Abu'l Fath,* given by Vilmar, p. lxxviii.
[77] I refer to his excellent treatment of Abu'l Fath's sources, p. lxxxv.

generally small importance. The Samaritans are certainly at the extreme of the oriental lack of historic sense, and the study of their annals provokes us to name them in the language of the Sirachide, " the foolish people that dwell at Shechem." Yet the remains of Samaritan literature in other fields must make us hesitate to condemn them too severely. We have to remember that between the period of their bloom and the date of the first extant known chronicle lie some six centuries. What of their earlier historical material has been lost, we do not know; it is possible that future finds may improve our opinion of their historical ability. The insipid traditions of the ignorant and debased community have preserved just such legends as please the ecclesiastical appetite of a provincial sect, whose life was intentionally lived apart from the world. Indeed we must bear in mind that what we possess are ecclesiastical annals, framed upon a theological scheme of history, and with the desire to edify; hence we have not to expect history in our sense of the word. When at last the keen Arabic spirit of historical research infected the Samaritans, so worthy and honest a chronicler as Abu'l Fath had little more to build upon than a residuum of inane tradition.

§12. SCIENTIFIC WORKS.

Following the example of Jewish scholars, the Samaritans felt the necessity of philological study, especially for the conservation of their sacred language. Hence Abu Said, probably the same as the translator of the Pentateuch, wrote his *Canons of the Scripture,* to correct certain mispronunciations of its language. The largest grammatical work is that of Abu Ischak Ibrahim ibn Faraj (surnamed " the Sun of the Sages "), of the XIIth Century. The work, called the *Tautia,* a technical Arabic name, embraces 164 MS pages, but is incomplete and disproportionate in its treatment. These two books show a slight dependence upon the Jewish grammarians. An abstract of the second work exists, in the Leyden MS that contains both, composed by Eleazar ben Phineas, who died in 1387.[78] Two MSS of lexical character exist; one is at Christ's College, Cambridge, composed by a Phineas, who was either the father or the successor of the aforesaid Eleazar, the other, which is at Paris, being a dictionary of the Hebrew of the Pentateuch, with the Arabic and Samaritan arranged along therewith in parallel columns. The two are said to correspond closely. Their MS dates are 1774 and 1476.[79]

The exigencies of the church year required sufficient astronomical science to calculate the calendar in advance for a certain term; this was necessary in order to bring the ancient lunar year into agreement with the solar year, which latter governed the course of the Hebrew sacred seasons. It was, as in the Jewish church, the duty of the priesthood to make such calculations and to publish the results among their coreligionists. As a rule these calendars appear to have been sent out semi-annually. In their European correspondence the Samaritans exhibited a painful anxiety in stating their reckonings to their " Brethren " and in inquiring after the calendar of the latter. Several such calendars have been published, and much material of the same kind exists in MS form.[80]

In the sphere of physical science the Samaritans pro-

[78] See Nöldeke's description of these works in *Ueber einige samaritanisch-arabische Schriften, die hebräische Sprache betreffend*, 1862, containing text and translation of Abu Said's treatise. Geiger has published extracts of Ibrahim's work in *ZDMG* xvii, 723. Comp. Nutt, *Sam. Targ.* 148.

[79] See Nutt, *Sam. Targ.* 150. Harkavy, *ibid.* 161, states that the lacunæ in the Paris lexicon may now be filled out from MSS in St. Petersburg.

[80] Tables have been published by Scaliger, *De emendatione temporum*, 657 (ed. 1629); de Sacy, *N. et E.* 135 (153); Heidenheim, *BS* iii, Beilagen, vi-viii. Cf. *N. et E.*, 34; *BS* iii, p. xxxvi; Nutt, *Sam. Targ.* 145. For the MS material, see *Journal asiatique*, xiv, 467; Harkavy, in Nutt, 162; *JE* x, 680.

duced several physicians of note whose works find a place in Arabic literature. One of these was Sadaka ibn Munajja ibn Sadaka, mentioned above, who wrote a commentary on the *Aphorisms* of Hippocrates. Another was Muhadhdhib ad-Din Yusuf ibn Abu Said ibn Kalaf. The latter had a nephew Abu'l Chasan ibn Gazal ibn Abu Said, who wrote on many subjects connected with natural history and was famous for his great library; he accepted Islam. Also Muwaffik ad-Din, another physician, wrote a commentary on the *Canon* of Avicenna. All these writers flourished in the XIIIth Century, and some of them are known• to have been connected with Damascus and its court.[81]

§ 13. RÉSUMÉ OF THE LITERARY ACTIVITY OF THE SA-
MARITANS.

The earliest literary monument of the Samaritans is their edition of the Pentateuch. In view of the frequent agreements with the Greek version and from the intrinsic excellence of many of the readings, we cannot doubt that it ,exhibits evidence of a comparatively early text. When we read in the Talmud of the Samaritan falsifications in the Law, it would seem that these had been long established, and accordingly we may judge that the Samaritan Pentateuch in its original form well antedates the formulation of a final text on the part of the Jewish church in Jerusalem. The Samaritan edition then goes back at least to the time of the pre-Christian centuries, when, as the Greek text shows, for example in the last chapters of Exodus, the text of the Law was still in flux.

This monument, important as it is to scholarship, is

[81] See Juynboll, *Hist. Sam.* 56; Nutt, *Sam. Targ.* 138, and the references in these places, especially Wüstenfeld, *Geschichte d. arabischen Aerzte*, 121. A number of medical fragments are said to be contained in the St. Petersburg collection; see Harkavy, in Nutt, 163.

however no indication of any literary activity on the part of the Samaritans in the first centuries of their community's existence, as the work was borrowed from the Jews, and the activity amounted to falsification. For other traces of pre-Christian theological literature we look in vain, although it cannot be denied that at the basis of much of the liturgy lies material which goes back at least to the beginning of our era; this is rendered probable by the correspondences traced in a former Chapter between the primitive Samaritan theology and the doctrines of early Judaism, especially in the fields of eschatology and Messianism.

The literary activity of the Samaritans may be divided into three periods, each of which was controlled and stimulated by external conditions. These are namely, the Greek, the Aramaic, and the Arabic periods.

A. THE GREEK PERIOD.

The first stimulus to a Samaritan literature appears to have been on Egyptian soil, where the necessity of apology toward Jews and Gentiles gave origin to a literature which was a reflex of the contemporary Jewish writings of the same character. Under Section 5 above have been indicated the slight traces we possess of a Hellenistic literature; to this is to be added that Midrashic material, doubtless of Egyptian Aramaic origin, which, as we have seen, underlay the original *Book of Joshua*. We may conceive that this activity of the Egyptian Diaspora was looked upon askance by the home-church, even as in Judaism, and that Samaria was little affected by the efforts of the exiled *littérateurs*.

B. THE ARAMAIC PERIOD.

So far as we are able to give any chronology, this period had its beginnings with the renascence which took place in the IVth Century, the age which is indissolubly connected in Samaritan tradition with the fame of Baba Rabba. The movement was one that followed after, and was a close parallel to, the Rabbinic activity which resulted in the Targums and Talmuds. To this period, and as its greatest monument, we have to assign the Samaritan Targum; vernacular Semitism was again raising its head against Hellenic influence, and asserted to itself the right of translating into the vernacular the obsolete Hebrew of the Scriptures. As contemporary of the great Samaritan reformer, Marka also appears in the IVth Century, and he remains the most prolific and influential writer, both in theology and in liturgical composition. The Aramaic period lasted down towards the XIth Century, when at last we find the Arabic influence in the ascendant.

C. THE ARABIC PERIOD.

The conquests of Islam disorganized the life of the Samaritan community and diminished whatever strength and spirit it possessed, so that it was long before the new empire exerted any beneficial effects upon the intellectual activity of the sect. But in the XIth Century Abu'l Chasan of Tyre, while writing hymns in the Aramaic, which seems to have been already obsolete, took the first steps towards the rendering of the Law in the language of the conquerors, and also, along with other writers, composed treatises upon the native laws. In the following century appeared the grammatical work of Ibrahim ibn Faraj, and the theological compositions of such men as Munajja. In the XIIIth Century was published Abu Said's classical and authoritative Arabic version of the Scriptures. The extensive Midrashic *Book of Joshua* was compiled about the same time. In the XIVth Century, which Cowley considers the age of "a sort of renascence of Samaritan literature," we have the only real historical work coming from a Samaritan, that of Abu'l Fath, and also the blossoming of a rich liturgical activity, which has continued to our own time but with accelerating degeneracy. As late as the XVIIIth Century theological literature flourished; we may instance the commentary of Gazal ibn Abu(1) Sarur. Since that time no important work has appeared, a cessation which is symptomatic of the moribund condition of the community.

In the Arabic period the priestly family at Nablus was a school of learning, at least of that very conservative order which perpetuates meagre annals; it was also the home of liturgical composition. But the real intellectual centres of the sect were in Egypt and at Damascus. While the *Toledas* are of native origin, the *Book of Joshua* hails from Egypt; the version ascribed to Abu Said also seems to have been of Egyptian origin.[82] To Damascus doubtless belonged the grammarian Ibrahim ibn Faraj, at least his scholastic connections would assign him to that city; there also flourished Munajja and the several physician-theologians. This famous centre of Islamic culture became the centre of Samaritan science, as Egypt had been of the Midrashic literature of the sect.

[82] Juynboll, *Orientalia*, ii, 116; Bloch, *Sam. -arab. Pentateuchüber-setzung*, 16.

ADDITIONAL NOTES.

A. THE NAME "SAMARIA."

The Assyrian form of Shomeron, שמרון, is Samerina, appearing first in Tiglath-pileser's inscriptions (Layard, 66, 18); the Aramaic is Shamerain, the Greek Σαμαρία Σαμαρεία. The relation of the Hebrew form to those given by foreign sources has not yet been explained. The Hebrew *o* in the first syllable is certainly secondary, the foreign renderings preserving the original vowel *a*. As for the final syllable, both -*ain* and -*on* (also -*un*) are frequent terminations in Palestinian place-names, and the two suffixes may be understood as original alternatives of the name. Or -*on* may have arisen from -*an*, the latter by distraction also undergoing a parallel change into -*ain*, -*en*. Winckler has suggested that -*on* (= -*un*) and -*ain* are related to one another as case-endings.

As for the foundation of the city, it must be assumed that the hill of Shemer was an ancient settlement, and that Omri bought from the clan inhabiting it the land he required for his buildings and fortifications; see Stade, *Der Name der Stadt Samariens und seine Herkunft, ZATW* v, 165. Compare David's transaction with Arauna the Jebusite, 2 *Sam.* 24. Shemer seems to have been a widespread clan-name, appearing as a clan of the tribe of Levi, 1 *Ch.* 6, 31, and of Benjamin, 8, 12, while Shimron is a family of Issachar, *Gen.* 46, 13, etc., and a town in Zebulun, *Jos.* 11, 1, etc. This is vocalized in *Jos.* 12, 20 by Cod. A. as Samron (cf. 19, 15), which would be the same as the original form of Omri's foundation. Thus more than one town " Samaria " existed on the early map, while a number of places with the same root are found in the Old Testament and on the modern map, e.g. Shamir, the modern Sumra, in Juda. The name then is more probably a derivation from a widespread tribe-name, than a local designation, as G. A. Smith suggests, rendering Shomeron as *Wartburg,* Watch Tower (*HG* 346). The Greek form recognizes the unessential and variable character of the last syllable in the Hebrew word. Only in some MSS to 1 *Ki.* 16, 24 and 2 *Esdras* 4, 10, do we find the Massoretic form imitated.

B. THE NAMES OF THE SAMARITANS.

The Samaritans usurp for themselves the theocratic name of Israel. They allow themselves to be called Samaritans only with a play upon the word. The word they use is Samerim, not the Old Testament Shomeronim, 2 *Ki.* 17, 29, which they never employ. Doubtless the word is the ancient gentilic for the place of Shemer; cf. the origin of Σαμαρεία from the latter, not from Shomeron. *Samerim* is the Samaritan equivalent of the Hebrew *shomerim,* " ob- servers," and it is in this sense the Samaritans use the word of themselves; thus, " We observe the holy Law and are called Observers," *N. et E.* 163 (175), or because they " observe " the Sabbath, *ibid.* This interpretation is an- cient. There is a reference to it in the Jewish antagonist's assertion that " there are no keepers of the Law here " (*Chol.* 6a; above, p. 191), and possibly in 2 *Chron.* 13, 11. It is frequently alluded to in the Fathers; e.g. Origen, *Homil. in Ezech.* ix, 1 (Migne xiii, 73) ; Eusebius, *Chron.* ii, *ann.* 1270; Jerome, *Epitaph. Paulæ,* 6 (M. xxii, 887) ; Epiphanius, *Hæres,* i, 9; etc.

Perhaps because of this interpretation the Jews rarely call their rivals Samaritans; exceptions are found in *Aboda Zara Jer.* 44d; *Bereshit R.* c. 32, etc. But they apply to them the opprobrious term Kuthim, as though they were identical with the colony imported from Babylon. No satisfactory explanation has been given for the choice of this special name; the Kuthites may have been the most important colony, Sanballat may have been of Kuthite origin (so Josephus), etc. The Samaritan explanation of this Jewish epithet is that their ancestors, returning from exile, came into a certain valley named Kutha (*Abu'l Fath*, 81).

The name preferred by Josephus for the sect is, very appropriately, Shechemites. In this connection may be discussed the name which Josephus alleges was used by the Samaritans of themselves in the time of the Antiochian persecution, *AJ* xii, 5, 5,— that of Sidonians. Michaelis would derive the connection from an assumed Kutha near Sidon (Juynboll, *Hist. Sam.* 35). I would suggest that the name arose from the attempt of Pagan Samaritans or renegade members of the sect to dissociate themselves from the unpopular Israelites, by connecting Samaria with the Phœnician Çimura (Çumur, Simirra; perhaps modern Sumura), appearing in *Gen.* 10, 18 in the gentilic Çemari and in the Greek thereto as Σαμαρεῖος.

C. THE FIRE-PURIFICATIONS OF THE SAMARITANS.

In *Lib.Jos.*, c. xlvii, *sub fin.*, the plea is made to Hadrian that the Samaritans " are accustomed to kindle a fire wherever a stranger has passed." An interesting illustration of this is given by Clermont-Ganneau (*Journal des savants,* ii, 41), who adduces the following quotation from Antonin de Plaisance, *circa* 600 A. C. (Gelzer, *Itinera Hierosolymitana,* 164): Descendentes per campestria, ciuitates uel uicos Samaritanorum; et per plateas, unde transuimus siue nos siue Iudæi, cum paleias (*sic*) vestigia nostra incendentes; tanta illis est execratio utrisque. A reference to the same custom is doubtless contained in the imperial prohibition against the Samaritans burning or destroying anything with fire, cited above, p. 112. This is the most unique custom the Samaritans possess, and I cannot trace its origin except to the universal idea of the purifying power of fire; cf. *Is.* 4, 4; *Mt.* 3, 11. According to Biruni (de Sacy, *Chrest. arabe,* i, 305) the Samaritan religion is a compound of Judaism and Magism; the latter imputation may refer to these fire-practices, but probably better to the legend of Simon Magus. Taglicht adduces (*Die Kuthäer,* 8) a Talmudic passage, *Taanit,* 5b, where the Kutim are called fire-worshippers, but he holds that the context demands כתיים, "the people of Kittim."

D. THE ALLEGED DOVE-CULT OF THE SAMARITANS.

The leading question in the early investigation of the Samaritans concerned the ancient allegation of the Jews that the Samaritans worshipped a dove on Gerizim. Huntington's inquiry on this point was regarded as an insult by the Samaritans; upon the beginning of the de Sacy correspondence Jewish informants still made the same charge against the sect (*N. et E.* nos. i and ii; see in general de Sacy's introduction to the volume, and Friedrich, *De Christologia Samaritanorum; Appendicula de columba dea Samaritanorum*). The accusation is now generally regarded as a sheer calumny, and the question has become one chiefly of archæological interest: What could have been the origin of the charge?

The Talmudic assertion of the accusation belongs to the IVth Century (see above, p. 169). In the interpretation given by *Sanhedrin,* 63b, of the deities worshipped by the colonists of 2 *Ki.* 17, no reference to the dove is found, although the deities are all zoologically explained. The Fathers are entirely silent on this score. The only point in Samaritan tradition which is in the least degree pertinent is the legend, *Lib.Jos.* c. 1, concerning a brazen bird placed by the Romans on Gerizim, which on the approach of a Samaritan cried *ibri,* i.e. "Hebrew," thus warning the guards. But this is a tradition concerning some mechanical oracle, of a kind witnessed to for antiquity. Reland, in his dissertation *De monte Garizim,* has carefully examined all the evidence concerning the ancient dove-cult. Selden, *De dis Syris, syntag.* ii, c. 3, *sub fin.,* made the happy suggestion that the cult must have been that of the goddess Semiramis; cf. *Diodorus Sic.,* ii, 20; Lucian, *De dea Syria,* c. 14; also Tibullus i, 8: Alba Palæstino sacra columba. Ronzevalle has recently followed up Selden's theory with a very interesting identification. In his article, *Inscription bilingue de Deir el-Qala'a,* in *Revue archéologique,* 1893, p. 29, he has put forth much evidence for the existence of a goddess, Sima or Shima, whom he identifies on the one hand with Semiramis, on the other hand with the Ashima of 2 *Ki.* 17. He suggests therefore that the Jewish accusation against the Samaritans may go back to the actual cult of the Hamathite deity Semiramis, under the form of a dove, practised by the Hamathite colony in Samaria. On the other hand this cult may have been introduced much later, in the age of Hadrian or subsequent syncretizing emperors. But to sum up, there is nothing to show for the legend that the Samaritan sect itself ever worshipped the dove.

ADDENDUM.

To p. 19. W. Max Müller thinks it probable that Shechem (*Skmm*) should be read in the narrative of a Syrian campaign of Usertesen III. of the XIIth Dynasty; see *Orientalistische Litteratur-Zeitung,* 1903, col. 448.

21

SAMARITAN BIBLIOGRAPHY.

(This list is necessarily confined, with some few exceptions, to books and articles dealing particularly with Samaritan subjects. General works, Histories, Introductions, etc., have been cited above in proper place.)

ABBOT, Ezra: In Smith's *Bible Dictionary,* Amer. ed. 1872–3, *s. v. Samaritan Pentateuch.*

ADLER, E. N. and SÉLIGSOHN, M.: *Une nouvelle chronique samaritaine.—REJ* 1902, Apr.–1903, Jan.; in extract, Paris, 1903.

ALMKVIST, H.: *Ein samaritanischer Brief an König Oscar.* In *Skrifter utgifna af k. human. Vetenskapssamfundet i Upsala,* vol. v, No. 2. Upsala, 1897. (With facsimile, and an alphabetic table by Euting.)

APPEL, M.: *Quæstiones de rebus Samaritanorum sub imperio Romano peractis.* Breslau, 1874.

BANETH, H.: *Des Samaritaners Marqah an die 22 Buchstaben den Grundstock der hebräischen Sprache anknüpfende Abhandlung.* Heft i. Berlin, 1888.

BARGÈS, J. J. L.: *Les Samaritains de Naplouse. Episode d'une pèlerinage dans les lieux saints.* Paris, 1855. (Appeared originally in *Revue de l' Orient,* i (1855), 81.)

—— *Notice sur deux fragments d'un Pentateuqe hébreu-samaritain.* Paris, 1865. (Noticed by Vilmar, *ZDMG* xxi, 288.)

BARTON, W. E.: *The Samaritan Pentateuch.—Bibliotheca Sacra,* lx (1903), 601. (With a list of the MSS at Nablus.)

———— *History and Religion of the Samaritans. By Jacob, son of Amram, High Priest of the Samaritans at Shechem.*— *Bibliotheca Sacra*, lxxvi (1906), 385. (To be continued; written by present highpriest in 1885.)

(BENGERS, T.) : *Samaritan and Syriack Alphabets with a Praxis to each.* London, 1814.

BERENS, B. : *Gentis Samaritanæ historiam et ceremonias proponit.* Halle, 1694.

BERNARD, E. : *Excerpta.* In *Acta eruditorum Lipsiensium*, 1691. (Chronological summary of Abu'l Fath, and table of highpriests. Bernard gave the translation of the Epistle of 1672 appearing in Ludolf, *Epistolæ Samaritanæ.*)

BJORNSTAHL, J. J. : *Ueber eine samaritanische Triglotte in der Barberinischen Bibliothek.*— Eichhorn's *Repertorium*, iii (1778), 84.

BLAU, O. : *Der Dekalog in einer samaritanischen Inschrift aus dem Tempel des Garizim.*— *ZDMG* xiii (1859), 275. (With notes by Rödiger.)

BLAYNEY, B. : *Pentateuchus Hebræo-Samaritanus.* Oxford, 1790.

BLOCH, J. S. : *Die samaritanisch-arabische Pentateuchübersetzung Deut. i-xi nach Handschriften und Noten.* Berlin, 1901.

BOWRING, J. : *Samaria and the Samaritans.* London, 1837.

BRUELL, A. : *Das samaritanische Targum zum Pentateuch.* With *Kritische Studien über samaritanische Manuscript-Fragmente des samaritanischen Targums in Oxford.* Frankfurt, 1875.

———— *Zur Geschichte und Literatur der Samaritaner.* Frankfurt, 1876.

BRUNS, P. J. : *Epistola samaritana Sichemitarum tertia*

ad Iobum Ludolfum. Helmstadt, 1781. Republished in Eichhorn's *Repertorium,* xiii (1783), 277.

———— *Ueber die Samariter.* In Stäudlin's *Beyträge zur Philosophie und Geschichte der Religion und Sittenlehre,* i, 78. Lubeck, 1797.

BUECHLER, A.: *Les Dositheens dans le Midrasch.—REJ* xlii, 220; xliii, 50.

BURTON, H.: *Christ and the Samaritans.—Expositor,* 1877, p. 186.

CAPELLUS, L.: *Diatriba de veris et antiquis Hebræorum literis.* 1645.

CASTELLUS, E.: (editor of the Samaritan Targum in the London *Polyglot,* with *Animadversiones,* vol. vi.)

———— *Lexicon heptaglotton,* etc. *Cum omnium grammaticis.* London, 1669.

CELLARIUS (Zeller), C.: *Horæ samaritanæ, hoc est, excerpta Pentateuchi Samaritanæ versionis . . . etiam Grammatica Samaritana.* Zeitz, 1682; 2d ed. 1705.

———— *Collectanea historiæ Samaritanæ quibus præter res geographicas, tam politia hujus gentis, quam religio et res litteraria explicantur.* Zeitz, 1688; also in Ugolini, *Thesaurus,* xxii.

———— *Historia gentis et religionis Samaritanæ.* Halle, 1699.

———— *Exercitatio, gentis Samaritanæ historiam et cærimonias, post ejusdem auctoris collectanea historiæ Samaritanæ, magis illustrans.* Halle, 1707. (An edition of Cellarius's works was published by Walch, Leipzig, 1712.)

CLERMONT-GANNEAU, C.: *Extrait d'une lettre de M. C. G. . . . . relative aux résultats de ses excursions; in Comptes rendus des premiers résultats de ses excursions.* In *Comptes rendus de l' Académie des Inscriptions et Belles Lettres.* Ser. iv. vol. ix (1881), 186.

—— *Rapports sur une mission en Palestine et en Phénicie entreprise en 1881.* In *Archives des missions scientifiques et littéraires.* Ser. iii. vol. ix (1882), 292; vol. xi (1885), 211 (with plate). (These three articles report the first Emmaus inscription.)

—— *Une nouvelle chronique samaritaine.*— *Journal des Savants,* ii (1904), 34. (Review of Adler and Séligsohn.)

—— *Inscription samaritaine de Gaza,* etc.— *Revue biblique,* 1906, p. 84.

COHN, N.: *Die Zaraath-Gesetze der Bibel nach dem Kitab al-Kafi des Jusuf Ibn Salamah.* Frankfurt, 1899.

CONDER, C. R.: *Samaritan Topography.*— *PEFQS* 1876, p. 182.

—— *Samaritan Customs.*— *Ibid.* 1887, p. 233.

—— and KITCHENER, H. H.: *Survey of Western Palestine Memoirs.* Vol. ii. *Samaria.* London, 1882.

COWLEY, A. E.: *The Samaritan Liturgy, and Reading of the Law.*—*JQR* vii (1894), 121.

—— *The Samaritan Doctrine of the Messiah.*—*Expositor,* 1895, p. 161.

—— *Some Remarks on Samaritan Literature and Religion.*— *JQR* viii (1896), 562.

—— in *Encyclopædia Biblica,* s. vv. *Samaria, Samaritans* (1903).

—— *Description of Four Samaritan Manuscripts Belonging to the Palestine Exploration Fund.*— *PEFQS* 1904, p. 67.

—— *Samaritana.* I. *Samaritan Dealings with the Jews based on Samaritan Fragments from Cairo Genizas.* II. *An Alleged (early) Copy of the Samaritan Pentateuch.*— *JQR* xvi (1904), 474.

—— *A Supposed Early Copy of the Samaritan Penta-*

teuch.— PEFQS 1904, p. 394. (On the same MS as the previous article.)

—— In *JE* (1905), *s. v. Samaritans.*

CRANE, O. T.: *The Samaritan Chronicle or the Book of Joshua.* New York, 1890 (Alden, pub.).

CRINESIUS, C.: *Lingua Samaritica ex Scriptura sacra fideliter eruta.* Altdorf (undated).

CURTISS, S. I.: in *Primitive Semitic Religion To-day.* Chicago, 1902. App. F.: *The Samaritan Passover.* (Description by an educated Syrian of the Passover in 1900.)

DEUTSCH, E.: in Smith's *Bible Dictionary,* Eng. ed., *s. v. Samaritan Pentateuch.*

DRABKIN: *Fragmenta commentarii ad Pentateuchum Samaritano-Arabici sex.* Breslau, 1875.

DRESDE, F. W.: *De usu Pentateuchi Samaritani ad emendandam lectionem Hebr.* 1783.

ECKSTEIN: *Geschichte und Bedeutung der Stadt Sichem.* Berlin, 1886.

EMMERICH, L.: *Das Siegeslied, eine Schrifterklärung des Samaritaners Marqah.* Berlin, 1897.

EUTING, J.: *Epigraphische Miscellen.* In *Sitzungsberichte der Preussischen Akademie,* 1885, p. 679 (treating of Emmaus inscription).

FALCONER, R. A.: *Is 2d Peter a Genuine Epistle to the Churches of Samaria?* — *Expositor,* 1902, p. 459.

FREUDENTHAL, J.: *Alexander Polyhistor und die von ihm erhaltenen Reste judäischer und samaritanischer Geschichtswerke.* Breslau, 1875.

FRIEDRICH, G. C.: *Discussionum de christologia Samaritanorum liber. Accedit appendicula de columba dea Samaritanorum.* Leipzig, 1821.

FUERST, J.: *Zur Differenz zwischen Juden und Samaritanern.— ZDMG* xxxv (1881), 132.

VON GALL, A.: *Ankündigung einer neuen Ausgabe des hebräischen Pentateuchs der Samaritaner.— ZATW* xxvi (1906), 293.

GARRATT (Canon): *The Samaritan Pentateuch.— Journ. Trans. of Victoria Institute*, xxxvi, 197.

GASTER, M.: *A Samaritan Sçroll of the Hebrew Pentateuch.— PSBA* xxii (1900), 240.

—— *The Hebrew Illuminated Letters of the IXth and Xth Centuries, and a Samaritan Scroll of the XIth Century. 8 Plates in gold and colors.* 1901.

GEIGER, A.: *Zur Theologie und Schrifterklärung der Samaritaner.— ZDMG* xii (1858), 132.

—— *Neuere Mittheilungen über die Samaritaner.— ZDMG* xvi (1862), 714 (criticism of *DVJ* i); xviii, 590; 813 (with revised text and translation of Prayer of Ab-Gelugah); xix, 601; xx, 143; xxi, 169 (text and translation of Litany of Marka); xxii, 528.

—— *Die hebräische Grammatik bei den Samaritanern.— ZDMG* xvii (1863), 718.

—— *Samaritanische Lesarten in der Halachah.— JZW* iv, 42.

—— (Interpretation of "Libonæan.")— *JZW* v, 115.

—— *Die gesetzlichen Differenzen zwischen Samaritanern und Juden.— ZDMG* xx (1866), 527.

GESENIUS, W.: *De Pentateuchi Samaritani origine, indole et auctoritate commentatio philologica-critica.* Halle, 1815.

—— *De Samaritanorum theologia ex fontibus ineditis commentatio.* Halle, 1823.

—— *Carmina Samaritana e codicibus Londinensibus et Gothanis (Anecdota orientalia,* fasc. i). Leipzig, 1824.

GOTTHEIL, R.: *Syriac and Assyrian.—Hebraica*, iii (1887), 187.

—— *The Method of Dating Samaritan Manuscripts.—JBL* xxv (1906), 29.

GRIMM, J.: *Die Samariter und ihre Stellung in der Weltgeschichte.* Munich, 1854.

GROVE, G.: *Nabloos and the Samaritans*, in F. Galton, *Vacation Tourists*, p. 336. London, 1862.

GRUENBAUM, M.: *Zu Awarta.—ZDPV* vi (1883), 195.

—— *Nachträgliches zu Nabulus und Garizim.—ZDPV* vii (1884), 131.

GUÉRIN, M. V.: *Description géographique, historique et archéologique de la Palestine: 2me partie, Samarie.* Paris, 1875.

HALÉVY, J.: *Mélanges de critique et d'histoire.* Paris, 1883. (No. xv on " Libonæan.")

HALL, I. H.: *On a Manuscript Fragment of the Samaritan Pentateuch.—JAOS* xi (1885), *Proc.* p. lxix.

HAMAKER, H.: *Aanmerkingen over de Samaritanen, en hunne Briefwisslung mit eenige Europesche Geleerden: ter Gelegenheid von eenen nog onbekenden Samaritaanschen Brief.* In *Archief von Kerkelijke Geschiedenis*, v. Amsterdam, 1834.

HAMBURGER, J.: In *REJud* vols. i, ii, *s. v. Samaritaner.*

HAMMOND: *The Samaritan Passover of the Year 1861.—Journ. Trans. of Victoria Institute*, xxxvi, 213.

HANOVER, S.: *Das Festgesetz der Samaritaner nach Ibrahim ibn Jakub. Edition und Uebersetzung seines Kommentars zu Lev. 23.* Berlin, 1904.

HARKAVY, A. J.: *The Collection of Samaritan MSS at St. Petersburg.* Appendix to Nutt, *Sam. Targ.*, 1874.

—— *Catalog der hebräischen und samaritanischen Handschriften der kais. öffentl. Bibliothek in St.*

Petersburg. Vol. ii. *Die samaritanischen Penta-teuchhandschriften.* Theil i. St. Petersburg, 1875. (In Russian.)

HEIDENHEIM, M.: *Untersuchung über die Samaritaner.—DVJ* i, 9; 374.

——— *Schreiben Meschalmah ben Ab Sechuah's an die Samaritaner.—DVJ* i, 78.

——— *Die Literatur der Samaritaner.—DVJ* i, 279; 421.

——— *Eine samaritanische Hymne.—DVJ* i, 290.

——— *Ueber den Gebrauch von* שרין *und* נשרי.—*DVJ* i, 406.

——— *Fragmente des Pentateuchs in der samaritanischen Liturgie. Genesis.—DVJ* i, 563.

——— *Der Traum des Priesters Abischa.—DVJ* ii, 81. (Cf. Petermann, *Gramm., Chrestom.* 24.)

——— *Gebet Ab Gelugah's.—DVJ* ii, 213.

——— *Appendix zu Gesenius' Carmina Samaritana.—DVJ* ii, 460.

——— *Die Litanei Markas.—DVJ* ii, 472.

——— *Nachrichten über die Samaritaner aus einem hand-schriftlichen Reisejournale aus dem 15. Jahrhundert.—DVJ* iii, 354.

——— *Samaritanische Passahlieder.—DVJ* iii, 357; 475.

——— *Wer war Symmachus?—DVJ* iii, 463.

——— *Der Dekalog in der samaritanischen Liturgie.—DVJ* iii, 486.

——— *Des Hohenpriesters Pinchas Gebet fur die samari-tanische Neumondsfeier.—DVJ* iii, 488.

——— *Samaritanische Festhymnen.—DVJ* iv, 110. (Including the *Midrash des Priesters Abraham,* and the *Midrash des Priesters Tobiahs.*)

——— *Zur Logoslehre der Samaritaner.—DVJ* iv, 126.

——— *Bemerkungen zu den Legenden Mosis.—DVJ* iv, 212. (Notes to Leitner's translation.)

——— *Gebete der samaritanischen Hohenpriester Markah und Amram.*— *DVJ* iv, 237.

——— *Erklärungen schwieriger Stellen des samaritanischen Targums.*— *DVJ* iv, 247.

——— *Die samaritanische Chronik des Hohenpriesters Elasar aus dem 11. Jahrhundert, übersetzt und erklärt.*— *DVJ* iv, 347. (The same as the *Chronicle Neubauer,* published two years earlier, and unknown to Heidenheim. A *Beilage* gives a comparison of the highpriestly tables in this chronicle and in *Abu'l Fath.*)

——— *Gebete des Hohenpriesters Amram.*— *DVJ* iv, 390. (Three hymns with text and translation.)

——— *Zur samaritanischen Angelologie und Astrologie. Ein samaritanisches Gebet.*— *DVJ* iv, 544.

——— *Bibliotheca Samaritana:* i. *Die samaritanische Pentateuch-Version. Die Genesis . . . unter Benutzung der barberinischen Triglotte.* Leipzig, 1884. ii. *Die samaritanische Liturgie.* Leipzig, 1885. iii. *Der Commentar Marqah's des Samaritaners.* Weimar, 1896.

——— *Ueber die Wichtigkeit der samaritanischen Literatur.* In *Verhandlungen der 29. Versammlung deutscher Philologen und Schulmänner in Zürich, 1887.* Leipzig, 1888; p. 148.

HESSEY, J. A.: In Smith's *Bible Dictionary,* Eng. ed., *s. v. Samaria.*

HILDESHEIMER, M.: *Marqah's Buch der Wunder nach einer Berliner Handschrift.* Berlin, 1898.

HILGENFELD, A.: *Der Taheb der Samariter, nach einer neu aufgefundenen Urkunde.*— *Zeitschr. f. Wissenschaftl. Theologie,* xxxvii (1894), 233. (With *Nachtrag, ibid.* 1895, p. 156, acknowledging Heidenheim's priority in publication of the hymn.)

HILLIGER, J. W.: *Summarium linguæ Aramææ i.e. Chaldæo-Syrosamaritanæ.* Leipzig, 1711 (?).

HOFFMANN, G.: *Lexicalisches.* כתב רעץ und כתב
ליבונאה — *ZATW* i (1881), p. 334. ליבון מלבן, *ibid.*
ii, 53.

HOTTINGER, J. H.: *Exercitationes anti-Morinianæ* de
Pentateucho Samaritano. Zürich, 1644.

——— *Smegma orientale.* Heidelberg, 1658. (P. 437,
discussion of *Book of Joshua.*)

——— *Dissertationum theologico-philologicarum fasciculus iii: De translationibus Bibliorum in varias linguas
vernaculas.* Zürich, 1660.

HOUBIGANT, C. F.: *Biblia Hebraica.* Paris, 1753; 2d
ed., Frankfurt, 1774. (Containing Samaritan variants.)

HUG, J. L.: *Beiträge zur Geschichte des samaritanischen
Pentateuchs.*— *Freyburger Zeitschrift,* 1834, No. vii.

HUPFELD, H.: *Beleuchtung dunkler Stellen alttestamentl.
Textgeschichte.*— *Theol. Studien und Kritiken,* i
(1830), 247. (P. 289 for the Rabbinic names for the
Samaritan and Jewish scripts.)

HUXLEY, H. M.: in *JE* x, 1674. (On Samaritan anthropology.)

HWIID, A. C.: *Specimen ineditæ versionis Arabico-Samaritanæ Pentateuchi e codice manuscripto Bibliothecæ
Barberinæ.* Rome, 1780.

JASTROW, M., Jr.: *On Assyrian and Samaritan.*— *JAOS*
xiii, *Proc.* p. cxlvi.

JUYNBOLL, T. G. J.: *Commentatio de versione Arabico-Samaritana et de scholiis quæ codicibus Parisiensibus
no. 2 et 4 adscripta sunt.* In *Orientalia,* ii, 115.
Amsterdam, 1846.

——— *Commentarii in historiam gentis Samaritanæ.*
Leyden, 1846.

——— *Chronicon Samaritanum, arabice conscriptum, cui
titulus est Liber Josuæ.* Leyden, 1848.

KAHLE, P.:   *Textcritische und lexicalische Bemerkungen zum samaritanischen Pentateuchtargum.* Leipzig, 1898.
—— *Fragmente des samaritanischen Pentateuchtargums, herausgegeben und erläutert.*— *Zeitschrift f. Assyriologie,* xvi (1902), No. 1; xvii, No. 1.
—— *Die arabischen Bibelübersetzungen. Texte mit Glossar und Literaturübersicht.* Leipzig, 1904. (With specimen of the Samaritan-Arabic Pentateuch, p. 25.)
KAUTZSCH, E.:   in Riehm's *Handwörterbuch des bibl. Alterthums,* 1884, *s. v. Samaritaner.*
—— in *RE²* xiii (1884), *s. v. Samaritaner.*
—— in *RE³* xvii (1906), ditto.
—— *Ein Brief des Hohenpriesters der Samaritaner Ja'kub ibn Harun.*— *ZDPV* viii (1885), 149.
KENNICOTT, S.:   *The State of the Printed Hebrew Text of the Old Testament Considered: Dissertation the Second, wherein the Samaritan Copy of the Pentateuch is vindicated,* etc. Oxford, 1759.
—— *Vetus Testamentum Hebraicum.* Oxford, 1776–1780. (Giving Samaritan variants. Also see *Dissertatio generalis,* at end.)
KIRCHHEIM, R.:   *Septem libri Talmudici parvi Hierosolymitani, quos nunc primum secundum M's e bibliotheca clarissimi Carmolii edidit in eosque commentarium composuit.* Frankfurt, 1851. (In Hebrew, and with Hebrew title-page.)
—— *Introductio in librum Talmudicum " de Samaritanis."* Frankfurt, 1851. (In Hebrew with Hebrew title-page: *Karme Shomron,* Contains historical sketch of the Samaritans, with a letter of Luzzato on the Samaritan script, a Hebrew translation of the *Book of Joshua,* a reproduction of Gesenius's *Carmina Samaritana,* with independent notes, etc.)
KLUMEL, M.:   *Mischpatim. Ein samaritanisch-arabisch-*

er Commentar zu Ex. 21–22, 15 von Ibrahim ibn Jakub. Berlin, 1902.

KNOBEL, A.: *Zur Geschichte der Samaritaner.* 1846.

KOENIG, E.: in *DB* Extra Vol. 68, *s. v. Samaritan Pentateuch.*

KOHN, S.: *Beiträge zur samaritanischen Pentateuch-Uebersetzung und Lexicographie.*—*MGWJ,* 1856–1857.

———— *De Pentateucho Samaritano ejusque cum versionibus antiquis nexo dissertatio inauguralis.* Leipzig, 1865.

———— *Samaritanische Studien,* Breslau, 1868. (Enlarged from the articles in *MGWJ,* 1856–7.)

———— *Zur Sprache, Literatur und Dogmatik der Samaritaner.* i. *Aus einer Pessach-Haggadah der Samaritaner.* ii. *Das Samaritanische Targum.* iii. *Die Petersburger Fragmente des samaritanischen Targum.* In *Abhandlungen für die Kunde des Morgenlandes.* Leipzig, 1876. (Reviewed by Nöldeke, *ZDMG* xxx, 343.)

———— *Zur neuesten Litteratur über die Samaritaner.*—*ZDMG* xxxix (1885), 165.

———— *Die samaritanische Pentateuchübersetzung nach der Ausgabe von Petermann und Vollers.*—*ZDMG* xlvii (1893), 626.

———— *Samareitikon und Septuaginta.*—*MGWJ* xxxviii (1894), pp. 1, 49.

KRAUSS, S.: *Dosithée et les Dosithéens.*—*REJ* xlii (1901), 27.

KUENEN, A.: *Geneseos libri cap. xxxiv priora ex Arabica Pentateuchi Samaritani versione.* Leyden, 1851. (Dissertation for doctorate.)

———— *Liber Geneseos secundum Arabicam Pentateuchi Samaritani versionem.* Leyden, 1851. *Libri Exodi et Levitici,* etc. Leyden, 1854.

LAGRANGE, M. J.: *Découverte d'une inscription en charactères samaritains à Amouas.*— *Revue illustrée de la Terre Sainte,* 1890, p. 339. *L' inscription samaritaine d' Amouas. Ibid.* 1891, p. 83. (Announcement of Lagrange's first Emmaus inscription.)

——— *Inscription samaritaine d'Amwas.*—*Revue biblique,* ii (1893), 114.

LEE, S.: Samaritan Hebrew text in *Biblia Sacra Polyglotta.* London, 1831.

LEITNER: *Die samaritanischen Legenden Mosis. Aus der arab. Handschrift des Britischen Museums übersetzt.*—*DVJ* iv, 185.

LEVYSOHN: (Russian translation, and facsimile, with introduction, of a Nablus MS of *Ex.* 20. Noticed by Abbot, Smith's *Bible Dict.* iv, 2812.)

LINCKE, K.: *Samaria und seine Propheten.* Tübingen, 1903.

LOEWE, (E. ?): Correspondence from Nablus, in *Allgemeine Zeitung des Judenthums,* iii (1839), Nos. 36, 39, 46, 47, 50, 56.

LOEWY, A.: *The Samaritans in Talmudical Writings.*— *PSBA,* 1879, Dec. p. 11.

——— *An Account given by a Samaritan, in A. D. 1713, of the Ancient Copy of the Pentateuch at Nablus.*— *Ibid.* p. 13. (Being a certification of a formal inspection of the sacred codex.)

LE LONG‹ *Bibliotheca Sacra.* Paris, 1723. (P. 541, translation of Kuenen's MS C of Arabic Pentateuch.)

LUDOLF, J.: *Epistolæ Samaritanæ Sichemitarum ad Jobum Ludolfum. Cum ejusdem Latina versione et annotationibus. Accedit versio Latina persimilium literarum a Sichemitis haud ita pridem ad Anglos datarum.* Zeitz, 1688.

(LUDOVICI, C. H.): *Targum Shomroni de Sepher Bereshit.* Halle, 1758. (Hebrew title. Contains *Gen.*

1–18 of the Sam. Pentateuch from the London Polyglot, cc. 1–3 in Samaritan script.)

LUDWICH, A.: *De Theodoti carmine Græco-Iudaico commentatio.* Königsberg, 1899.

MACEWEN: (a visit to the Samaritan Passover.)— *Good
Words,* 1894, p. 50.

MACLER, F.: *Note sur une nouvelle manuscript d'une
chronique samaritaine.—REJ* 1905, p. 76.

MARGOLIOUTH, G.: *Descriptive List of the Hebrew and
Samaritan MSS of the British Museum.* London,
1893.

———— *An Ancient MS of the Samaritan Liturgy.—
ZDMG* li (1897), 499.

———— *Catalogue of the Hebrew and Samaritan MSS in
the British Museum.* Part I. London, 1899.

———— *An Early Copy of the Samaritan Hebrew Pentateuch.—JQR* xv (1903), 632.

MASCLEF, F.: *Grammatica Hebraica. Accessunt tres
grammaticæ, Chaldaica, Syriaca et Samaritana.* 2d ed.
Paris, 1743.

MAZADE, C.: *Dissertation sur l'origine, l'âge et l'état
critique du Pentateuque samaritain.* Geneva, 1830.

MERX, A. J.: *Carmina Samaritana e codice Gothano.* In
Atti della Reale Accademia dei Lincei; iii, 1, p. 550;
2, p. 161. Rome, 1887.

———— *Ein samaritanisches Fragment über den Ta'eb oder
Messias.* In *Actes du Huitième Congrès International des Orientalistes tenu en 1889 à Stockholm et
à Christiania: IIme partie, section i,* p. 119. Leyden,
1893.

———— *Samaritanisch.* In Bänsch-Drugulin, *Marksteine
aus der Weltlitteratur.* Leipzig, 1902. (Portion of
Passover liturgy, with transcription and interpretation.)

MILLIUS, S.: *De caussis odii Judæos inter atque Samaritanos.* Leyden, 1743. (No. xiv. of *Dissertationes selectæ.*)

MILLS, J.: *Three Months Residence at Nablus, and an Account of the Modern Samaritans.* London, 1864. (With account of the Passover.)

MONTGOMERY, J. A.: *Notes from the Samaritan.*—*JBL* xxv (1906), 49.

——— *Were the Samaritans Worthy or Unworthy?*— *Sunday School Times,* 1906, p. 383.

MOORE, G. F.: *On a Fragment of the Samaritan Pentateuch in the Library of the Andover Theological Seminary.*—*JAOS* xiv (1890), *Proc.* p. xxxv. (This MS has since been removed.)

MORINUS, J.: (in edition of the LXX, Paris, 1628, readings of the Samaritan Pentateuch.)

——— *Exercitationes ecclesiasticæ in utrumque Samaritanorum Pentateuchum. De illorum religione et moribus,* etc. Paris, 1631.

——— (Editor of Samaritan Pentateuch in Paris *Polyglot,* 1645. But for the date, see v. Gall, *ZATW* 1906, p. 293.)

——— *Opuscula Hebræo-Samaritica.* With *Grammatica Samaritana,* and *Lexicon Samaritanum.* Paris, 1657.

——— translation of Samaritan Epistles to Scaliger, posthumously published in R. Simon, *Antiquitates ecclesiæ orientalis.* London, 1682.)

MOULTON, W. J.: *The Samaritan Passover.*—*JBL* xxii (1903), 187.

——— *Das samaritanische Passahfest.*—*ZDPV* xvii (1904), 194.

DE MUIS, S.: *Assertatio veritatis Hebraicæ adversus J. Morini Exercitationes.* 1631.

——— *Assertatio altera.* 1634.

——— *Castigatio animadversionum Morini.* 1639.

MUNK, E.: *Des Samaritaners Marqah Erzählung über den Tod Mosis.* Königsberg, 1890.

MUSIL, A.: *Sieben samaritanische Inschriften aus Damaskus.* In *Sitzungsberichte der kaiserl. Akademie der Wissenschaften in Wien*, cxlvii, i. Vienna, 1903.

NESTLE, E.: *Zu den samaritanischen Typen.*— *ZDMG* lvii (1903), 568.

NEUBAUER, A.: *Chronique samaritaine, suivie d'un Appendice contenant de courts notices sur quelques autres ouvrages samaritains.*— *Journal asiatique,* 1869, 385. (Reprinted in 1873 as extract No. 14.)

———— *Un commentaire samaritain inconnu (Genèse i à xxvii, 10).*— *Journal asiatique,* 1873, 341. (Also in reprint along with the preceding article.)

———— *Catalogue of the Hebrew MSS in the Bodleian Library and in the College Libraries of Oxford, including MSS in other Languages which are written with Hebrew characters, ... and a few Samaritan MSS.* Oxford, 1886.

NEUMANN, W.: *Studien über zwei Blätter aus einer alten samaritanischen Pentateuchhandschrift.* In *Abhandlungen aus dem Jahrbuch der Leo-Gesellschaft,* 1896. Vienna, 1896. (Reviewed *Am. Journ. Sem. Lang.,* xiii, 317.)

NICHOLLS, G. J.: *A Grammar of the Samaritan Language, with Extracts and Vocabulary.* London, 1858.

NICOLL, A.: *Notitia codicis Samaritano-Arabici in Biblioth. Bodl. adservati Pentateuchum complectentis.* Oxford, 1817.

———— and PUSEY, W.: *Bibliothecæ Bodleianæ codicum manuscriptorum orientalium catalogus.* Oxford, 1821–1835.

NOELDEKE, T.: *Ueber einige samaritanisch-arabische Schriften, die hebräische Sprache betreffend.*— *Göt-*
22

tinger Gelehrte Nachrichten, Nos. 17, 20. 1862. (Also in separate imprint.)

NUTT, J. W.: *Fragments of a Samaritan Targum edited from a Bodleian MS. With an introduction, containing a Sketch of Samaritan History, Dogma, and Literature.* London, 1874. (With an Appendix by Harkavy.)

OTHO, G.: *Synopsis institutionum Samaritanarum, Rabbinicarum, Æthiopicarum, et Persicarum.* Frankfurt, 1702; 2d ed. 1717; 3d ed. 1735.

—— *Palæstra linguarum orientalium.* Frankfurt, 1702. (*Gen.* 1-4 is given in the Samaritan Hebrew and Samaritan Targum, the latter with Latin translation, and a Samaritan glossary. The texts of the London *Polyglot* are used.)

PAULUS, H. E. G.: *Commentatio critica exhibens e Bibliotheca Oxon Bodl. specimina versionum Pentateuchi septem Arabicarum.* 1789.

—— *Zur Geschichte des samaritisch-arabischen Pentateuchs.* In his *Neues Repertorium,* Jena, 1791.

PAYNE-SMITH, R.: *The Samaritan Chronicle of Abu'l Fatch, the Arabic text from the MS in the Bodleian Library with a literal English translation.—DVJ* ii, 303, 431. (The publication was abandoned upon the discovery that Vilmar published the whole text in that year, 1865; see *DVJ* iv, 347.)

PETERMANN, J. H.: in *RE*[1] *s. v. Samaritaner* (1860).

—— *Reisen im Orient,* vol. i, Leipzig, 1860. (P. 233, Samaritan Passover; p. 260, stay at Nablus.)

—— *Versuch einer hebräischen Formenlehre nach der Aussprache der heutigen Samaritaner nebst einer darnach gebildeten Transcription der Genesis.* In *Abhandlungen f. d. Kunde des Morgenlandes,* v, No. 1.

Leipzig, 1868. (Reviewed by Nöldeke, *ZDMG* xvii, 718.)

—— *Pentateuchus Samaritanus ad fidem librorum Mss. apud Nablusianos repertorum.* Berlin, 1872–1891. *Genesis* (1872) and *Exodus* (1882), by Petermann; the remaining books were completed by K. VOL-LERS: *Leviticus,* 1883; *Numbers,* 1885; *Deuteronomy,* 1891. (This work gives the Samaritan Targum.)

—— *Brevis linguæ Samaritanæ grammatica, litteratura, chrestomathia, cum glossario.* (*Porta Linguarum Orientalium.*) Carlsruhe and Leipzig, 1873.

PICK, B.: *Horæ Samaritanæ; Collection of Various Readings of the Samaritan Pentateuch Compared with the Hebrew and other Ancient Versions.*— *Bibliotheca Sacra,* xxxiii (1876), 264; 533; xxxiv, 79; xxxv, 76; 309.

PLUMPTRE, E. H.: *The Samaritan Element in the Gospels and Acts.*— *Expositor,* 1878, p. 22.

(PONCET, M.): *Nouveaux éclaircissements sur l'origine et le Pentateuque des Samaritains.* Paris, 1760.

RAPPOPORT, S.: *La liturgie samaritaine. Office du soir des fêtes.* (*Texte samaritain et traduction arabe.*) *Précédé d'une étude sur la liturgie samaritaine.* Paris, 1900. (The preface alone has appeared.)

—— *Deux hymnes samaritains.*— *Journal asiatique,* 1900, p. 289.

RAVIS, C.: *A Discourse of the Oriental Tongues, viz. Ebrew, Samaritane, etc., together with a Grammar of the said Tongues.* London, 1649.

RELAND, H.: *Dissertationes:* iii. *De Monte Garizim;* vii. *De Samaritanis.* In *Dissertationes miscellaneæ,* Utrecht, 1706; 2d ed. 1713. Also in Ugolini, *Thesaurus,* vii; xxii.

—— *Dissertationes quatuor de nummis quibusdam vete-*

rum Hebræorum qui ab inscriptarum literarum forma Samaritani appellantur. Utrecht, 1706. (With a letter from J. B. Ott. A fifth dissertation published under title: *De nummis . . . . dissertationes quinque,* Utrecht, 1709. These reprinted, with a sixth dissertation by R., and others by J. Harduin, J. Gagner, in Ugolini, *Thesaurus,* (xxviii.)

———— Palæstina, vol. ii, *s v. Sichem,* Utrecht, 1714; 2d ed. 1716.

ROEDIGER, E.: (*in Hallesche Allgemeine Literatur-Zeitung,* 1845, p. 658, giving Consul E. G. Schultz's report of discovery of the Nablus Decalogue inscription, with plates.)

———— *Schlussbemerkung über die samaritanischen Inschriften.*—*ZDMG* xiv (1860), 632. (See also BLAU.)

ROGERS, E. T.: *Notices of the Modern Samaritans, illustrated by Incidents in the Life of Jacob esh-Shelaby, Gathered from Him and Translated.* London, 1855.

ROGERS (MISS), E. T.: *Domestic Life in Palestine.* (With account of her brother Consul Rogers' attendance at Samaritan Passover in 1862.)

ROSEN, G.: *Ueber samaritanische Inschriften.*— *ZDMG* xiv (1860), 622. (With plates of the Nablus inscriptions of the Decalogue and the Ten Words.)

———— *Ueber Nablus und Umgegend.*— *ZDMG* xiv (1860), 634. (With excellent map.)

———— *Alte Handschriften des samaritanischen Pentateuch.* — *ZDMG* xviii (1864), 582. (With plates.)

ROSENBERG, J.: *Lehrbuch der samaritanischen Sprache und Literatur.* Vienna, 1901. (Reviewed by Schwally, *Theol. Lit.-Zeit.* 1902, No. 9.)

DE ROSSI, J. J.: *Specimen variarum lectionum sacri textus. Appendix de celeberrimo Samaritano tritaplo sacri textus* (p. 165). Rome, 1782.

DE SACY, S.: *Litteræ Samaritanorum ad Iosephum Scaligerum datæ ex autographis Parisinis.* In Eichhorn's *Repertorium,* xiii (1783), 257.

—— *Commentarium de versione Samaritana Arabica librorum Mosis.* In Eichhorn's *Allgemeine Bibliothek,* x, 1. Leipzig, 1800.

—— *Mémoire sur l'état actuel des Samaritains.* In *Annales des voyages et de la géographie,* 1812. Expanded in the prefatory treatise in *N. et E.* xii. Translated into German in Wachler's *Neue Theologische Nachrichten,* Oct. 1813, and in Stäudlin and Tzschirner's *Archiv f. alte und neue Kirchengeschichte,* i, 3, Leipzig, 1814.

—— *Chrestomathie arabe.* Paris, 1806. (With extract from Makrizi's *History of Egypt,* including an important section upon the Samaritans.)

—— *Mémoire sur la version arabe des livres de Moïse à l'usage des Samaritains et sur les manuscrits de cette version.* In *Mémoires de l'Académie des Inscriptions et des Belles Lettres,* xlix, 1. Paris, 1808. (Enlarged from *Commentarium* above.)

—— *Correspondance des Samaritains de Naplouse, pendant les années 1808 et suivant.* In *Notices et Extraits des MSS de la Bibliothèque du Roi,* xii, 1. Paris, 1831. (For contents, see above, Chap. I, notes 14, 18.)

ST. CLAIR, G.: *The Samaritans. I. Their Number. II. The Ancient Copy of the Law.*— *PEFQS* 1888, p. '50.

SAMPEY, J. R.: *The Samaritans.*— *Biblical World,* 1899, p. 188.

A SAN AQUILINO, A.: *Pentateuchi Hebræo-Samaritani præstantia in illustrando et emendando textu masorethico.* Heidelberg, 1783.

SCALIGER, J. J.: *De emendatione temporum.* Leyden, 1583; 1598; Geneva, 1629, etc.

SCHNURRER, C. F.: *Samaritanischer Briefwechsel.* In

Eichhorn's *Repertorium,* ix (1781), 1. (For contents, see above, Chap. I, note 14.)

―――― *Probe eines samaritanischen biblischen Commentars, über 1 B. Mos. xlix.*― *Repertorium,* xvi (1785), 154.

―――― (In Paulus' *Memorabilien,* ii, 54, extract of *Abu'l Fath,* 60–76, Vilmar's pagination; do. in Paulus' *Neues Repertorium,* i, pp. 93–108.)

―――― (Translation of the Samaritan Epistles of 1808, in *Mines de l'Orient,* i. Vienna, 1811.)

SCHULZ, J. C.: *De implacabili Judæorum æque ac Christianorum in Samaritas odio commentatio.* Wittenberg, 1756.

SCHWARZ, F. J.: *Exercitationes historico-criticæ in utrumque Samaritanum Pentateuchum.* Wittenberg, 1756.

SIMON, R.: *Antiquitates ecclesiæ orientalis.* London, 1682. (Contains the Samaritan Epistles to Scaliger, and the correspondence between Morinus and P. della Valle.)

―――― *Concerning the Carraites and Samaritans, written in French and translated into English* (by Simon Ockley). In L. di Modena, *History of the Present Jews,* 1707.

SKINNER, J.: *Notes on a Newly Acquired Samaritan Manuscript.*― *JQR* iv (1902), 26.

SMITH, W. ROBERTSON: in *Encyclopædia Britannica,*[9] *s. vv. Samaria, Samaritans.*

SOBERNHEIM, M.: *Samaritanische Inschriften aus Damascus.*― *MDPV* viii (1902), 70.

SPIRO, J.: *Étude sur le peuple samaritain.*― *Revue chrétienne,* v (1897), 263.

SPOER, H. H.: *Description of the Case of the Roll of a Samaritan Pentateuch.*― *JAOS* xxvii (1906), 105.

STADE, B.: *Der Name der Stadt Samariens und seine Herkunft.— ZATW* v (1885), 165.

STAFFORD, R. G.: *The Samaritan Passover.— PEFQS* 1903, p. 90.

STANLEY, A. P.: *The Samaritan Passover.* Appendix iii to *The Jewish Church,* vol. i. (Recorded for the year 1862.)

STEINSCHNEIDER, M.: *Die arabische Literatur der Juden.* Frankfurt, 1902. (For Samaritan Arabic literature, see p. 319ff.)

—— *Supplément aux catalogues des Mss hébreux et samaritains de la Bibl. Impériale.— Zeitschrift f. hebr. Bibliographie,* vi (1902). Reprinted Frankfurt, 1903.

STOEHR, H.: *Theoria et praxis linguarum sacrarum, sc. Samaritanæ, Hebr. et Syr., earumque harmonia.* Augsburg, 1796.

TAGLICHT, I.: *Die Kuthäer als Beobachter des Gesetzes nach talmudischen Quellen nebst Berücksichtigung der samaritanischen Correspondenz und Liturgie.* Berlin, 1888.

THOMSON, J. E. H.: *The Samaritans.—Expository Times,* xi (1900), p. 375. (For the year 1898.)

—— *The Samaritan Passover.—PEFQS* 1902, p. 82.

TRUMBULL, H. C.: in *Oriental Social Life;* p. 371: *The Samaritan Passover.* Philadelphia, 1894.

TYCHSEN, O. G.: *Disputatio historico-philologico-critica de Pentateucho Ebræo-Samaritano.* Bützow, 1765.

—— *Die Unächtheit der judischen Münzen mit hebräischen und samaritanischen Buchstaben.* Rostock, 1779.

—— *Untersuchung ob R. Saadjah Haggaon Verfasser der arabischen Uebersetzung des Pentateuchs in den Polyglotten sey.— Eichhorn's Repertorium,* xi (1782), 82.

UHLEMANN, F.: *Institutiones linguæ Samaritanæ ex anti-quissimis monumentis erutæ et digestæ, quibus accedit chrestomathia Samaritana cum glossario.* Leipzig, 1837.

DELLA VALLE, P.: *Viaggi.* Rome, 1650. A German translation, *Reisebeschreibung*, Geneva, 1674; English translation, *The Travels of Pietro della Valle in India*, by Havers; republished by the Hakluyt Society, London, 1892. The Italian has also appeared at Brighton, England, 1843.

VERSCHUIR, J. H.: *Dissertationes philologicæ exegeticæ.* (No. iii. on the Ebal-Gerizim question.)

VILMAR, E.: *Notizen zum Briefwechsel der Samari-taner.*— ZDMG xvii (1863), 375.

——— *Abulfathi annales Samaritani.* Gotha, 1865.

VAN VLOTEN, W.: *Specimen philologicum quod continet descriptionem cod. MS. Bibliothecæ Lugduno-Batavæ, partemque inde excerptam versionis Samaritano-Arabicæ Pentateuchi Mosaici.* Leyden, 1803.

VOGELSTEIN, H.: *Shechem and Bethel.*— JQR iv (1892), 513.

DE VOGÜÉ, M.: *Nouvelle inscription samaritaine d'Am-was.*— *Revue biblique*, v (1896), 433. (Announcing Lagrange's second Emmaus inscription.)

VOLLERS, K.: see PETERMANN.

——— *Katalog der islamischen, christlich-orientalischen, jüdischen und samaritanischen Hss. der Universitäts-Bibliothek zu Leipzig, mit einem Beitrag von J. Leipoldt.* 1906.

WALTON, B.: *Biblia Polyglotta.* London, 1657. Prolegomenon xi: *De Samaritanis et eorum Pentateucho eiusque versionibus.* (The Prolegomena have been frequently re-published: by Heidegger, Zürich, 1673; Dathe, Leipzig, 1777; Wrangham, Cambridge, 1828.)

WARREN, C.: *Underground Jerusalem.* London, 1876. (Chap. X describes visit to the Samaritans and their Passover.)

WATSON, W. S.: *A Critical Copy of the Samaritan Pentateuch, written in A. D. 1232.*— *Hebraica,* ix, 216; x, 122. (Collation with Blayney's text. Cf. *Presbyterian and Reformed Review,* 1893, p. 656.)

———— *A Samaritan Manuscript of the Hebrew Pentateuch written in A. H. 35.*— *JAOS* xx (1899), 173. (Probably identical with the one described by Rosen, *ZDMG* xviii, 586.)

WILSON, C. W.: *Ebal and Gerizim.*— *PEFQS* 1876, p. 66. (With plan of ruins on Gerizim.)

WILSON, J.: *Lands of the Bible,* Edinburgh, 1843. (ii, 688, a facsimile of a Samaritan Ketuba.)

WINER, G. B.: *De versionis Pentateuchi Samaritani indole dissertatio critico-exegetica.* Leipzig, 1817.

———— in his *Realwörterbuch* (ed. 3, 1848), *s. v. Samaritaner.*

WRESCHNER, L.: *Samaritanische Traditionen mitgeteilt und nach ihrer geschichtlichen Entwickelung untersucht.* Berlin, 1888.

WRIGHT, WILLIAM: (Editor of *Oriental Series,* London, 1875, of Palæographical Society's *Facsimiles of Manuscripts and Inscriptions.* Plates xii, xxviii, lxxxix, reproduce Samaritan MSS.)

———— (Note on Samaritan tablet in the Leeds Philosophical and Literary Society Library. With reproduction. *PSBA* vi (1883), Nov. p. 25.)

WRIGHT, W. ALDIS: *Communication sur un manuscrit contenant un fragment du Thargoum samaritain.* — *Journal asiatique,* 1870, p. 525.

———— and SCHILLER-SZINNESSY: *A descriptive List of the Arabic, Persian, and Turkish Manuscripts in the Library of Trinity College, Cambridge, by E. H.*

346   *BIBLIOGRAPHY*

Palmer, with an Appendix containing a Catalogue of the Hebrew and Samaritan Manuscripts in the same Library (by W. and S.-S.). Cambridge, 1870.

YUNG, R.: *Toledot Adam* (in Hebrew). *The Hexaglot Pentateuch, with the Corresponding Samaritan, Chaldaic, Syriac and Arabic.* (Edinburgh ?)

ZACHARIAE, J. F.: *De Samaritanis eorumque templo in monte Garizim.* Jena, 1723.

ZOTENBERG, H.: *Catalogue des MSS hébreux et samaritains de la Bibliothèque Impériale.* Paris, 1866.

An Account of the Samaritans in a Letter to J. . . . M. . . . . 1714.

Annales de philosophie chrétienne, Nov. 1853. (Contains the Samaritan memorials in Hebrew and Arabic addressed to the French government in 1842, with translation.)

Note on the Newly Discovered Samaritan Stone.— PEFQS 1873, p. 118.

The Samaritan Stone at Gaza.— Ibid., 157.

Il Pentateucho Samaritano e l'autenticità dei libri mosaici.— Arc. di litt. bibl. ed or. v (1883), No. 12, p. 350.

It may be noticed here as a curiosity that on the Commencement Programme of Harvard College for 1771 (July, 17) appears " A Dialogue in the Samaritan language." Nothing is now known concerning the title or nature of the dialogue, nor the name of the students concerned. In the previous year a Chaldaic dialogue was given. These efforts were the result of the impetus given by the foundation of the Hancock Professorship of Hebrew in 1764.

INDEX OF BIBLICAL REFERENCES.

347

INDEX OF TALMUDIC CITATIONS REFERRING TO THE SAMARITANS.

Under each Tractate are given the references: (1) to the Mishna; (2) to the Babylonian Gemara; (3) to the Jerusalem Gemara; (4) to the Tosefta. Doubtful references to the Samaritans are interrogated.

BRIEF INDEX OF LITERARY REFERENCES TO THE SAMARITANS IN ANCIENT AND MEDIÆVAL LITERATURE.

(Exclusive of Biblical, Talmudic and Samaritan Sources.)

GENERAL INDEX.

A

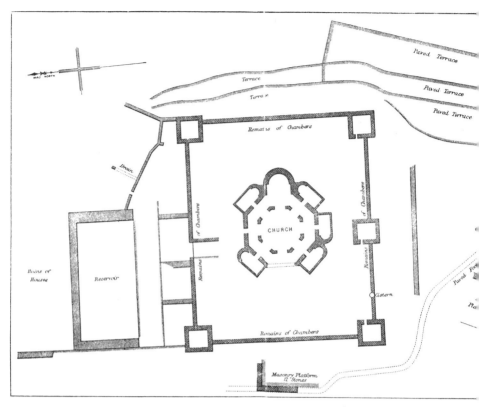

MAGNETIC NORTH

Paved Terrace

Terrace

Paved Terrace

Terra ?

Paved Terrace

Remains of Chambers

Drain

Remains of Chambers

of Chambers

CHURCH

Remains

Ruins of Houses

Reservoir

Cistern

Paved For

Pla

Pla

Remains of Chambers

Masonry Platform
12 Stones

PLAN O

Prepared by C. W. Wilson for

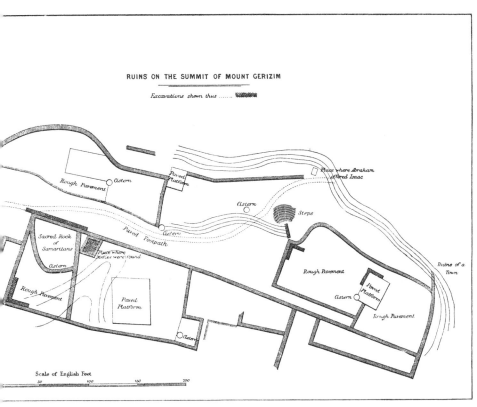

RUINS ON THE SUMMIT OF MOUNT GERIZIM

Excavations shown thus ....

Rough Pavement

Cistern

Paved Platform

Place where Abraham offered Isaac

Cistern

Steps

Paved Footpath

Cistern

Sacred Rock of Samaritans

Cistern

Place where bodies were found

Rough Pavement

Rough Pavement

Cistern

Paved Platform

Ruins of a Town

Paved Platform

Rough Pavement

Cistern

Scale of English Feet

50   100   150   200

GERIZIM.

Fund (see *PEFQS* 1873, p. 66.)